# Preserving Food

*An Essential Guide to Canning, Preserving, Smoking, Salt Curing, Root Cellaring, and Fermenting*

# Contents

# Part 1: Canning and Preserving

*What You Need to Know to Can Vegetables, Fruit, Meat, Poultry, Fish, Jellies, and Jam. Along with a Guide on Fermenting, Dehydrating, Pickling, and Freezing for Beginners*

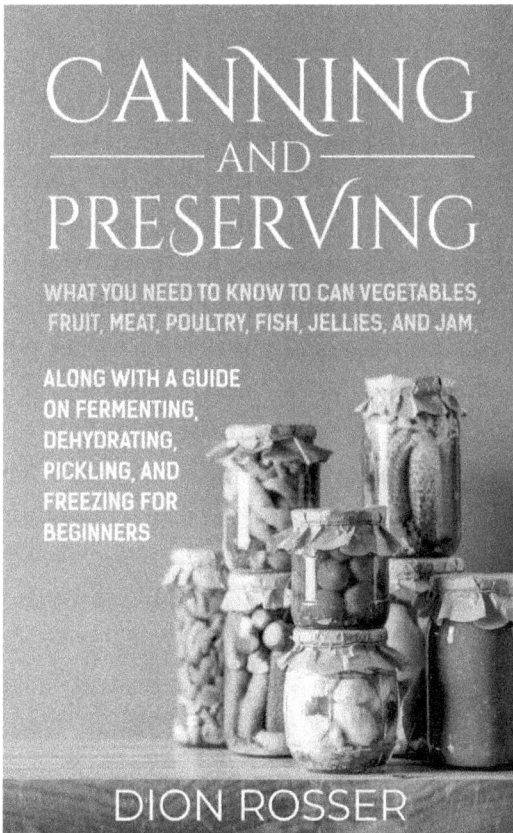

# Introduction

This book explores the various methods of canning and preserving food. It explains how you can pick, ferment, freeze, pickle, can, and dehydrate various foods. These include fruits, vegetables, meat, poultry, seafood, jellies, and jams. Many fruits and vegetables are seasonal, meaning they are not available or are less abundant in some seasons than in others. Many types of food spoil quickly at room temperature, in the presence of oxygen. By preserving food, you can keep it fresh for a longer period without it being contaminated by chemicals or harmful microorganisms. If implemented carefully and correctly, the food will retain its nutritional value, color, texture, consistency, and flavor. That is why thousands of years ago, humans started adopting methods to preserve food to safely consume it later. Besides delaying spoilage, making all types of food available throughout the year, and diversifying your diet, preserving partially processed food can save you a lot of time and energy when preparing it later.

This book is suitable for beginners and experts alike. It discusses and explains the purpose of each preserving method, how they work, and the benefits they offer. In this book, you will find hands-on and step-by-step instructions on how to prepare your food with different preservation techniques and how to apply them. The information is thorough, specific, and straight to the point, which will allow you to put it into practice confidently. The book provides advice on the type of equipment, tools, and containers that you should use. It also offers tips and tricks on selecting the best produce and overcoming potential issues along the way. You will find several simple recipes and clear directions that will help you to perfect the food preservation process.

Additionally, the book will teach you how to correctly use the food after it has been preserved to make sure it maintains its quality. The information in this book is up-to-date and compatible with modern-day technology. It is also highly accessible and applicable—no over-the-top equipment or procedures are required. The information is divided into clear, concise sections to help you easily comb through and find the details you're searching for. This way, you can use it as a guide or manual as you get to work. You will find numerous examples to ensure you carry out procedures successfully. The book uses common and understandable language, and any jargon or specific terms are clarified and simplified.

This book is meant to be fun and easy to read. Not only does it provide extensive knowledge and helpful guidelines, but it's also filled with interesting facts and information. You will gain general knowledge, find generic and diverse tips to help you in the kitchen, and, of course, you will master the art of canning and preservation. This book aims to be a firsthand, attainable, and reliable handbook. It presents accurate and real information. The procedures are neither oversimplified nor exaggerated in terms of functionality, practicality, nor implementation. This way, you will know exactly what to expect before you jump right in. The book is designed to help you get the most out of your food and decrease food wastage. It intends to help you overcome everyday issues and find solutions to the most common problems you may encounter in the kitchen. It's a friendly guidebook for anyone looking to make their time in the kitchen less of a headache.

# Chapter 1: Introduction to Canning and Preserving

It's funny how we always crave our favorite fruits and veggies during their off-season. Not being able to satisfy those cravings can be quite frustrating. But it doesn't have to be that way. Canning and preserving your favorite food can give you a way out. Canned and preserved food can taste just as good and be almost as fresh as the day you first preserved them. The best thing about this is that the process is quite straightforward, and many things can be canned and preserved—jams and jelly, fresh fruit and vegetables, meat and pickles. And all this can be done without adding any artificial preservatives.

Preserving food is a process that has been around for centuries. Modern technology has been a boon, making life very simple for us. While we can simply head out to the supermarket to pick out what we need, our ancestors had to preserve food to survive the winter. Historical evidence shows that people in the Middle East would preserve food by drying it in the sun as far back as 12,000 BC. While that process took a lot of time, it saved people from starving in the winter. The practice of drying food, especially fruit, was also common practice in ancient Rome. The Romans were very fond of dried food. In regions where there wasn't enough sunlight available, they built "still houses," making it feasible. Different approaches were used in different regions based on the means available to their inhabitants.

While preserving and canning food may seem to be one and the same, they are actually two very different processes. Preservation of food has been done for thousands of years. However, the process of canning food was developed quite recently in comparison. Canning food dates back to the 1800s and was invented by French confectioner Nicolas Appert in 1809. This procedure was invented in response to a need to preserve food for the Army and the Navy.

Canning and preserving food offers numerous benefits. While preserved food can easily be purchased from the market, commercial products neither offer the same quality nor the satisfaction of preserving food on your own. In addition, they usually are more expensive and often contain artificial preservatives. Whether you grow your own food or purchase food in bulk, food preservation can help you to stock up, save money, and enjoy your favorite foods all year long.

# How is Canning Different from Preserving?

Canning and preserving food have gained widespread popularity, with more and more people appreciating the benefits. While the two terms are often used interchangeably, they are quite different from each other. Not only are the processes different, but they also offer different results. While preserved food may last a few weeks in a refrigerator, canned food can last a lot longer.

### Preserving Food

Preserving food is a method of prolonging its life by destroying any active bacteria and inhibiting bacterial growth. This is done by treating the target food with heat, acid, salt, sugar syrup, or, in some cases, even smoke. The medium used to preserve food naturally depends on the kind of food being preserved. Sugar syrup is often used to preserve foods like fruits, jams, and jellies. Whereas vinegar and oil are used to preserve pickled vegetables. This allows for extending their shelf life by a few weeks and, in some cases, even a few months. However, one may still need to store them in a refrigerator. Even herbs like basil leaves, bay leaves, oregano, curry leaves, and coriander can be preserved by sun-drying or simply drying them in a microwave.

Drying fruits and vegetables is also considered preservation, where the objective is to dehydrate them. The removal of water helps inhibit the growth of bacteria, yeast, and mold. This is probably the oldest method of food preservation, one that has been practiced for many centuries. Traditionally this was done by leaving food out in the sun, and sometimes even by air drying, smoking, or wind drying. This process takes quite a lot of time. Modern technology like electric food dehydrators, microwaves, and freeze-drying have made the process much faster and simpler.

### Canning Food

Methods of preserving food had already existed well into the 1700s, but none of those forms were ideal for use in the military. There was a need to develop faster, more reliable methods to make both transportation and storage easy. It was towards the end of the 1700s when a need for better ways of preserving food arose. Napoleon Bonaparte needed a way to keep his armies well-fed and kick-started the search for a better way of preserving food. But the solution only came into existence in the early 1800s with the invention of the food canning process. The process of canning food came into existence when Frenchman Nicolas Appert responded to a call from the French government to develop a solution to help support the army. Over time, canning became extremely popular and is now used for preserving fruits, vegetables, soups, gravy, sauces, and meat.

The canning process involves sealing a can or jar with a combination of what needs to be preserved and a liquid, which is water. This process aims to kill any microorganisms present in the food and subsequently seals the food from the external environment to shield it from any further growth. These are the very same microorganisms that cause the food to spoil, and by killing them, the shelf life of food can be extended significantly. This is done by first sealing the contents in a container and subjecting it to heat and pressure. When the jar is subsequently cooled, the air inside is cooled and compressed, sealing the contents completely from the external environment. This protects the food from microorganisms and any further contamination. Compared to preserving food by storing it in a solution like vinegar, or sugar syrup, canning offers a higher shelf life. It does not require the canned food to be preserved in a refrigerator.

# Benefits of Canning and Preserving

Canning and preserving used to be common practice. But over time, the usage of these techniques decreased significantly. The fact that you have access to almost every kind of fruit and vegetable, even when they are off-season, has made these processes redundant. However, there are numerous benefits to canning and preserving your favorite fruits and veggies at home.

### Prevents Decay

Canning food helps to prevent decay. The canning process introduces various chemical changes like moisture, acidity, salinity level, and pH level of the food, killing any active microorganisms and preventing further growth. Preserving food can extend its shelf life for weeks, while canning can help prevent long-term decay, increasing the shelf life for years.

### Economically Feasible

Buying food can be somewhat expensive. Growing it yourself can help you to save money. Unfortunately, fresh vegetables and fruits spoil quickly if you do not take measures to slow that process down. Canning and preserving food allows you to enjoy your homegrown produce for a long time, helping you to cut down your expenses. Not only is homegrown food cheaper, but food that is preserved and canned at home is also very economical compared to frozen foods available for purchase.

### Taste and Flavor

On top of being more economical, canning and preserving food at home retains a higher quality, which improves the taste. In addition, pickling food can introduce a distinct flavor that you can tweak to your preference.

### Healthier Than Commercial Products

Consuming canned food may not be as healthy as consuming fresh food, but it is better than preserved food purchased from commercial establishments. When you carry out the canning and preservation process at home, you can be certain of the ingredients used and attest to their quality. This is not the case with commercially canned products, and, by purchasing them, you can often end up with a lower than expected quality. Food canned and preserved at home will always be as healthy, if not healthier, than what you can purchase from retail stores.

### Environmentally Friendly

Canning and preserving food can help to reduce your carbon footprint. This is because it can help you preserve excess food that would otherwise go to waste. By growing your own vegetables, you can also ensure there are no artificial preservatives and pesticides in your food. In addition, you also help to reduce the impact on the environment from large-scale commercial farming practices, and transporting vegetables from farmers to distributors, distributors to retailers, and retailers to your home.

# Common Approaches for Canning Food

There are various approaches to canning and preserving food, each having their own upsides and downsides.

When it comes to canning, three methods are commonly used. These methods have been scientifically tested and proven to keep food safe and consumable for a long time. While the process of these three approaches may be different, they all follow the same principle.

### 1. Using a Boiling Water Canner

The boiling water canner is an ideal solution for the canning of food that has high acidity. The food is first placed in a jar which is then placed in boiling water. The heat from the boiling water helps kill bacteria and other microorganisms. This approach is generally used for canning fruits, jams, jellies, tomatoes, salsas, chutneys, and pickles. However, the same water canner may not be suitable for all types of food, and some may be specifically designed for jams and jellies.

## 2. Using a Pressure Canner

A pressure canner is generally used with vegetables and fruits that have low acidity. This is because it heats the food to a higher temperature and is more effective at killing microorganisms, helping preserve the food for a long duration despite a low acid concentration. Thus, a pressure canner is the perfect tool for potatoes, beetroots, green beans, corn, carrots, pumpkin, and meat. Two different types of pressure canners are generally used—a dial gauge pressure canner and a weighted pressure canner. In the dial gauge pressure canner, you can directly read the pressure from the pressure gauge and subsequently adjust the pressure by varying the heat. In the weighted pressure canner, the weighted gauge begins to hiss when a preset pressure is reached, which can then be used to adjust the flame and pressure as required. While both devices provide you feedback regarding the pressure in the vessel, a pressure gauge-based canner offers better control.

## 3. Using a Steam Canner

Unlike pressure canners, steam canners are used for fruits and vegetables that have a high acid concentration. The steam in an atmospheric steam canner can reach the temperature of boiling water and is just as safe for food canning.

It is important to note that it is always better to invest in specialized equipment for canning instead of rudimentary techniques such as heating in an oven or sealing hot food in a jar. These can be dangerous and ineffective.

# Common Approaches for Preserving Food

Just like canning, there are different ways of preserving food items. Many of these processes can be easily performed by using equipment available at home. Here are some of the commonly used methods for preserving food.

### 1. Freezing

Freezing food you want to preserve is one of the most straightforward and simple ways of increasing its life span. However, there is more to it than simply placing it in your freezer. Before you decide to freeze your food, it has to be prepared. When it comes to fruits, they can either be frozen directly or with a sugar solution. Freezing them with sugar can help to prevent discoloration and keep them fresher. Vegetables, on the other hand, must be cooked and blanched before being frozen. This involves heating them and then immediately immersing them in cold water. Doing this helps keep the vegetables fresher and prevents their aging. Finally, once the needed preparation is done, the food can be frozen, ideally in vacuum-sealed bags, as those can help prevent ice developing.

## 2. Drying

Drying foods essentially refers to dehydrating them. This can be done through various methods that include sun drying, wind drying, and using an electric food dryer. You can also use your microwave in some cases. For example, basil leaves can easily be dried and stored by placing them between paper towels and microwaving them in short bursts of a few seconds each. But you must be cautious because a microwave is not designed for this, and leaving it on for too long can burn the leaves, causing them to lose their flavor and aroma.

## 3. Fermenting

Fermentation of food has been done in a lot of cultures. Your favorite wine is made out of fermented grapes, and your favorite beer is made from wheat or sometimes even bread. But fermenting food doesn't just yield alcohol—it is also used to preserve food. For example, cabbage is fermented to make kimchi. Fermenting food also results in the formation of numerous vitamins and minerals. It makes certain foods more nutritious than their unfermented counterparts and makes them more desirable to some people.

## 4. Pickling

Pickling is the process of preserving food in vinegar, sugar, and other acids, which preserves it and gives it a distinct taste. It is commonly performed worldwide, and the process often includes using different spices to yield different flavors.

There are many different ways of canning and preserving different fruits and vegetables, each offering their own set of benefits. While canning offers long-term storage, preserving food not only helps extend its shelf life but, at times, also makes it more nutritious and desirable. Both techniques are quite easy to execute, but there are a few things you should keep in mind as they are crucial in helping your food retain its freshness and taste. You also need to use the right equipment to ensure the best results. From here on out, you will be introduced to various techniques and tricks that will help you to ensure your food lasts and tastes fresh. Canning and preserving food will not only help you to save money but will also help you to lead a more sustainable life by reducing your carbon footprint and reducing food wastage.

# Chapter 2: Canning and Preserving Supplies

Now that you've had a small introduction to canning and preserving, it's time to get you acquainted with the supplies you will need. These are divided into four sections. First, the ingredients you'll be using regularly. Second, the appliances that will help you cook, can, and puree. Third, the necessary and extra tools and utensils you'll be working with. And fourth, everything storage-related, from jars to bubble poppers. All of that, along with a little surprise for those with a mind for business.

## Ingredients

### Pectin

Pectin is an ingredient common in all canning recipes. It is used to thicken fruit juice, leaving you with jam as your end product. While it is a natural component of any fruit, some fruits contain very little amounts, like cherries, while others contain large amounts, like apples. That's why you will often need to add powdered pectin to make any kind of jam. During the cooking process, it is released/added to the juices. Once in the juices, you should add the proper concentrations of lemon juice and sweetener to activate its gelling properties.

## Bottled Lemon Juice

That's right, bottled lemon juice. For pectin to become gel-like, it needs a specific acidic concentration. When it comes to fresh lemons, you can never accurately tell how acidic they are, as it heavily depends on many variables related to the lemons' growing conditions. Bottled lemon juice provides a perfectly regulated alternative with a consistent pH (acidic concentration). That's why you'll find that most recipes call for bottled lemon juice, and that's why you should stick with it for better, more consistent results.

## Sweetener

Who doesn't like a little sugar in their bowl? Sweeteners, whether sugar or honey, play an important part in the canning process for many reasons. In sweet preserves, the added sweetness amplifies the flavor of the fruits and counteracts the taste of vinegar. In savory preserves and pickles, it complements the acidity and adds a certain depth to the flavor. Sugar also contributes to producing a tastier, brighter-looking jam, jelly, or preserve, with much better consistency. That said, it is completely safe to cook without sugar, but make sure you use no-sugar pectin.

## Vinegar

Adding white vinegar or apple cider vinegar is essential when it comes to pickling. However, depending on your use, you will either want to use high-quality vinegar or simply get the cheapest option out there. If you'll be using vinegar for pickling or adding a specific taste to a preserve, use the good vinegar and make sure it contains at least 5% acetic acid. On the other hand, if you'll only be using the vinegar to keep your jars from clouding during packing, the quality of vinegar you use won't matter (it won't come into contact with the fruits/vegetables).

## Spices

If you will be playing with fruits and vegetables, don't forget to experiment with different flavors. Spices go a long way when matched with the right fruit/vegetable. The only thing you need to remember is to add the spices in their whole form (seeds, sticks, leaves) without grinding them. The flavor spreads more evenly when the spices are added whole, and even if the flavor isn't as powerful, it will be consistent. You can simply adjust quantity as desired.

### Pickling Salt

What separates this type of salt from others is that it has no added chemicals, like iodine or other agents. As opposed to table salt, pickling salt doesn't affect the color of pickling water or the vegetables themselves. While other salt varieties won't hurt, as long as the salt you're using has added chemicals, your liquid won't be as clear.

# Appliances

### Water Bath Canner

What gives these canners an edge are two things: their large size and the fact that they come with a rack. The large size allows for canning the larger pint jars—several jars at a time, too. Meanwhile, the presence of a canning rack means you won't have to go and buy a separate one to protect your jars while canning. You should, however, keep in mind that this canner is the most suitable method for canning fruits and vegetables that are high in acidity. When it comes to low-acid produce, it's better to use a pressure canner.

### Pressure Canner

Comparisons have often been made regarding the differences between pressure canners and water bath canners. The core difference is that pressure canners allow you to cook at very high temperatures by trapping steam inside and pushing water beyond its boiling point. The process is fast and efficient at deactivating all potentially harmful microorganisms. Pressure canners are the best for low-acid fruits and veggies because the extremely high temperature guarantees the death of certain bacteria known for producing the botulism toxin. In acid-rich fruits, the acid prevents bacteria growth and, in turn, toxin formation.

### StockPot

Stockpots are the most versatile tool you'll find. Not only are they extremely useful during the cooking process, but if you don't have a canner and are not fully invested in buying one, stock pots are a great alternative. Granted, they are a lot smaller, but large stock pots can help you fill out a jar or two at a time. It's not too shabby for a substitute. Although, you will have to improvise when it comes to canning racks. Fold a kitchen towel and place it at the bottom of the pot. That way, your jars won't crack under the heat.

### Slow Cooker

The slow cooker is the extreme opposite of a pressure cooker. It's perfect for turning fruit into complete mush. So, if you like fruit butter, salsas, and sauces, you'll love a slow cooker. More importantly, it's the best appliance to use if you don't appreciate the steam and the heat that a pressure cooker produces. Imagine cooking in a cool kitchen. That's the dream, right? Slow cookers are the perfect appliance for keeping your butter/preserve warm as you can it. Just set them to low and let them do their job.

### Food Mill

Think of a food mill as a manual food processor. But it does a better and finer job when it comes to straining, grinding, and pureeing. If you aren't a fan of seeds, a mill is one thing you'll need to separate seeds from fruit chunks. When it comes to fruit butter, too, a food mill can help you puree the larger fruit parts and strain out the skin. It's especially helpful when it comes to making apple butter, jellies, and tomato-based sauces.

# Utensils and Accessories

### Colander

If you're planning on working with a large batch of fruits or vegetables, then you have a lot of washing, peeling, and rinsing to look forward to. Having a large enough colander will save you a lot of time and effort during those initial processes. Even deeper in the canning process, as you drain the hot fruit from its juices, you're still going to need a colander, more specifically, a stainless steel one. While plastic is cheaper, it can melt when exposed to high temperatures.

### Jelly Bag

If one of the things you have your heart set on making is jelly, do yourself a favor and buy this type of strainer. The fine pores strain the liquid mixture, separating the solid components from the fruit juice, which can then be boiled with pectin, sugar, and lemon juice to make the jelly. You can also use a mesh strainer to achieve similar results, but it will take a little longer.

### Wooden Spoon

Wizards wield staffs, and canners wield long wooden spoons. Because you're going to be doing a lot of stirring, you need a wooden spoon with a comfortable grip. You may have heard that wooden spoons retain bacteria. It's true; they do. After washing your spoon, don't use a cloth to dry the wooden spoon, but let it air dry to avoid any contamination from the cloth.

### Knives

When it comes to peeling and slicing fruits, any knife will do, but some knives will make the job a lot easier than others. If you're not looking for accuracy, a chef's knife will do. For a more demanding task, like slicing or peeling small fruits, you want a paring knife. It is smaller, shorter, and lighter, making it easier to handle.

### Peeler

Rather than using a knife to do the job, try using a hand-held or table-top peeler. You can also find specially designed peelers/corers that can help you easily de-core an apple. Unless you are an old-school chef who operates faster with a knife, or someone who appreciates a challenge, save yourself the hassle and invest in a peeler.

### Towels

You are going to need many of them. Canning is a messy job, regardless of how neat you are or how organized you try to be.

### Ladles

As mentioned before, plastic melts when exposed to high temperatures for a long time. A stainless-steel ladle is definitely the better option for you.

# Storing

### Jars

This is where your artistic side will get to shine. There are a variety of jars with different designs that come in different sizes. While the designs vary from one manufacturer to another, the sizes are pretty much standard, ranging from as little as 4 oz.

(quarter pint) to as large as 128 oz. (gallon). Here are the most common sizes and their uses:

- 4 oz. jars: used for gifting preserves and storing baby purees.

- 8 and 12 oz. jars: used for storing jams, jellies, and preserves.

- 16 oz. (pint) jars: ideal for salsas and sauces.

- 32 oz. (quart) jars: ideal for pickled fruits and vegetables.

As for jar mouths, there are only two sizes: wide mouth and regular mouth. Wide mouths are perfect for storing pickles and bulkier canned products. If you intend to pickle whole or halved cucumbers, you shouldn't store them in a regular-mouthed jar for practicality's sake. Meanwhile, regular mouth jars will work just fine if you're storing a jam or preserve.

### Lids and Rims

Every jar comes with its own lid and rim, but it doesn't mean you need to buy a jar to get a lid and rim. Each jar you reuse saves a lot of money and helps the environment, so, rather than buying entirely new jars, just buy a pack of rims and lids, mostly lids, to match with the jars you reuse. While the rim won't need to be replaced unless it starts rusting, the lid will have to be changed with each use. Lids are specially designed and lined with a sealing compound that seals a jar only once. Of course, you can opt for reusable lids, but they are a bit more expensive. It all depends on whether you are selling/giving away your jars or strictly keeping them for yourself.

### Funnels

This nifty little gadget will save you a lot of trouble when it comes to transferring your preserves from pot to jar. When buying a funnel, opt for a wide-mouthed canning funnel. Most regular funnels have a wide mouth and a narrow neck. While you need a wide mouth to prevent spillage, fruits, veggies, and viscous liquids will get stuck in a narrow neck. On the other hand, a canning funnel has a wide neck that fits inside regular and wide mouth jars, making it easy for chunky liquids to flow through. You'll realize a canning funnel's true value once you start ladling your first batch.

### Canning Rack

Having a canning rack for your jars is essential to carry out a proper canning process. To heat your jars (jar processing), you'll have to place them on a metal rack inside a water bath canner or a regular pot. If you place your jars directly on the bottom of the pot, you'll risk the jars breaking as glass doesn't react well to direct, excessive heat. In other words, a canning rack ensures the safe distribution of heat. Since the accessory is simply an elevated metal platform with a basic purpose, you are more than free to improvise. Canning rack substitutes include cooking racks, towels, and steaming racks.

### Bubble Popper

After you fill up your jars with jam, you'll notice a few air bubbles. It's important to pop these bubbles to avoid upsetting the ratio between air and occupied space. When the jars are heated a second time, for vacuum sealing, the heat is supposed to apply pressure to the air molecules so that they escape the jar, sealing it. Trapped air bubbles interrupt this process, which is why you'll often notice that most recipes insist on bubbling. A bubble popper is a plastic tool that does the job perfectly. You could also use a wooden chopstick or a thin plastic spatula.

# Budgeting

As you can see, canning is not cheap. This shouldn't be a problem if you are only looking for a hobby—you'll only need to know how to spread out your budget to get the necessary appliances. However, if your aim is to turn this into a profitable business, you will need to do some calculations before investing. It's all about expense projection.

Expenses are divided into two types: fixed and variable expenses.

• Fixed expenses are those which will cost you the same amount, whether you're making large quantities or not. These include the prices of the appliances used for storing, like freezers and fridges. Even the cost of electricity required to operate a freezer, as well as the costs of appliance repair, should be included in your fixed costs equation.

• Variable expenses are those which vary according to the quantity you're producing. Let's say you make a 9-pint batch of peach jam. You'll have to buy roughly eleven pounds of peaches. You'll also have to buy enough jars, lids, and rims. Your utility bill will also increase according to how much gas/electricity you use. Meaning, the more you produce, the more your variable expenses will increase.

When figuring out a budget and the pricing of your product, you'll need to calculate an average of your expected fixed and variable expenses.

| Fixed Costs | |
| --- | --- |
| *Item* | *Total / Batch* |
| Equipment (freezer, fridge, etc.) (cost/expected lifespan) | |
| Fixed equipment—operation costs | |
| Yearly equipment repair budget | |
| | |
| Total Cost per Jar (total fixed cost/number of jars) | |
| **Variable Costs** | |
| *Item* | *Total / Batch* |
| Ingredients | |
| Variable equipment—operation costs | |
| Packaging (Jars, rims, lids, labels) | |
| Delivery (if applicable) | |
| | |
| Variable Cost per Jar (total variable cost/number of jars) | |

The sum of the two tables should make for your expected starting cost. In research done by the University of Florida in its *Food and Resource Economics Journal*, a 2018 budgeting study found that an 8-half-pint-jar batch of strawberry jam costs $26.46 per batch. It also took a price of $3.31 per jar only to break even (no profit or loss). This will likely vary with market pricing. Nevertheless, costs vary from one person to another depending on whether they can find ways to cut costs (buying in bulk, saving on operational expenses by cooking in large batches, and reusing jars).

# Chapter 3: Picking the Best Ingredients

Now that you know about all the supplies that you'll be needing to start your canning and preserving adventure, it's time to move on to the most important element, the ingredients. The quality of your ingredients is key if you want great results. There's a common misconception that the produce used doesn't need to be fresh or of high quality if it's going to be preserved or fermented. This is completely wrong. Picking the right ingredients is more of a science-backed skill that you should learn more about before giving it a go. This chapter will give you lots of tips and tricks to start with until you gain some solid knowledge to identify the best ingredients at first glance. To make it easier for you to follow up, we'll classify ingredients into three categories—fruits and vegetables; meat, poultry, and fish; and finally, jams and jellies. Let's get started:

## Fruits and Vegetables

Fruits and vegetables are the most common ingredients used for preserving as they are relatively easiest to handle. Though it can be a lengthy process, you'll find it very useful to grow your own produce and enjoy your summer veggies during the cold winter months. Tomatoes, cucumbers, and squash are essentially summer vegetables. However, with the preservation methods that you'll learn throughout this book, you'll be able to enjoy them year-round. While most fruits and vegetables can be preserved, some give better results than others. As a general rule, high acidity makes for a better candidate for canning and preserving. This includes berries, apples, peaches, pears, plums, and nectarines. As for the vegetables, tomatoes, potatoes, mushrooms, and carrots top the list of the best-performing preserving ingredients. Regardless of your ingredient pick, you can follow some general guidelines to select the most suitable ones. Here are the top factors that you have to consider when choosing your fruits and vegetables:

- **Ripeness:** your produce should be fully ripe. Otherwise, you'll be disappointed that the taste and texture are off. If you usually buy your produce from local vendors, consider making a deal with them to set you aside some that will fare well with preserving.

- **Free of defects:** one bad piece of fruit or vegetable can invite harmful bacteria to fester and ruin your entire batch. So, be extra-cautious when deciding which ones to use. Choose produce that is not bruised or damaged, and which feels sturdy to your touch. You should also consider its skin and flesh color—it has to be bright and healthy, showing no defect signs.

- **Aromatic:** aroma is a very important element that sets apart good produce from bad produce. When you're at the market, put your sense of smell to work. A quality mango should fill the air around you with its intoxicatingly sweet and overpowering smell. The same goes for watermelon, honeydew, and peaches, just to name a few. In general, a more pronounced aroma most probably means higher quality produce.

• **Chemical-free:** this shouldn't be a problem if you're growing your produce yourself. However, organic, chemical-free fruits and vegetables can be quite expensive to buy at the market. But, they make much better ingredients for preservation. Besides, when you're looking to preserve produce, you're only making a one-time bulk purchase. So, it's not going to have a big impact on your bank account at the end of the month.

• **In-season:** this might be an obvious factor. However, it's worth reminding yourself to use in-season ingredients if you want the best results with canning or freezing or any other preservation method. If you're a pasta lover and can't imagine ever running out of fresh tomato sauce, you should preserve your tomatoes during summer. Tomatoes love sunshine and clear air, so they grow best during the summer months. However, given the high demand, you might want to make some special arrangements to get the quantity you need for preservation. Make sure to plan ahead and have all the preservation supplies and tools at hand to make the most of your juicy summer tomatoes.

Fruits and vegetables are very versatile when it comes to preservation. The method that you choose comes down to your preference. However, here are a few suggestions recommended by preservation fanatics.

If you want to give canning a go, we mentioned above that berries, apples, and pears make for excellent options due to their high acidity. Whole tomatoes remain the most common choice.

If you're more interested in fermenting, root vegetables like carrots, beetroots, turnips, and radishes, and of course, the super healthy fermented cabbages (sauerkraut) should all be on your list. They all withstand the fermentation process incredibly well and can fulfill your dietary probiotics requirements much better than any supplements. Fermented fruits are more of an acquired taste—not everybody seems to enjoy them. However, plums, peaches, and apricots are typical choices for fermentation as their color and shape stay intact. Fermented apricot leather is especially famous in the Arab world, where it is used to make one of the infamous Ramadan drinks, Kamar Eldin.

Dehydrating fruits and vegetables is one of the oldest preservation techniques. Dehydrated bananas, apples, strawberries, and mangoes are some of the healthiest snack options to pick up at the supermarket. Zucchini and sweet potato chips are also all the rave right now. However, they'll cost you some serious cash if you get used to treating yourself to these tasty crisps. By the end of this book, you'll be able to prepare them yourself for a fraction of the price.

Freezing is the universal option for produce. In fact, it's believed to be the healthiest among all the preservation options, since frozen foods retain around 97% of nutrition. The list of freezable fruits and vegetables is very long and includes strawberries, berries, bananas, kiwis, peas, corn, broccoli, cauliflower, and winter greens.

## Meat, Poultry, and Fish

Many people are unaware of the fact that you can safely preserve meat at home. It's actually a great way of making sure you always have some canned beef on hand to prepare your favorite soup or noodle dish. Just as with fruits and vegetables, there are a few important factors to bear in mind when choosing which meats, poultry, or fish to preserve. Always make sure your meat is:

- **Fresh:** while you can preserve pre-frozen meat, it's better to choose meat that has just been butchered for the best result. Don't spare any time or effort scouring your neighborhood until you find the best local butcher. Ask to see all the necessary tags and licenses to ensure that your meat is top quality.

- **Low-Fat:** lean meats and poultry preserve better than fatty meats. The extra fat lingering around the canning jar gets in the way of proper sealing and increases the chances of your meat going bad. Prep your meat accordingly before you start preservation. Cut out any excess fat and get rid of bruises.

- **Boneless:** if you're canning beef, lamb, or pork, it's recommended that you get rid of the bones. However, for chicken, duck, and other kinds of poultry, there's no need for deboning.

Below, you can find some examples of the kinds of meat you can use and the most appropriate preservation method for each.

### Venison Cubes or Strips

Having some pre-prepared jars of preserved venison cubes will save you a lot of time in the kitchen. Canning is the favored method for this specific meat cut. You can either go for a raw or hot pack. As the name suggests, if you use a raw pack, you won't need to precook your venison—simply adding some canning salt on top of your raw meat in a jar will get the job done. Remember not to add any kind of liquid to your raw meat as it releases its own juices with time.

If you're a fan of the caramelized meat flavor, canning with a hot pack will satisfy your taste buds. This method is done by giving the venison cubes a quick sear before placing them in the jar. You'll notice that the jar will fit more meat with this method as the heat makes the meat cubes shrink in size.

### Ground Beef

You don't have much choice with ground beef—you'll have to use a hot pack. Use an electric meat grinder or a manual one if you want to make up for missing any workouts. Grind your beef chunks, then heat the meat to a nice brown color on the stove, optionally with chopped onions and garlic if you like the taste. Add the liquid of your choice (tomato juice, water, or broth) to your ground beef and bring the mixture to a boil. Once the liquid is reduced and the ground beef takes a nice brownish color, divide it into canning jars, adding some canning salt on top. Again, you can choose whether to add water or broth, then seal the jars and pop them into your preheated pressure canner.

## Sausages

Sausages are perhaps the most commonly used meats for fermentation. Despite having a bad reputation amongst health fanatics, who usually complain about their high-sodium content, they're still wildly popular worldwide. In fact, fermented sausages were found to contain a significant amount of heme-rich protein. If you fancy this kind of meat, preparing it at home can be a good way for you to control the sodium content. After getting rid of the fat in your meat, you can spice it using your favorite herbs and spices, then add a bit of sugar. Sugar will help with the production of lactic acid that is essential for the fermentation process. You can then stuff your casings with the ground meat mixture, making sure to remove the air bubbles. Hang the sausages to air-dry somewhere with high humidity. After a few days, you should be able to enjoy your homemade fermented sausages.

## Chicken

Chicken, duck, or turkey are all great choices for raw pack canning. Unlike hot pack canning, which tends to over dry the tender poultry meat, the raw pack keeps the meat moist and juicy. Keeping the bones in or taking them out is your choice. However, you have to remove all the skin.

For safety reasons, it's better to use chicken that has been dressed and chilled. When canning poultry, a rule of thumb is to always go with bigger birds, since they tend to be packed with more flavor that remains intact with preservation. From here onwards, the process is pretty much the same as the canning of venison. After cutting the chicken, you simply put it in the jar, add some canning salt, and hold off on the liquid. Along with every other kind of white meat, chicken also fares well with dehydration, thanks to its low-fat content.

### Fish

If you fish for your own shrimp and tuna, you don't necessarily need to freeze or can them as you may already be accustomed to. Dehydration is an excellent and relatively easy preservation method to enjoy shrimp, tuna, and even imitation crab. To kill off any harmful bacteria, you have to make sure you dry your fish at 145 degrees Fahrenheit. You should also remember to remove any excess fat to avoid rancidity.

### Clams

Many people love claims but hardly have access to them. If you're a fan of this seafood delicacy, you can preserve your own clams at home. Canning clams is a simple process, but it does include several steps. First, you should keep the clams alive until you're ready to start canning. After washing and scrubbing the shells really well, steam them for a few minutes until they pop open. Next, scrape off the meat and set the clam juice aside. Give the meat a good wash and boil it in hot water with some lemon juice and half a teaspoon of citric acid. After boiling for two minutes, strain the water and add the clam meat into the canning jars. Then add the clam juice that you saved earlier on top of the meat, seal the jar, and you're all done.

### Jams and Jellies

To make delicious jams and jellies, you have to be picky with the ingredients you choose. Some fruits may seem like they will make for a good base to prepare your jams. However, small details like their acidity and water content affect the final result. To help you make the right choice while grocery shopping, you should use the tips below:

- Choose fruits that are firm and free of any defects. Ripe fruits have good amounts of pectin, which is responsible for the stickiness and gooiness of jams after they are set.

- Give the fruits a taste test. Whenever possible, you should always try to give the fruits a taste before buying them to ensure that the flavor is just right.

- Purchase the right quantity. There's really no point in going overboard with the quantity of fruit you buy on account of its freshness. Cooked fruit will not be good to eat for too long without being preserved. Aim to buy the exact amount of fruit that you'll be using in your jams and jellies.

- Choose in-season fruit to prepare good quality preserves.

- You can opt for frozen fruit to prepare jams. Whether homemade or store-bought, all you have to do is thaw your fruit ahead of time, so you'll be able to crush and use them for preservation.

If you want to try your hand at making jams and jellies, you'll be happy to know that there are many options to choose from.

Grapes, apples, berries, pears, and of course, strawberries are only a few of the fruits that you can use to make jams and jellies.

As you can imagine, choosing high-quality ingredients will make a world of difference in the final results. If you're a beginner, the whole thing may seem a little intimidating at first. However, if you use the tips mentioned above and use them as your personal guide when you are at the market, you'll be much more confident when you head back to your kitchen. The idea is to look for the best ingredients you can get your hands on. Don't think that there won't be much of a difference in the end, because as you well know, there will be. In the next chapter, you will go on a journey to dig deeper into what water-canning is all about. You'll understand everything about the water-canning process, how and when to use it, and all the necessary supplies that you'll be needing.

# Chapter 4: Water Bath Canning

So, you've learned how to pick the best ingredients to make delectable jams and jellies. You've bought the supplies, and your set-up is perfect. Now it's time to get your pantry stocked with jars of your homemade creations that your whole family will enjoy. The first thing you need to master at this stage is water bath canning, which will help you get shelf-stable jams and pickles free of any preservatives. This chapter will focus on the water bath canning process and help you figure out the details step by step. While it may sound like a pretty daunting exercise for a first-timer, it's actually a lot of fun once you get the hang of it.

### First Things First...

A quick reminder before you start this process: water bath canning is only truly effective with foods naturally high in acid, including most fruit preserves like jams, jellies, fruit canned in syrup, and most kinds of pickles. Of course, you should not venture into jam-making without making sure that you are relying on a recipe from a reliable source. Never attempt to undertake this process with non-acidic vegetables, soup, different kinds of stocks, meat, fish, or poultry. These require more complicated processes utilizing a pressure canner. Water bath canning does not apply to these kinds of food.

# Equipment and Set-Up

With that warning out of the way, we can get to the more interesting stuff. Let's start with the equipment you'll need and the proper way to set up. A few things are probably already in your kitchen, which is great—you don't always need to invest in pricey equipment and can simply work with what you have. And, while there are pre-made canning kits available for sale, you don't have to splurge since you can easily rely on things already available in your home. This can definitely help you save money in the long run.

### Simple Set-Up

You'll need a few basic things: a tall pot (the sort you'd use to boil lobster or prepare shellfish, for example) and a rack to fit inside the pot. Of course, you'll also need a whole bunch of canning jars with two-piece lids—the most popular kind is simple mason jars.

You will also require a ladle, a funnel to help with all your canning endeavors, a timer, some tongs, a clean spatula, and lots of clean towels. Although it's a less environmentally friendly way to carry out the process, you can use paper towels.

### Additional Equipment

The list above is technically all you need to get started. However, other tools can help to streamline the process. Some of these items are a lid caddy to help you keep lids organized, and a magnetic lid wand, which can be a lifesaver. This handy tool helps you to remove the sterilized canning lids from the boiling water to prevent contamination, all while keeping your fingers away from hot water. This will keep you from having to suffer through a bunch of unnecessary burns when making your way quickly through the jam or jelly canning process. Also, you may need a canning rack with handles to help make things a bit easier, and a stovetop or electric kettle will also be useful when you need to add more hot water quickly.

### Starting the Process

The first thing you need to do is place the rack at the bottom of the tall pot—the rack helps to keep all the jar bases at a safe distance from the bottom of the pan. Instead of burning or breaking the jars, the water can evaporate and escape around the jars, which prevents them from shaking and knocking against each other, causing them to break. Add enough water to cover the jars, at least one inch above the lids. Turn on the heat and bring the water to 140 degrees Fahrenheit. If you are hot packing, make sure the water is at least 180 degrees. Use a thermometer to get the necessary accuracy. You can begin this part of the process while the food to be canned is being prepared.

### Filling the Jars

This sounds like such a straightforward step that it's almost laughable. However, filling the jars with preserves is the more detail-oriented part of the job, and it needs to be done carefully.

First, you need to check the jars and rims to ensure they don't have any chips or imperfections after being inside the pot. Also, make sure to use new lids that haven't been used before. The rings can never be reused—they're really only good for one go.

A quick tip: look at the instruction manual for the jars and lids before using them. Some may require you to heat the jars lightly in a water bath while the lids are kept in a separate container of hot water. The ever-popular mason jars have recently changed their recommendations, stating that this step is no longer necessary when using them. But many other brands still require that this initial step is performed the old-school way, so check first.

All jars and lids need to be cleaned with hot, soapy water, rinsed, and properly dried right before filling them up. If this seems too cumbersome, you could also run the jars through a cycle in the dishwasher. This will ensure that they are cleaned with the hottest water possible, maintaining the "bath" element crucial to stabilizing jams and jellies.

After washing, you'll need to work fast so that your canning jars and lids remain at the required temperature. Quickly fill the canning jars, leaving an adequate amount of space at the top between the food and the rim of the jar. Usually, somewhere between a quarter of an inch and an inch is safe. Be sure to check your recipe for the exact details, since this can also vary according to the different recipes you may be using.

### Topping Things Off

Once you've added the concoction, be sure to run a clean spatula along the interior of the jar to help release any trapped air bubbles. Then, make sure to wipe any trace of the food off the rims using a clean, moist towel. As they say, the devil is in the details, and wiping away any trace of the food off the rims will allow for much better contact between the lid and jar, which will give you the perfect seal.

Next, you'll want to place the round canning lids onto the jars. If you manage to get a magnetic lid wand, you'll find that this will be a huge help. It allows you to grab them one at a time quickly and efficiently. Basically, you'll want to screw them onto the jars as steadfastly as possible so that they are screwed tight. However, you also want to make sure they are not so tight that too much air escapes the jars, which may compromise the quality of your food.

## Processing the Jars

Next, you'll have to boil the jars in the same way outlined above, this time with the jam or jelly inside. In the first step, it was done primarily to sanitize everything before adding the food. In this step, however, it's meant to further stabilize the product inside in a natural manner, without the addition of preservatives, unlike most store-bought products.

This time, you just need to load the jars onto the rack and lower it into the water bath slowly. If your rack doesn't have handles—a tool that comes in handy when adding your jars into already boiling water—then use tongs to place them. Be careful and make sure the jars are kept vertical so that the food doesn't come into contact with the rim of the jars. Again, there should be at least one inch of water above the top of the jars. If you don't have enough water, quickly boil some in a kettle and pour it into the pot. Be sure not to keep the jars too close—you will want to keep at least half an inch of space between each of them.

When you're done, turn up the heat and bring the water to a full, rolling boil, putting the lid on the pot. Start the timer according to the recipe you're following and keep a close eye on what comes next. Most canning recipes will ask that you boil a water bath for about ten minutes. Keep in mind that the processing time doesn't begin until after the jars are fully submerged, and the water has come to a full boil. If the water is boiling too much, causing the jars to shake and rattle, then reduce the heat till it boils at a gentler pace. But make sure that it is still boiling.

### The Cool Down

When the processing time for your water bath canning has ended, turn off the heat, let the jars find their equilibrium, and settle for about five minutes. Set the timer again to help you keep track.

Then, remove the jars from their rack using the tongs, lifting them vertically, and be very careful not to tilt them. They're at a vulnerable stage, so be careful with them. Otherwise, the food will touch the lid, something you do not want at this stage since you're still trying to make sure everything will be shelf-stable, with a perfect seal.

Transfer the jars to a cooling rack, or simply place many towels on the counter to protect your surfaces from the hot glass. Make sure to keep a distance of at least one inch between each jar. The towels or cooling rack is very important because you don't want the temperature of the jars to drop suddenly. The temperature shock can cause them to break. Make sure that your jars are left without anyone shaking them or moving the contents around for at least twelve to fourteen hours until they've completely cooled. Any movement at this juncture will cause the lids to flex, which can break the seal, so keep them still. Once in a while, the lid will make a small sound. This is the seal settling with the new temperature and is generally a good sign.

### Storage

Once you've let them cool, test the seal by gently lifting the jar by gripping the seal—you should be able to easily lift the jar from the lid. If the lid falls, then put it in the fridge and make sure to consume the food right away. Otherwise, you'll be leaving your work out to rot. If you haven't left the jars out for too long, you can get the contents reprocessed within 24 hours.

If all goes well with the seal, wash and wipe down the jars with a moist cloth and store them in a cool, dark place. They can be safe to eat for at least a year after you're done. Now your family can enjoy the fruits of your labor any time and taste the freshness of sweet strawberries even when they're not in season, or have the best kosher pickles without having to go to a deli. Preserves made at home have a distinct flavor that cannot be replicated elsewhere. Once you've managed the process of canning in water baths, you will be well on your way to having a perfect harvest all year round.

# Chapter 5: How to Pickle Any Fruit and Veggie

Pickling is a food preservation technique that dates back to 2400 B.C., according to the New York Food Museum. Four-thousand years ago, the Mesopotamians couldn't preserve their foods for long periods, given that freezing technology did not yet exist. They were often at the mercy of their yield. You could say that the frustration of throwing away food one month and starving to death in the next pushed them to innovate. They started putting their foods in containers with vinegar. Some also started using brine as a preservation liquid, and it worked.

These extremely acidic, salty solutions worked because they created an inhospitable environment for bacteria and fungi to grow. Microorganisms can only survive in specific temperatures, acidity, and salinity levels. Any drastic change will deactivate them, if not kill them. That's why people boil milk to sterilize it, use a pressure canner to sterilize low-acidity fruits, and put cucumbers in brine/vinegar.

Over the years, what started as a necessity, became a way of life and a luxury and delicacy. People realized that pickling changed the texture and taste of a vegetable and fruit. Not just that, but they also discovered the full power of spices when it came to adding flavor. Put two and two together, and there you have it, the origins of pickling.

When Napoleon, needing to provide sustenance for his army, asked for a preservation method, Nicolas Appert stepped in. In 1809, he simply suggested removing air from the jars before sealing them. In other words, he suggested water bath canning to create a vacuum seal.

About 91 years later, in 1900, another food preservation method—fermentation—gained prominence. Compared to pickling, fermentation relied on the acid produced by good bacteria within the fermented foods, rather than adding vinegar or any other external source. As you can see, both methods are based on the same concept of creating an inhospitable environment for harmful bacteria, but the techniques can be very different.

This chapter is solely dedicated to the culinary art of pickling. So, get ready to learn the ins and outs of the pickling process. By the end of the chapter, you'll be able to pickle and can any type of food you want.

### What You Will Need

There are two types of pickling: quick pickling and regular pickling (the pros' choice). The main difference between the two is in canning. The brine is made and added to the vegetables in a jar with quick pickling, then put in a fridge. The pickles only last for about a month. On the other hand, regular pickling uses a higher vinegar concentration and, more importantly, involves a water bath canning procedure. The procedure removes oxygen from the jar and vacuum seals the pickles. Combined with the vinegar, the water bath canning keeps the pickles safe to consume for up to a year (no refrigeration needed). Not to mention, regular pickles have a stronger, more multi-dimensional flavor.

Regardless of the process you choose to try out, you will need a few basic ingredients: white vinegar or apple cider vinegar—dealer's choice—pickling salt, sugar, whole spices, and water. It goes without saying that you also need the food that you will be pickling.

Both processes also have one instrument in common, and that's a saucepan for preparing the pickling brine. As for your jars, it entirely depends on what you want to pickle. Whole veggies/fruits, like cucumbers, require large jars (16 oz. or larger) with a wide mouth, so you don't struggle when packaging them or taking them out. You can use regular mouth jars for smaller/chopped-up foods, like onions and carrots.

If you want to follow through with the longer canning process, you will need a few more things. As mentioned before, you need a water bath canner because it's where the process takes place. Second, you need a canning rack or a folded kitchen towel to place under the jars when they are heating up. Third, loads and loads of water, and a little more vinegar. Last but not least, a couple more towels for when the hot jars are out of the canner.

Quick pickling should seem much more appealing right about now, especially after knowing all the work required for regular pickling. Quick pickling does save a lot of time and effort, but before you opt for the shortcut, consider the scenic route. It's hard work, but you'll be much more satisfied with the end product.

**Preparing the Brine**

Brine is the pickling liquid. It's the vinegar, salt, sugar, and water combination that makes or breaks a pickle. Suffice to say, you have got to make a fine brine—no pressure. As important as they are, brines are simple, and the key is to get all the ratios right. When starting, you want to learn how to make a basic brine—not too sugary, not too acidic. As you start experimenting with different fruits and vegetables, you can tweak the ratios to accentuate the flavor of the food you are pickling.

**Ingredients**

- 1 cup of white or apple cider vinegar (at least 5% concentrated)

- 1 cup of water

- 1 Tbsp. of pickling salt (not table salt). You can also substitute pickling salt for kosher salt. The conversion ratio is 1:1.5 (pickling to kosher salt). In other words, exchange each tablespoon of pickling salt with 1.5 tablespoons of kosher salt.

- ½ cup of sugar

Pro tip: if you can't estimate how much brine you'll need, pack your jars with the fruits/vegetables, then fill them up with water. Pour the water back into a measuring cup, note the amount, and split it between vinegar and water.

**Directions**

1.      Put all of your ingredients in a saucepan over high heat. Add your herbs and spices if you want to add any.

2.      Bring the mixture to a boil while stirring the sugar and salt until they've dissolved completely.

3.    Turn off the heat and divide the mixture across your jars (filled with veggies). Make sure you leave about ½ an inch of space between the top of the jar's contents and the inside of the lid.

4.    Stop here if you are quick pickling. Wait for the jars to cool down before you put them in your fridge. Eat after a day or two to get a stronger flavor.

5.    If you are regular pickling, you'll need to de-bubble your jars because the air bubbles compromise the vacuum seal. Tap the jars lightly on your counter, then stick a bubble popper (a wooden chopstick/utensil will do, too) around the sides of the jar to remove any air pockets. You might need to top off your veggies with more brine after the air escapes.

6.    Wipe the jars clean for a better seal and start the canning process.

This brine mixture will allow you to pickle anything you want without having to change the ratios. Still, you're free to adjust them to your personal taste.

Note: While quick pickling ratios are flexible, canning ratios are not as flexible. Keep in mind that each canning recipe and brine ratio is designed to maintain a certain level of acidity to preserve food safely from botulism-producing bacteria. When tweaking your recipes, make sure you maintain a ratio of 1:1 (vinegar to water). You can always increase the amount of vinegar or decrease the water, but don't dilute the vinegar. As for the other ingredients, you're free to improvise however you want.

### The Possibilities Are Endless

What can you pickle? Aside from human body parts—for legal purposes—you can pickle anything. Vegetables: from asparagus to zucchini. Fruits: from blueberries to grapes to watermelons. Amsterdam is known for its pickled herrings, Louisiana for its pickled pork, and Germany for its pickled eggs, which have made their way to Britain and the United States with the Pennsylvania Dutch. In other words, the possibilities are endless and overwhelming.

# Best Veggies for Pickling

• **Cucumbers (technically a fruit):** the cucumber is so famously pickled that it has become the face of the word "pickles." There are several ways to pickle a cucumber. You can cut the bitter tips and pickle them whole or slice them vertically in halves or quarters. If you're feeling a little cheeky, you can go for pickle chips. Use a crinkle knife and cut your cucumbers in circles.

• **Red Onions:** pickled onions are beautiful. They are a little sweet, a little sour, and can make a regular burger taste like a million bucks. Just thinly slice your onions into semi-circles and consider increasing the sugar in your brine just a little.

• **Asparagus:** definitely an interesting choice of vegetable, and you've got to blanch them first to soften them. Drop the stems in salted boiling water, wait for about three minutes, then drop them in iced water for at least five minutes. Make sure your jar is tall enough, though.

# Best Fruits for Pickling

• **Peaches:** all picnic fruits bow before pickled peaches. Boil one cup of vinegar with two cups of sugar (no need for salt or water), then add the peeled peaches into the mix. Cook until the peaches are soft, and there you have it. For a special touch, boil 3-5 cinnamon sticks with the vinegar-sugar-peach mixture.

- **Apples:** what goes well with a scoop of ice cream? Pickled apples. Use a basic brine and go easy on the salt (1 tsp. instead of 1 tbsp.). Boil your ingredients, then bring them to a simmer before you add the apple wedges. A few cinnamon sticks will go along nicely with the apples, too.

- **Blueberries:** the perfect companion to all things cheese, from cheesecakes to brie sandwiches and salads. Add the vinegar and spices first, then pop the blueberries into the saucepan once you bring the liquid down to a simmer. Let cook for five minutes until the berries start swelling, and no matter what, don't stir.

Shake the pot to move the berries around, but don't stir, or you will damage the fragile berries. Turn off the heat and let cool for a minimum of eight hours before you drain the berries and ladle them into jars. Next, put the drained liquid back into the saucepan, add the sugar, and boil for three to four minutes for a syrupy brine. Finally, pour the brine over the berries and seal the jars.

# Interesting Combinations

Who said you couldn't pickle more than one veggie/fruit together? There are endless combinations. It's all about finding the things that go together. Sweet fruits go well with spicy veggies, like peaches and habanero peppers. Another complementary power couple is apples and ginger slices. If you're not much of a sweet tooth, you can pickle avocados with chili; the perfect mix between buttery and spicy. Once you run out of complementary pairs, try putting together fruit/veggie groups that share a similar feel, like peaches, plums, and grapes, or carrots and onions.

As mentioned before, the options are endless. It's all up to your imagination. As long as vinegar occupies at least 50% of your brine, you can put anything in that jar. Go ahead and try out these fruits and veggies, or go rogue from the start. Who knows, you might stumble upon a delicious pickling recipe. It's time to get creative.

**For an Extra Kick**

Every master pickler knows their way around a spice cabinet. Dill, hot pepper flakes and black peppercorns can turn a two-dimensional jar of cucumber pickles into a taste fest. Pickled plums coupled with cinnamon sticks, star anise, and cloves can spread warmth through your body with every bite. That's the power of herbs and spices.

| Spices | Herbs |
|---|---|
| Hot Pepper Flakes | Rosemary |
| Cinnamon Sticks | Dill |
| Star Anise | Mint |
| Mustard Seeds | Lavender |
| Fennel Seeds | Basil |
| Coriander Seeds | Thyme |
| Bay Leaves | Cilantro |
| Vanilla Bean | Marjoram |
| Ginger Root | Parsley |

The most important thing to remember when dealing with herbs and spices is to trust your senses. Take your time testing out various spice and herb combinations. Play around with the different flavors and intensities as much as you want, but remember to always use whole herbs and spices. Ground spices always result in a cloudy, unappealing brine. Other than that, there are absolutely no wrong answers.

## What to Do with a Half-Full Jar

Once you've eaten your way through your first jar of pickles, you're going to face a tough decision. How do you bring yourself to throw out the tasty brine you worked so hard to make? The good news is, you don't have to. If you're going to learn how to make the brine, it's only fair to learn how to make the most out of it, and there are, figuratively, a million ways to do so.

### More Pickles

If you properly pickled the first batch of pickles, why not use the leftover brine to quick pickle a second batch? It will save you a ton of time, effort, and money.

### Instant Salad Dressing

Have you ever wanted to put together a quick, refreshing salad to balance out a cheesy/creamy meal, but got turned off at the thought of preparing a dressing? Just pour a little brine over your selection of chopped veggies and enjoy.

### Alcohol it Up

Who said you can't get drunk on pickle juice? Two parts vodka or gin (two shots/2 oz.), one-part pickle juice (1 oz.), some ice, and a pickle slice as garnish—and you have one pickle-tini recipe you'll want to try.

Pickle brine can also serve as a secret ingredient for the Bloody Mary recipe you've been trying to perfect for years. It's acidic and salty, with just a hint of sugar that can unlock a whole new range of flavor.

If you're not a fan of cocktails, chase your whiskey with a shot of pickle juice to rid yourself of the taste and the burn. The acid in pickle juice neutralizes the taste of alcohol.

## The Morning After

After having all those cocktails, you should be expecting a hangover, but it shouldn't be a problem. Pickle brine helps with that, too. After your body is sucked dry of its water content and your whole electrolyte concentration is off-balance, you're going to need a dose of electrolytes. What's better than vegetable water, vinegar, and salt to replenish your electrolytes? However, before you dig in, cut the brine with more water or club soda. Too much acid can irritate your stomach lining.

With this information in your back pocket, nothing can stand in your way of becoming a master pickler. You only need practical experience, and there's only one way to get that, so bring out the jars and get pickling.

# Chapter 6: How to Make Homemade Jam and Jelly

Besides pickling, making jam and jelly are the most popular ways to preserve fruit. If you manage to get your hands on some good quality ingredients, it's quite easy to prepare these enjoyable, sweet fruit spreads. You can store them for a couple of weeks without canning, but if you seal them with water bath canning, they can last till the next season.

This chapter focuses on teaching you how to make homemade jelly or jam from any fruit in a few easy steps. You might find the process a bit overwhelming at first. Still, nothing can outweigh the benefits of preparing these natural products yourself. They won't contain any artificial colors, flavors, or preservatives, after all. And honestly, despite all the artificial flavor enhancers in the store-bought spreads, homemade ones taste a lot better. Plus, it costs far less to make your own fruit spreads and store them in your pantry than to buy them from a store.

# The Supplies You Will Need

To make your own jam or jelly, you will only need some fruit (fresh or frozen), sugar, water, acid, and pectin. The last ingredient is optional for some jams but necessary for making jelly. You will also need at least one saucepan large enough to cook the fruit, some sterilized glass jars with lids and screw bands, and a cheesecloth if you are making jelly. After you have all your supplies, arm yourself with patience, because cooking can take a long time. Especially if you plan on making a large batch of jam without using any pectin.

# The Difference between Jam and Jelly

Although made with the same ingredients, jams and jellies have different consistencies. A jelly typically tends to be much smoother and firmer than a jam and has a clearer appearance. The reason for the difference lies in the process of making these two spreads. The finished jelly contains only fruit juice, without pulp, while the finished jam has the whole fruit inside. That is also why it takes longer to make jam. The less homogenous the mixture is, the more time it takes to achieve an even thickness for the perfect spread. Other than that, jellies and jams are made from the same fruits, taste similar, and have almost identical nutritional values, which is why they are interchangeable in recipes.

# Making Homemade Jam

The main difference between store-bought and homemade jams is in the quality and the quantity of the ingredients. Making your own jam at home gives you the option to choose how much sugar and pectin you want to add—if any. Some fruits have naturally high sugar content, so you might find that you won't need to add any to your jam, depending on your taste. But keep in mind that not adding extra sugar will make the thickening process even slower. And if you add pectin to thicken your jam, you will definitely need the sugar as well. This is because the bond between the sugar and the pectin will give your jam the perfect consistency.

### What is Pectin?

Pectin is the natural fiber in fruits that, when combined with added sugar, helps the liquid inside a jam or jelly to reach a thick consistency, which makes them spread evenly on bread. However, this doesn't mean you have to add pectin to your fruit while cooking when making jam. You can learn how to make jam with or without pectin.

# Making Jam with Pectin

The good thing about adding pectin to your jam is that you won't have to worry about the type of fruit you choose. While tart fruits are high in pectin, sweeter ones have not as much, and without added pectin, it can take ages for the jam to thicken. If you are going with low pectin fruit, such as peaches, apricots, or tropical fruit, you will need to use some pectin in the mixture. You can reduce the amount of pectin you add by choosing ripened fruit and adding lemon or apple juice. These acids can act as boosters for pectin release. You will also have to make sure you add the right amount of sugar along with the pectin, because the pectin cannot work without it. The more pectin you add, the more sugar you will need.

Here is your guide to making jam with pectin:

- **Clean and dice the fruit:** wash the fresh fruit under running water before cutting it into small pieces. After that, put the fruit pieces in the saucepan. Besides the size of the chunks, the type of fruit you use can also determine how long it takes for the pectin to act, so keep that in mind when you cut it up. Aim to cut low pectin fruit into smaller chunks to spend less time making your jam.

- **Combine with sugar:** pectin works best with granulated sugar. Make sure to properly combine it with the fruit before heating it. Powdered pectin should also be added at this point. Using a blender or food processor to break up the sugar and the pectin can make them dissolve much faster. Alternatively, you can use preserving sugar, which will help you to store your jam for longer in your pantry. If you use frozen fruit, your first step will be to let it thaw, and add the sugar afterward to avoid burning it.

• **Boil the mixture:** after melting the sugar, increase the heat under your pan to the highest setting to bring the mixture to a full boil. At this stage, you can mash frozen fruit while stirring it with a wooden spoon. If you use liquid pectin, add it to the boiling mixture and let it boil for at least fifteen minutes. Lower the heat to medium and add an acid, such as lemon juice, stirring the jam often until thickened. With pectin, this shouldn't take more than an hour.

• **Skim and jar the jam:** when pectin reacts with sugar, it tends to make a lot of foam on the surface of the jam. Some of this foam will remain, even after the jam is cooked, and you will have to skim the surface to avoid air bubbles in your spread. While you do that, the jam will probably be cool enough for you to scoop it into sterilized glass jars. If you want to store it in the fridge, let the jam cool down to room temperature and properly seal the jar first. Or you can proceed with a canning method to preserve it for even longer.

## Making Jam without Pectin

Instead of adding pectin to your jam, consider using fruits that are naturally high in pectins, like apples, blackberries, cranberries, pears, and plums. The lack of pectin will make the process a little slower, as the jam will need more time to thicken, but it will also make for one less ingredient to worry about. Plus, taking the pectin out of the recipe can eliminate the need for sugar as well. Without all that added sugar, this jam recipe could be a great alternative if you cannot consume refined sugar due to any health reasons. If you have chosen fruit with low pectin and are worried about not creating a thick enough jam, you can add an alternative thickening agent, such as chia seeds.

Here is how to make jam without pectin:

• **Wash and cut the fruit:** before you use fresh fruit for your jam, you need to rinse it under cool, running water right before cooking it. After that, cut the fruit into either halves or fourths and put them in the pan. The size of the pieces will determine how fast they cook, so you want to make them as small as possible. You can even blend the fruit with a food processor if needed. If you are using frozen fruit, you can skip this step.

• **Add a sweetener:** the rule of thumb is to add one tablespoon of sweetener for every cup of fruit you use, but you can use less or more depending on your preference. Although table sugar is the most commonly used sweetener, you can opt for a healthier alternative, such as honey or coconut sugar. With fresh fruit, you can add the sugar or sweetener right after you cut it up. When cooking with frozen fruit, you will have to thaw out the fruit first, or the sugar will burn while cooking.

• **Cook the fruit:** place the pot with the fruit and the sugar over a heat source. Bring the mixture to the boiling point and let it boil for at least fifteen minutes, mixing occasionally. After that, reduce the heat to medium-low and continue to stir until the jam thickens. As the fruit cooks, you will notice some bubbles of foam appear on the top. When the bubbles become smaller, your jam is as good as it gets. Depending on the amount of fruit you used, this can take anywhere between thirty minutes and three hours.

• **Cool down and store:** once your jam reaches the consistency you like, remove it from over the heat immediately. You can now sprinkle and stir in some chia seeds to achieve a thicker spread. Let the jam cool, then scoop it into your sterilized glass jars. If you want to freeze or store the jam for a longer period, you can add a little bit of lemon juice at this point. Cover the jars with a tightly sealed lid, let it cool to room temperature, and then place in the fridge.

# Making Homemade Jelly

Essentially, jelly consists of the same ingredients as jam: fruit, sugar, and pectin. However, when making jelly, you will need to separate the fruit juice from the pulp. This process removes the added texture and some of the natural pectins from the fruit. Because of this, the use of pectin is a must in jelly-making. Even if you use a high pectin fruit such as a citrus fruit or some berries, you will need the additional pectin to form a solid, translucent spread from your fruit juice.

Here is how to make jelly at home:

- **Prepare your fruit:** wash your fruit in cold water under a tap and cut it up if needed. Put the fruit in a large saucepan along with some water. The amount of water you add depends on the softness of your fruit, but it shouldn't be more than 1 cup per pound of fruit.

- **Boil the fruit:** bring the fruit and water to a boil, then reduce the heat to cook on a medium setting. Stir it occasionally until you notice the fruit has softened, and you crush the pieces to extract the juice. The cooking time depends on the fruit you have used, and it may take anywhere from five to thirty minutes.

- **Strain the juice:** when the fruit is cooked, remove it from the heat and let it cool. Place a cheesecloth over a sieve and strain the cooked fruit and water mixture over another saucepan. Let the liquid seep through naturally, even if it takes a long time.

- **Heat the juice:** mix in two tablespoons of lemon juice with the fruit, and if you are using powdered pectin, add that as well. However, if you are using liquid pectin, you should add it when your juice is already hot as it takes less time to melt. Bring the juice to a boiling point while stirring it frequently.

- **Add the sugar:** lower your heat and add a cup of sugar for every cup of juice. If you opt to add an acid, such as lemon or apple juice, you can reduce sugar by a third. On the other hand, tart fruit juice may require a little more sugar, depending on your preference.

- **Cook until jellied:** continue boiling your juice until it begins to thicken. When that happens, you will need to stir it constantly so it doesn't clump up. Due to the added pectin, the jelly will form pretty quickly and visibly. After it has formed, remove it from the heat source.

- **Jar it while hot:** unlike with jam, you shouldn't wait for your jelly to cool down, as this will make it harder to handle. Skim off some excess foam after it's cooked, but you should scoop or pour it into containers while the jelly is still hot and somewhat workable. Remember to leave the jars open to allow the steam to escape before sealing them with sterile lids.

# Tips for Making the Perfect Homemade Jam or Jelly

### The Best Fruit to Use

Although you can turn almost any fruit into excellent jellies and jams, the fruit you choose will determine the need for the rest of the ingredients. For example, granny smith apples and blackberries are the best fruits to make jam for beginners. They have higher acid and pectin content than any other fruit, and you can get a lot of jam from them. Raspberries and strawberries are also great for making jam if you remember to combine them with pectin and sugar. For a thick jelly, use plums, peaches, or even cantaloupes. Or you can think outside the box and use dandelion or mint instead. While they technically aren't fruit, they are inexpensive and can add a delicious flavor to your jelly.

## Mix and Match

Sometimes the best results will come when you begin to mix flavors. Not only that, but by combining high pectin fruit with low pectin ones, you can further reduce the amount of pectin and sugar that you will need to add. Mixing pears and apples can increase the overall pectin content while counteracting the tartness of your jam or jelly. Adding pomegranate to your blueberry jam can act as a strong emulsifier, plus the flavors come together wonderfully. Berries, in general, blend well together when used to make jelly. Besides fruit, you can add some other food elements to your jams and jellies. Combining oranges with ginger or adding a small number of hot peppers into a jelly can bring joy to your taste buds and ease your digestion.

## Avoid Artificial Sweeteners

When used in a large quantity, artificial sweeteners can actually turn bitter, something you definitely don't want for your sweet fruit spreads. And even if a sweetener gives you the taste you want, the pectin cannot bond to it as it will to the sugar, and your jam or jelly can end up runny. This can happen with some natural sweeteners as well, so be careful when choosing.

# Chapter 7: Pressure Canning

Pressure canning is used to safely and effectively can low acid foods like fruits, vegetables, soup, and meat. Due to the increasing popularity of multi-utility pressure cookers, many people believe that pressure cooking can be used for canning. However, that is not the case. The process of pressure cooking might be similar, but it isn't the same as pressure canning.

You'll need a pressure canner like the Presto 16-Quart Aluminum Pressure Canner to successfully increase your food's shelf-life. Unlike high-acid foods like jam and pickles, low-acid foods are prone to more potent bacteria. Simple water-bath canning won't be sufficient for canning your batch of beans, soups, or veggies safely.

Pressure canning can be frightening, especially if you're a beginner. This chapter underlines the science behind it, the differences between water bath canning and pressure canning, and the importance of proper equipment to make the process less intimidating. It also talks about the types of products that can be preserved, step-by-step instructions to operate a pressure canner safely, and things to avoid while using the canner.

### What Is a Pressure Canner?

Like a pressure cooker, a pressure canner is a large pot that can be locked shut with a lid. High pressure is built up inside the container when intense heat is applied to it through a burner. A pressure canner generates higher boiling temperatures by increasing the pressure. By processing low-acid foods in a pressure canner, they can be sterilized and stored in your cabinets for a longer duration of time.

Pressure canners have a regulator. The regulator can either be a one-piece pressure regulator, dial-gauge regulator, or weighted-gauge regulator. The weighted gauge or dial on a pressure canner lets you control the amount of steam generated inside the canner simply by turning the burner heat up and down. All pressure canners have a knob or dial-like regulator that allows you to control the pressure inside the canner.

### How Do Pressure Canners Work?

A pressure canner uses pressure to create temperatures that are way higher than boiling temperature. This helps to heat and process low-acid foods effectively to last longer when sealed and stored appropriately. If you're using a weighted-gauge pressure canner, you can set a weight on the steam valve corresponding to a pressure of five, ten, or fifteen PSI. On passing the set weight, the pressure canner releases a small amount of steam to stabilize the pressure. However, a weighted-gauge pressure canner only gives three weight settings. On the other hand, in a dial-gauge pressure canner, you get more options to control the pressure and maintain an intermediate temperature level.

# The Difference between Water Bath Canning and Pressure Canning

There are two types of canning methods. The first is called Water Bath Canning, which does not require any special equipment, except for the canning jars. However, the pressure canning method requires a specialized device known as a pressure canner. You must understand that both these methods are utilized for different purposes. That said, each of these methods has different procedures to be followed for different types of foods. If you use the correct method and procedure, you can easily and satisfactorily preserve your food.

The process of water bath canning involves a large pot, usually filled with boiling water. Tightly sealed jars of food are completely immersed in the boiling water bath for the required amount of time, as specified in the canning recipe. The jars are then allowed to cool down until a vacuum seal is created. A boiling water bath can only heat the food to the boiling temperature and is well suited for acidic foods like pickled vegetables, fruits, and preservatives.

The pressure canning method involves a pressure canner with features like a pressure valve, vent, and screw gauges. This method is perfect for canning less acidic foods like certain vegetables and meat with a near-neutral or alkaline pH level. Apart from the equipment used, the main difference is that food can be heated up to higher than boiling temperatures if you use the pressure canning method.

## The Importance of Proper Equipment

It is critical to know that. To process your food safely, you must choose the appropriate canning method for the type of food you want to preserve. Low-acid or alkaline foods like animal products, soup stocks, and unpickled vegetables cannot be processed in a boiling water bath. You'll need a pressure canner because alkaline foods are more receptive to bacteria that can only be sterilized at temperatures higher than the boiling temperature.

Remember this: all alkaline foods must be processed in a pressure canner. In contrast, all acidic foods like pumpkin, tomatoes, and pickled vegetables can be safely processed in a boiling water bath. It is also important to note that you should use glass jars instead of metal cans for domestic-use food preservation.

## Foods that Qualify for Pressure Canning

As mentioned before, foods acidified using vinegar or citric acids, like pickled vegetables, do not require pressure canning. While all types of foods that have an alkaline or low-acidic pH can be safely processed in a pressure canner. Here's a list of foods that qualify for heavy-duty pressure canning.

- **Beans:** all types of beans like baked beans, black beans, green beans, navy beans, and pinto beans can be preserved by pressure canning.

- **Meat/seafood:** all kinds of meat like seafood, poultry, beef, chicken, and pork can be processed in a pressure canner.

- **Broths:** both meat and vegetable broths and stocks have low acid levels that qualify them for processing in pressure canners.

- **Soups:** stews or soups made with low-acid ingredients like onions, mushrooms, and peppers can be preserved by pressure canning.

- **Vegetables:** pumpkin, potatoes, carrots, sweet corn, and other veggies can be chopped and preserved for long periods by pressure canning.

# Supplies Needed for Pressure Canning

If you're trying to increase the longevity of your low-acid foods, pressure canning is the best method to use. But, to do that, you'll need some supplies. First of all, you'll need to purchase a pressure canner, which can cost you anywhere between $100 and $500, depending on the quantity of food you want to be able to process per batch. Plus, you'll need some canning jars, lids, bands, and other canning accessories, like jar lifters, canning filters, ladle, potholders, and kitchen towels. One key requirement for pressure canning is a traditional or gas stove with coil heating units. You'll also require a chopping board, countertop space for preparing food, and a place to keep the empty jars. Once you're done processing and canning the food, you'll require shelf space to store your delicious creations.

# Step-By-Step Instructions for Pressure Canning

Here are some simple steps you need to follow to safely and effectively process foods by pressure canning.

### 1. Pre-Canning Check

Before you start the pressure canning process, ensure you've gathered all the materials that you're going to need. This includes freshly washed glass jars, a canner lid, canner trivet, and other canning accessories. Ensure there aren't any cracks or leaks in the canning jars and that they properly fit the lids.

### 2. Preparing Your Foods

Depending on the food you're trying to process, some recipes require you to pre-cook the food to preserve its taste and texture. At the same time, some instruct you to directly add your food into the canning jars and place it in the pressure canner. The best way to ensure the proper canning of your food is to follow the instructions provided in tried and tested canning recipes.

### 3. Pre-Heating the Pressure Canner

The water level in a pressure canner needs to be enough to fill the canner's chamber with steam and prevent the pressure canner from running dry during the process. Start by adding water to the canner as per the device's instructions. Add the canning trivet to prevent your jars from coming into direct contact with the heated bottom of the canner. You can then begin pre-heating the pressure canner until the temperature rises to 140 F - 180 F. It is important to note that the canner's temperature must be similar to that of the jars. Otherwise, you risk breaking your jars due to thermal shock.

### 4. Loading the Canner

While your pressure canner pre-heats, you can start preparing your food and then fill your canning jars using a ladle and funnel. Ensure you have enough headspace in your jars as per the canning recipe. Tightly turn the lids of your jars with your fingertips. Make sure the lids are tight enough that no food can leak into your canner. At the same time, however, the lids should be loose enough for air to escape when the jars cool down and create a vacuum. Now you can load your jars on top of the canning trivet in your pressure canner with a jar lifter.

If your jar contents leak into the pressure canner, this can be because of too little headspace, or the lids are screwed on too tightly.

### 5. Sealing the Pressure Canner

Once you've loaded your food jars in the pressure canner, leave the vent open and turn on the heat. Let the entire chamber of the canner be filled with steam. Wait until you see a constant flow of steam coming out of the vent for at least ten minutes before closing the vent. If you fail to do this properly, your canner can be left with cool air pockets. This will give improper canning results and partially unprocessed food.

### 6. Maintaining the Pressure

Bring the canner's pressure up to the required level and start the timer once that level has been reached. Maintain the recommended pressure from your canning recipe for the required amount of time. When the time is up, turn off the heat and leave your pressure canner as it is for some time. This is to let the pressure canner and the contents within cool down. Avoid rapid cooling of the canner because it can break the jars inside.

### 7. Release the Steam and Remove the Jars

Check the pressure on the gauge of your pressure canner. If it has come down to 0 PSI, there's no more increased pressure in the canner, and you can safely release the steam through the vent before opening the lid. Safely remove the jars and place them on kitchen towels to cool on your countertop.

Be careful, as the contents of the jars will still be pretty hot for a long time, so you best let the jars cool off overnight. Check and double-check the seals on your jars. Remove the canning rings if they're still on. You can then store the sealed jars in your pantry to be used within 12-18 months.

# Things to Avoid

Pressure canning can go very wrong very fast if you overlook any of the safety instructions or forget to follow a step. There's a huge margin for error in the process of pressure canning. To summarize the most common safety precautions, here's a list of things to avoid while operating a pressure canner.

### 1. Changing the Temperature Too Quickly

The temperatures of the canner and the food being placed in it must be regulated to match one another. If the jars you place inside the chamber are cooler than the canner, they can crack from the sudden temperature change.

## 2. Rushing the Process

Pressure canning requires that you invest a lot of time if you want to execute the process properly. There are a lot of instructions to be followed and precautions to be taken. If you're impatient and try to rush the process, things will most definitely go unpleasantly. Give the process the necessary time to avoid any complications with canning and to ensure your personal physical safety.

## 3. Leaving No Headspace

It is necessary to leave the recommended amount of headspace for the contents in your canning jars. If there's not enough headspace, the boiling contents of the jars will hit the lids and cause them to loosen. This will allow liquid to flow out of the jars. You may even experience excessive liquid loss, where more than half of the jar's contents leak out.

## 4. Releasing Pressure Manually

Unlike pressure cookers, you cannot let off steam within a heated pressure canner manually. Do not try to release the canner's pressure in any way if you've just turned off the burner. Doing so may result in the jars inside the pressure canner breaking. The super-hot steam can also cause severe burns if you try to release the pressure manually.

## 5. Using an Instant Pot for Canning

Multi-utility appliances like the Instant Pot must not be used for pressure canning. There are two reasons for this. The first reason is that these countertop appliances cannot maintain the even pressure required for safe canning. The second reason is they don't support canning trivets which are crucial to keeping the jars safe from the heated bottom of the pot. As a result of thermal shock, glass jars are bound to break in an Instant Pot.

# Tips for Perfect Pressure Canning

Are you canning your foods just to preserve them longer or to preserve them in a way that maintains their taste and texture? Pressure canning, if performed according to instructions, can be an extremely satisfying experience. Here are a few tips to help you preserve your delicious foods perfectly.

## 1. Learn to Use the Pressure Canner

Read the instruction manual of your pressure canner carefully before using it. Understand its functionalities and requirements. If you have a dial gauge pressure canner, have the dial inspected for accuracy every 8-12 months. If your pressure canner hasn't been used in a long time, get it inspected for leaks.

## 2. Inspect the Jars

Clean your canning jars with hot water and soap. Rinse them well. Check for cracks or nicks on your jars. Make sure the lids fit perfectly on the jar heads. With a spatula, release the air bubbles between the jar and the food, if there are any. As per directions, leave a headspace of ¼", ½", or 1" in your canning jars. Always use a jar lifter when placing the jars in boiling water or removing them from the canner. Instead of using old-fashioned jars or used peanut butter jars, try mason-style jars to store your canned foods.

## 3. Label Your Canned Food

Once you're done pressure-canning your delicious recipes, label the jars with the content name and date. Don't forget to mention the canning year on the label. It may seem silly to some, but it's easy to lose track of the food stored in your pantry. Labeling the jars will help you to identify the ingredients of the jars and whether or not they have expired. It's easy to label your canned food as soon as it cools down and very helpful when you stumble upon a canning jar far in the future!

# Chapter 8: How to Can Fish

Give a man a fish, and you feed him for a day; teach a man to can fish, and he can make it last for an entire year!

Canning is a safe and easy preservation method for fish that has been around for hundreds of years. In fact, the first reported instance of canning was done by Nicolas Appert—the French inventor who is also known as the "father of canning"—who invented this method solely to preserve fish. The science behind canning fish is quite simple. By cleaning the fish and packing them in disinfected, air-tight jars, you slow down their spoilage. This environment prevents the growth of microorganisms such as bacteria and mold, which keeps the clean pieces of fish safely edible for up to a year.

Apart from being convenient and cost-effective, canned fish has many health benefits that even rival fresh fish at times. They have high protein content, are rich with omega-3 fatty acids, and tiny, tender fish bones that you can safely eat, making canned fish one of the best sources of pure calcium out there. Therefore, it is quite common to can the highest quality yields to be consumed when the weather is too cold for fresh meats and food, especially in countries with really cold winters. It is more or less similar to cured meats that make the end product different, delicious, and more valuable than fresh meats.

# Types of Fish Ideal for Canning

Fish are relatively easy to preserve, some being easier than others, and they keep their flavors and nutrients well after the canning process. However, no matter which type of fish you plan to can and preserve, it is important that you select top-quality, fresh fish. Like any other fresh meat, fish can be susceptible to tissue decomposition if not handled and preserved well. Always use freshly caught fish for canning. If you use wild-caught fish, try to keep them alive for as long as possible if you plan to preserve them later. They start the deterioration process soon after they leave the water. Once you have them, clean and preserve them as soon as possible to create the best-canned fish. Here are a few species of fish that are ideal for canning.

### Mackerel

Mackerel is an affordable fish with a taste similar to tuna and salmon. They are easy to catch and can be found near piers and rocks in large flocks, ideal for preserving. They are rich in healthy fats and have a decent number of bones that become tender during canning. While fresh mackerel can be somewhat chewy, canned mackerel is tender and has a distinct yet mild flavor.

### Salmon

Salmon is a popular fish for canning because of its delicious taste, high omega-3 fatty acid content, and potent antioxidants that give its uniquely appetizing color. Wild-caught salmon are often the best choice for canning since they have fewer contaminants and are more nutritious. Once properly canned, salmon has a light color and texture, with a pleasantly mild flavor.

### Herring

Herring are small, bony, and naturally oily, making them great for canning. The excess moisture in the fish escapes and combines with the salt and makes for a deliciously tender and flavorful meal when you cook and eat them later. Due to their size, flavor, and moist texture, canned herring takes little to no preparation or cooking.

### Trout

Trout is a member of the salmon family and is a popular fish among hobby fishermen since they are widely available in creeks and rivers. Fresh trout has tender and flaky flesh with a mild nutty flavor. They have ample flesh and can be smoked or brined before canning to add more flavor if needed.

### Steelhead

Steelhead is also a type of salmon with a nice orange flesh and milder taste. A great source of low-fat protein, steelheads are anadromous fish that spend parts of their lives in freshwater and others in saltwater. The flesh is tender and moist, making the canned fish flavorful with great texture.

## Blue

Bluefish are large marine fish with mild, flaky flesh packed with intense flavor. They make rich and succulent canned fish, often tasting even better than fresh counterparts since the preservation makes the strong flavor milder and more pleasant. Due to their ample flesh, bluefish give a great yield as canned fish, which can be used to make plenty of food, including fish cakes, soups, pasta sauces, or croquettes.

# How to Make Great Canned Fish

Now that you have your fish—fresh fish is always the best option, but thawed frozen fish can also be canned—it's time to gather the equipment and ingredients and start the canning process.

### Equipment

- Filleting knife.

- Hardwood cutting board.

- Wide mouth canning jars and self-sealing lids with rings.

- Pressure canner.

Note: As mentioned in the previous chapter, a pressure canner is a big pot with a secure lid, with a dial or a gauge that helps you regulate the steam pressure. Be careful when you use the pressure canner since the pressurized steam can be hotter than boiling water. Every pressure canner on the market comes with its own set of directions. Read your manual several times and follow the exact directions when you use it. Before every fish canning session, check if your pressure canner is in good condition. The vent should always be clean and open, and the pressure gauge should be accurate. Doing a trial run with a few inches of water to check the performance of the pressure canner is recommended before every canning session.

As for the jars, you can use straight-sided mason-type canning jars with a tight lid. If you are using jars that have been used previously, thoroughly clean them using hot, soapy water to remove any residue. For your preserves to retain their quality, the lid should be perfectly secure on the rim of the jar. Check for any nicks or cracks on the rims and discard any damaged jars. Get self-sealing lids to secure the jars and replace them if you use them for a second time. You can reuse jars and rings if they are not damaged or bent.

Every piece of equipment used in the canning process, including the knives and the hardwood cutting board, should be cleaned well with warm, soapy water, rinsed, and properly dried.

### Ingredients

- Fish
- Salt
- Water
- Vinegar (optional)

### Preparation

If your fish is frozen, put it in the refrigerator until it is completely thawed before getting started. Rinse fresh or thawed fish well in clean, cold water. You can add some vinegar to the water to help remove any slime. Gut the fish and remove the head, fins, scales, and tail without damaging the skin or flesh. You can keep the bones in since the pressurization tenderizes the bones, making them a good source of calcium. Use a generous amount of water to wash and clean the fish that you will be canning. If you are not going to start the canning process immediately after preparing the fish, store it in a refrigerator until you are ready.

## Packing

Clean and disinfect your canning jars. Cut your fish into chunks that can fit into the jars. If you are using a type of fish where the skin stays on, arrange the pieces in the jars with the skins facing outwards to make the finished product look nicer. If the fish skins are touching the insides of the jar, it can be difficult to clean after use. You can simply face the skins inwards if you want to avoid the few extra minutes of cleaning after finishing the jar. If you are using standard 1-quart canning jars, pack the chunks of fish tightly, leaving about one inch of unfilled space at the top. Use a plastic spoon to align the product inside for a tighter pack. If you prefer some added flavor, add about one to two teaspoons of salt to each jar. You can also add small amounts of your favorite herbs and spices, such as paprika and garlic powder, to the jars as well. When you can halibut, add a couple of spoons of olive or vegetable oil for better moisture.

Once you pack the fish in, use a clean, damp cloth or a paper towel to remove any oils or residue from the edge of the jar. Secure the lid and the rings properly. Read and follow any specific guidelines from the manufacturers of your canning jars and lids. They should neither be too tight nor too loose. If you over-tighten the lids, it can lead to the jars breaking and discoloring the fish, since air will not escape through the tight lids during processing.

## Processing

Add water to the bottom of the pressure canner until it is three inches deep. Put the rack on the bottom and place the closed jars on the rack. Check any specific instructions in your pressure canner manual on arranging the jars for more efficient processing. Fasten the canner cover. The directions for processing fish in the pressure canner vary according to the jar size, fish type, and canner brand. Always check the instructions from the manufacturer. For standard quart jars, heat the canner on high for about 20 minutes until you can see steam coming through the open vent in a steady stream. If the steam is not steady enough, let it heat up a little more. Let the steam flow out for about ten more minutes. This makes sure that the heat spreads evenly inside the canner. The time it takes for a steady stream of steam to come out may be thirty minutes or more, depending on the size of your canning jars and the temperature of the fish.

When the heat becomes even, close the lid vent using an oven mitt or hot pad and set the weighted gauge. Depending on the manufacturer, there should be three sections in your weighted gauge. Turn up the heat until the pressure reads 10 pounds for a weighted gauge pressure canner. Keep adjusting the heat to maintain a steady pressure from the beginning to the end. If you are using quart jars, it may take about 160 minutes of processing with 10 pounds of pressure for most fish. If you are located at over 1000 feet altitude, use up to 15 pounds of pressure.

### Cooling

Once the recommended processing time is over, remove the canner from the heat and let it cool. Allow the pressure to drop naturally until the gauge shows zero pounds of pressure. Most pressure canners nowadays come with a lid lock that automatically unlocks when the pressure drops to zero. Wait a few more minutes and slowly open the vent using a heating pad or oven mitt. Open your lid so that the escaping steam faces away from you. Take the jars out one by one using tongs or a jar lifter. Do not try to tighten the lids if they appear to be loose. It takes some time for the lids to seal while cooling. Check the lids after about twelve hours to see if they have been sealed properly. You can remove the rings and wash them if you want to reuse them later. If a lid has not sealed after twelve hours, remove the fish and use a different jar to process them within twenty-four hours. You can place the unsealed jars in the freezer until you can process them again.

## Storing

Wash the surface of your sealed jars and wipe them dry. Label them with the processing date and the type of fish, if you are canning more than one type. Store the jars in a cool, dry place.

# Chapter 9: Canning Poultry and Meats

Poultry and meat canning is easy if you know how to do it. You won't find it much different from canning veggies and other vegetarian foods. Not only does canned meat and poultry stock your pantry, but it allows you to prepare quick meals when needed. Imagine the convenience of having a canned jar ready to be opened to add in to one of your delectable meat or poultry recipes, without the need to prepare the meat or chicken.

Besides convenience, canning meat or poultry products is a must-have skill that will save you space in your freezer and keep you prepared with ready-to-go food that you are sure to cherish.

However, canning poultry and meats is only healthy and possible with pressure canning because these foods have very low pH levels (less than 4.6). Using water baths or steam canning will not be enough to heat the food in the can, making it unsafe for storage.

Many of you may feel intimidated by the process of pressure canning, but following the below instructions will help you to secure your food safely for years.

# Canning Chicken

Every poultry product that you want to can will require the same steps, so let's understand the process by knowing how to can chicken. You need to first do the preparation work for the chicken-canning recipe.

# Preparation Work before Canning Chicken

Store-bought chicken is seasoned and refrigerated, so you can use it as soon as you buy it. However, if you plan to use freshly butchered chicken, season it first. Then, let it chill for six to twelve hours before you start canning it. Make sure you thaw the chicken pieces before you use them if they were frozen.

Next, choose the canning options you want to use for the chicken.

### Hot or Raw Pack?

In the hot pack option, you first cook the chicken lightly and then put it into canning jars with some of the hot liquid and preserve it. The raw pack method requires you to put raw chicken chunks into the jars and preserve them. While both methods are safe to preserve chicken, the hot pack one makes the chicken last longer.

Note that you don't have to cook the chicken too much because pressure canning will do that for you. That's why it's more convenient to go for raw pack canning.

### Bone-in or Boneless?

It's your choice whether to keep the bones intact in the poultry meat or not. Either way, it will not make any difference to the quality of the canned chicken. However, a boneless chicken will give you more space for food. In addition, chicken pieces with bones will require you to use more effort to fit them inside the jars properly. Using boneless meat will give you the advantage of storing somewhat uniform chicken cubes in the jars.

# Equipment and Ingredients for Canning Chicken

It's always a good idea to start canning food after cleaning the kitchen counter, preparing the area, and setting the equipment up. Canning requires adequate space to keep all the tools, jars, and other equipment neat and tidy to ensure maximum hygiene.

Here's what you'll need to have ready before you start the canning process.

• Chicken (boneless or bone-in, certain parts or the full chicken chopped into chunks).

• Salt (completely optional, most people add it to enhance the flavor of the poultry meat).

• Canning utensils.

• Canning rings, lids, and jars (pint or quarts – depending upon your canning requirements).

• Pressure canner.

• Clean rag.

If you want to can chicken for one meal, using pint-sized jars may be the best choice. However, if you don't mind using leftovers, quart could work too. Now, let's look at the recipe.

# Chicken Canning Recipe

Prep Time: 30 min

Cook Time: 90 min

Total Time: 2 hours

**Directions:**

1. Start by preparing the pressure canner. Pour water in the canner up to several inches, and start heating the water at low heat.

2. Chop the chicken (bone-in or boneless) into small pieces to make them convenient enough to fit in the jars. If you like, you may remove the chicken skin. As mentioned earlier, it will be easier to fit boneless pieces in the jars, as pieces with bones will require some adjustment.

3. For the raw pack method, fill the jar with the chopped chicken pieces in raw form. You may add 1 tsp. of salt for quart jars or ½ tsp. of salt for pint jars to enhance the flavor.

4. If using the hot pack method, steam, bake, or boil the pieces very lightly (2/3rd of the way cooked) before adding them to the jars.

5. In both cases, pour hot water or broth over the packed chicken pieces. Make sure to leave 1 inch of headspace between the rim and the poultry.

6. Use the air-bubble removal utensil, a chopstick, or plastic knife to remove the air bubbles trapped among the chicken pieces. Avoid a metal knife as it can scratch the glass jars and damage them.

7. Use a clean cloth to properly wipe the residue from the jar rims.

8. Place the lid and close the ring over the jar. Ensure that the lid is just closed finger-tight.

9. For jars with boneless chicken, set the canning process to 75 minutes for pint jars and 90 minutes for quart jars. For canning bone-in chicken, set the process to 65 minutes for pint jars and 75 minutes for quart jars.

10. If you are using a dial-gauge pressure canner, can at 11 lbs. or 12 lbs. of pressure. If using a weighted gauge canner, can at 10 lbs. of pressure or at 15 lbs. of pressure.

Now, let's look at a recipe for canning meats other than poultry.

# Meat Canning Recipe

Prep Time: 1 hour

Cook Time: 2 hours

Total Time: 3 hours

**Directions:**

1. Make sure you are using chilled meat. Properly thaw the meat if frozen. You can either use a microwave or cold water to thaw it.

2. If the meat is strong-flavored, soak it in brine (1 tbsp. of salt per quart jar of water) for 1 hour. Rinse the meat and remove excess fat. Chop the meat into chunks, cubes, or wide strips.

3. If you use the hot pack method, make sure to precook the meat by browning, stewing, or roasting it in a little bit of fat. Don't cook it completely.

4. Place the rack in the pressure canner. Pour water in the pressure canner to a few inches, and get it boiling.

5. Pack the prepared meat or raw meat in the jars cleanly, leaving 1 inch of headspace at the top of the jar. Make sure the meat is not packed too tight in the jar because you want the liquid to flow freely around the meat.

6. Add salt to the jars (1/2 tbsp. to pint jars and 1 tbsp. to quart jars) if desired.

7. Pour a few inches of boiling water into each jar.

8. Use a clean rag to wipe the rims and make sure they are dry. Run your finger around the rim to remove knicks or salt particles, because such elements can disrupt the sealing process.

9. Affix the lid and rings on the jars and place them into the pressure canner.

10. Place the jars on the rack so that they are a few inches above the base of the pressure canner to prevent damaging the jars.

11. Set the pressure canner to start building pressure, keeping the gauge off. Allow the canner to build up steam and vent out for 10 minutes before placing the weighted gauge.

12. After the steam has vented out, keep the pressure building until the dial gauge shows 10 lbs. of pressure when operating at sea level. If you are located at 1,000 feet or more above sea level, let the pressure in the gauge increase up to 15 lbs.

13. For pint jars, keep the pressure for 75 minutes. For quart jars, retain the pressure for 90 minutes. After the appropriate time passes, allow the canner to release the pressure naturally.

14. Once the canner releases the pressure, open the lid, facing away from the steam that will be released. Use canning tongs to vertically pick up each jar.

15. Place them on the counter and let them cool and seal for 24 hours. Once sealed, you can remove the rings and store the sealed jars as needed.

Note: Instead of chunks, strips, or pieces, you can also use ground meat for the process. You should only use a pressure canner for meat and poultry, or it will not work properly. As mentioned before, low-acidic foods (with pH lower than 4.6) require a high level of heating to ensure that the bacteria is killed off completely. Otherwise, it can lead to botulism.

# How to Practice Safe and Efficient Meat and Poultry Canning

There is no doubt that pressure canning is a convenient, efficient, and quick way to store meat and poultry for later consumption. It saves you the trouble of going to the store to buy ingredients, wasting a lot of your time. Additionally, it's a convenient way to keep food with you in case of an emergency.

However, if you don't follow the steps for pressure canning carefully, you may end up damaging your health. That's why it's important to follow the below-mentioned tips for canning poultry and meat safely and efficiently.

### Make Sure You Are Using the Right Equipment

It's important that you only use a pressure canner for processing meat and poultry products. Don't use a steam canner or water bath canner for these foods. The pressure canner should have a high-quality weight or dial gauge. Next to the canner, ensure that you have new jar lids. Follow the safety rules and protocols listed in the pressure canning manual to properly use the equipment.

### Prepare for a Large Batch

Canning meat can take a lot of time, so make sure you have enough room for a large batch. That way, you can save time and effort and avoid the need to can frequently. If you have to buy a pressure canner first, make sure to invest in a large model that will allow you to process several jars at a time. Using a large canner will help you to increase your efficiency.

### Don't Be Afraid of Using a Pressure Canner

Many people are afraid of pressure canning because it feels like the equipment may explode any minute. However, that's not the case at all. If you follow the simple instructions for using a pressure canner, you won't have any problems. After one or two canning batches, you will find it to be the most reliable equipment for preserving meat in the long term.

### Enhance the Meat Flavors

If you want the canned chicken or meat to have a good flavor, use dried herbs or salt when processing the meat in jars. Herbs and spices tend to improve the flavor of food if preserved for a long time. One of the best examples is pickles, which a lot of people enjoy eating. You may also use green herbs, but that usually changes the meat color to a shade of green, which may not look very appetizing. If that's the way you see things, too, go for dried herbs instead.

### Preserve Strategically

Make sure you know the right quantity of meat that you want for the canning process. If you or your family don't consume a lot of meat, it will be useless to can and store a lot of canned meat. In such a case, you may just use the freezer to preserve the meat or chicken and utilize the canning space for other foods.

## Can What You'll Use

Preserve meat that you will be using in your dishes later. Make sure to know what you and your family consume the most. It would be useless to preserve beef chunks if you only eat white meat, for example. Likewise, preserve meat in the right form, such as chunks, strips, or ground, as per your liking to add to specific dishes later.

### Prepare Each Jar in the Right Quantity

Most families have an idea about the average amount of food each member consumes. Keep that in mind when selecting the canning jar sizes to have enough meat for the meals you will make later. For instance, use a 1½-pint or wide-mouthed jar to store loaf-style meat or bologna so that you find it easy to take out the meatloaf as per your needs.

### Keep the Rings Affixed

Most canning experts advise removing the ring from canned jars containing pickles, jellies, or jams when storing them. This prevents the rings from rusting or becoming infested with insect nests. However, you may want to keep the rings intact on jars with canned meat to add an extra layer of protection against rodents. This depends on where you store your jars. Also, ensure that the jar lids and rings are completely dry before storing them.

### Cooking Meat before Canning is Optional

Most people preserve meat after cooking it a little to be ready for specific recipes when opened. However, it's completely optional to do so. You can use the raw-pack method for canning poultry and meat without any issues. If you want, you can add spices or salt to enhance the flavor of the raw meat.

### Monitor the Meat Jars before Consuming

Even if you have successfully followed the steps of pressure canning meat or poultry, you should still habitually check the stored jars for any signs of inadequacy. Discard the meat immediately if you notice anything unusual. When you plan on using the meat for a recipe, make sure to reheat the meat and stock by boiling the ingredients at 140° F for at least 10 minutes. Do this even if the preserved meat in the jar appears to be completely fine. This removes any possibility of infection in the preserved food, making it safe for consumption.

### Remove the Jars in a Vertical Position

It's important to keep the jars upright whenever you handle them so that the pressure built up in the jars with the meat can be sealed efficiently. Tipping the jars or placing them unevenly can compromise the sealing process.

Pressure canning sure does need practice, but the benefits of doing so can be fruitful. It's important to follow the necessary safety tips to ensure maximum efficiency when preserving or using the food. Unlike other foods, meat and poultry items require extra care because they are not acidic, making them more vulnerable to bacterial growth if prepared carelessly. Note that using a pressure canner is not as challenging as preserving the meat safely in jars. Pressure canning is a safe and fun process that will let you keep food for months and years without worrying about shortages at the time of need.

# Chapter 10: How to Ferment

For thousands of years, even before developing alcoholic drinks, humans have been, unknowingly, fermenting food. The fermentation process of dairy was likely a natural occurrence because of the innately present microflora and the hot climate. Researchers even suggest that hanging goat milk bags over the backs of camels was the world's first yogurt production process. It wasn't until 1856 that the science behind fermentation was understood. That year, Louis Pasteur, a French chemist, linked yeast to the fermentation process.

Later in 1910, Elie Metchnikoff, a Russian bacteriologist, brought new information regarding fermentation to light. He suggested that since Bulgarians consumed more fermented dairy than other nations, they had a longer average lifespan of 87. His observations suggested that fermented food is considered beneficial to human health. Further investigations revealed that Lactobacillus acidophilus, the bacteria found in fermented dairy, survives inside the human gut and remains very active. Throughout the 1900s, fermentation was used popularly as a food preservation method. By storing food in an oxygen-free environment, they were able to keep food from spoiling. Undesirable bacteria can't survive anaerobic environments, while desired bacteria thrive.

For the past forty years, give or take, considerable research regarding the health benefits associated with the consumption of "good" bacteria has been conducted. Several links were made between benefits, including detoxification and improved digestion, and the consumption of friendly bacteria. You may have heard about the endless probiotic products available, from supplements to beverages, which have become popular in today's health and fitness world. Probiotics are a commercial trend right now, and it's nothing to be upset about. Fermentation comes with great benefits, donates a very strong, unique flavor to food, and is a great way of preserving food. That is why it is no surprise that you are interested in learning how to ferment your food. One thing to keep in mind before jumping right in is that fermentation is substantially modulated decay.

### What Is Fermentation?

In simple terms, fermentation is a metabolic process where the activity of microorganisms results in a change in food and drinks. This change is usually desirable as it is used to add flavor, increase health benefits, preserve food, and more. Although the word "ferment" is derived from the Latin word "fervere," which means "to boil," the fermentation process can occur without the presence of any heat.

### How Does It Work?

Good bacteria survive by feeding on carbohydrates for fuel and energy. Adenosine triphosphate (ATP) and similar organic chemicals transport this energy to each part of the cell whenever needed. ATP is generated when microbes respire—they can produce ATP most efficiently through aerobic respiration. When glucose is converted to pyruvic acid—a process called glycolysis— aerobic respiration starts but on the condition that sufficient oxygen is present. On the other hand, fermentation is a process that's similar to anaerobic respiration, which occurs without the presence of oxygen. The production of ATP is also possible in such an environment. This is because the fermentation process results in lactic acid production and other various organic molecules that result in ATP. In this case, good bacteria also feed on carbohydrates, starches, and sugars, releasing carbon dioxide, alcohol, and organic acids, which preserve the food and give it flavor. Individual microbes and cells generally can alternate between the two energy production modes, depending on the surrounding environment.

### What Goes on in the Process?

As mentioned above, fermentation is an anaerobic process when oxygen is absent and good microorganisms, like bacteria, yeast, and mold, are present to acquire energy from fermentation. In fact, some yeast cells, like Saccharomyces cerevisiae, favor fermentation over aerobic respiration when enough sugar is present, even in the abundance of oxygen. As the fermentation process takes place, good microbes break starches and sugars down into acids and alcohol. This preserves food, allowing us to store it for prolonged periods without it spoiling.

The enzymes that fermentation provides are also vital for digestion. Humans are born with a specific number of enzymes, and as we age, they decrease. Fermented food provides us with the enzymes necessary to break foods down. Fermentation helps with pre-digestion as well. As microbes digest starches and sugars, they break down the food before we even consume it.

# Types of Fermentation

There are generally three types of fermentation that you can use: lactic acid fermentation, ethanol or alcohol fermentation, and acetic acid fermentation. In the lactic acid fermentation process, the bacteria and yeast strains convert sugars and starches into lactic acid, requiring no heat. Since this is an anaerobic chemical reaction, pyruvic acid uses the nicotinamide adenine dinucleotide + hydrogen, or NADH. A similar process is carried out by human muscle cells during strenuous activity. Lactic acid bacteria are necessary for producing and preserving food, especially wholesome and inexpensive food. Impoverished nations rely heavily on this fermentation method. Kimchi, sourdough, pickles, sauerkraut, and yogurt are all made using this fermentation method.

During the ethanol or alcohol fermentation process, pyruvate molecules and the product of glycolysis are broken down by yeasts. Carbon dioxide molecules and alcohol are the products of broken-down starches and sugars. This fermentation method is used to make wine and beer. The acetic acid fermentation process ferments the sugars and starches of fruits and grains into vinegar and other condiments with a sour taste. Wine vinegar, apple cider vinegar, and kombucha are examples of the resultants of this process.

# Stages of Fermentation

The stages of the fermentation process can vary according to what you are fermenting. However, there are generally two fermentation stages: primary fermentation and secondary fermentation. Primary fermentation is a relatively brief phase, during which the microbes quickly begin to work on raw ingredients like dairy, vegetables, or fruit. The surrounding liquid, such as the fermented vegetables' brine, contains microbes that prevent food colonization from the putrefying bacteria. Carbohydrates are converted into acids and alcohols by yeasts and similar microbes.

During the longer fermentation stage, or secondary fermentation, carbohydrates, the microbes' and yeast's food source, becomes scarcer, causing them to die off. The alcohol levels rise as well, and this phase usually lasts anywhere between several days and weeks. Alcoholic beverages are made by winemakers using secondary fermentation. The chemical reactions between the microbes and their environment are highly affected by the varying pH of the ferment—the pH can change drastically from what it initially was. Once the alcohol levels reach 12% to 15%, the yeast is killed, and no further fermentation occurs. Distillation is then needed to get rid of the water and condense the alcohol to increase the concentration.

## Benefits of Fermentation

There are many benefits associated with fermented products. One of the key benefits is that digestive, health-friendly bacteria in the gut can be restored by the probiotics generated in the fermentation process. This may help reduce numerous digestive problems. For instance, a study from the *World Journal of Gastroenterology* suggests that probiotics can help relieve Irritable Bowel Syndrome (IBS) and reduce the severity of bloating, diarrhea, constipation, and gas by increasing the amount of Lactobacillus and Bifidobacterium in the gut. The high probiotic content found in fermented foods can also boost the immune system and reduce the risk of several infections. Probiotic food can help speed up the recovery process if you're ill. Most fermented food is high in zinc, iron, and vitamin C, all great for the immune system. The broken-down nutrients in food resulting from the fermentation process can make food much easier to digest. That is why those who suffer from lactose intolerance can consume fermented food like kefir and yogurt. Antinutrients such as lectins and phytates found in grains, nuts, seeds, and legumes are broken down and destroyed during the fermentation process. Antinutrients can disrupt nutrient absorption. Research published in *Nutrients Journal* as part of a study funded by the European Regional Development Fund linked Lactobacillus rhamnosus and Lactobacillus gasseri, and other probiotic strains to reduced body fat and weight loss. Lactobacillus helveticus and Bifidobacterium longum were also linked to reduced symptoms of depression and anxiety. Fermented food may also help to lower total LDL cholesterol and blood pressure, lowering the risk of heart disease.

# Choosing the Right Equipment

To prepare your vegetables for fermenting, you need to invest in a quality knife or food processor. If you are fermenting food that ferments in its own juices, such as sauerkraut, you will need a pounding tool. This will help you to compress and break apart your food in the fermenting vessel. Your choice of jars and containers will heavily depend on the type of food that is being fermented. Glass containers are easy to find and are ideal in the sense that they don't scratch easily and are free of chemicals such as BPA. Ceramic containers are typically great for large batches of fermented vegetables, as they range from 5 to 20 liters in size. Porcelain containers are generally safe, as long as you avoid pieces that are not food grade, like decorative pottery or vases. You should avoid plastic containers as they are easy to damage and scratch, easily harboring bacteria. Plastic also usually contains harmful chemicals that can impact your food. To ensure that oxygen is kept out and the gases from fermentation don't escape, you must make sure that your lid is sealed tightly. Using an airlock, a tight lid or a cloth cover are the most popular options. Airlocks are great because they reduce the risk of yeast and mold formation. Tightly sealing the lid is a good option, too. However, you may need to burp the jar daily to rid it of carbon dioxide buildup. Cloth covers may suffice, as well, but they may lead to the formation of mold and yeast.

# Preparing the Vegetables

There are several ways in which you can prepare your vegetables for the fermentation process. The first is grating—you can either use your hand or a processor to grate your vegetables. Grating works well for crunchy or hard vegetables and can allow the salt to rapidly penetrate the vegetable because of the large surface area that it creates. If you grate your vegetables, it's unlikely that you'll need to add brine. You will also usually end up with a relish texture when done grating. Chopping your vegetables is also another option. Typically, the recipe that you follow should specify the size that you should chop your vegetables. However, if not specified, you can chop according to your preference. Most of the time, chopped vegetables demand salt brine. The time they take to culture will depend on their size. The third method is slicing. If you are working with firm vegetables, you can slice them thinly. If not, slice your soft vegetables into larger pieces. This will allow them to maintain their shape as they ferment. Sliced vegetables take a reasonable amount of time to ferment— not too slow and not too quick. The last method would be leaving your vegetables whole. Some vegetables such as Brussels sprouts, radishes, and green beans work best that way. Some recipes may suggest that you drown the whole vegetable in brine, while other larger vegetables may require special culture treatment.

## Salt, Whey, and Starter Culture

Salt prevents bad bacteria from growing as it pulls out the moisture in the food and allows the natural bacteria that exist on the vegetable to carry out the fermentation process. This results in a slower fermentation process, ideal for cultured vegetables that need to be stored for more time. Salt also enhances the flavor of the vegetables and leaves them crunchy to bite, as it hardens the pectins in vegetables. Although salt-free ferments are more bio-diverse, they result in mushy vegetables and even mold. Various freeze-dried starter cultures can be used alone without salt. You can also use some kind of bacterial starter to speed up the fermentation process. Since whey is dairy-based, it may not be suitable for everyone. If you decide to use it, make sure that it's fresh and well-strained because it can lend its flavor to the vegetable. You can add salt to the whey for flavor and crunch.

## Brine and Fermentation Recipe

1. To make the brine, you will need to follow a ratio of two tablespoons of salt to one quart of water. If the temperature is above 85 degrees, add one more spoon of salt. Stir well and set aside.

2. Prepare your vegetables in the desired method.

3. Gather your preferred spices. You can use fresh herbs, onions, and garlic.

4. Add the herbs, onions, and garlic to the bottom of your container.

5. Add mesquite leaves, black tea, horseradish, oak, or grapes to keep your vegetable crisp.

6. Place the prepared vegetable on top of the flavorings, ensuring there's 2 inches headspace between it and the top of the jar. Pour the brine over the vegetable, covering it by at least 1 inch.

7. Use an inverted plastic jar lid or a glass weight to keep your vegetable below the brine as it ferments.

8. Use your preferred lid to seal the jar tightly. Place it at 65-85 degrees Fahrenheit for around ten days (depending on your preference). The longer the time, the sourer the vegetables.

9. Burp your jar frequently if needed.

10. Once you are done, move the jar to a cold storage area.

## Preventing Cross-Contamination

To prevent your cultures from cross-contamination, you should keep them at least 4 feet away from each other. Make sure that all your tools and your environment, in general, are clean. Rinse everything thoroughly to rid it of soap residue. You should always avoid antibacterial detergents and soap when fermenting and never allow your pets inside the kitchen. You should empty the space from anything that can be spilled easily and keep the ferment away from bacteria sources (garbage cans, sink drains, or soiled laundry).

Fermentation is a great way to preserve your vegetables, add other health and nutritional benefits to them, and give them a unique flavor. Fermentation is a process that has been carried out for thousands of years. Many studies are still being carried out to discover more about fermentation and its benefits. Besides aiding in digestion and boosting immunity, fermentation has also been linked to weight loss, boosting mental health, and lowering the risk of heart disease. There are several fermentation processes and vegetable preparation procedures that you can choose from—

it all comes down to your preferences. You can experiment with several fermentation recipes. As long as you make sure you're using the right equipment, sealing the lid tightly, burping it when needed, and taking the necessary precautions to prevent cross-contamination.

# Chapter 11: Dehydrating as a Method of Preservation

In this chapter, you will learn about a secret to food preservation that people have been using for thousands of years in times of emergency and famine: dehydrating. It turns out a dehydrated potato isn't as bad as it sounds (unless you take it personally).

Centuries ago, the only means of preserving food was to dry it, specifically to use it in winter, when it was impossible to grow fresh harvest. It's said that food dehydration originated among Middle Eastern and Oriental cultures, as it enabled ancient men and women to preserve their food sources. Egyptians used the desert heat to dry their fish and meat, and around the year 700 AD, the Aztecs began salting and sun-drying their tomatoes to conserve their freshness. Later, the Italians started to dry their tomatoes on their rooftops as well.

Dehydration is the removal of the moisture in food through evaporation to prevent microorganisms from spoiling it. Microorganisms love moist environments, so by destroying their shelter, we extend our food's shelf life.

We're all familiar with dried fruits and jerky—these are actually commercially dehydrated foods that we've come to love and consume regularly. Commercial food industries perform more efficient dehydrating processes, so the dehydrated foods that we buy can last up to ten years. Foods dehydrated at home last for shorter periods, depending on the type of food. But drying food at home is very convenient and retains the foods' nutritional value. There are many other reasons to do it at home.

DIY food dehydration:

● It can allow you to dehydrate and preserve your favorite foods safely, without harmful additives or artificial colors.

● It provides you more control over the quality and process.

● It can prove to be a lot cheaper because you'll be able to produce larger quantities any time you like.

● It is quite enjoyable, especially if you add your own touches and do it with family and friends.

**Why Dehydrate Food in General?**

1. Dehydrating preserves perishable foods like fresh fruits and meat, allowing you to carry them around anywhere.

2. Drying food shrinks its size while retaining the nutrients so that you can store more food in less space.

3. Dried food can reduce the time you spend cooking. You can prepare all your vegetables and legumes at once, dehydrate them, then easily rehydrate later.

# Best Foods to Dehydrate

• Bananas: we're all guilty of buying more bananas than we need when we go grocery shopping, and of course, they over ripen in no time. So, it's quite convenient to peel those bananas, cut them into slices, dehydrate them, and voila! Banana chips that can last for months. Who doesn't love those?

• Apples: a nutritious fruit that, when dried, can last up to three years and can even be preserved for much longer if frozen. Dried fruits are also healthy snacks and can be added to your breakfast oatmeal.

• Beans, peas, corn, lemon: You can throw them in soups or stews, and they rehydrate immediately as you're cooking.

• Other vegetables: dried, crunchy vegetables can be dipped in sauces, grated in casseroles and salads, or even blended and used as powders (onion powder, garlic powder, etc.)

• Walla Walla onions: many people love these onions. Some even eat them like apples, but, unfortunately, they are difficult crops—their harvest lasts for only a few weeks in summer every year. Lucky for you, you can wait for the Walla Walla season, buy these tasty French onions and dehydrate them. You won't have to wait for the next season because you'll have enough supply of these sweet onions to last you the rest of the year.

• Meats: years ago, Americans decided to smoke dry meat, and, from there, jerky was invented. These thin strips of meat are very popular and delicious snacks. Dehydrating jerky at home is more economical than buying it. Finished jerky products cost about $32 per pound, while homemade jerky will cost you only $12.50 per pound. You can use any type of meat to make jerky (beef, lamb, or poultry). If you're a huge fan of jerky, here's a mouthwatering recipe!

# Jerky Recipe

1. Soak the meat in vinegar, drain it, and marinate with soy sauce, salt, black pepper, and onion powder. You can add any spices you love to enhance its flavor (chili, garlic powder, or red pepper). For a sweet and sour jerky, add ¼ cup of maple syrup.

2. Place in a Ziploc bag and refrigerate for four hours or a whole day to allow the flavors to be absorbed.

3. Take the bag out and cut your meat, making sure it's uniformly sliced. Then lay the strips on the dehydrator tray and dry at 160°F for 4-6 hours. (Warning: your kitchen is going to smell amazing!)

4. Blot the meat with paper towels during the dehydration process to absorb any fat.

5. Once it reaches the level of dryness you desire, the jerky is good to go!

• Did you know that you can dehydrate your grain products? You can cook your pasta like you normally do, drain it well, spread it evenly on your tray, and dehydrate at 135°F until it's crispy and brittle. Rice can be cooked in non-fat broth before drying for an excellent taste.

- Even sauces can be easily dehydrated, spaghetti sauce, curry sauce, and salsa. They'll come in handy whenever you're too busy to make dinner. All you have to do is add some water and reheat them, and they'll rehydrate back instantly, so you can just add them to your pasta.

# How to Dehydrate Food

There are various techniques for food dehydration, but regardless of the technique used, dehydration requires a few basic conditions. An adequate amount of heat to dehydrate the moisture, dry air to absorb it, and enough circulation to get rid of the vapor.

### 1. The Traditional Way

The traditional way of drying food would be sun drying. It's how food dehydration started and how it was done for thousands of years. Sun-drying is the easiest and cheapest way to dehydrate food, especially fruits and vegetables.

- Sun drying is ideal if you live in a hot area, but it won't work in humid or cold areas.

- All you have to do is set the food out on a tray, cover it with a cloth, expose it to direct sunlight and leave it for 3-4 days to dry.

The downside of this dehydration method is that it relies on the weather, so if temperatures drop below 85 degrees Fahrenheit, microorganisms can thrive and spoil your food.

### 2. Dehydrators

Dehydrators produce the best results out of most drying methods, as they have electric heating elements and air vents. Moreover, they are safe and cost-effective. A dehydrator can provide an adequate amount of heat to dehydrate the food but not enough heat to cook it (125-150 degrees F). There are a plethora of different brands and models that can give you satisfactory results. But you need to consider a few things when you're buying a dehydrator:

• Heating element: some dehydrators have the heating element on top, blowing the heat currents downwards. If the heating element is on the top or bottom, you'll have to flip the food every couple of minutes to ensure an even distribution of heat.

• Fans: your best option would be a box-type dehydrator that blows the heat currents from the back to the front and has dual fans, as it will provide a more balanced circulation inside, and there won't be a need for rotation. This makes the unit more efficient and achieves better results.

• Temperature settings: the adjustable temperatures feature is a must to dehydrate different ingredients. Many dehydrators even have timers to shut down the machine and prevent it from overheating.

- Capacity: the larger the capacity, the better. A 9-tray capacity would be ideal and will hold a lot of food. But it all depends on your preferences and how much food you'll be drying.

- Other features: If you want trays that are dishwasher safe, avoid dehydrators made of plastic and look for metal ones instead. However, they are more expensive. Some dehydrators also have transparent glass doors so that you check up on the food without opening the machine.

### 3. Kitchen Oven

- Ovens take much longer to dry food when compared to dehydrators because they often don't have fans. However, you can place a fan nearby.

- Your oven should go as low as 140 degrees so that your food doesn't cook instead of dry, but some ovens don't go that low.

- You can use an oven thermometer to know the exact drying temperature, as oven dials usually don't give accurate readings.

- Don't close the oven door completely. Prop it open a few inches.

### 4. Air Drying

Air drying takes place in enclosed spaces, unlike sun-drying. It's similar to a greenhouse, where you can control the environment during the process. You can do it in a well-ventilated attic or a dry room. Mushrooms, peppers, and herbs are all best to air-dry. But this technique may not be successful for all foods.

# Storing Dehydrated Foods

The shelf life of dried food depends on storage conditions.

•After the dehydration process, you should leave the food to cool for about forty minutes.

•To make sure that the food is ready to be stored, check for its dryness. Fruits should feel like leather when you touch them and be slightly translucent, while vegetables should be brittle.

•Choosing proper storage containers is essential as it prolongs shelf life, saves nutrients, prevents bugs and microbes from reaching the food, and keeps moisture out. Use metal or glass containers with tight, insect-proof, and well-insulated lids.

•Check the food within a week or two. If there's any moisture present, you could take the food out and redry it.

•Dried food should be kept in dark, cool, and dry places. Avoid light, as it breaks down the food and makes it lose its flavor, shortening its shelf life.

•Fruits have double the shelf life of vegetables. Most fruit can be stored for a year, while vegetables only last for six months on average. Meat lasts up to two months only.

# Dehydrating Do's and Don'ts

1. Some foods shouldn't be dehydrated, like dairy products, as the probiotics can result in food poisoning. Foods like eggs are susceptible to salmonella bacteria, and the high heat used in dehydration increases that risk. Generally, food high in fat doesn't dehydrate well, as fats don't have much moisture. Hence, they can't evaporate, leading to the food going rancid.

2. Many foods with a waxy coating, like fruits and vegetables (berries, grapes, tomatoes), should be blanched first. Blanching is plunging food from boiling water into cold water. This process preserves color, nutrients, stops enzyme activity, slows ripening, and prevents food from spoiling or rotting quickly.

3. Keep in mind that some types of food are susceptible to oxidation, like apples and pears. You can juice any citric fruit like lemons or oranges and apply it as a pre-treatment solution. Another option would be adding a teaspoon of ascorbic acid to some water to soak the fruits in before drying them—this can help prevent most food from browning.

4. You have to use the right temperature. Too high of a temperature can result in case hardening, which dries the food's exterior and prevents the interior from drying and removing the moisture properly. In contrast, low temperatures cause the growth of bacteria and molds.

5. Don't turn up the heat when you want to speed up the drying process. It's better to slice or cut your food into smaller pieces.

6. Different foods have varying dehydration temperatures, so avoid grouping different foods together.

7. Meat and poultry need around 160 degrees Fahrenheit, fruits and vegetables need 125-135 degrees Fahrenheit, while grains and pre-cooked meats need 145 degrees Fahrenheit.

8. Don't leave the food out for too long to avoid the moisture from re-entering, and if the container is musty, it's better to throw it away or sterilize it.

9. The only vitamin that gets damaged in the dehydration process is vitamin C. So, keep vitamin C supplements on your shelf if you won't get enough from all the dried food you'll be eating.

# Chapter 12: Freezing

From frozen vegetables to ready-made meals, almost any food you can think of can be found in the freezer section at the grocery store. Frozen food has been rapidly growing in popularity, offering more variety than ever since it was first introduced in the 1930s. Frozen food serves as a convenient alternative to cooking from scratch—it is time-saving, easy to cook, and can usually be prepared in multiple ways. Besides the practicality that it offers, freezing food is a great way to preserve it. Many people choose to cook and freeze large batches of food, allowing them to safely store it for long periods and reheat it whenever needed. Freezing has been used as a method to preserve food since prehistoric times. Even back then, people frequently preserved their hunt using ice and snow.

Many people believe that freezing can negatively impact the food's nutrient content. However, this is not always the case. If you blanch or submerge your fruits and vegetables in boiling water before freezing them—a method that deactivates yeasts and enzymes that may contribute to spoilage—15% to 20% of their vitamin C content can be lost. This isn't usually a problem since frozen fruits and vegetables are usually frozen right after harvesting when in peak condition. This makes them higher in nutrient content than other fresh crops that take time to be sorted, transported, and distributed. This process slowly strips them of their nutrients and vitamins. As a matter of fact, green vegetables and soft fruit can lose around 15% of their vitamin C content every day when stored at room temperature. This means that frozen and fresh fruits and vegetables end up with around the same vitamin C content.

If you freeze poultry, meat, or fish, there will be almost no mineral or vitamin loss. This is because vitamins A and D, minerals, and protein are not impacted by freezing. However, when they defrost, they lose liquids that contain mineral salts and water-soluble vitamins. If you don't recover the lost liquid, it will be completely stripped away during the cooking process.

# How and Why Freezing Works

By freezing your food, you are delaying enzyme activity that leads to spoilage, as well as preventing harmful microorganisms, such as mold and yeast, from growing. This helps keep your food safe from spoilage for longer and keeps it safe for consumption. Microorganisms need the water content present in food to survive and grow. When this water turns into ice crystals upon freezing, it becomes inaccessible to them. However, you must keep in mind that some—or the majority—of the microorganisms, excluding parasites, can survive the frozen environment. This is why you must always handle your frozen food very carefully, before freezing and upon defrosting. Generally, food can last anywhere between 3 to 12 months in your freezer without spoiling or losing its quality. The specific duration depends on the type of food and the product label. If applicable, check the label and instructions for directions, special requirements, and suitable duration.

# Tips on Freezing

## Freezing Fruits

If you want to freeze your fruits, make sure to remove cores, stems, and other inedible parts of the fruit before washing, drying, and slicing them up. You should then place a single layer of fruit on a baking tray lined with a silicone sheet liner or compostable parchment paper. Place the fruit in the freezer for about two to three hours—or until it's completely frozen. While this step is not necessary, it is highly recommended. Freezing your fruit in a tray with a baking sheet will ensure that it won't stick together when frozen again. Ending up with a large blob of frozen fruit slices can be a pain. After it's done freezing, you can transfer the fruit slices into the container of your choice. Frozen fruit typically lasts for a long time, though it's best consumed within six to nine months.

You can either thaw the fruit or use it frozen in your recipes (if apt). Some fruits, like grapes and blueberries, are very delicious when consumed frozen. If you want to thaw your fruit, make sure to thaw only the amount that you want. The consistency of the fruit can be changed when frozen and then thawed. Freezing it for the second time may be a bad idea. You can either transfer the fruit to your fridge so that it thaws at its own pace or by running cold water over the container.

## Freezing Vegetables

To freeze your vegetables, you will need to trim off the roots, stems, and other blemished areas. If you are working with vegetables that come with outer layers, like beans or peas, you should remove them. If you usually peel, core, or de-seed any of your vegetables, do so before freezing as well. Make sure that your vegetables are washed, dried, and then chopped. As mentioned above, some vegetables work best when blanched—boil some water in a pot and then submerge your vegetables in it. Keep the vegetables in long enough so that they are still firm and not cooked through. If you are working with herbs or greens, they should turn a brighter green color and wilt slightly. Scoop the vegetables out of the pot and transfer them into an ice bath. This is necessary to "shock" the vegetables, interrupting the cooking process. After your vegetables cool down, make sure to pat them dry to prevent any freezer burns. Some vegetables, like celery, bell peppers, and onions, don't need to be blanched, so make sure to find out what's best for the vegetables you are freezing. Like fruit, you should freeze your vegetables on a baking sheet before transferring them to your desired container. If properly frozen, vegetables can last around eight to ten months and should be thawed in the refrigerator or under cold water.

## Freezing Fresh Meat

When freezing fresh meat, avoid freezing large amounts at once, as this helps to make the freezing and thawing processes easier. Cut and store meat in meal-sized portions to prevent it from being exposed to bacteria and make sure that it thaws easily. You should always freeze meat as fast as possible. To ensure that you are packaging your meat correctly, use a vacuum sealer or aluminum foil, plastic wrap, airtight Ziploc bags, or freezer wrap to double wrap meat cuts. Never thaw your meat at room temperature, as this makes it more vulnerable to collecting bacteria. You can thaw your meat in the refrigerator, a cold-water bath, or the microwave. Meat that has been thawed in the refrigerator can be refrozen. If you thaw it in a cold bath, make sure to change the water every thirty minutes to protect it from bacteria. Microwaving is ideal if you are under a time crunch. However, it can change the meat's consistency and texture.

### Freezing Seafood

When it comes to seafood, freezing is not a one-size-fits-all process. For every 500 gm of lobster, cook in salted water for eight minutes, drain, and cool. Place in a plastic bag, cover it with brine, seal, and freeze. Scallops need to be rinsed under cold water and free of sand and their shell. Drain, place in a plastic bag, seal, and freeze as well. For clams and mussels, rinse them to get rid of sand, then steam them over medium heat so that the shells open slightly. Shuck them, place them in a plastic bag, cover them in brine or the strained cooking liquid, seal, and freeze. Oysters must be shucked, rinsed, and reserved in liquid. You should then pack them and their liquid in a plastic bag, then seal and freeze them. Finfish should generally be gutted and rinsed under cold water. Wrap small fish in baking sheets, then freeze them—large fish should be frozen on a baking sheet, dipped in ice-cold water, and returned to the freezer. Repeat multiple times, wrap well, and freeze. It's recommended that you cover steaks and fillets with brine solution before freezing in a plastic bag or container. The recommended freezing time varies based on the type of seafood, though seafood usually lasts between three to six months when handled correctly. You can thaw seafood in the refrigerator or under cold water—don't unfreeze until you're ready to cook.

### Freezing Eggs and Dairy

You can freeze your eggs for up to one year. To freeze the eggs, you should remove the shells and scramble them well. Pour the mixed eggs into an ice cube tray, wrap them well using saran wrap, and freeze. After they freeze, you can either leave them in the tray or transfer them into another container. Eggs need to be thawed in a refrigerator. Milk can be frozen. However, keep in mind that it may separate when thawed. Make sure to remove 1 ½ cups per gallon when freezing the milk. This will guarantee that the milk doesn't burst the container or overflow when it expands. Frozen milk can last up to one month and can be thawed in the refrigerator. Make sure to shake it well before you use it.

# Freezing Soups, Broths, and Stews

You can use rectangular plastic containers to freeze your soups, broths, and stews. Line your container with saran wrap and make sure that it hangs over the sides. Fill it up with a pre-measured amount of soup/ broth/ stew, and then place the container on a rimmed sheet pan. Freeze them flat, flip out the container, and wrap the saran wrap around your frozen soup, broth, or stew. You can place the wrapped product in a Ziploc bag. To thaw, heat it over low or medium heat until it thaws completely.

### Which Containers to Use

Ideally, you should use re-sealable freezer bags, glass storage containers that come with airtight lids, or plastic deli containers to freeze your food. Some wide jars are also suitable for freezing. However, in all cases, make sure you read the label to ensure they're freezer friendly. You should also leave one-inch headspace between the lid and whatever you are freezing. Keep in mind that when you freeze liquids, they expand. In which case, glass containers, if not freezer-safe, may become hazardous and shatter. This is why random glass jars may not be the best option if you are freezing milk or sauces. Besides unreliable glass, their seals may not be airtight. As explained above, the best packaging method and most suitable type of container depends on the food you are freezing. If you choose the correct containers and follow packaging and thawing procedures, you will avoid off-flavors. You should also stick to the recommended freezing period to maintain flavor, texture, and consistency.

## Freezer Tips

Your freezer should always be kept at -18°C or below the suggested temperature. While refrigerators may not function when they are full, deep freezers function better when packed tightly. Don't confuse this with overloading, however. Overloading your freezer can block the vents, reducing their lifespan. It may also damage your food due to blockage of air circulation, catalyzing bacterial growth. Over packing your freezer can also impact its energy efficiency. To avoid freezer burns, messes, or spills, ensure that everything is packed in suitable and freezer-safe containers. You should always avoid placing hot food in the freezer. This is why you should run your vegetables under cold water or place them in ice baths before freezing. Placing hot food in the freezer will raise the freezer temperature. Not only will this negatively impact your freezer, but it may also ruin other food, as it could end up melting or producing water. When the food thaws and refreezes incorrectly, it can develop an off-taste. This could also mess with its consistency and even attract bacteria. You should always make sure that your food is completely thawed before you cook it. Don't refreeze your food after it has been cooked.

To prevent your freezer from over packing, you should frequently empty it and rid it of all expired products. Store-bought frozen food often comes in bulky, useless boxes. Tossing these boxes out and replacing them with Ziplocs or freezer bags can help you to save space. Another excellent freezer organization tip is storing everything vertically instead of laying it flat. You will be surprised by how much space you will gain. Besides, keeping things vertically will allow you to have a better view of everything. You can also use paper clips strategically to hang things from the shelves and store the larger items at the bottom of your freezer.

## What to Do When a Freezer Stops Working

If the energy goes out or your freezer stops working for whatever reason, there are a few things that you should do to ensure that your food doesn't go bad. If you know that the issue can be fixed within a day, then make sure to keep your freezer shut. Every time you open your freezer, cold air will escape, and warm air will flow in. If your freezer doesn't have a thermostat, you should get a compatible one. This way, when the freezer stops working, you will determine the status of your food. As long as your freezer doesn't go above 4°C, it should be safe. However, keep in mind that not all food is the same and that this is just a general rule. If your freezer isn't fixed within a day, you should take some alternate protective measures. One of the easiest options is to ask a friend, neighbor, or family member if they have any room in their freezer. Make sure to transport your food in an icebox. You can also use dry ice to keep your freezer temporarily cold. However, be very careful when handling dry ice to avoid chemical burns. Use gloves to wrap the dry ice in newspapers or towels before placing it in the freezer. You can also use insulated coolers or an icebox to keep your food at home. Make sure that the temperature doesn't rise above 4°C.

Freezing has been used for centuries as a food preservation method. It is a great way to ensure that you have ready-made, safe food whenever you don't feel like cooking. It is also a great way to preserve fruit and vegetables for later consumption. Many people freeze off-season fruits to have access to them all year round. For instance, they may freeze mangoes during summer to make fresh mango juice during winter when unavailable at the markets. Freezing comes with endless advantages. However, to ensure that your food remains bacteria-free, doesn't develop an off-taste, or change its texture and consistency, you must keep several things in mind. Based on the food you are handling, follow through with the suitable preparation, packing, freezing, and thawing procedures. You should also make sure to use freezer-safe containers suitable for the type of frozen food you will put inside them to steer clear of potential hazards.

# Conclusion

Around 1.3 billion tons of food are wasted around the world each year. Many people buy food that stays forgotten at the back of the pantry. Others may buy an excessive amount of food because they overestimate their needs. Regardless of the reason, food spoilage and waste remains among the most popular problems our world faces. Another issue we encounter is seasonal dietary restrictions or limitations. Many fruits and vegetables are seasonal. They are only available or more abundant during specific times of the year. This could be a major problem for some people if their diet heavily depends on specific seasonal foods. For others, craving a food item when it's less abundant can be a minor inconvenience. Whichever problems you're facing, they can be fixed through canning and preserving.

Now that you have read this book, you probably know everything there is to know about canning and preserving. It's time to get your hands on a canner, mason jars, a food processor, a dehydrator, a juicer, and any other supplies you may need. Make sure to select the right supplies for the job, though! For instance, if you're freezing your food, make sure to invest in freezer-safe containers, or get the right jars and lids if you plan to ferment. Before you jump right in, make sure that you conduct the right preservation technique for the type of food, your needs, and desired outcome. Knowing exactly what you expect from the process will help you to figure out which technique is the most suitable. Following through with the right procedure will help to guarantee a successful preservation experience. When it's time to use your preserved food, you should also refer to the instructions when needed.

Understanding how you can preserve your food will surely change your life. As you put all this information into practice, you will find that the time you spend in the kitchen drastically decreases. You will also notice that less food is being wasted, your diet is becoming more diverse, and your grocery shopping bills are decreasing. When you preserve your food at home, you control everything that occurs throughout the process. Being aware of the equipment used, the cleanliness of the supplies, the general environmental conditions, and, of course, avoiding the additives that suppliers use will keep your mind at ease. It is a great way to ensure that your family's health remains a top priority, while still benefiting from everything that preservation has to offer. While processing and implementing all this information in real-time may feel very overwhelming at first, preserving your food will become a habitual and regular kitchen routine.

Whether you want to save your chicken broth for later or make batches of semi-cooked food to prepare whenever you need it, you will automatically put all your knowledge into practice. Besides, if you ever feel stuck, you will always have this friendly handbook to turn to. Filled with simple, delicious recipes and step-by-step directions, you will eventually master the art of making delicious homemade jams and nutritious preserved goods. Whether you are into pickling or fermenting, you will find a way to give your food a unique flavor and please your family's taste buds. Knowing how to preserve your own food may just be the skill that you never knew you'd need until you started it.

# Part 2: Smoking and Salt Curing

*What You Need to Know About Preserving Meat, Game, Fish, and More!*

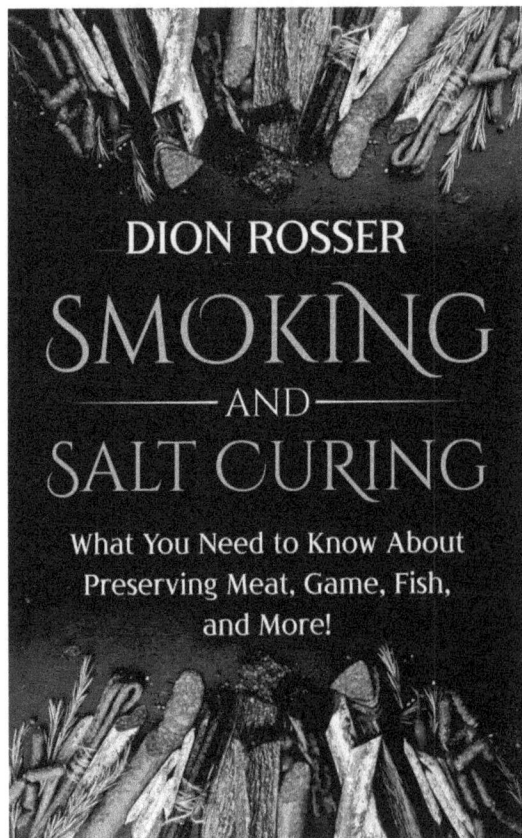

# Introduction

The art of preserving meat, fish, game, and poultry is not a modern concept. Our early ancestors worldwide were known to preserve the fish and game they harvested to prolong its shelf life. In tropical regions, they used sun drying, and in colder regions, different meats were frozen using ice. Even though these techniques seem rudimentary, they paved the way for modern methods of preserving food. Food preservation includes a variety of techniques designed to avoid food spoilage due to different factors.

The most popular food preservation methods are smoking and salt curing. You can pretty much smoke and cure everything ranging from freshly caught game and fish to store-bought meats! The sky is truly the limit once you get the hang of it. "Smoking and Salt Curing: What You Need to Know About Preserving Meat, Game, Fish, and More!" will teach you how to do it all!

Whether you are a hunter, or an angler looking to cure and smoke your fresh catch, or a home cook interested in making delicious smoked meats at home, this is the perfect book for you. This book will act as your guide every step of the way. This book is your one-stop-shop for all information from helping you understand the history, meaning, elements, and methods of food preservation to learning in detail about smoking and salt curing. You will be introduced to the basics of smoking and salt curing before moving on to learning the guidelines for meat, game, fish, and poultry preservation.

Once you are armed with all the theoretical knowledge you need, you will explore the delicious recipes in this book. All the recipes are divided into different categories based on protein. These recipes are not only easy to understand but are simple to follow. You can start whipping up delicious meals at home in no time! You need only to gather the required ingredients after selecting a recipe that appeals to you. Follow the simple instructions, and voila!

So, are you excited to learn about the art of food preservation? If yes, let's get started immediately.

# Chapter 1: Introduction to Food Preservation

Our ancestors were used to oscillating between periods of bounty and scarcity. The dire need to make it through scarcity acted as the catalyst that triggered preserving food. With the advent of agriculture and modern farming practices, the concept of famine is slowly vanishing from modern memory. However, there is still a need to keep food fresh from the time it is harvested until consumption. This is where food preservation techniques step into the picture. Whether it is to increase the shelf life, reduce the risk of contamination by pathogens, or retain the natural qualities of food items, food preservation serves various purposes.

Food preservation is a process that prevents decay or food spoilage, making it fit for storage and future use. It is also known as the state a food has managed to retain over a prolonged period without contamination traces. This, of course, while holding on to its natural properties in flavor, nutritional value, texture, and taste.

# History of Food Preservation

From the moment food is harvested, it starts degrading. Our early ancestors, for the sake of survival, had to ensure they had sufficient sustenance to get through the cold months. They froze meat on ice in the freezing climate while the food was dried under the sun in tropical regions. This primary food preservation technique gave them the confidence and security required to put down their roots and form communities. They no longer had to worry about instantly consuming fresh kill or new harvest. Instead, they preserved it for later.

Due to the extremely cold temperatures in some regions, freezing was the ideal method for preservation. This eventually led to the invention of ice houses for storing the ice needed to preserve food. This later was transformed into iceboxes – further modified in the late 1800s for freezing foods. Clarence Birdseye, an American inventor and naturalist, discovered that frozen vegetables and fruits taste better when they were quickly frozen at relatively low temperatures.

As civilizations grew and developed, science also prospered. One of the novel techniques for preserving food was canning. A vacuum seal is created within the canning jar after the food is processed at high temperatures and cooled down. This technique destroys pathogens and inactivates any enzymes present within the ingredients. Foods that are canned and vacuum-sealed properly ensure microorganisms cannot enter the jar. This technique was introduced by a French man named Nicolas Appert during the 1790s.

During Napoleon's reign, in 1795, a significant reward was offered to anyone who could develop a new method to preserve food. Appert was given this reward in 1809 when he discovered canning for preserving foods. He believed the success of canning was because all air was eliminated during the preserving process, increasing the shelf life of food. Louis Pasteur proved him wrong in 1864 after discovering a direct relationship between pathogens and food spoilage.

Another notable achievement in the field of food preservation was the contribution made by Robert Ayers in 1812. He opened the first cannery in the United States. In 1858 the Mason jar was patented by John L. Mason. These achievements paved the way for several other innovations in the field of home food preservation. In 1915, Alexander H. Kerr patented a two-piece metal canning lid still used today. The popularity of home food preservation has not died down with time.

## Principles of Food Preservation

With food preservation, some simple principles are standard regardless of the method used.

The first principle of food preservation is to prevent or possibly delay the decomposition of food by keeping microorganisms or pathogens away from it. It essentially means using different techniques to remove traces of microorganisms, prevent their growth, or destroy them.

The second principle is preventing self-decomposition of food or delaying it for as long as possible. Whether it is the destruction of enzymes or delaying any chemical reactions, this simple process prevents food from decomposing on its own.

The third principle of food preservation is to prevent any damage caused due to physical or external reasons such as mechanical causes or damage caused by rodents or insects.

## Detecting Spoiled Food

Whether it was takeout or a home-cooked meal, chances are there would have been some leftovers. Maybe the food didn't taste as fresh as it did the previous night, or you stumbled across a mold-covered casserole during routine cleaning. Learning to identify whether the food has gone bad or not is a helpful skill. If you don't want an upset stomach or something more severe, never eat food that's gone bad. Besides this, identifying whether something specific has gone bad or not can reduce food wastage and help save a few dollars.

The most obvious sign the food has gone bad is mold. Meats and dairy products are especially susceptible to mold. From a layer of white fuzz to black or green spots, mold comes in different forms. As soon as you see mold, throw the food item away. Similarly, discard all foods coated with a slimy film. If the meat looks and feels damp, it is a bad idea to put it in your mouth! Watch out for any changes in the texture and color of food. If the item has been discolored, it is a clear sign of oxidation. One final tip to identify whether the food has gone bad or not is the smell. If the food smells rancid or different from how it smelled previously, it has gone bad!

# Causes of Food Spoilage

The primary motivation for preserving food is to increase its shelf life and prevent instant degradation. From the moment the producers harvest or slaughter flood, it started degrading. The most common reasons for food spoilage are physical damages and chemical changes.

If the food is damaged, bruised, or even punctured due to external factors, it is termed *physical damage*. Any damage caused by microorganisms or insects is included in this. At times, the physical damage caused by insects – such as puncturing or bruising the foods – can increase the risk of pathogen contamination.

But oxidation, growth of microbes, and change in enzymes within food products are known as chemical changes. If iron is left exposed to elements such as water and air, rust forms through a process known as oxidation. This process applies to food too. Oxidized food generally turns rancid.

Enzymes are helpful chemicals present in animals and plants responsible for their growth and functioning. Even after harvest, these enzymes don't stop working. This reaction of enzymes changes the texture and flavor of the ingredients.

The third common cause of food spoilage is microbial growth. The three common microorganisms that harm food are mold, bacteria, and yeast. The greenish spots on old bread or a fuzzy white layer on dairy products signify mold growth. Mold doesn't discriminate and can easily spoil all types of foods. If the food seems slimy or starts bubbling, it is a sign of yeast growth. As with mold, yeast doesn't discriminate either. Another pathogen that spoils food is bacteria. Bacteria tend to multiply rapidly and make the food unsafe for consumption.

# Importance of Food Preservation

What pops into your head when you think of food preservation? Do you perhaps think of canned or dehydrated foods, or maybe frozen foods? Well, there is so much more to it than this. Food preservation is not a new concept, and it has been around since time immemorial.

Whenever you are learning something new, the best way to motivate yourself is by concentrating on its benefits. Here are all the benefits of preserving food.

## Reduces the Risk of Contamination

Perhaps the most obvious benefit of food preservation is it reduces the risk of contamination by pathogens. Whether it is salmonella, E Coli, or other pathogens, different types of bacteria tend to spoil and degrade food. By preserving it, you are essentially inhibiting the growth of such harmful pathogens. It, in turn, reduces the risk of food-borne diseases.

## Retains Quality

An important benefit of food preservation is that it helps retain the quality of the ingredients. When food starts deteriorating, as it normally does with time, it goes bad. If you notice any signs discussed in the previous section, it is unfit for consumption. The food is unsafe to eat, and its taste, appearance, and texture are significantly altered. Food preservation techniques help retain the natural qualities of ingredients, including their nutritional value, texture, and taste, to a great degree.

## Increases Shelf-Life

Another benefit of food preservation is that you get to enjoy seasonal ingredients all year round. It also helps reduce your grocery bills as wasting food is quite expensive. Using different preservation methods, you can save meats, vegetables, fish, and pretty much anything you desire well past their expected expiration dates.

Besides all this, preserving food can increase your sense of satisfaction. When you learn about the different techniques in this book and follow the simple recipes, you can start preserving food in no time! You will certainly feel a sense of pride when you do the job and do it well!

# Chapter 2: Methods of Food Preservation

The concept of refrigeration became commonplace only during the last couple of decades. Before that, different techniques were employed for increasing the shelf life of foods. Some of these techniques date back thousands of years. Drying, salting, and pickling are food preservation techniques that not only increase the shelf life of foods but change their flavor, appearance, and texture. The change isn't undesirable, however, like the one caused when food goes bad. They are classic techniques and are still favored today because of their unique transformative properties. In this chapter, we'll look at some of the most common food preservation techniques.

# Freezing

When foods are chilled and stored at least 10°F, it is known as freezing. All foods, including dairy products, vegetables, eggs, nuts, seafood, and fully cooked foods, can be stored using this method. To try your hand at freezing, understand that it differs from tossing the ingredients into the freezer compartment of a regular refrigerator. A regular refrigerator supports temperatures between 10-32°F while freezing requires a temperature of at least 10°F. It is an easy process, provided you can invest in a deep freezer, which is a rather expensive purchase.

# Canning

Canning essentially includes two processes known as pasteurizing and vacuum sealing. The first is pasteurizing, where food is heated for a specific duration at a specific temperature to eliminate pathogens, including harmful bacteria. This cooking process also prevents the activity of enzymes in the food. Once the ingredients are pasteurized, they can come to room temperature before moving on to the final stage - vacuum sealing. The pasteurized foods are placed in special glass jars designed for this purpose. Most foods, including seafood, meats, vegetables, fruit, and even some cooked foods, can be stored using this technique.

# Drying

Perhaps one of the most used preservation techniques for prolonging the shelf life of foods is drying. With drying, foods are dehydrated to remove excess moisture present within. This process reduces the risk of any microbial activity. Fruits, vegetables, legumes, nuts, and even seafood are commonly preserved using this technique.

# Fermenting

Fermenting is a very common process that encourages cultivating good pathogens that preserve the food instead of spoiling them. Different types of foods, including vegetables, meat, seafood fruits, common legumes, eggs, and dairy products, can be easily fermented. Yes, you are increasing the growth of desirable bacteria and other pathogens to discourage the growth of unhealthy ones. For instance, wine is made from fermented grapes, yogurt is only fermented milk, while cured sausages refer to fermented meats.

# Salting

Salting was quite a popular method of preserving food before the advent of modern refrigeration. It helps preserve food by drawing out all the moisture present within. When there is no moisture left, bacteria and other pathogens cannot develop or survive. It, in turn, increases the shelf life of the ingredients. There are two types of salting - dry and wet salting. In dry salting, food is covered in salt and left in a cool and dry place. When the salt draws out moisture present in the food, you might need to pour out the accumulated liquid and replace the lost salt.

But in wet curing, food is placed in a salt and water mixture known as brine. The ingredients are left to soak in the brine in a cool and dry place. More flavors can be easily incorporated into the foods by adding peppercorns or Juniper berries to the brine. Since the food is preserved in salt in one form or other, the result can be incredibly salty. So, the salted food might need to be reintroduced to water or reconstituted to remove the excess salt to be fit for consumption.

# Pickling

Pickling helps preserve food by using an edible antimicrobial solution that prevents the growth of pathogens. Food is immersed in a solution that contains alcohol, salt, or acid. The most common foods that are pickled include eggs, legumes, fruits, vegetables, certain meats, and seafood. You need no special equipment for pickling. However, if pickled foods are stored carelessly or preserved at room temperature, they can become unsafe for consumption. This technique usually combines other preservation methods such as refrigeration, canning, or fermentation.

# Curing

Curing involves flavoring and preserving food, especially fish and meat, by adding a mixture of salt, sugar, and nitrites or nitrates. Salt is believed to inhibit the growth of microorganisms responsible for decomposing food. It helps draw the water out of microbial cells through a process known as osmosis. If the population of bacteria is reduced, food automatically becomes safer for consumption. Curing encourages the growth of desirable bacteria belonging to the Lactobacillus genus. Here's a fun fact- bacteria belonging to this genus are commonly found within our digestive tract and are good for our digestive health.

This brings us to the next ingredient commonly used in curing- sugar. Sugar also limits the growth of bacteria and their existing population. Even if certain types of bacteria are considered good, too much of anything is seldom good. Sugar adds an interesting flavor and smell to the preserved food, making it more enjoyable. The nitrates or nitrites kill harmful pathogens while adding a tangy flavor to the meat. They also help retain a pinkish or reddish tinge to the meat. The most used nitrate is sodium or potassium nitrate. These nitrates bind with iron atoms present within the food and prevent oxidation. You will learn more about this technique in the subsequent chapters.

# Smoking

Smoking is a wonderful preservation technique that improves the appearance, texture, and flavor of the food stored. It is also used as a drying technique. Smoking pairs perfectly with curing and acts as a flavor enhancer. Compared to unsmoked meats, the likelihood of smoked meats turning rancid, getting oxidized, or growing mold is quite low. You will learn more about this food preservation technique in the later chapters.

# Sealing

Sealing is a food preservation process where the air is kept out to delay the decaying processes triggered by different pathogens. This technique simply delays but does not stop the process of decay, though. Sealing is commonly used with other preservation techniques such as freezing and drying. Fat and vacuum sealing are the most common sealing techniques.

# Potting

Potting is an old British food preservation technique still used in certain parts of France. The idea is simple. The meat is first prepared and thoroughly cooked before shifting for storage. After the meat is fully prepped, it is placed in a ceramic crock or any other pot for storage. The crock used is fully sterilized to deter the growth of bacteria. After the meat is placed in it, all fats collected are melted and poured into the crock. As soon as the fat covering the meat solidifies, it is ready for storage. The crock is then stored in a cool and dry location, such as a root cellar.

# Tips To Remember

Here are some food safety guidelines you should always follow while curing and smoking meats. It doesn't matter whether you are interested in preserving poultry or fish. These rules are still applicable. Please follow them for your own safety.

The first rule is to thoroughly wash your hands with soap and water for at least 20 seconds before and after working. Always wash your hands after changing tasks. If you do any specific activity which can contaminate your hands, don't forget to wash them. The same rules apply even if you sneeze or use the washroom.

Ensure the equipment and workspace you will use to prepare the food are completely clean before you start using them. Sterilize all the equipment with hot soapy water to ensure there are no traces of pathogens. Remember, the idea is to preserve the meat. If these meats are exposed to pathogens in any form, the risk of contamination obviously increases.

Whenever you are using cutting boards, always wash them first. Wash them with hot water, soap, and rinse them. You can also sanitize them using a solution made of water and chlorine. Add one tablespoon of chlorine bleach to one gallon of water or one teaspoon for 4 cups of water. Spray or dip the cutting boards in the solution and let them air dry.

If you are using any frozen meat, ensure it is perfectly thawed before you use it. To thaw the meat, you should not leave it outside and let it thaw. Instead, place it in the refrigerator at a temperature of around 40°F. If you use any raw meat, always keep separate cutting boards for it. It's not just the cutting board. The work surfaces need to be different too. You can always color coordinate the boards to remember which ones are used for different types of meat. Raw meat can quickly become a breeding spot for all sorts of pathogens, and unless you are careful, you cannot reduce the risk of contamination, especially cross-contamination.

Before you preserve meat, ensure it is perfectly cooked. To do this, you must check its internal temperature. You will learn about the different internal cooking temperatures for different types of meat in the following chapters. Pay extra attention to the temperatures for cooking and storing them. You can use a food thermometer to check whether the meat is cooked properly or not. In fact, investing in a food thermometer is a good idea if you want to smoke meat.

After cooking, ensure you let the meat cool down to at least room temperature before preserving. Never put warm or hot meat in the fridge. While storing it in the freezer, always use freezer-safe containers and food-grade plastic. The stored meat should not be directly exposed to air.

# Chapter 3: Smoking Meat

As explained, there are several preservation techniques commonly used for increasing the shelf life of different products. One such food preservation technique is smoking. This is a great way to treat foods by preventing any spoilage caused by pathogens. Smoking is a preservation technique that promotes the shelf life of the product and improves its flavor profile. It helps flavor, cook, and preserves the food by exposing it to steady smoke. Smoke is generated by burning plant material such as wood or even hardwood. While it is mostly a commercial process, it can be carried out at home provided you have the right equipment.

## Methods of Smoking

The two methods are commonly used for smoking are hot and cold smoking.

In hot smoking, the food is directly exposed to smoke in a controlled environment. Smoked foods can be cooked or reheated as and when required. They are also ready for consumption with no further cooking. The usual temperature range for hot smoking is between 125-180°F. When food is exposed to this temperature, it's normally cooked internally. The ideal temperature for most cooked meats is around 180°F. So, if the ingredients are exposed to hot smoke, you can consume them immediately. Foods tend to retain their moisture and texture at this heat level while a smoky flavor is added. If the temperature increases beyond this, foods can lose their moisture, and the fat starts drying. Usually, smoking is used combined with other preservation techniques such as curing or drying. For example, once foods are salt-cured, they are smoked to increase their shelf life.

This brings us to the next smoking method known as cold smoking. This is more of a flavor enhancer than a cooking technique. It is commonly used for improving the flavor of chicken breast, pork chops, scallops, steak, and even salmon. The temperature used for this is between 68-90°F. The temperature is maintained at this level with the aim of moisture retention. It is not meant for food preservation. It's simply about adding a smoky flavor to the food. So, foods that are cold smoked shouldn't be consumed immediately, and instead, they need to be cured before they are cold smoked. When meats are cured, the moisture in them is removed, which prevents bacterial growth. Once the meat is cured and preserved using any other technique, it can be cold smoked.

# Benefits of Smoking Meats

Smoke is believed to have antioxidant and antimicrobial properties. This means that any pathogens present on the surface of meat are eliminated, as are their chances of reappearing. However, smoking cannot be used as a standalone preservation technique. The problem is that the compound of smoke only sticks to the outer surface of the food, and it does not penetrate the meat or the food you are trying to preserve. So, the antioxidant and antimicrobial properties of smoke are restricted to the external surfaces of the meat. This is why smoking needs to be combined with other preservation techniques such as salt curing or drying.

Whenever wood is burned, its smoke contains phenol and certain phenolic compounds believed to be natural antioxidants. Oxidation is a process that occurs when the structure of the molecules is changed due to oxygen exposure. A common example of damage caused by the oxidation of food is rancidity. Food goes bad when left exposed to the elements for prolonged periods. So, the helpful compounds in wood smoke curtail the rancidification of fats present in meat, fish, and even poultry. This, coupled with antimicrobial agents such as formaldehyde, acetic acid, and several other helpful organic acids, reduces the pH of smoke. The usual pH of smoke is around 2.5. This low level of pH makes it difficult for pathogens to survive.

Besides prolonging the shelf life of food, smoking also elevates the flavor profile. Smoked meats are simply delicious! Once the meats are smoked and preserved, they can be stored for up to one year at the right temperature! This gives you easy access to the required ingredients whenever you want to cook. This certainly makes the meat more appetizing and flavorful. The color of the meat also changes once it is smoked. The meats seem shinier and redder. This simply makes them more appealing.

# Risks to Consider

Too much of anything is bad. Everything needs to be balanced in every aspect of your life, which is true for diet. Eating too much of anything is not good for your body. So, eating too much smoked food is certainly not good for you. A common reason is the active compounds released from wood during smoking dries out the food. This essentially means the substances from smoke are incorporated into your food. Increased consumption of smoked food is associated with an increased risk of different types of cancers. Read on to learn more about the disadvantages associated with smoking food.

Smoking is a tedious process that requires specific equipment and plenty of attention. It can be a little expensive in terms of the resources involved. Keeping the moisture content low must be a priority while smoking. If not, it increases the risk of pathogen contamination. While smoking, if the fire is too hot, or if there isn't sufficient heat or smoke, the meat can quickly go bad before it is properly smoked.

Potential carcinogens can also be present in smoked food. This is due to the transference process responsible for smoking. Apart from the helpful phenols released by burning wood, certain hydrocarbons known as polycyclic aromatic hydrocarbons (PAHs) are also released. PAHs are believed to be food contaminants that increase the risk of gastrointestinal cancer. In recent research undertaken by the American Chemical Society, a simple way to reduce the risk of exposure to carcinogens is by taking a leaf from the auto industry's playbook. The zeolite filters used in automobiles filter harmful compounds and reduce air pollution. By using such filters fitted to smokers, the risk of carcinogens can be reduced. Once again, it is important to note the real problem starts if you consume too much smoked meat. Eating it occasionally is not harmful.

However, it is worth noting that the research is not definitive, and more evidence is needed to prove the case.

# Chapter 4: Basic Things to Note Before Smoking

The modern concept of smoking food is a continuation of an age-old technique of food preservation. Before chemical preservatives and refrigeration were invented, smoke was used to extend the shelf life of ingredients, especially meats. In the previous chapter, you were introduced to the different reasons smoke is believed to be a preservative. From acetic acid and formaldehyde to the low PH level, smoke has several antioxidant and antimicrobial properties that prolong its shelf life. It's not just about prolonging the shelf life, but it also reduces any risk of contamination.

These days, smoking is mostly about tenderizing meats and enhancing their flavor. However, it doesn't mean you can't use it to preserve food. Once you get the hang of smoking, don't restrict yourself to meat. These days, nuts, vegetables, fruits, and even different types of cheese are smoked! Before you smoke food, here are some important things you should consider.

# Consider the Cut of the Meat

Whenever you think about smoking something, it's important to determine the ingredient you wish to smoke. From poultry and different types of meat to fish, different things can be smoked. Why is it important to consider the cut of the meat here? Depending on the thickness of the cut, the time required for smoking will differ. The most common cuts used for smoking include all the motion muscles. For instance, spareribs from the belly, loin, beef brisket, and ribs are the most common meat cuts chosen for smoking.

For smoking, it is always better to choose fatty cuts. Fat helps the meat absorb the delicious smoky flavors. So, whenever you choose any meat to smoke, look for cuts with plenty of fat and connective tissue. Choosing fattier cuts keeps the meat tender and moist. When the fat starts melting, it bastes the meat in its juices. This further elevates the flavor profile while easily incorporating the smokiness into the chosen meat.

As you read through the different chapters on food preservation discussed in this book, a point to remember is that smoking is the final step in the preservation process. Whether it is fish, poultry, meat, or game, the ingredients are first salt-cured before they are smoked.

# Selecting the Wood

If you want good results from smoking, pay extra attention to the wood used. Yes, wood type plays an important role here. Different types of wood tend to pair with different flavors of the meat and would need to complement the flavor of the meat. Let us look at some common woods used for smoking.

Apple wood has a fruity and sweet taste. It is rather mild and pairs brilliantly well with poultry, ham, and fish. Another commonly used wood for smoking is alder. Alder has a delicate flavor profile and natural sweetness that elevates the flavor of pork, fish, poultry, and all other types of light meats. The best way to incorporate some hearty smokiness into red meats and ribs is to use hickory. This is the most popular word used in barbecues. Hickory's pungent and strong smell perfectly complements the hardness of red meats. This brings us to another commonly used wood- oak. Oak is ideal for large cuts of meat smoked for extended periods. It offers a good smoky flavor that is not overpowering. Whether it is brief brisket or game meats, this is a great choice of wood. Mesquite is also popular, but it can be overwhelming. Mesquite should be used just like peppers in cooking. It is ideal for short durations when used in combination with other woods.

Maple has a light and sweet taste that pairs well with ham and poultry. Be careful while using maple, however, because it can darken the color of meat. As with mesquite, maple is used with other woods such as oak and apple. Pecan has a pungent fruity flavor but use it sparingly. It also doesn't burn quite as hot as other woods, making it ideal for smoking larger cuts of meat. To improve the color of any meat, add some cherry wood. It pairs brilliantly with pork and beef.

If in doubt, always choose oak or alder. These are the safest bets for smoking meats.

## Select the Smoking Method

As explained, there are two types of smoking methods available. Depending on the results you are trying to achieve, the smoking process you need to choose will differ. For instance, if you aim only to infuse the smell of smoke into the meat, choose cold smoking. On the other hand, if you want to cook the meat thoroughly, choose hot smoking.

# Brining

During the smoking process, meat tends to dry out. This is one reason why placing the meat in brine is a wonderful idea. A solution of water and salt is known as brine. Depending on the cut of the meat, the quantity of brine required will differ. Brining meat is a great way of ensuring lean cuts of meat do not dry out during the smoking process. If you decide to brine the meat, it becomes easier to preserve it. If you are interested in immediately consuming the meat, this step is optional. You will learn more about using brine for different meats in the subsequent chapters.

# Select the Smoker

Now that you have decided on your meat, how you want to smoke it, the type of wood, and when you want to consume it, all that's left for you to do is select the right smoker. Selecting the wood was one aspect of deciding how to go about the smoking process. So now, it's time to determine the smoker that will work well for you. The most common smokers on the market are gas-fired barbecue pits and electric ones.

# Stick Burners

Stick burners rely solely on wood as their fuel source. In the previous section, you were introduced to the different types of wood paired with different meats. Carefully go through the list and select one combination that appeals to you. Once you have the wood ready, you simply need to place them on the stick burner. These burners require the most attention compared to all the others mentioned in this section. Because you need to pay constant attention to the food while it's on the burner, a steep learning curve is involved.

And most cheap variants from any local hardware or departmental store are not good at retaining heat and are rather flimsy. There are higher-end stick burners available made of heavy-duty materials. However, they can be rather expensive.

# Electric Smokers

Electric smokers use an electric heating rod. It helps ignite the wood pellets present inside the smoker. The wood pellets serve a dual purpose here. They act as a heat source to cook the meat and as a flavor enhancer. When the wood pellets are placed into the firebox, the heat can be regulated using a thermostat. The heating element of these smokers produces smoke instead of an open flame. Since there is no combustion here, its smoke is different in flavor compared to live fire.

# Pellet Smokers

These are similar to a pellet grill or a kitchen oven. They come with an embedded thermostat that can be used for regulating the smoker's temperature. All you need to do is simply place the smoker where you want, plug it into a socket, set the ideal temperature, and let the smoker do the rest. You don't have to constantly check on the smoker to ensure the meat doesn't burn, thanks to the adjustable thermostat. In a pellet smoker, pellets made of compressed sawdust are pushed into a firepot next to the smoker's internal mechanism, which then combusts in the firepot to produce the required heat and smoke. These smokers are incredibly easy to use. That said, the flavor produced by a live fire cannot be replaced or even duplicated by any other smoker models.

# Gas Smokers

The next category of smokers includes gas-fired ones. As with electric smokers, these use propane or any other natural gas for ignition. The gas-fired units can be used for hot and cold smoking meats. These smokers usually have a water pan that helps retain moisture in the meat while cooking or smoking it. This means the meat isn't at risk of drying out quickly. Gas smokers offer great control over the cooking temperature, but they produce no smoke.

# Kettle Grills

This is a live-fire piece of kitchen equipment that most home cooks are familiar with. If you are a little careful and use it smartly, it can be used for smoking meats at home. However, these grills are not ideal for slow-smoking meats. For instance, you can create an indirect heat source by restricting the charcoal or wood chips to one-half of the grill. You can place the meat on the other side. Similarly, keep a thermometer nearby to ensure the meat is cooking properly. You will learn more about the different cooking temperatures for different meats in the following chapters.

# Charcoal Smokers

Charcoal smokers include the most popular smokers, such as the stainless-steel Weber Smokey Monkey, Pit Barrel cooker, other drum smokers, and ceramic kamado ovens such as the Big Green Egg. When compared to a stick burner, these don't require that much attention but are not entirely hands-off either. After the coal is lit, you will need to adjust the temperature using the built-in dampers for controlling the airflow. Most of the smoke will be produced from the charcoal, but you can always add some extra wood chips for flavoring the meat. While doing this, it's important to remember that wood smolders instead of combusting, and the smoke given out by it might not be as flavorful as those produced by a stick burner.

Charcoal is the fuel source for these smokers. Simply ignite the charcoal and leave it in the smoker until the ash is left. This is similar to grilling meats on a barbecue. The food must be placed on racks once the coal is hot enough. Close the smoker and let it cook. This is perfect for hot smoking meats.

If you are considering buying a smoker, there are a few factors you need to remember. The most obvious one is your budget. If you are just getting started with smoking meats, stick to the basics for now. Once you get the hang of it, you can always invest in a higher-end version. To learn to barbecue and smoke, starting with a charcoal smoker is a good idea. They are affordable and easy to use. The next factor to consider is the fuel type used by the smoker. This factor is in tandem with the previous one. Once again, it is better to stick with charcoal to get the hang of barbecuing and grilling meats.

But if convenience is the sole priority, a pellet smoker is a worthy investment. Consider the usual size of the meat to be smoked before buying a smoker. If you are interested in smoking large cuts of meat or game meat, you will need a considerably bigger smoker.

# Chapter 5: Salt Curing

How do you usually keep your meat safe? The answer is you refrigerate it. Well, refrigeration is a relatively new invention. Before refrigerators were introduced, curing was the technique most used to preserve meat. Salt-cured meats are popular even today, not just out of necessity but also because of their unique taste. You can make different types of cured meats such as bacon, sausage, ham, and corned beef at home if you know how curing works.

Curing is essentially a technique that uses salt to preserve the meat. Remember, in the previous chapter, we mentioned that pathogen contamination or growth of living organisms such as bacteria results in food spoilage? Salt helps kill them and prevents this process. If any pathogens start ingesting the meat and metabolizing it, the meat's texture, color, and flavor start changing. These are all telltale signs of food spoilage.

So, how exactly does salt help preserve the food? Salt removes all the moisture or water present within the meat cells through a process known as osmosis. Osmosis has two beneficial effects. The first effect is it dries the meat, and the second is it kills all the pathogens. It's important to remember that salt here doesn't mean regular table salt. Instead, it refers to a combination of salt, salt cures, and a little sugar.

The most common types of salt-cured meats are bacon, ham, and corned beef. Apart from this, pancetta, liverwurst, summer sausage, salami, and chorizo are also salt-cured meats. Even if the time taken to salt-cured meats is stretched to several weeks, the flavor it produces is worth it. During curing, different enzymes in the meat undergo various chemical changes that build the meat's flavor. Besides this, the salt used in curing further elevates its natural flavor. This, coupled with sugar, herbs, and spices, further balance the flavors and elevates them to the next level. If salted meat is smoked later, it creates a wonderful and well-rounded flavor profile. Salted meats aren't cooked. Some salted meats are further dried to ensure they are fit for consumption.

# Curing Agents and Mixtures

The most common curing agents are salt, nitrates, nitrites, and sugar. You also have the option of purchasing readymade cure mixtures. Salt was commonly used for curing meats before saltpeter replaced it. It's believed that during the 1600s, it was discovered that a mixture of saltpeter and salt was a better and effective way to preserve meat. The potassium nitrate present in the saltpeter kills bacteria responsible for botulism. The nitrate also retains the pink color of the meat. This is what our ancestors believed. It turns out, the reasons for the pink color and the extended shelf life are not as straightforward.

You will learn more about the different types of salts used, commercially produced curing mixture, and alternatives in the next chapter.

# Benefits of Curing

The most obvious benefit of salt curing is to prolong the shelf life of ingredients. For instance, if the meats are properly cured and later dried or smoked, their shelf life increases by a couple of months. If stored at the right temperature, cured meats are fit for consumption for almost a year! This is a great way to preserve meats, poultry, fish, and even game meats.

Another advantage of salt curing is it kills any harmful pathogens in the meat. The salt dries out the meat and removes any traces of moisture. When this happens, the pathogens are automatically killed. The meat becomes inhospitable for disease-causing pathogens.

Salting is also a great way to elevate the flavor and texture of certain meats. Once the meats are cured, they can be cooked in different ways. For instance, bacon tastes different from a regular strip of pork belly, doesn't it? This is due to the curing process it undergoes.

# Risks to Remember

It was a popular belief that nitrites and nitrates have carcinogenic properties. This widespread belief resulted from a rather flawed experiment conducted back in the 70s. Even though this risk has been debunked as a myth, the damage was done. In 2003, WHO (World Health Organization) issued a clarification stating there was no association between cancer risk and nitrites or nitrates. Most natural foods, including vegetables such as carrots, spinach, lettuce, and celery, are sources of nitrites. So, don't worry about nitrites.

Perhaps the most significant risk you must take into consideration while salt curing meats is the presence of pathogens. Clostridium botulinum is the bacteria responsible for Botulism. Botulism can be deadly, and it is more dangerous than food pathogens such as E Coli or salmonella. Botulism is a food-borne illness, and the bacteria causing it is commonly found in soil. The microbe by itself is not harmful. The problem is with the neurotoxin it produces. Bacteria can produce this toxin in an anaerobic environment.

Any environment devoid of oxygen is known as an anaerobic environment. For instance, the environment inside the tissue of cured meat or meat being cured is anaerobic. With fresh meat, you don't have to worry about botulism. The real trouble starts when you are curing and preserving meat. To prevent botulism, there are three methods available. The first is salting and dehydrating. The second method is to reduce the environments' pH or create an acidic condition that inhibits the microbe's growth. The third idea is to pressure-can the meat. Whenever you are using any meat, you can avoid the risk of Botulism by curing and then smoking it.

One way to kill this bacterium is by submerging it in brine or keeping it in the dry salt curing mix. This, coupled with temperature control, will make the cured meats safe for consumption. Curing should take place in a temperature-controlled environment. The ideal temperature to be maintained is between 36-40°F to prevent the growth of pathogens.

Cured meats are safe for consumption. That said, those with any existing cardiovascular disorders, including high levels of cholesterol and blood pressure, should severely restrict their consumption of cured meat. Cured meat is rich in sodium, and this can further worsen any existing blood pressure problems.

Always keep the salt cures out of the reach of children. Nitrites and nitrates aren't carcinogenic agents, but children shouldn't directly consume them. Their digestive systems, especially the helpful bacteria in the digestive tract, aren't yet developed to digest nitrites and nitrates.

Don't try to cure meat at home without using curing salt. Without the salt cure, the desirable action of nitrites and nitrates doesn't occur. Unless the nitrites in the cure react with the meat, the meat proteins aren't broken down, and if this doesn't happen, nitric oxide isn't produced. Nitric oxide prevents the growth of harmful pathogens and removes all their traces. You will learn more about all this in the next chapter.

# Chapter 6: Basic Things to Note Before Salt Curing

You might be quite tempted to skip to the recipes about preserving different ingredients. Before you do this, it is important to know the basic steps involved in salt curing. It is not just about understanding the concepts. You must also understand the different methods, types of curing salts, and so on. If you are a beginner, do not skip this chapter.

## Types of Salts to Use

To understand how curing works and the different salt you can use, you need a brief chemistry lesson. When selecting the salt used for curing, there are many options available, and the evidence is often conflicting. In the past, regular salt was used to cure meat, but during the 1600s, saltpeter was added to the curing mixture. Saltpeter is the common name for sodium nitrate or potassium nitrate. However, saltpeter does not directly preserve the food. Salt is mainly used to preserve the food. However, certain types of bacteria can't be killed by salt alone. As such, saltpeter is added to protect against them. Bacteria in the food eat the nitrates in the saltpeter, and in this process, nitrites are produced. After this, another reaction further occurs, which turns these nitrites into nitric oxide. Nitric oxide starts bonding with various proteins present in the meat. This makes the meat pink and reduces the risk of oxidation. Nitric oxide is essentially preserving the meat while killing the deadly spores of Botulism and other harmful bacteria. Whenever you are using saltpeter, it is always used along with salt. Saltpeter is not a salt substitute.

This brings us to something that is commonly known as pink salt or Prague powder. It is another name for saltpeter, used for curing meat. It is known as pink salt because a food coloring is added to it, so consumers do not mistake it for normal salt. The pink hue of the cured meat resulting from salt-curing isn't associated with the red dye mixed in the cure. Remember, it is the activation of nitric oxide, which gives the meat a pink hue. Prague powder #1 and Prague powder #2 are two types of pink salts. They are also known as pink salt #1 and pink salt #2, respectively. The former contains around 93% common table salt, and the rest is sodium nitrite. If you are cooking meat, poultry, or fish after curing it, choose Prague powder #1. But pink salt #2 contains 4% sodium nitrate, 6.25% sodium nitrite, and the rest is table salt. This is used as a dry cure for meats that will not undergo any further cooking processes, such as prosciutto.

Besides this, some recipes use Morton Tender Quick. It is a mixture of salt, sodium nitrite, sugar, and sodium nitrate. It is not dyed pink like its counterparts. If you are using this at home, ensure that you keep it separate from the regular table salt. A common mistake most beginners make is that they believe all curing salts are the same. Curing salts are not interchangeable, so please do not make this mistake. If a curing recipe uses a specific curing salt, follow the instructions. Don't try to change it. The salts are chosen based on the preservation process involved.

Now that you understand the different types of curing salts used for food preservation, it's time to address some worries most have about curing salts. It's a common misconception that curing salts are extremely toxic. Curing salts are only toxic in large and excessive quantities. Curing salts are not meant for direct consumption. You're not supposed to inhale it or rub it over your eyes. It should be kept out of children's reach. Don't worry about all of this because home curing recipes do not call for such massive quantities of salt. Also, you are not exposed to it constantly, and therefore, it does not threaten your health.

Another common worry regarding nitrites is their association with an increased risk of cancer. Nitrites are found in natural foods. They are more common than you might have believed. For instance, you will consume more nitrites in a single serving of spinach than from a serving of salami.

The only concern to worry about when curing meats is the risk of botulism. Apart from that, there's nothing else to worry about. The risk of Botulism reduces when you follow the curing recipe properly and maintain the required salting and smoking temperatures.

There are alternatives to curing salts. The only reason to use curing salts is to eliminate all traces of Botulism spores in the meat. You can cure using regular salt, but there are a few issues you need to be aware of. The presence of iodine in regular or table salt is a major issue. Table salt is always iodized, and iodine can lend a weird taste to the cured meat. Other anti-clumping active ingredients in table salt make the dry cure lumpy. If you use it to make the brine, there might be sediments in it. When using regular salt for curing the meat, stick to the recipe and ensure you choose non-iodized salt.

If you are using regular salt, pay attention to the size of the salt granules. This can affect the amount of salt that goes into a recipe. For instance, a cup of kosher salt is about 5-8 ounces, while one cup of table salt equals 10-ounces. So, one cup of table salt is a different measurement as kosher salt. An efficient way to measure the ingredients whenever you are curing meats at home is to use a weighing scale.

If you are looking for a natural source of nitrate, choose celery juice. Celery juice has natural nitrates. In the curing process, celery juice triggers a reaction similar to saltpeter. However, this isn't a substitute for the results produced using saltpeter.

# Curing Options to Consider

You have three options for curing meats using salt. Namely, dry curing, wet curing, and injecting. The safest option available for curing at home is wet curing. Let us learn more about these options and how they work.

## Dry Curing

The most common preservation technique for curing meats is dry curing. Remember when you were introduced to the different curing mixtures in the previous section? Now, you simply need to rub the meat with the curing mixture, place it in a container, and cover it with more curing mix. The meat must then be placed in the refrigerator or any other cold space where a steady temperature of 36-40°F can be maintained. Regulating the temperature and humidity are the most crucial aspects of curing meat. So, pay extra attention to it.

## Wet Curing

To cure limited quantities of meat, wet curing should be your go-to option. It is especially helpful if you will be cooking the cured meat again. For this, you need to make a brine solution and simply submerge the meat in it. The brine removes the excess moisture and helps create an ideal balanced that prevents pathogen breeding. You can easily regulate the salt used with this method. This method ensures that the salt has evenly seeped into the meat and there are no salt pockets created in it. While wet curing the meat, store it in the fridge or freezer. The meat must always stay submerged in the brine, and you must keep turning it every few days, so it is evenly exposed to the brine. The meat shouldn't be exposed to air. Preferably, use a separate storage area for curing meats to prevent cross-contamination.

### Injecting

As the name suggests, you will essentially be injecting salty brine into the meat using a syringe. It is slightly difficult to ensure the brine is evenly distributed with this method, especially if you don't have the required professional equipment. As a DIY solution, this rarely is recommended. One common problem with this method is it can create salt pockets in the meat.

# Equipment Needed

Whether it is dry curing or smoking meats, you'll need some basic equipment. The most important aspect of curing meats is a cool area or a fridge. Temperature regulation is a crucial part of curing. If you're not careful, improper temperature increases the risk of pathogens breeding on your meats. This makes the final product unfit for consumption. The usual temperature required for curing and storing meats is less than 40°F - anything more than this and the risk of pathogen contamination increases. So, you will need a refrigerator, freezer, or any cold area where you can maintain this temperature for as long as the meat is being cured and stored.

# Tips to Remember

The time required to cure the meat depends on the bone and fat in the meat and its thickness. For instance, thin cuts of meat can be cured quickly, while thicker cuts take longer. You can add a variety of herbs, spices, and other ingredients to the curing mixture. However, do this only after you get the hang of the basic curing process and have understood the recipes well.

Whenever you place any meat in the refrigerator for curing, ensure you label the container with the date clearly. It is easy to forget when you might have placed a specific batch in the fridge.

The temperature in the refrigerator should be between 36-40°F for best results and safety.

If the meat is too salty after curing, soak it or boil it in water to get rid of the excess salt. You can reduce the curing time if the meat becomes too salty on the first attempt.

It's important to understand that cured meat is still raw. So, you will need to cook it after curing before it is fit for consumption.

# Chapter 7: Guidelines for Meat Preservation

An important aspect of curing and smoking meats ensures that the essential nutrients are not lost. Since the meat is not exposed to direct heat and is instead cooked at low temperatures, its nutrients are preserved. The texture and integrity of the meat are also preserved. Adding a wonderful smoky aroma simply elevates the flavor profile of the meat altogether. Smoking also helps tenderize the meat making it easier to eat. Once you follow all the different steps discussed in the following section, the meat is ready for consumption. The savory, tender, and smoky flavors of the meat will make it simply irresistible. Besides this, all harmful pathogens are killed, and the risk of the meat going bad is drastically reduced.

Before you learn about curing meats, the three aspects you need to focus on are temperature, sanitation, and storage. Meat is not cooked until its internal temperature reaches around 160°F. Don't forget to check whether the meat is fully cooked or not before you consume it. Overcooked meat is hard and tough like rubber, but undercooked meat increases the risk of food-borne illnesses. Microbial growth usually occurs in temperatures between 40-140°F. Once the meat is ready, ensure that you store, cure, and age it at a temperature less than 40°F.

Whenever you store the meat, make sure that all the cooked products are separated from the raw ingredients. When stored close together, the juices from one container or ingredient can transfer to another, increasing the risk of contamination. All the utensils used, include the equipment and workspace, must be thoroughly sanitized and cleaned before and after each use. Now, let's look at the different steps of preserving meat.

# Selecting The Meat

Before you concentrate on preparing and preserving the meat, the first step is to select the right meat. Whenever you are purchasing meat, ensure it is not discolored. If purchasing poultry, check the area under the wings, and if there are any blood clots or bruises, check for better meat options. Poultry rarely has any odor, and if there is any, don't purchase it. Red meat has a specific odor, and it usually depends on the type of meat you want to purchase. Even if it has an odor, it should never be overpowering. There should be no slimy coating on the meat, and the flesh should be springy. Here is a simple finger test you can use. Poke the flesh with your finger. If it bounces back, it is fresh. Use this simple test to check meats before purchasing.

# Curing

You will need food-grade salt, curing compounds, and meat. Alternatively, you can also purchase commercially prepared cure mixes and carefully follow the instructions on the package. To preserve meat, ensure you are starting with fresh and high-quality meat. Curing is not a method to salvage any meat close to going bad or has bacterial growth. You need not age the meat before curing it because this process and smoking will tenderize the meat itself.

Food-grade salt contains no additives- especially iodine, and this is what you should be using. If the salt has any traces of impurities, the results will not be as desirable. Before you start curing the meat, ensure it has sufficient fat content. If the meat is lean, a wet cure will be better. If you are purchasing any cure mixtures, ensure it contains nitrate for dry-cured products that are not smoked, cooked, or refrigerated. If the meat needs to be cooked, smoked, or canned, use nitrate mixtures. You can use 1o z of nitrite for 100 lb. of meat, whereas you can use 3.5 oz of nitrate for 100 lb. of meat.

You need to be extra careful whenever handling nitrates and nitrites. Nitrites become toxic if you exceed the recommended limit. As a rule of thumb, always remember one gram of sodium nitrite is lethal for an adult human. To avoid any confusion, it is better to use curing mixtures instead of working with pure nitrites.

# Dry Cure

Decide on whether to dry or wet cure the meat. If you are dry curing, start by trimming any excess fat but leave a few layers so the meat doesn't dry out. If the meat has a rather thick layer of fat, penetrate it with a fork so the dry cure can enter the meat easily. Take your chosen cure and hand rub this mixture all over the meat.

Place the meat in a container laid out with parchment paper. Place something heavy on top, such as weights or a cast iron pan, to ensure the meat goes deeper into the curing mixture while leaving a small gap for flow. Transfer the meat to the refrigerator for around ten days. Once it is ready, remove it from the refrigerator, rinse it with water, and now the meat is ready for smoking.

If you are curious about making a dry rub, you can add salt, curing salt, sugar, and any spice you want to use. For instance, you can add cumin, black pepper, paprika, dry mustard, onion powder, cloves, and even Bay leaves to the rub.

# Wet Cure

If you want, you have the option of wet curing the meat. It essentially means the meat will be immersed in a salt water-based liquid or brine. As a rule of thumb, the meat needs to stay in the brine solution for 12 hours per pound of weight. If the meat weighs 4 pounds, it needs to stay in the brine for 48 hours. The meats ideal for brining are the ones that tend to lose moisture during the cooking process, such as lean cuts of pork and beef.

To start brining, once again, it's important to trim any excess fat, especially the dangling bits. Place the meat in a brining bag or a sealable container that is big enough to hold the meat and the brine. The container shouldn't be filled to the brim, and there should be some space for movement. If you are using premixed brine, follow the instructions when mixing the brine cure with water. If not, you can make the brine at home.

The simplest brine recipe calls for 4 cups of water mixed with 1 cup of food-grade salt and ¼ cup of sugar. Increase the proportions based on the portions you will need. Start by heating two cups of water with salt and sugar. Once the ingredients dissolve, remove them from heat. Let this mixture come to room temperature and add the rest of the water. Place this brine mixture in the refrigerator to chill until needed. Other ingredients that can be added to the wet cure are apple cider, fresh citrus, and herbs, honey, vegetables, ginger, etc. If the mixture has at least 20% salinity, it will prevent the growth of microbes.

Let us get back to brining the meat. While the meat is stored in the refrigerator, keep turning it in the brine daily to ensure it is evenly cured. Whenever you are ready to remove the meat from the refrigerator, take it out and rinse it with water until the excess salt has washed away. The meat must be patted dry before it can be smoked. If you don't want to smoke it immediately, store it in the refrigerator until ready by wrapping it in cheesecloth.

# Smoking

Now that the meat is cured, it's time to smoke it. Whether or not you have a smokehouse or use a backyard smoker, the heat, airflow, and moisture need to be well balanced. While doing this, pay specific attention to the internal temperature of the meat you are smoking. Smoking does not work as an effective preservation technique if the meat is not cooked properly. So, the first condition is that the meat should be thoroughly cooked. As explained, between the temperatures of 40-140°F, meats are at a higher risk of attracting pathogens.

The ideal internal temperature of fresh beef is between 145-170°F, depending on whether you like it rare, medium, or well done. This range is applicable for fresh lamb and veal. For ground meat and meat mixtures of turkey and chicken, the internal cooking temperature must be 165°F. If the ground meat or meat mixtures are made of pork, veal, and beef, the internal temperature must be 160°F. The ideal internal temperature for a whole chicken, turkey, duck, and goose is 180°F. For pork, the ideal internal temperature to ensure cooking is between 169-170°F.

Once the meats have reached their desired internal temperature, cool them quickly to 40°F. After this, keep it refrigerated. Try to reduce handling cooked meats if they are meant for storage.

# Storage

Once the meat is cured and smoked, it is time to store it. You can store it for two weeks in the refrigerator and for a couple of months in the freezer. Refrigerate the meat within two hours of smoking. The best way to store meat is by wrapping it in butcher paper or plastic wrap. Butcher paper comes away easier than plastic wrap. After this, wrap it in a layer of aluminum foil and place it in the coldest part of the freezer. Store it at a steady temperature of around 40°F. If you want to consume it afterward, always heat it to an internal temperature of 160°F instead of tasting it right away. This is important for your safety.

# Chapter 8: Guidelines for Game Preservation

Some might hunt for sport while others hunt to feed their families. If you don't want to consume game meat immediately, learning to preserve it is important. From field dressing the animals to transporting and preserving them, you need to pay attention to different aspects of this process. If you're not careful, this simply increases the risk of pathogen contamination, which can harm your health.

The most important aspect of preserving game meat is to regulate its temperature. Bacteria and other pathogens are present everywhere. Temperature plays a crucial role in their ability to survive. The most common temperature range for bacterial growth is between 40-140°F. If the temperature is less than 40°F, it is too cold for bacteria to grow. This is the reason for using a refrigerator or freezer while preserving game.

Once the game meat is ready, it must be stored in a freezer at 0°F and will last for almost a year. You must remember to cook game meat to its ideal internal temperature to preserve it. Once this temperature is reached, the bacteria in it are destroyed, which prevents food-borne illnesses. Once the meat is cooked, it needs to be cooled down rather rapidly before refrigeration. Now that you are aware of the different temperatures to pay attention to, it's time to start processing and preserving the wild game.

# Aging

Game meat is usually tougher than regular meat obtained from domestic animals. Wild animals are more active and exercise for longer periods while foraging for food, escaping predators, and their surviving in general. The tenderness of the meat is associated with the location of the muscle and the age of the animal. Healthy and young animals have the most tender meat. The condition of the animal before slaughter also affects the quality of the meat. For instance, if the animal was running a long distance before it was killed, the meat tends to be sticky, gummy in texture, and darker. The energy stored in the muscle of these animals is higher, and this increases their muscle pH. As there is an increase in pH, the meat quality reduces while increasing the risk of bacterial growth.

This is one reason why it was suggested that game meat must be aged first. Aging is a simple process that tenderizes the meat while enhancing its flavor. In aging, the carcass or the meat cuts are placed in an environment with controlled temperatures and humidity levels for several days. When this happens, the enzymes present in the meat start breaking down, and the complex proteins become simplified.

If the meat doesn't have much fat, you don't have to age it, or it will dry out. If you are directly cooking the game meat by stewing, braising, or roasting, you don't have to age it because these processes will tenderize the meat. To age the meat, you will need to place it under a temperature of 40°F for up to 7 days to improve its tenderness. Pay specific attention to this temperature range. If it is above this range, it increases the risk of pathogen contamination. You can speed up this process by increasing the temperature, but this increases the risk of contamination.

# Curing

You can either carve the carcass on your own or get a butcher to do it. Once the meat is ready, it's time to start curing. You can cure it with a dry rub, place it in a brine mix, or inject it with brine. These are the three methods of curing you were introduced to in the previous chapter. You can add salt, salt brine, sugar, spices, and any other ingredients you want for curing.

Once again, pay attention to the temperature at which you are doing all of this. Whether or not you are making dry curing mix at home or purchasing a readymade one, coat the meat thoroughly with it. To opt for a wet cure, you can place it in the brine solution. Injecting is rarely recommended for home curing operations. For fattier cuts of meat, choose a dry rub, while the leaner ones do well with wet curing. Once you've applied the mix to the meat, place refrigerate it at a controlled temperature of less than 40°F. As a rule of thumb, you will need to cure the meat for seven days per inch of thickness. If the meat is about 2 inches thick, it will need to cure for 14-days.

# Smoking

Once you have cured the meat, it is time to smoke it. The ideal wood types to smoke game meats are hickory, oak, maple, pecan, and even mesquite in moderation. While smoking meat, especially the larger cuts or large game, consider its size and dimensions. This makes all the difference. The ideal temperature of the smoker must be maintained between 225-300°F and cook the meat until it reaches an internal temperature of 165°F. This process can take 8 hours or even longer. The time for smoking depends on the size and thickness of the meat. Once the meat is smoked, it is time to store it.

# Storage

After the meat is smoked, cool it and wrap it in butcher paper and aluminum foil. Transfer it immediately into the freezer. Store it at a temperature of 0°F. The shelf life of the meat depends on the storage temperature. Don't transfer warm meat into the freezer and wait until it cools down. Also, air is your enemy while preserving meat. Whenever you store any meat in the freezer, ensure you wrap it in butcher or freezer paper or place it in Ziploc bags. You need to do this to avoid freezer burns. The idea is to preserve the meat without letting it come into direct contact with the cold air in the freezer. This is especially true for meats that will stay in the freezer for prolonged periods. One piece of equipment you can consider investing in, provided you are interested in curing and smoking regularly, is a vacuum sealer. It helps suck out any air from the bag or container used for securing and storing meats.

# Chapter 9: Preserving Your Fish

One of the oldest ways to enjoy and preserve fish is by smoking them over the flame. The wonderful smoky aroma of the wood coupled with the delicate meat of freshly caught fish is quite brilliant. In this chapter, let's look at the simple steps you should follow for preserving fish at home.

## Selecting the Fish

For preserving fish, starting with fresh catch is always the best. Compared to factory-farmed variants available on the market these days, fish caught in the wild is always better. The fresher the fish, the better the result produced. If you are lucky enough to get your hands on some freshly caught fish, try to keep it alive for as long as you possibly can. After this, thoroughly clean the fish and chill it so it doesn't go bad. This is especially true during warmer months when the temperature starts increasing. In such conditions, fish tends to go bad quite quickly. Don't forget to carefully store the cleaned fish and place it in an ice cooler. As a rule of thumb, you need two pounds of ice per pound of fish.

Fatty fish can absorb a smokier flavor. So, any naturally fatty fish such as trout and salmon are good options. You can either use the whole fish or parts of it for smoking. Usually, fillets with the skin are the ideal choice for smoking. It's important to consider the wood you will be using. Depending on your preference, you can choose any wood of your choice. Usually, alder is used for smoking salmon. However, any other wood, such as oak and mesquite, works well too.

## Preparing the Brine

If you are making the brine at home, you need to add 2.23 lb. of salt to one gallon of water; the concentration or the strength of the brine used for soaking fish matters a lot. As a rule of thumb, dissolve one cup of salt in seven cups of water per 2-3 pounds of fish. You can always use a commercially available brine mixture. Simply follow the instructions on the packing if using a store-bought mix. To make the brine at home, combine the salt and water over low heat until the salt is fully dissolved. If the brining process takes less than 4 hours, then the ideal temperature of the brine should be less than 60°f. If it takes longer, the temperature shouldn't be higher than 38°F.

Once you have prepared the brine, it is time to make a dry rub. This step is entirely optional. Using a dry rub will further enhance the flavor of the cured fish. A simple dry rub is a Cajun spice mix that includes various spices that lend a mellow kick and flavor to the preserved fish.

## Preparing the Fish

If you are using fish purchased from the market, you don't have to do anything here. You simply need to keep it on ice or place it in the fridge until you can use it. But if you are using freshly caught fish, you need to clean and prepare it. Remove the scales by scraping the dull edge of the knife against the grain of the scales. The next step is to remove the head, tail, and face. Rinse the body cavity, remove all the tissue and blood present inside. Once it's clean, cut fillets from the fish. Alternatively, you can also use the whole fish after thoroughly cleaning its body cavity.

## Place It in the Brine and Rinse

Thin pieces of fish are about ½-inch thick at their thickest point and should be soaked for a maximum of ten minutes in brine. In comparison, fish over ½-inch thickness need around 30-40 minutes of soaking time. This is an important process and keeps the fish fully submerged for the desired duration. If you are placing the brine in the fridge to maintain the desired temperature, don't forget to cover it with plastic wrap. This ensures the smell of the fish does not mix with everything else in the refrigerator. Fish is quite light, and fillets are even lighter. They tend to float to the top of the bowl. To prevent this, place another bowl on top to ensure they stay submerged. The bowl holding the fish and brine shouldn't be too tightly packed. There must be room for the fish to circulate instead of getting cramped up.

After patiently waiting for the fish to soak in brine, it is time to prepare it. Remove it from the brine bath, rinse it under cool water, and dry it. The simplest and efficient way to do this is by patting them dry using paper towels. Alternatively, use grease racks and place the fish on them. Wait for around 2-3 hours or until a shiny skin or pellicle has formed on the fish. This ensures the natural juices from the fish are not lost during the smoking process. Once the fish is dry, it's time to apply the dry rub. This is entirely up to you. If you don't feel like adding any spice rub, skip the step. Before you apply the spice rub, don't forget to coat the fish lightly with a layer of butter, so the spice rub sticks to the fish evenly.

### Smoke the fish

While smoking the fish, the ideal temperature should be less than 150 °F. Maintain this temperature for the initial 1-2 hours of smoking. After 2 hours, turn the heat up to 200°F and continue smoking. The fish is thoroughly cooked once it reaches an internal temperature of 165°F. It's always better to smoke the fish at a low temperature to preserve the flavor and texture. To keep the grates of the smoker clean and don't want the fish to stick to it, use aluminum foil. Place the fillets or fish on the aluminum foil with the skin side up while smoking it. If you are using skinless fillets, use a solid surface such as a wooden plank to ensure the fillets don't fall into the smoker. To regulate the smoker's temperature, especially if it tends to heat beyond 200°F, put some ice in a pan and place it inside the smoker.

# Enjoy the Fish!

Once the fish is brined and smoked, it is time to enjoy it! Serve it with some baked potatoes or fries for a classic fish and chips meal. It also pairs well with crusty bread and butter, salad, and some flavored rice! If you don't want to eat it immediately, you can store it for later. To do this, wrap the smoked fish in foil or wax paper. When placed in the refrigerator, it can stay for up to 10 days. To prolong its life, you can place it in the freezer.

# Chapter 10: Preserving Your Poultry

Nothing compares to the wonderful aroma and taste of smoked or cured poultry such as smoked duck or cured chicken. The salt, sugar, and nitrites present in the curing mix cure the poultry while preserving its flavor. The nitrites in the cure help retain the pinkish hue of the meat and prevent the growth of pathogens. Once you cure the meat, it can be refrigerated for up to 2 weeks. A point to remember with poultry, any uncured smoked meats should be stored for the same duration as any other regular cooked meat. In this chapter, let's look at all the different steps you can follow for preserving poultry.

## Select Good Quality Poultry

As with other types of meat, starting with fresh and high-quality poultry is a must. Using good-quality ingredients makes all the difference if you want good results. For instance, choose grade-A poultry, considered the best available on the market, and use it within an hour of slaughter.

# Prepare the Brine Solution

As you have learned by now, you can either make the brine solution at home or purchase a readymade mix. To make a brine solution at home for poultry, for one gallon of water, you must add 1.6 ounces of saltpeter, 0.9 lb. of non-iodized salt, and 2.4 ounces of brown or white sugar. Ensure the temperature of this mixture is 45-50°F. You can use a sodium chloride Salometer to measure the salt levels and temperature of the brine. Thoroughly mix the solution and make sure all the ingredients have dissolved completely.

A commercially prepared mixture contains the correct proportions of salt, sugar, and nitrites. This is a faster and easier procedure. If you are using a commercially prepared mixture, dissolve 1 lb. of cure mixture into a gallon of water or carefully follow the brining directions given on the packaging.

# Inject the Brine

As opposed to other meats, poultry is usually injected with brine then soaked in it to hydrate the meat instead of just soaking in it. However, birds that weigh less than 3 lb., such as quails or similarly small birds, need not be brine injected and can just soak in the brine directly.

Now that the brine mix is ready, you can start injecting it into the bird. You need to inject a measurement of brine solution equivalent to 10% of the carcass's total weight. For instance, if a turkey weighs 15 lb., it needs 1.5 lb. of brine. This step is crucial because you must ensure the brine is equally distributed within the carcass. While injecting brine, you need to concentrate on different areas and not just go about randomly stabbing the carcass. While brining birds that weigh around 3-9 lb., such as capons, broilers, and pheasants, brine must be injected in three places. The birds are injected in each half of the breast, two sites on the thighs, and one on each of its drumsticks. About 60% of the brine must be injected into the breast region, 30% into the thighs, and rest into the drumsticks. Birds that weigh over 10 lb., such as turkeys, are injected into five sites. Larger birds follow the same injecting sites as smaller birds, namely, the breasts, the thighs, and the drumsticks. And you must inject the larger bird in either side of its back and once in each wing. About 50% of the brine must be injected into the breast for large birds, 25% into the thighs, 10% each into the drumsticks and wings, and the rest into the back.

# Let the Poultry Soak

Now, this step is all about patience. Once you have injected your poultry, place it in either a plastic or stainless-steel container (food-use quality). Ensure the remaining brine is at a temperature between 34-36°F and cover the bird with it. You will need around a 5–10-gallon mixture of brine for curing two turkeys or over three broilers. You will need sufficient brine so the bird is immersed in it. Place the poultry inside an insulated ice chest to retain the desired brine temperature. You can always add more ice to maintain the temperature. However, remember the proportions of the cure must be maintained as more ice is added. As mentioned, quail and other similarly small birds need not be injected with brine and can be directly placed in the brine solution. Small birds need to stay immersed in brine for 4-6 hours, while small broilers that are not injected need about 4-8 hours in brine. Broilers, pheasants, capons, and turkeys weighing less than 10 lb. need to stay in the brine for 24-36 hours, while bigger birds need 48-72 hours.

# Draining and Netting

Once the poultry is cured for the desired time, remove it from the brine solution, drain it, and let it dry for 15 minutes. There should be no extra brine left in its body cavity. If you have a conventional smokehouse, place them on stockinette and have them hanging breast-side down. If you are using a backyard barbecue smoker or cooker, you need not do this. Instead, tie the bird's legs together using a piece of string or twine, tuck its wings towards the breast, and let it dry out. This helps the bird retain its shape even after cooking.

# Smoking

Once the bird is almost dry, place it in the backyard smoker or the smokehouse. The ideal temperature for this step is around 170°F. Smoke can be applied only when the bird is completely dry. If you don't let the bird dry out completely, the carcass will have a streaked look after being smoked. Don't be in a rush and slowly cook the bird on a low fire while generating plenty of smoke. While smoking, keep the bird as far away from the heat source as you possibly can. The best woods for smoking poultry are pecan, green hickory, oak, mesquite, and other fruitwoods.

The time taken for smoking poultry depends on the thickness of the meat, whether it is deboned or not, and its fat content. Other factors are the external weather conditions and the insulation on the smoker. The smoker and the fuel it uses also influence the cooking time. Besides this, another factor you need to consider is whether the meat was at room temperature before you started smoking it or not. It usually takes 4-5 hours to smoke a whole turkey, whereas a whole chicken only takes 2-3 hours.

# Complete the Cooking Process

When the bird has reached the desired color, increase the temperature to 200-225°F to complete the cooking process. Check the internal temperature of the bird. It is not fully cooked unless it reaches an internal temperature of 162-165°F in the fleshy muscles. You can also check whether the bird is fully cooked or not by twisting the leg quarter. If it moves freely, the bird is fully cooked. Don't be alarmed if the bird's size shrinks by

20% or so during the cooking process. Brining and smoking remove the salt and moisture present on the inside resulting in the size reduction.

## Storage

Once you have followed all the steps for brining and smoking, it's time to store the cured poultry. You don't have to cook it any further, and it can stay refrigerated for up to two weeks. This is the same timeframe applicable to other cured meats as well. To store it for longer than 2-weeks, ensure it is kept in the freezer at 0°F. If the poultry is packed, cured, smoked, and stored properly, it can retain its quality and flavor for up to one year.

# Chapter 11: Poultry and Meat Recipes

## Smoked Chicken

Ingredients:

If using brine:

- 8 cups water
- 1 whole chicken (2 pounds), rinsed
- ½ cup Fette Sau dry rub

If using dry rub:

- ½ cup Fette Sau dry rub or as much as required
- 1 whole chicken (2 pounds)

For Fette Sau dry rub:

- 6 tablespoons packed dark brown sugar
- ¼ cup ground espresso beans
- 1 tablespoon garlic powder
- ½ tablespoon ground cumin
- ¼ cup kosher salt

- 1 tablespoon freshly ground black pepper

- ½ tablespoon ground cinnamon

- ½ tablespoon cayenne pepper

**Directions:**

1. To make Fette Sau dry rub: Mix sugar, espresso beans, garlic powder, cumin, salt, black pepper, cinnamon, and cayenne pepper in an airtight container. Close the lid and shake the container to mix well. Use as much as required and store the remaining.

2. Place the spice container in a cool area. It can last for two months.

3. Dry the chicken well with paper towels. You should dry it inside as well as on the outside.

4. If you use brine for the chicken, combine water and Fette Sau dry rub in a stockpot.

5. Place the pot over high heat. Stir until all the sugar and salt dissolve completely. Turn off the heat and let the brine cool completely.

6. Pour the brine into a non-reactive container and chill for 3 – 4 hours.

7. Place chicken in the chilled brine and place the container in the refrigerator. Let it chill for 4 – 8 hours.

8. Have a wire rack placed on a rimmed baking sheet.

9. Take the chicken out from the brine and dry it with paper towels. Place it on the wire rack. Discard the brine.

10. Now place the chicken on the rack along with the baking sheet in the refrigerator. After 6 hours, take it out from the refrigerator for smoking.

11. If you are using only a dry rub, keep the chicken on a rimmed baking sheet. Sprinkle the dry rub all over the chicken. Use only as much rub as required, suiting your taste.

12. Set up your smoker and preheat it to 225°F. Place the chicken into the smoker and smoke the chicken. Add wood chunks or wood chips as and when required. See that the temperature of the smoker is maintained between 200°F and 225°F. Follow the manufacturer's instructions for adding wood chips.

13. The time for smoking chicken is approximately 45 minutes per pound. So roughly for 1 - 1-½ hours. When done with the smoking, the internal temperature in the center of the chicken leg should show 165°F when checked with an instant-read thermometer.

14. Place the chicken on your cutting board. Give it a rest for about 10 - 15 minutes.

15. You can now cut, shred or chop the chicken and use it. For a crisp skin, you can roast the whole chicken in an indirect method on the grill. Cover the grill while roasting. You can also crisp it up in an oven at 450°F.

# Smoked Chicken Wings

## Ingredients:

- 1 ½ pounds chicken wings, separated into drums and flats
- ¾ tablespoon baking powder or cornstarch
- 1 tablespoon kosher salt
- ½ cup Franks Red hot sauce
- 2 tablespoons butter
- 1 ½ tablespoons poultry rub
- 9 ounces IPA beer
- 10 tablespoons brown sugar
- 2 tablespoons butter

## Directions:

1. Place the wings into a Ziploc bag. Add ½ tablespoon rub, 2 tablespoons of brown sugar, and salt in the bag—drizzle 6 ounces of beer over the chicken.

2. After sealing the bag, turn the bag around a few times so that chicken is well coated with the marinade. Keep the bag in the refrigerator for 12 - 15 hours.

3. Take out the wings from the bag, dry the wings by patting them with paper towels, and then transfer them to a bowl. Sprinkle cornstarch and remaining rub over the wings.

4. Place the wings on a baking sheet lined with aluminum foil.

5. Set up your smoker and preheat it to 150°F. Place the wings in the smoker on the grill grate, and smoke them for 30 minutes. Add wood chunks or wood chips when required (follow the manufacturer's instructions on

how to use the wood chips). See that the temperature of the smoker is maintained between 145°F and 150°F.

6. Next, set the temperature of the smoker to 350°F and cook for another 40 – 45 minutes.

7. Meanwhile, combine red-hot sauce, butter, remaining brown sugar, and remaining beer in a small saucepan. Cook the sauce mixture until it is reduced to half of its original quantity.

8. Take out the wings from the grill and add them into a large serving bowl. Drizzle sauce mixture on top and toss well.

9. Serve.

# Smoked BBQ Korean Chicken Wings

**Ingredients:**

For brine:

- 1 quart water
- ¼ cup sugar
- ¼ head garlic, sliced
- 5 black peppercorns
- ½ cup sea salt
- ½ lemon
- 2 sprigs thyme

For wings:

- 1 tablespoon olive oil
- 1 ½ pounds chicken wings

For sauce:

- ¼ cup gochujang paste
- 3 tablespoons honey
- 1 tablespoon lime juice
- 2 tablespoons butter, melted
- ½ tablespoon grated ginger
- ¼ cup soy sauce
- 1 tablespoon rice wine vinegar
- 1 tablespoon sesame oil
- 2 cloves garlic, minced

To garnish:

- 1 green onion, thinly sliced
- 3 tablespoons sesame seeds

**Directions:**

1. Pour water into a saucepan. Add salt and sugar and heat over high flame. Stir often until sugar and salt dissolve completely.

2. When the brine solution begins to boil, turn off the heat. Add lemon, thyme, garlic, and peppercorns and stir.

3. Let it cool completely. Transfer the brine into a container. Drop the chicken wings into the container. Cover the container and keep it refrigerated for 4 - 8 hours.

4. Take out the chicken wings from the brine and dry them by patting them with paper towels.

5. Brush oil over the wings.

6. Set up your smoker and preheat it to 275°F. Place the chicken in the smoker on the grill grate, and smoke the chicken wings for 30 minutes. Add wood chunks or wood chips when required (follow the manufacturer's instructions on how to use the wood chips). See that the temperature of the smoker is maintained between 250°F and 275°F.

7. Next, set the smoker's temperature to 375°F and cook for an additional 50 - 60 minutes or until the internal temperature of the chicken shows around 170°F to 175°F.

8. Meanwhile, make the sauce: For this, combine gochujang paste, honey, lime juice, butter, ginger, soy sauce, vinegar, sesame oil, and garlic in a saucepan. Heat the mixture over medium flame and let it come to a simmer. Turn off the heat.

9. Add wings into the sauce. Toss well. Add green onion and sesame seeds and toss well.

10. Serve immediately.

# Smoked Herb Chicken

**Ingredients:**

- 1 whole chicken (about 2 pounds), rinsed
- ½ chopped tablespoon fresh parsley
- ½ tablespoon chopped fresh basil
- ½ tablespoon chopped fresh oregano
- ½ tablespoon chopped fresh chives
- 2 tablespoons butter, chopped into pieces

**Directions:**

1. Dry the chicken well with paper towels. Dry it inside as well as on the outside.

2. Loosen the skin all around the breast of the chicken. Place the pieces of butter in different places below the skin.

3. Mix parsley, basil, oregano, and chives in a bowl. Place half the herbs below the skin and stuff the remaining inside the chicken.

4. Set up your smoker and preheat it to 200°F. Insert the chicken in the smoker and smoke the chicken. Add wood chunks or wood chips as and when required. (Follow the manufacturer's instructions on how to use the wood chips). See to it that the temperature of the smoker is maintained between 150°F and 200°F.

5. The time for smoking chicken is approximately 45 minutes per pound. So roughly after 1 – 1-½ hours, the chicken should be smoked. When you are done with the smoking, the internal temperature in the center of the chicken leg should show 165°F when checked with an instant-read thermometer.

6. Place the chicken on your cutting board. Let it rest for about 10 - 15 minutes.

# Smoked Pulled Chicken

**Ingredients:**

- 2 ½ pounds chicken thighs, boneless
- 2 - 3 tablespoons BBQ rub
- ¼ cup BBQ sauce

For brine:

- ½ cup kosher salt
- 1 quart water

To make sandwiches: Optional

- Red onion slices
- 4 seeded or brioche buns
- Any other toppings of your choice

**Directions:**

1. Combine salt and water in a brining bucket. Once the salt is completely dissolved, add chicken thighs into the bucket.

2. Transfer the brining bucket into the refrigerator. Let it chill for an hour.

3. Dry the chicken well with paper towels.

4. Set up your smoker and preheat it to 225°F. Place the chicken thighs in the smoker, on the racks, leaving a gap between the thighs and smoke the chicken thighs. Add wood chunks or wood chips as and when required. (Follow the manufacturer's instructions on how to use the wood chips). See to it that the temperature of the smoker is maintained between 200°F and 225°F.

5. When you are done with the smoking, the internal temperature in the center of the chicken thigh should show 165°F when checked with an instant-read thermometer.

6. Place the chicken on your cutting board. Cover loosely with aluminum foil. Let it rest for 10 – 15 minutes.

7. Shred the meat with a pair of forks. You can now use the chicken for salads or soups, etc.

8. For BBQ flavored chicken sandwiches: Place the shredded chicken in a bowl. Pour BBQ sauce over it and toss well.

9. Serve over buns with onion slices and any other toppings of your choice.

# Smoked Chicken Salad

Ingredients:

- 2 - 3 cups smoked, shredded chicken

- 2 oranges, peeled, separated into segments, deseeded, chopped

- 2 cooked beetroots, cooled, peeled, chopped into cubes

- Chopped cilantro

For dressing:

- 1 teaspoon honey

- 1 tablespoon yogurt or sour cream

- ¼ teaspoon Dijon mustard

Directions:

1. For smoked chicken, follow the recipe for smoked herb chicken, or smoked pulled chicken, or smoked chicken in this chapter.

2. Combine chicken, oranges, beets, and cilantro in a bowl.

3. To make the dressing: Combine honey, yogurt, and Dijon mustard in a bowl. Pour dressing over the salad. Toss well and serve.

# Brunswick Stew

**Ingredients:**

- 2 pounds smoked meat of your choice
- 1-pound smoked chicken
- 6 large potatoes, peeled, cut into cubes
- 2 pounds corn kernels
- 2 tablespoons cider vinegar
- 2 cans chopped tomatoes
- 2 onions, chopped into chunks
- 4 tablespoons Worcestershire sauce
- 2 tablespoons sugar
- 2 tablespoons tomato paste
- Pepper to taste
- Salt to taste

To serve: Optional

- Cooked rice
- Crusty bread

**Directions:**

1. Set up your oven and preheat it to 260°F.

2. Place half the potatoes into the food processor bowl and process until smooth. Transfer into a bowl.

3. Add half the corn into the food processor bowl and process until smooth. Transfer into the bowl of potatoes and mix.

4. Place onions into the food processor bowl and process until smooth. Transfer into the bowl of potatoes and corn and mix until smooth.

5. Place all the meat, remaining chopped potatoes, remaining corn, vinegar, tomatoes, pepper, Worcestershire sauce, sugar, tomato paste, and salt into a Dutch oven.

6. Pour blended potato mixture into the pot and stir. Close the lid. Place the Dutch oven in the oven and cook for 5 - 6 hours.

7. Check on it after 4 hours. If the stew is looking very dry, add some water. If it is watery, uncover and cook until the desired thickness is achieved.

8. Serve over rice or with crusty bread.

# Smoked Turkey

**Ingredients:**

- 10 -12 pounds turkey

For brine:

- 1 cup kosher salt
- ½ bottle white wine
- 2-3 navel oranges
- 2 large onions, chopped
- 3 bay leaves
- ½ bottle red wine
- 2 cups chicken broth
- 2 tablespoons whole peppercorns
- 2 tablespoons whole cloves
- Cloves from ½ head garlic, peeled, chopped

After brine:

- Vegetable oil, as needed
- Freshly ground pepper to taste
- 3 - 4 cloves garlic, chopped
- 3-4 tablespoons soy sauce
- ½ apple, cored, quartered
- 1/8 large onion, chopped

**Directions:**

1. Add salt and about 2 quarts of boiling water into a large stockpot or brining bucket. Add red wine, white wine, and broth. Juice the oranges and add the juice into the brining bucket. Add the peels of the oranges, garlic,

onion, peppercorns, bay leaves, and cloves. Stir the brine solution until the salt dissolves completely.

2. Place the turkey in the brine breast side down in the bucket.

3. Place the turkey with brine in the refrigerator for at least 12 hours. The turkey may turn purple in color, but that is nothing to worry about. In fact, it will taste even better.

4. Remove the turkey from the brine and pat it dry with paper towels. Rub oil over the turkey. Brush soy sauce all over the turkey and rub it well into it.

5. Sprinkle a generous amount of pepper all over the turkey. Keep the turkey on the rack in a turkey pan.

6. Stuff the inner hollow cavity (the cavity should be cleaned, so remove everything from the cavity beforehand) with onions, garlic, and apple.

7. Take two large sheets of foil and fold one of its ends into a point. Place this point in between the legs of the turkey.

8. Brush oil on the foil that will touch the turkey while covering it. Fold the foil over the body of the turkey.

9. Set up your smoker and preheat it to 500°F. Place lava stone under the grill grates.

10. Place the turkey in the smoker along with the pan on the grill grate. Close the lid and smoke the turkey for about 30 minutes. Add wood chunks or wood chips as and when required (follow the manufacturer's instructions on how to use the wood chips). See that the temperature of the smoker is maintained between 450°F and 500°F.

11. Remove the turkey from the grill and lower the temperature of the grill to 325° F.

12. Place a meat thermometer in the thickest part of the meat. Place the turkey back in the grill. Cover and cook until the temperature of the thermometer reads 165° F in the thickest part of the breast area.

13. Remove the turkey from the grill and let it sit for 45 minutes (do not uncover the turkey).

14. Uncover the turkey.

15. Cut into slices and serve.

# Smoked Chicken Breast

**Ingredients:**

- 3 tablespoons table salt or 5 tablespoons kosher salt
- 1 quart water
- 1 ½ teaspoons minced garlic
- 1 - 2 sprigs of fresh thyme
- ¼ cup brown sugar
- 1 chicken breast, bone-in, skin-on
- 2 thin lemon slices
- 1 - 2 sprigs of fresh rosemary

**Directions:**

1. To make the brine: Combine water, brown sugar, and salt in a container.

2. Stir until sugar and salt dissolve completely.

3. Insert the chicken into the brine. Make sure the chicken is immersed in the water. Place something heavy on the chicken, if necessary, to keep it submerged.

4. Keep the container in the refrigerator for 7 - 9 hours. Take it out of the refrigerator about 30 minutes before smoking.

5. Set up your smoker and preheat it to 225°F for 15 minutes.

6. Take out the chicken from the brine and dry it with paper towels. Discard the brine.

7. Rub the chicken with garlic. The skin of the chicken is to be loosened.

8. Place the lemon slices, garlic, and herbs between the skin and meat.

9. Place the chicken on the grill and smoke the chicken. Add wood chunks or wood chips as and when required. See that the temperature of the smoker is maintained between 200°F and 225°F. Follow the manufacturer's instructions for adding wood chips.

10. When done with the smoking, the internal temperature in the center of the chicken breast should show 160°F when checked with an instant-read thermometer.

11. Place the chicken on your cutting board. Let it rest for about 10 – 15 minutes.

12. Slice or shred and serve.

# Baked Potato and Smoked Chicken Casserole

Ingredients:

- 2 ¼ pounds red potatoes, cubed
- ½ pound pulled smoked chicken
- 4 slices bacon, cooked until crisp, crumbled
- ¾ cup sour cream
- Red pepper sauce to taste
- 1 ½ tablespoons olive oil
- ¼ teaspoon freshly ground pepper
- 6 tablespoons BBQ sauce
- 4 ounces shredded sharp cheddar cheese
- ¼ cup chopped green onions
- Salt to taste

Directions:

1. Preheat the oven to 400°F.

2. Grease a baking dish with some cooking spray and prepare the potatoes for baking.

3. Place potatoes in a bowl. Drizzle oil over them. Sprinkle salt and pepper and toss well.

4. Spread the potatoes in the baking dish.

5. Place the baking dish in the oven and bake for 20 minutes. Stir and continue baking for another 20 minutes or until the potatoes are crisp on the outside and fork-tender inside.

6. Combine smoked chicken and BBQ sauce in a bowl and spread over the potatoes.

7. Scatter bacon and cheese on top.

8. Put the baking dish back into the oven and bake for 10 to 12 minutes or until the cheese melts and is bubbling.

9. Drizzle sour cream on top. Scatter green onions on top. Drizzle some hot pepper sauce to taste and serve.

# Penne with Smoked Chicken and Mascarpone

**Ingredients:**

- ½ pound penne pasta

- 1 tablespoon sherry vinegar

- 4 ounces young green beans, cut into 1 ½ inch pieces, blanched for about 2 minutes

- 1 shallot, thinly sliced

- Crushed red pepper to taste

- 1 tablespoon minced parsley

- ¼ cup mascarpone cheese

- ½ tablespoon extra-virgin olive oil

- 4 ounces zucchini, cut into 1 ½ x 1/3-inch sticks

- ½ pound boneless smoked chicken breast, remove skin and fat, shredded

- Salt to taste

**Directions:**

1. Cook pasta according to the directions on the package of pasta.

2. Retain about ¼ - ½ cup of the cooking liquid and drain off the rest. Set the pasta aside.

3. Cook mascarpone cheese and vinegar in a stainless-steel saucepan on low heat. Once the mixture melts, turn off the heat and keep it covered.

4. Place a nonstick skillet over medium heat. Pour oil into it and let it heat up. Once the oil is hot, add the zucchini and green beans and cook until tender.

5. Add shallots and cook until light brown.

6. Stir in smoked chicken, salt, and crushed red pepper and heat thoroughly. Transfer into a large bowl.

7. Add cooked pasta into the bowl of chicken. Add mascarpone cheese sauce mixture and retained pasta cooked liquid and toss well.

8. Garnish with parsley and serve.

# Chopped Salad with Smoked Brisket

**Ingredients:**

For dressing:

- 2 tablespoons red wine vinegar
- Salt to taste
- ¼ cup extra-virgin olive oil
- ½ tablespoon minced garlic
- Freshly cracked pepper to taste

For salad:

- 3 cups chopped lacinato kale or Romaine lettuce
- ½ cup halved cherry tomatoes
- ½ red bell pepper, chopped
- 2 – 3 cups pulled or chopped smoked brisket (refer to smoked brisket recipe in this chapter)
- ½ cup chopped red cabbage
- ½ small red onion, thinly sliced
- ½ cucumber, peeled, sliced

**Directions:**

1. To make the dressing: Place garlic, vinegar, salt, and pepper in a bowl and whisk until well combined.

2. Pour oil in a thin drizzle, whisking all the time. Keep whisking until the dressing is emulsified.

3. To make the salad: Place Romaine lettuce or kale, tomatoes, bell pepper, cucumber, cabbage, and onion in a bowl and toss well.

4. Add dressing and stir until well combined.

5. Divide salad into plates. Scatter brisket on top and serve.

# Cured Beef and Pickle Sandwich

**Ingredients:**

- 2 gherkins, cut into thin slices lengthwise

- 2 teaspoons honey mustard or medium-hot mustard or more to taste

- 4 slices of whole-wheat bread or any other bread of your choice

- ¾ cup pastrami (refer to pastrami recipe in this chapter)

**Directions:**

1. Smear 1 teaspoon mustard on one side of 2 of the bread slices.

2. Place pastrami and gherkin slices over the bread slices.

3. Cover with the remaining bread slices and serve.

# Loaded Grilled Italian Sandwich

**Ingredients:**

- 2 loaves (16 ounces each) Italian bread, halved lengthwise
- 4 cloves garlic, peeled
- 2 cups roasted red bell peppers
- 12 ounces sliced provolone cheese
- 24 ounces kalamata olives, drained
- 1 cup marinated artichokes
- 2 tablespoons oil from the marinated artichokes
- 12 ounces salami slices
- 4 cups arugula

**Directions:**

1. Scoop out the insides of the bread halves to resemble boats. Make sure the outer part of the bread is not pinched or torn. The scooped bread can be used in another recipe that needs breadcrumbs.

2. Place olives, garlic, and oil from artichoke hearts in a blender and blend until smooth.

3. Spread the artichoke puree on the cut side of the bread halves, filling the scooped part as well. Use all the mixture.

4. Place cheese slices over the bread halves.

5. Place the salami, roasted red peppers, and arugula on the bottom halves of the loaves.

6. Close the sandwiches with the top half of the loaves.

7. Preheat the oven to 350°F.

8.  Take 2 large sheets of aluminum foil. Place a sandwich on each and wrap them completely.

9.  Bake for 15 – 18 minutes. Unwrap and bake for about 5 minutes.

10. Cut into 3-inch slices and serve.

# Corned Beef Hash

## Ingredients:

- 1 ½ tablespoons unsalted butter
- 1 ½ cups finely chopped corned beef
- 1 tablespoon chopped fresh parsley
- ½ cup chopped onion
- Salt and pepper to taste
- 1 ½ cups cooked, chopped potatoes
- Fried eggs or poached eggs to serve

## Directions:

1. Place a cast-iron skillet over medium flame. Add butter and let it melt.

2. Once butter melts, add onion and cook until pink.

3. Stir in corned beef and potatoes. Now spread the beef moisture all over the pan and raise the heat to medium-high heat.

4. Press the mixture with a metal spatula, making sure not to stir. Let it cook for a few minutes.

5. Once the underside is brown, flip sides. Add more butter if required. Press the mixture once again, making sure not to stir. Let it cook until brown.

6. Turn off the heat. Add a generous amount of pepper and some parsley and stir.

7. Serve with eggs, either fried or poached.

# Corned Beef Cottage Pie

**Ingredients:**

For mashed potatoes:

- ½ pound potatoes, peeled, quartered
- 1 tablespoon butter
- 3 tablespoons milk
- Salt to taste

For corned beef filling:

- ½ cup diced onions
- ¾ - 1 tablespoon ketchup
- 1 tablespoon chopped fresh parsley
- 1 ¼ cups finely diced corned beef
- 1 tablespoon butter
- ½ teaspoon Worcestershire sauce or to taste
- ¾ cup chicken or beef broth
- 1/8 teaspoon dried thyme
- Salt to taste
- Freshly ground pepper to taste

For topping:

- 2 tablespoons dried breadcrumbs or 3 tablespoons fresh breadcrumbs

**Directions:**

1. To make mashed potatoes: Boil potatoes in salted water until soft.

2. Combine butter and milk in a saucepan and heat over a low flame. When the butter melts, turn off the heat and mix well. Cover and keep it warm.

3.   Drain off the water from the cooked potatoes and add it back into the pot.

4.   Keep the pot over medium flame. Pour the milk mixture into the pot. Using a potato masher, mash the mixture, adding some more milk if required.

5.   Add salt and pepper to taste. Turn off the heat. Keep the pot covered until you make the filling.

6.   While you are making the filling, preheat the oven to 400°F.

7.   To make the filling: Melt butter in a skillet placed over medium flame.

8.   Cook onions in the butter until light golden brown. Stir in broth, ketchup, Worcestershire sauce, thyme, and parsley and cook until the broth in the pan is reduced to half of its original quantity.

9.   Stir in corned beef and lower the flame. Cook until nearly dry. Add salt and pepper to taste and turn off the heat.

10.  Spread the mixture into a baking dish. Spread the mashed potatoes over the meat layer.

11.  The next layer will be cheese and breadcrumbs right on top.

12.  Place the baking dish in the oven and bake until golden brown on top.

# Pepperoni Pasta Bake

**Ingredients:**

- ½ pound dry pasta
- 1 small onion, diced
- 2 cloves garlic, minced
- ½ can (15 ounces can) diced tomatoes, drained
- ¼ cup grated parmesan cheese
- 1 cup marinara sauce
- 1 cup shredded mozzarella cheese, divided
- 15 – 20 pepperoni slices, halved
- ½ tablespoon olive oil
- ¼ teaspoon dried oregano

Optional toppings:

- 4 – 6 leaves fresh basil, chopped
- ¼ cup shaved parmesan

**Directions:**

1. Follow the directions on the package and cook the pasta in salted water. Turn off the heat. Drain off the cooking water and add the pasta back into the cooking pot.

2. While the pasta is cooking, preheat your oven to 375°F.

3. Meanwhile, pour oil into a skillet and heat over medium flame. When the oil is hot, add onion and cook until pink.

4. Stir in oregano and garlic and cook until you get a nice fragrance. Turn off the heat. Transfer this mixture into the pot of pasta. Add tomatoes, marinara sauce,

parmesan cheese, most of the mozzarella and pepperonis. Stir until well incorporated.

5.  Grease a baking dish and add the pasta mixture to the baking dish. Top with retained mozzarella cheese.

6.  Place the baking dish in the oven for about 20 minutes or until the cheese melts and is starting to brown.

7.  Serve hot.

# Pepperoni Meatloaf

**Ingredients:**

- 6 cups chopped pepperoni
- ½ cup sliced pepperoni or more if desired
- 2 cans (15 ounces each) tomato sauce
- 1 cup grated parmesan cheese
- 6 tablespoons dried minced onions
- 2 tablespoons garlic powder
- 1 teaspoon dried tarragon
- 2 pounds extra-lean ground beef
- 1 ½ cups cracker crumbs
- 4 eggs
- ¼ cup French fried onions
- 3 teaspoons dried oregano

**Directions:**

1.   Preheat your oven to 350°F when you start preparing the meatloaf.

2.   Place ground beef, tomato sauce, chopped pepperoni, cracker crumbs, eggs, parmesan cheese, dried minced onions, garlic powder, oregano, tarragon, and French-fried onions in a bowl and mix until well combined. Do not mix for too long, as the meat will get tough.

3.   Place the mixture in a large loaf pan. Use two smaller loaf pans if you do not have a large one. The top of the loaf should be smooth. You can use a spatula to do so.

4.   Place the meatloaf in the oven and bake for about an hour or until the meat is not pink anymore. When the loaf is cooked, the temperature in the middle of the meatloaf should show 160°F on a meat thermometer.

5.   Now top with the pepperoni slices and continue baking for another 5 minutes.

6.   Take it out from the oven and let it cool.

7.   Cut into slices and serve. Store leftovers in an airtight container in the refrigerator until use. Consume within 4 – 5 days.

# Smoked Pork Ribs

**Ingredients:**

- 2 racks of baby back ribs, trimmed
- BBQ sauce, as needed (optional)

For the rub:

- ½ tablespoon ground pepper
- 1 tablespoon Hungarian sweet paprika
- 2 tablespoons celery salt
- 2 teaspoons kosher salt
- 1 tablespoon onion powder
- 2 tablespoons garlic powder

For bath:

- 1 tablespoon brown sugar
- 2 tablespoons apple juice or cider
- 1 tablespoon apple cider vinegar
- 2 tablespoons butter, cubed

**Directions:**

1. Dry the ribs by patting them with paper towels.

2. To make the rub: Combine all the spices, celery salt, and kosher salt in a bowl.

3. Sprinkle the rub all over the ribs.

4. Set up your smoker and preheat it to 225°F. Place the ribs in the smoker and smoke the ribs for about 3 hours. Add wood chunks or wood chips as and when required. (Follow the manufacturer's instructions on how to use the wood chips). See that the temperature of the smoker is maintained between 200°F and 225°F.

5. Take a large sheet of foil or use two sheets of foil. Place the ribs on the foil. Top with brown sugar, apple juice, vinegar, and butter. Wrap the ribs tightly. If you are using two sheets of foil, place one rib on each foil. Divide the brown sugar, apple juice, vinegar, and butter among the ribs and place them on top. Wrap tightly.

6. Place the packets in the smoker and cook for 2 hours.

7. Without sauce: Unwrap and brush ribs with the cooked liquids. Roast for some time until crunchy, making sure to baste with the cooking liquid a few times. Let the ribs rest for 15 minutes. Cut into slices and serve.

8. With sauce: Brush some BBQ sauce over the ribs, and roast for 15 minutes. Repeat this process 3 more times (i.e., brushing ribs with BBQ sauce and roasting for 15 minutes).

9. Let the ribs rest for 15 minutes. Cut into slices and serve.

# Smoked Pork Tenderloin

**Ingredients:**

- 12 tablespoons butter
- 4 pork tenderloins (1 pound each)

For brine:

- ½ cup salt
- 6 tablespoons honey
- 4 cups water

For the rub:

- 2 tablespoons brown sugar
- 2 teaspoons garlic powder
- 4 teaspoons kosher salt
- 1 teaspoon chili powder (optional)
- ½ tablespoon ground pepper
- 2 tablespoons paprika
- 1 tablespoon onion powder

**Directions:**

1. Pour water and honey into a saucepan, add the salt, and stir. Place the saucepan over medium flame. When the brine is warm, turn off the heat and let it cool completely.

2. Place pork tenderloins in a brining bucket or large stockpot. Pour the brine over the pork.

3. Place the brining bucket in the refrigerator for 8 to 10 hours.

4. Take out the pork tenderloins from the brine and dry them by patting them with paper towels.

5. Discard the silver skin from the tenderloins.

6.   Sprinkle spice rub all over the tenderloins and tie them up with a butcher string.

7.   Set up your smoker and preheat it to 180°F. Place the tenderloins in the smoker and smoke them for about 3 hours or until the internal temperature of the meat in the thickest part shows 120°F on an instant-read thermometer or meat thermometer. Add wood chunks or wood chips as and when required. (Follow the manufacturer's instructions on how to use the wood chips). See to it that the temperature of the smoker is maintained between 170°F and 180°F.

8.   Next, raise the temperature of the smoker to 400°F and cook the tenderloins until the internal temperature of the meat in the thickest part is 160°F.

9.   Once cooked, remove them from the smoker and place on your cutting board. Tent loosely with foil and let it rest for 15 minutes.

10.  Cut into slices diagonally.

# Smoked Pulled Pork

**Ingredients:**

- 3 - 4 pounds bone-in pork shoulder

- 2 tablespoons pork rub or add more to taste

- 1 tablespoon avocado oil or olive oil, or any other oil of your choice

**Directions:**

1. For pork rub, you can use your own favorite rub, homemade or store-bought. You can also use the rub from the recipes for smoked pork ribs or smoked pork tenderloin.

2. Rub oil all over the meat. Sprinkle rub all over and rub it well into it.

3. Set up your smoker and preheat it to 225°F. Place the meat in the smoker and smoke them for about 3 - 4 hours or until the internal temperature of the meat in the thickest part shows 160°F on an instant-read thermometer or meat thermometer. Add wood chunks or wood chips as and when required. (Follow the manufacturer's instructions on how to use the wood chips). See to it that the temperature of the smoker is maintained between 200°F and 225°F.

4. Next, wrap the meat with butcher paper and place it back in the smoker. Smoke the meat until the internal temperature of the meat shows 200°F - 205°F on the thermometer.

5. Take out the meat from the smoker and do not remove the butcher paper.

6. Wrap the meat with a layer of aluminum foil and keep it in a cooler for resting. Let it rest for 2 - 5 hours.

7.   Remove the meat from its wrapping and shred the meat with a pair of forks. You can serve it over buns along with BBQ sauce or any other toppings of your choice like coleslaw, lettuce, cheese, tomatoes, etc.

# Smoked Brisket

**Ingredients:**

- 14 - 16 pounds whole brisket
- 6 - 7 tablespoons BBQ rub
- 3 - 4 tablespoons garlic-infused olive oil

**Directions:**

1. Leave about ¼ inch of fat and trim off the remaining fat from the brisket.

2. Apply a generous amount of garlic-infused oil all over the brisket and rub it in well.

3. Set up your smoker and preheat it to 225°F. Place the brisket in a roasting pan in the smoker and smoke the brisket until the internal temperature of the meat in the thickest part shows 160°F on an instant-read thermometer or meat thermometer. The approximate timing is 1 - 1 ½ hours of smoking per pound of meat. Add wood chunks or wood chips as and when required. (Follow the manufacturer's instructions on how to use the wood chips). See to it that the temperature of the smoker is maintained between 200°F and 225°F.

4. Once the internal temperature of 160°F is reached, wrap the meat in butcher paper and keep it back in the smoker. When the internal temperature shows 200°F, take it out from the smoker.

5. Do not remove the butcher paper.

6. Wrap the meat with a layer of aluminum foil and keep it in a cooler for resting. Let it rest for 2 - 5 hours.

7. Remove the meat from its wrapping and slice it against the grain and serve.

# Coffee-Rubbed Texas-Style Brisket

Ingredients:

- 2 tablespoons ground coffee

- 2 tablespoons dark brown sugar

- 4 teaspoons ancho chili powder

- 2 teaspoons onion powder

- 2 teaspoons freshly ground pepper

- 2 tablespoons kosher salt

- 4 teaspoons smoked paprika

- 2 teaspoons garlic powder

- 2 teaspoons ground cumin

- About 9 pounds flat-cut brisket (about 3 inches thick)

Directions:

1. Mix coffee, salt, and all the spices in a bowl. Rub this mixture all over the brisket.

2. Set up your smoker and preheat it to 225°F. Place the brisket in a roasting pan in the smoker and smoke the brisket until the internal temperature of the meat in the thickest part shows 160°F on an instant-read thermometer or meat thermometer. The approximate timing is 1 - 1 ½ hours of smoking per pound of meat. Add wood chunks or wood chips as and when required. (Follow the manufacturer's instructions on how to use the wood chips). See to it that the temperature of the smoker is maintained between 200°F and 225°F.

3. Once the internal temperature of 160°F is reached, wrap the meat in butcher paper and keep it back in the smoker. When the internal temperature shows 200°F, take it out from the smoker.

4.   Do not remove the butcher paper.

5.   Wrap the meat with a layer of aluminum foil and keep it in a cooler for resting. Let it rest for 2 – 5 hours.

6.   Wrap the meat with a layer of aluminum foil and slice it against the grain.

7.   Serve it along with the juices collected while smoking.

# Irish Smoked Beef Brisket

**Ingredients:**

- 6 pounds rolled brisket
- 1 cup brown sugar
- ½ cup vegetable oil
- 4 tablespoons lemon juice
- 2 tablespoons ground black pepper
- 4 cloves garlic, crushed
- 2 teaspoons dried chili flakes
- 2 bottles Guinness
- 1 cup water
- ½ cup Worcestershire sauce
- 2 tablespoons cooking salt
- 2 tablespoons soy sauce
- 2 large onions, sliced

For sauce:

- 2 tablespoons vinegar
- 8 teaspoons cornstarch mixed with ½ cup water
- 6 teaspoons English mustard

**Directions:**

1. To make the marinade: Combine brown sugar, oil, lemon juice, pepper, garlic, dried chili flakes, Guinness, water, Worcestershire sauce, salt, soy sauce, and onions in a bowl.

2. Once combined, transfer the marinade into a large Ziploc bag or food-grade plastic bag.

3. Place brisket in the bag and make sure to seal the bag well. Place the bag in the refrigerator for at least 12 hours or longer if possible. Turn the bag over every 30 - 40 minutes.

4. Remove brisket from the marinade and retain the marinade.

5. Set up your smoker and preheat it to 225°F. Place the brisket in a roasting pan in the smoker and smoke the brisket until the internal temperature of the meat in the thickest part shows 160°F to 170°F on an instant-read thermometer or meat thermometer. The approximate timing is 1 - 1 ½ hours of smoking per pound of meat. Add wood chunks or wood chips as and when required. (Follow the manufacturer's instructions on how to use the wood chips). See to it that the temperature of the smoker is maintained between 200°F and 225°F.

6. Once the internal temperature of 160°F is reached, wrap the meat in butcher paper and keep it back in the smoker. When the internal temperature shows 200°F, take it out from the smoker.

7. Do not remove the butcher paper.

8. Wrap the meat with a layer of aluminum foil and keep it in a cooler for resting. Let it rest for 2 - 5 hours.

9. To make the sauce: Pour retained marinade into a saucepan. Add vinegar, cornstarch mixture, and English mustard.

10. Place the saucepan over medium flame. Stir constantly until the sauce is thickened to the desired consistency. Remember, the sauce will thicken even more once cooled.

11. Wrap the meat with a layer of aluminum foil and slice it against the grain and serve with sauce poured on top.

# Pulled Chuck Roast with Grilled Onions

Ingredients:

- 2 - 3 chuck roasts (3 pounds each)
- 4 tablespoons Texas style rub or more to taste
- 2 tablespoons olive oil + extra to grill
- Bread slices or burger buns, as required
- ½ teaspoon kosher salt per pound of meat
- 4 medium onions, halved, thinly sliced
- Butter, as needed for the sandwiches
- 1 can cream of mushroom soup
- 2 cans beef broth

Directions:

1. Rub salt all over the chuck roast. Next, rub Texas-style rub all over the roast.

2. Place the roast in a roasting pan and keep it refrigerated for 8 - 9 hours.

3. Start up your smoker and preheat it to 240°F. Place the roasting pan in the smoker and smoke the chuck roast until the internal temperature of the meat in the thickest part shows about 145° - 1 50°F on an instant-read thermometer or meat thermometer. The approximate timing is 1 - 1 ½ hours of smoking per pound of meat. Add wood chunks or wood chips as and when required. (Follow the manufacturer's instructions on how to use the wood chips). See to it that the temperature of the smoker is maintained between 225°F and 240°F.

4. Pour beef broth and cream of mushroom soup into a large foil pan. Stir until well combined.

5. Now transfer the chuck roast into the foil pan. Keep the foil pan in the smoker and let the meat cook until the internal temperature of the meat shows 175° F in the meat thermometer.

6. Wrap the chuck roast with foil and continue cooking until the internal temperature of the meat shows around 208° F or until the meat is cooked through.

7. Take out the foil pan along with meat from the smoker. Do not unwrap the meat and leave it to rest for 1 – 2 hours.

8. Now unwrap and shred the meat with a pair of forks.

9. Meanwhile, grill the onions in your smoker. For this, drizzle a little oil over the onions and mix well. Place onions on a griddle and grill the onions.

10. Spread butter on both sides of the bread slices and grill the bread slices on the griddle as well.

11. To assemble: Place a little meat and little grilled onions between 2 slices of bread and make sandwiches.

# Smoked Lamb Ribs

**Ingredients:**

- 2 racks lamb ribs, trimmed of fat
- 2 tablespoons onion salt
- 4 teaspoons freshly ground pepper
- 2 tablespoons garlic salt
- 2 tablespoons mixed dried herbs
- Olive oil, as needed

**Directions:**

1. Combine onion salt, pepper, garlic salt, and mixed dried herbs in a bowl.

2. Take some olive oil and brush it all over the ribs. Cover the ribs with herb mixture. Place it into a roasting pan and let it rest for 30 minutes.

3. Start up your smoker and preheat it to 225°F with indirect cooking. Place the roasting pan in the smoker and roast for 3 - 4 hours.

4. The internal temperature of the meat in the thickest part should show 110°F when the meat is cooked through.

5. Place lamb ribs on your cutting board. When you can manage to handle it, cut the meat between the bones.

6. Serve.

# Smoked Meatloaf

**Ingredients:**

- 4 pounds ground beef
- 4 stalks celery, finely diced
- 6 cloves garlic, minced
- 4 tablespoons Worcestershire sauce
- 2 teaspoons red wine vinegar
- 2 tablespoons minced fresh rosemary
- 3 - 4 teaspoons salt or to taste
- 2 cups onion, finely chopped
- 2 carrots, grated
- 4 cups panko breadcrumbs
- 1 cup red wine
- 6 eggs
- 2 tablespoons minced fresh thyme
- ½ tablespoon paprika
- 1 cup ketchup
- 2 teaspoons olive oil

**Directions:**

1. Pour oil into a pan and heat over medium-low heat. When the oil is hot, add onion, celery, and carrots and cook until onions are pink.

2. Stir in garlic and sauté for a few seconds until you get a nice aroma. Remove the pan from the heat.

3. Start up your smoker and preheat it to 350°F.

4. Fix the paddle attachment to a mixer. Place ground beef in the mixer and mix. Add sautéed vegetables and mix until well combined. Add an egg and mix well. Repeat this with all the eggs, mixing one at a time and mix well each time.

5. Add thyme, rosemary, wine, breadcrumbs, vinegar, and spices. Mix well.

6. Grease 2 large loaf pans with butter and divide the meat mixture into the pans.

7. Place the loaf pans in the smoker and smoke for 20 minutes. Add wood chunks or wood chips as and when required. (Follow the manufacturer's instructions on how to use the wood chips). See that the temperature of the smoker is maintained between 340°F and 350°F.

8. Remove the loaf pans from the grill and brush ketchup liberally on the top.

9. Smoke for another 10-12 minutes, adding more wood chunks if necessary.

10. Cook until the meat thermometer shows 155 ° F.

# Beef Salami

**Ingredients:**

- 2 pounds ground beef
- 2 teaspoons Morton table salt
- 1 teaspoon freshly ground pepper
- ¼ teaspoon ground nutmeg
- 3 level teaspoons Morton Tender Quick mix
- 1 teaspoon mustard seeds
- 1 teaspoon garlic powder
- ½ teaspoon liquid smoke (optional)

**Directions:**

1. Combine ground beef, salt, pepper, nutmeg, Morton Tender Quick mix, mustard seeds, garlic powder, and liquid smoke if using in a bowl. Mix until well incorporated.

2. Divide the mixture into four equal portions and shape into logs about 1 ½ inches in diameter.

3. Wrap each portion of the meat in cling wrap or aluminum foil. Keep them in the refrigerator for 8 - 9 hours.

4. Uncover the meat and place them in a broiler pan.

5. Set up the temperature of your oven to 325°F. Place the broiler pan in the oven and bake for 50 - 60 minutes or until the internal temperature of the meat reads 160°F on an instant-read thermometer.

6. Cool completely. Wrap them in foil or cling wrap and keep it refrigerated. You need to consume it within 3 - 5 days. Place it in the freezer if you want it to last longer.

# Herbed Sausage

**Ingredients:**

- 2 pounds lean ground beef
- 4 tablespoons dry red wine
- 2 teaspoons dried basil, crushed
- 1 teaspoon mustard seeds
- ¼ teaspoon onion powder
- 3 level teaspoons Morton Tender Quick mix
- 2 teaspoons freshly ground pepper
- 6 tablespoons grated parmesan cheese
- 2 teaspoons dried oregano, crushed
- ½ teaspoon garlic powder

**Directions:**

1. Combine ground beef, dry red wine, basil, pepper, onion powder, Morton Tender Quick mix, mustard seeds, parmesan cheese, garlic powder, and oregano in a bowl. Mix until well incorporated.

2. Divide the mixture into four equal portions and shape into logs of about 1 ½ inches diameter.

3. Wrap each portion of the meat in cling wrap or aluminum foil. Keep them in the refrigerator for 8 - 9 hours.

4. Uncover the meat and place them in a broiler pan.

5. Set up the temperature of your oven to 325°F. Place the broiler pan in the oven and bake for 50 - 60 minutes or until the internal temperature of the meat shows 160°F on an instant-read thermometer.

6. Cool completely. Wrap them in foil or cling wrap and keep it refrigerated. You need to consume it within 3 - 5 days. Place it in the freezer if you want it to last longer.

# Mexican Chorizo

**Ingredients:**

- 2.2 pounds pork butt, freshly ground
- 2 teaspoons cayenne pepper
- 2 tablespoons ground cumin
- ½ teaspoon ground cloves
- 2 teaspoons dried oregano
- 2 teaspoons salt
- 6 tablespoons apple cider vinegar
- 2 tablespoons paprika
- 2 tablespoons garlic powder
- 2 teaspoons ground coriander
- 1 teaspoon ground cinnamon
- 1 teaspoon dried thyme
- 1 teaspoon ground black pepper
- Natural hog casing, as required, soaked in water for 30 minutes, drained, rinsed

**Directions:**

1. Grind the meat in a grinder.

2. Add all the spices and vinegar along with meat and mix on low speed for about 2 minutes.

3. Fill the meat mixture into the hog casings. Twist at the point you would like the length of the sausage to be. Make sure to tie the ends of the sausage.

4. Prick with a sterilized needle wherever you see air pockets. Dry the sausage with a clean towel and hang it in a cool and dry area for 1 hour.

5. Set up your smoker and preheat it to 160°F. Places the sausages in the smoker and smoke them for about 3 - 4 hours or until the internal temperature of the meat in the thickest part shows 160°F on an instant-read thermometer or meat thermometer. Add wood chunks or wood chips as and when required. (Follow the manufacturer's instructions on how to use the wood chips). See that the temperature of the smoker is maintained between 150°F and 160°F.

6. Have an ice bath ready. Remove the sausages from the smoker and immerse them in the ice bath for a while.

# Smoked Pastrami

**Ingredients:**

- 6 - 7 pounds brisket

For pickling spice:

- 1 ½ tablespoons black peppercorns
- 1 ½ tablespoons mustard seeds
- 1 ½ tablespoons allspice berries
- 1 ½ teaspoons ground ginger
- 2 bay leaves, torn
- 1 ½ tablespoons coriander seeds
- 1 ½ tablespoons red chili flakes
- 1 ½ tablespoons whole cloves
- 1 ½ teaspoons ground mace
- 2 sticks cinnamon, crushed

For brine:

- 6 quarts water
- 1 ½ cups white sugar
- 15 cloves garlic, crushed
- 2 ¼ cups kosher salt
- 6 teaspoons pink curing salt (Not Himalayan pink salt)
- 10 pounds ice

For pastrami rub:

- 6 tablespoons black peppercorns
- 2 tablespoons yellow mustard
- 6 tablespoons coriander seeds

**Directions:**

1.	For pickling spice: Combine mustard seeds, coriander seeds, and black peppercorns in a skillet and toast over a high flame until you get a nice aroma, taking care not to burn the spices.

2.	Turn off the heat and spread the spice mixture on a napkin. Let it cool for a few minutes.

3.	Transfer the spices into a mortar and pound with a pestle until crushed.

4.	Transfer the crushed spice into a bowl. Add allspice berries, ginger, bay leaves, chili flakes, cloves, mace, and cinnamon and stir.

5.	To make the brine: Pour water into a pot and add white sugar, garlic, kosher salt, pink curing salt, and six tablespoons of the pickling spice mixture.

6.	Place the pot over high flame. Stir until sugar and salt dissolve completely. When it begins to boil, turn off the heat.

7.	Place ice in a brining bucket. Add brine mixture and let it cool completely—place the brisket in the bucket. Place the bucket in the refrigerator for 4 to 6 days.

8.	Take out the brisket from the brine and rinse well under cold running water. Dry the brisket with paper towels.

9.	Combine black pepper and coriander in a mortar and pound with a pestle until coarsely ground.

10.	Spread a thin layer of yellow mustard all over the brisket. Sprinkle the coriander and pepper mixture all over the brisket.

11.	Set up your smoker and preheat it to 250°F. Place the brisket in a roasting pan in the smoker and smoke the brisket for 5 hours.

12. Raise the temperature of the smoker to 300°F. Wrap the brisket with aluminum foil and place it back in the smoker. Smoke for 2 - 3 hours until the internal temperature of the meat in the thickest part shows 160°F on an instant-read thermometer or meat thermometer. (Follow the manufacturer's instructions on how to use the wood chips). See that the temperature of the smoker is maintained between 225°F and 250°F.

13. Unwrap and let it rest for a while

14. Slice the meat against the grain.

# Salt Cured Ham (Old-Fashioned Preserving)

Ingredients:

- 6 tablespoons ground red pepper
- 6 cups brown sugar
- 12 cups curing salt
- 6 tablespoons ground black pepper
- 2 fresh hams

Directions:

1.   Combine salt, black pepper, red pepper, and brown sugar in a bowl.

2.   Rinse the ham with cool water and pat dry with paper towels.

3.   Take a deep tray and spread some curing mixture in it. It should be at least ¼ - ½ inch in height from the bottom of the tray.

4.   Keep ham over the curing mix in the tray. Make slits at the hipbone and hock joints and pack these slits with curing mix.

5.   Sprinkle the remaining curing mix all over the ham and rub it well into it. Place the tray in a cool place for 18 days. Maintain the temperature between 36°F to 40°F. It can be a refrigerator or a cooler with ice in it.

6.   Rinse cured ham with cool water and pat dry.

7.   The ham is now ready to be smoked.

8.   Start up your smoker and preheat it to 225°F. Place the ham in a roasting pan in the smoker and smoke for about 2 hours. Add wood chunks or wood chips as and when required. (Follow the manufacturer's

instructions on how to use the wood chips). See that the temperature of the smoker is maintained between 200°F and 225°F.

9.  Now wrap the ham in a double layer of aluminum foil and place it back in the smoker.

10. Smoke the ham until the internal temperature of the meat in the thickest part shows 140°F.

11. Take out the ham from the smoker and let it rest covered in foil for 30 minutes.

12. Slice and serve with the cooked juices collected in the foil.

# Canadian Bacon

**Ingredients:**

- 2 boneless pork loins, trimmed of fat
- 1 teaspoon granulated sugar for every pound of pork loin
- 1 tablespoon Morton Tender Quick mix for every pound of pork loin

**Directions:**

1. Combine Morton Tender Quick mix and sugar in a bowl. Sprinkle this mixture all over the pork loins and rub it well into the loins.

2. Place the loin in a large Ziploc bag or food-grade plastic bag. Seal the bag tightly and place it in the refrigerator for curing. It should be ready in 3 – 5 days.

3. Take out the meat from the bags and place it in a container filled with cold water.

4. After 30 minutes, remove the loin from the container and dry it with paper towels.

5. Place it on a tray in the refrigerator for some time, so the meat dries a bit.

6. Take out the pork loin and slice it into 1/8-inch-thick slices.

7. Brush a skillet with some oil and heat it over low heat. Cook the meat slices in the pan until brown all over and cook in batches.

8. Serve.

# Deli Style Corned Beef

**Ingredients:**

- 1 beef brisket (8 – 12 pounds), trimmed of fat
- 4 tablespoons brown sugar
- 2 teaspoons ground paprika
- 2 teaspoons ground allspice
- 10 tablespoons Morton Tender Quick mix
- 2 tablespoons ground black pepper
- 2 teaspoons ground bay leaves
- 1 teaspoon garlic powder

**Directions:**

1. Combine brown sugar, paprika, allspice, Morton Tender Quick mix, pepper, bay leaves, and garlic powder in a bowl.

2. Rub the spice mixture all over the brisket.

3. Place the brisket in a large Ziploc bag or food-grade plastic bag. Seal the bag tightly and place it in the refrigerator for curing. It should take five days for every inch thickness of the meat. So, if the meat is 2 inches thick, it should take ten days.

4. Take out the meat from the bag and place it in a Dutch oven. Pour enough water to cover the meat.

5. Place the Dutch oven over high flame. When the water begins to boil, lower the heat and cook until meat is tender. It should take about 4 to 5 hours.

# Pepperoni

**Ingredients:**

- 2 pounds lean ground beef
- 2 teaspoons liquid smoke
- 1 teaspoon mustard seeds
- ½ teaspoon crushed red pepper
- ½ teaspoon garlic powder
- 3 level teaspoons Morton Tender Quick mix
- 1 ½ teaspoons freshly ground pepper
- 1 teaspoon fennel seeds, lightly crushed
- ½ teaspoon anise seeds

**Directions:**

1. Combine ground beef, pepper, crushed red pepper, Morton Tender Quick mix, mustard seeds, garlic powder, fennel seeds, anise seeds, and liquid smoke in a bowl. Mix until well incorporated.

2. Divide the mixture into four equal portions and shape into logs of about 1 ½ inches diameter.

3. Wrap each portion of the meat in cling wrap or aluminum foil. Keep them in the refrigerator for 8 – 9 hours.

4. Uncover the meat and place them in a broiler pan.

5. Set up the temperature of your oven to 325°F. Place the broiler pan in the oven and bake for 50 – 60 minutes or until the internal temperature of the meat shows 160°F on an instant-read thermometer.

6. Cool completely. Wrap them in foil or cling wrap and keep it refrigerated. You need to consume it within 3 - 5 days. You can also place it in the freezer, and it will last longer.

# German-Style Cured Pork Chops (Gepockelte)

Ingredients:

- 1 tablespoon Morton Tender Quick mix for every pound of chops

- 2 loins or rib chops (about ½ - ¾ inch thick)

Directions:

1. Sprinkle Morton Tender Quick mix all over the chops and rub it well into the loins.

2. Place the loins in a large Ziploc bag or food-grade plastic bag. Seal the bag tightly and place it in the refrigerator for about 2 hours for curing.

3. Take out the meat from the bag and rinse it well with cold running water.

4. Brush a large skillet with some oil and heat it over medium heat. Cook the chops in the pan until brown all over. Pour about half a cup of water and keep the pan covered with a well-fitting lid. Cook until meat is tender, over low heat. It can take about an hour to cook.

5. Serve.

# Salt Beef

**Ingredients:**

For brine:

- 10 cups water
- 4 bay leaves
- 1 teaspoon black peppercorns
- 1 teaspoon ground mace
- 14.1 ounces salt
- 7 ounces sugar
- 6 cloves garlic, sliced

For meat:

- 2.2 pounds beef topside
- 4 stalks celery stalks, coarsely chopped
- 2 onions, chopped
- 4 bay leaves

**Directions:**

1. To prepare brine: Combine water, bay leaves, black peppercorns, mace, salt, sugar, and garlic in a large saucepan.

2. Place the saucepan over high flame. When the mixture begins to boil, turn off the heat, and let it cool completely.

3. Pour the brine into a stainless-steel container or ceramic container. Place beef in it and keep the container covered in the refrigerator for 8 – 9 hours.

4. Take out the beef from brine and keep it in a large saucepan. Discard the brine. Add onion, bay leaves, and celery, and cover the meat with water. Keep the saucepan over high flame.

5. When the mixture begins to boil, lower the flame, and cook on low heat for a few hours until meat is cooked and tender. It can take 5 – 8 hours.

6. Take out the meat from the saucepan and place it on your cutting board. When cool enough to handle, cut into thin slices.

7. Use it in making sandwiches or serve with mashed potatoes or serve with greens or use in salads.

# Cured Corned Beef

**Ingredients:**

For pickling spices:

- 2 tablespoons whole allspice berries
- 2 tablespoons coriander seeds
- 2 tablespoons whole black peppercorns
- 18 whole cardamom pods
- 4 teaspoons ground ginger
- 2 tablespoons mustard seeds
- 2 tablespoons red pepper flakes
- 4 teaspoons whole cloves
- 12 large bay leaves, crumbled
- 1 stick cinnamon

For brine:

- 1.32 pounds kosher salt or 4 cups Diamond crystal brand kosher salt or 7 tablespoons Morton's kosher salt
- 6 tablespoons pickling spices
- 1 quart water
- 10 teaspoons pink curing salt (not Himalayan pink salt)
- 1 cup brown sugar

For brisket:

- 2 tablespoons pickling spices
- 1 beef brisket (about 9 – 10 pounds)

**Directions:**

1. To toast spices: Combine allspice berries, coriander seeds, peppercorns, cardamom pods, cloves, red pepper flakes, and mustard seeds in a pan and toast over medium flame until you get a nice aroma, taking care not to burn the spices. Turn off the heat and transfer it into a mortar.

2. Crush the spices lightly with a pestle and transfer them into a bowl. Add bay leaves and ginger and mix well.

3. To make the brine: Take out about 6 tablespoons of the spice mixture and add into a large pot. Add cinnamon, salt, brown sugar, and water. Place the pot over high flame.

4. When the mixture begins to boil, turn off the heat and let it cool completely. Keep the brine in the refrigerator for 5 – 6 hours.

5. Lay the brisket in a large pan or container. Pour chilled brine over the meat. The meat should be immersed in brine. You can also keep it in a large food-grade plastic bag. Seal the bag tightly and keep the bag in a container.

6. Next, place the brisket in the refrigerator to cure for 5 to 7 days. Turn the brisket over daily. If you have kept it in the plastic bag, turn the bag around once daily.

7. To cook corned beef: Once the brisket is cured, take it out from the brine and rinse it well with cold running water.

8. Place the brisket in a large pot. Pour enough water to cover the meat by at least an inch. If you do not like salty brisket, pour more water into the pot.

9. Stir in pickling spices. Place the pot over high flame. When water boils, cooks on a very low flame until meat is fork-tender.

10. Turn off the heat and cool completely. You can use it now or keep it in the refrigerator for 6 – 7 days.

11. Cut the meat across the grain and serve.

# Potato Cakes Stuffed with Cured Meats

Ingredients:

- 2.2 pounds potatoes, peeled, cut into thin slices

- 3 - 4 tablespoons butter

- 7 ounces cheese

- 2 tablespoons olive oil or more if required

- 8 - 12 slices cooked ham or salami or any other cured meat of your choice

Directions:

1. Set up the temperature of the oven to 450°F and preheat it.

2. Add oil and butter into a large ovenproof pan and heat over medium flame. Swirl the pan to mix up oil and melted butter.

3. Place a layer of potatoes all over the bottom of the pan, slightly overlapping, in a clockwise direction. There should be no space between the potato slices.

4. Place another two layers of potatoes similarly over the first layer. Sprinkle salt and pepper over the third layer of potatoes.

5. Next, place half the cured meat over the $3^{rd}$ layer of potatoes. Place another 2 more layers of potato slices. Sprinkle salt and pepper.

6. Layer with cheese. The next layer will be the remaining meat. Place another 2 - 3 layers of potatoes. Sprinkle salt and pepper. If any more slices of potatoes are remaining, layer them as well. Turn off the heat.

7. Shift the pan into the oven and bake for about 30 minutes or until brown on top and cooked through.

8. Cut into slices and serve.

# Stir-Fried Bamboo Shoots and Cured Ham

**Ingredients:**

- 4 tablespoons vegetable oil

- 6 ounces cured pork belly, thinly sliced

- ½ cup Anhui yellow wine

- 4 green garlic shoots, sliced

- 2 teaspoons cornstarch mixed with ¼ cup water

- 2 inches fresh ginger, peeled, grated

- 4 large fresh bamboo shoots, discard outer leaves, thinly sliced

- ½ teaspoon sugar

- 2 fresh long red chilies, thinly sliced

- Water or stock, as required

**Directions:**

1. Pour oil into a wok and heat over medium-high flame. When oil is hot, add ginger and stir-fry for about half a minute or until you get a nice aroma.

2. Stir in cured pork belly and cook until brown.

3. Transfer the ginger and pork belly into a bowl and place the wok back over the heat.

4. Place bamboo shoots in the wok. Add a bit of oil if necessary and sauté for a couple of minutes.

5. Stir in sugar, wine, garlic shoots, chili, and stock.

6. Add in cornstarch mixture. Keep stirring until thick. Add cured pork belly mixture and mix well.

7. Serve.

# Chapter 12: Fish and Game Recipes

## Smoked and Cured Salmon with Orange Zest

Ingredients:

- 2 center-cut salmon fillets (2 pounds each)
- 4 tablespoons light brown sugar
- Zest of 2 oranges, finely grated
- 5 tablespoons kosher salt
- 2 teaspoons ground coriander
- 4 tablespoons vodka

Directions:

1. Spread ½ cup small wood chips on the bottom of the smoker and start it up following the manufacturer's instructions. Set it on high heat.

2. Keep the drip tray and rack over the chips. In a minute or two, smoke will be coming out from the smoker.

3.   Lay salmon fillets on the rack, with the skin side down on the rack. Close the smoker and let it smoke for 20 seconds. Shift the salmon away from heat and let it smoke for 30 seconds.

4.   Remove salmon fillets from the smoker and keep them in a glass baking dish.

5.   Rub the vodka all over the salmon.

6.   Then combine brown sugar, salt, orange zest, and coriander in a bowl. Rub this mixture all over the salmon.

7.   Cover the dish and place it in the refrigerator. Turn it every day for the next 2 days (3 days in all, from keeping it in the refrigerator to turning it daily for 2 days).

8.   Rinse the salmon fillets well with water and pat them dry with paper towels.

9.   Cut the salmon into thin slices on the bias and serve.

# Smoked Trout

**Ingredients:**

- 3 trout's (¾ pound each) cleaned
- Salt to taste
- Freshly ground pepper to taste
- 3 lemon halves

**Directions:**

1.   Set up your smoker to 375°F and preheat it. Sprinkle salt and pepper over the trout as well as inside and place it in a pan. Keep the pan in the smoker and smoke the trout for about 30 minutes or until cooked and visibly opaque.

2.   Serve with lemon halves.

# Smoked Sturgeon

**Ingredients:**

- 1 ½ - 2 pounds sturgeon, trimmed of fat or dark meat, cut into large rectangular blocks

- 2 tablespoons sugar

- ½ tablespoon garlic powder

- ½ cup kosher salt

- ½ teaspoon ground mace

- 2 - 3 tablespoons whiskey or brandy or more if required

**Directions:**

1. Combine salt, sugar, garlic powder, and mace in a plastic or stainless-steel container.

2. Place fish pieces in it and turn it around so that the fish is well coated with the curing mixture. If the weight of each block of fish is around 1 pound, cure it for an hour in the refrigerator. If it is ½ pound, cure it for 30 minutes.

3. Place the container in the refrigerator accordingly.

4. Take out the fish blocks from the container and rinse well. Dry the blocks by patting them with paper towels.

5. Place a rack on a baking sheet and place the fish on it. Do not cover the fish. Place the rack along with the baking sheet in the refrigerator for 18 - 24 hours.

6. Start up your smoker and preheat it to 160°F. Place the fish on the rack in the smoker and smoke for 2 - 4 hours, or the way you prefer it to be smoked. Add wood chunks or wood chips as and when required. (Follow the manufacturer's instructions on how to use the

wood chips). See that the temperature of the smoker is maintained between 150°F and 160°F.

7.   Once smoked, let it cool completely. Place it in a Ziploc bag or food-grade plastic bag. Remove all the air from the bag. You can vacuum seal the bag if possible and store it until ready to consume.

# Smoked King Crab Legs

**Ingredients:**

- 2 ½ pounds King crab legs

For basting butter:

- ½ cup butter
- 1 tablespoon lemon pepper seasoning
- 2 tablespoons lemon juice
- 1 tablespoon garlic powder or minced garlic

For the spice mix:

- 2 tablespoons salt
- 1 teaspoon paprika
- ½ teaspoon peppercorns
- ½ teaspoon red pepper flakes

**Directions:**

1. Start up your smoker and preheat it to 225°F.

2. To make basting butter: Combine butter, lemon pepper seasoning, lemon juice, and garlic powder in a microwave-safe bowl. Place the bowl in the microwave. Heat for a few seconds until butter melts.

3. Add salt, paprika, peppercorns, and red pepper flakes into the bowl of the melted butter mixture and stir until well combined.

4. Place crab legs on the rack in the smoker. Smoke for 30 minutes, basting with basting butter mixture every 10 minutes. Add wood chunks or wood chips as and when required. (Follow the manufacturer's instructions on how to use the wood chips). See that the temperature of the smoker is maintained between 200°F and 225°F.

5.   Now increase the temperature of the smoker to 350°F. Cook for 2 minutes. Flip sides and cook for another 2 minutes.

6.   Serve it right out of the smoker.

# Smoked Tilapia

**Ingredients:**

- 2 tilapia fillets, cleaned, boneless
- Pepper to taste
- 2 cloves garlic, minced
- Lemon slices to serve
- Kosher salt to taste
- 1 tablespoon chopped fresh basil
- ½ tablespoon olive oil

**Directions:**

1. Start up your smoker and preheat it to 170°F.

2. Mix basil, salt, pepper, olive oil, and garlic in a bowl. Brush this mixture all over the fillets.

3. Place the fish in the smoker and keep the vent open. Add wood chunks or wood chips as and when required. (Follow the manufacturer's instructions on how to use the wood chips). See that the temperature of the smoker is maintained between 160°F and 170°F.

4. Remove it from the smoker after 1-½ hours.

5. Serve with lime slices.

# Cured Salmon Gravlax

**Ingredients:**

- 2 tablespoons white peppercorns, crushed

- 16 ounces rock salt

- 1 salmon (4 pounds), sashimi-grade, skin-on, boneless

- 2 cups chopped dill

- 16 ounces white sugar

For the mustard cream sauce:

- 1 cup heavy cream

- 4 teaspoons mustard powder

- 2/3 cup Dijon mustard or hot mustard

- Salt to taste

- Pepper to taste

To serve:

- Lemon wedges

- Rye bread slices or any other bread slices of your choice, toasted or crackers

- ½ cup chopped dill

**Directions:**

1. Mix white peppercorns, sugar, salt, and dill in a bowl.

2. Take two large sheets of cling wrap and place them on your countertop in such a manner that they are overlapping slightly.

3. Place half the salt mixture on the cling wrap and spread it so it resembles the salmon.

4.   Lay salmon over the salt, with the skin side on the salt. Spread remaining salt all over the salmon.

5.   Now cover the salmon with extra cling wrap. If it is not covering completely, use some more cling wrap to wrap up the salmon.

6.   Keep the wrapped salmon in a large container. Place a heavy cutting board on the salmon and place 3 – 4 cold drink cans on the cutting board to weigh the salmon down. Keep this entire setup in the refrigerator.

7.   After 12 hours, take the salmon and the entire setup out and place it on your countertop.

8.   Remove the weights and cutting board. Do not remove the cling wrap.

9.   Flip the salmon over and put the cutting board and cold drink cans back over the salmon. Place this entire setup back into the refrigerator.

10.   Repeat steps 7 – 9 once again, so in all, this curing process is to be done for 36 hours. This is a medium cure.

11.   Remove the cling wrap and remove the excess salt mixture by scraping it off. Rinse the salmon well and dry it by patting it with paper towels.

12.   If you have time, place the salmon in a container and place it in the refrigerator for 3 to 12 hours. Do not cover the salmon this time and let it dry.

13.   Cut the salmon at an angle. You are not supposed to eat the skin, so cut it accordingly.

14.   To make the mustard sauce: Combine heavy cream, mustard powder, Dijon mustard, salt, and pepper in a bowl.

15.   Serve salmon slices with bread. Scatter dill on top. Serve with mustard sauce and lemon wedges.

# Kelp-Cured Blue Mackerel with Fennel Salad

**Ingredients:**

- 1 whole blue mackerel, headless, remove pin bones, gutted, made into 2 fillets
- ½ cup rice wine vinegar
- ½ teaspoon brine from a jar of preserved lemons
- ½ tablespoons finely chopped chives
- 3 tablespoons broken pomelo segments
- ½ tablespoon fine salt
- 2 sheets dried kelp (kombu)
- Extra-virgin olive oil, to drizzle
- Microgreens like red garnets, shallots, etc.

For dressing:

- 1 tablespoon mirin
- ¼ teaspoon finely chopped red Asian shallots
- 2 tablespoons soy sauce
- ¼ teaspoon finely grated ginger
- ½ teaspoon finely grated lemon zest

For salad:

- 1 young fennel bulb, shaved
- 1 tablespoon fresh lemon juice
- Salt to taste
- Freshly ground black pepper to taste
- ¾ tablespoon extra-virgin olive oil

## Directions:

1. With the flesh side facing up, lay the fish fillets on a tray. Sprinkle it with salt. Keep in the refrigerator for 30 minutes.

2. Add rice wine vinegar into a bowl. Dip the fish fillets in the vinegar one at a time and keep them on a plate—brush remaining vinegar over the kelp sheets.

3. Brush lemon juice on the flesh side of mackerel and keep each on a piece of kelp, with the flesh side touching the kelp.

4. Cover mackerel with the remaining 2 pieces of kelp and place them on a tray. Keep the tray covered with cling wrap and keep it in the refrigerator for 3 - 8 hours, depending on how much time you have on hand.

5. To make the dressing: Whisk together mirin, shallots, soy sauce, ginger, and lemon zest in a bowl. Cover and set aside for a couple of hours for the flavors to fuse.

6. Sprinkle salt and pepper over the fennel. Drizzle lemon juice and olive oil over the fennel and toss well. Spread over a serving platter.

7. Discard the skin from the mackerel and cut it into very thin slices across the grain.

8. Place mackerel slices over the fennel—drizzle dressing over the fennel and mackerel.

9. Sprinkle chives, pommel, and microgreens over the salad. Trickle some extra-virgin olive oil on top and serve.

# Marinated and Smoked Venison Tenderloin

## Ingredients:

- 4 venison tenderloins (6 – 8 ounces each) remove silver skins

- ½ cup extra-virgin olive oil

- 2 teaspoon brown or Dijon mustard

- 1 small onion, diced

- 2 teaspoons dried rosemary

- 2 teaspoons cracked black pepper

- 2/3 cup dry red wine

- 2 tablespoons soy sauce or tamari

- 2 teaspoons honey or maple syrup

- 4 cloves garlic, minced

- 2 teaspoons sea salt

## Directions:

1. Combine olive oil, mustard, onion, rosemary, pepper, red wine, soy sauce, honey, garlic, and sea salt in a bowl.

2. Take 2 – 3 large Ziploc bags and put the tenderloins in them. Drizzle the marinade over the tenderloins. Seal the bags after removing extra air from the bags.

3. With the bag sealed, massage the meat so that the meat is coated with the marinade. Keep the bags in a dish and chill for 8 – 12 hours.

4. About 20 minutes before starting the smoker, take out the meat from the refrigerator.

5. Take out a grill rack from the smoker and place it over paper towels.

6. Set up your smoker and preheat it to 250°F. Keep the top vent open. Place the venison on the rack and discard the marinade. Place the rack in the smoker and smoke the venison until the internal temperature of the meat in the thickest part shows between 140°F - 150°F on an instant-read thermometer or meat thermometer, depending on how you like it cooked. Add wood chunks or wood chips as and when required. (Follow the manufacturer's instructions on how to use the wood chips). See that the temperature of the smoker is maintained between 240°F and 225°F. It should be cooked in 2 - 2 ½ hours.

7. Once cooked, place the venison on your cutting board. Cover loosely with foil.

8. After about 20 - 25 minutes, cut into thin slices and serve with a side dish of your choice.

# Smoked Venison Jerky

**Ingredients:**

- 10 pounds venison meat, trimmed of fat, rinsed, cut into ¼ inch thick slices across the grain
- 1 cup water
- 1 cup soy sauce
- ½ cup brown sugar
- 2 tablespoons Morton Tender Quick mix
- 3 teaspoons Cajun spice mix
- 2 tablespoons garlic powder
- 2 teaspoons cayenne pepper
- 2 tablespoons ground black pepper
- 2 teaspoons celery salt

**Directions:**

1. Combine water, soy sauce, Morton Tender Quick mix, brown sugar, Cajun spice mix, garlic powder, cayenne pepper, black pepper, and celery salt in a bowl. Stir until brown sugar, and Morton Tender Quick mix dissolves completely.

2. Place venison in a large bowl. Drizzle half the marinade over it and stir until well combined.

3. Drizzle the remaining marinade over the venison and stir until well combined. Set aside for a couple of hours to soak.

4. Grease the smoker racks with some oil. Place the racks over baking sheets. Place the venison strips along with the marinade in a colander to drain.

5.    Set up your smoker and preheat it to 200°F. Place meat strips on the racks and keep the racks in the smoker, along with the baking sheets. Smoke for 3 - 4 hours or until dry and a bit pliant as well. Add wood chunks or wood chips as and when required. (Follow the manufacturer's instructions on how to use the wood chips). See that the temperature of the smoker is maintained between 160°F and 200°F. It can take anywhere between 2 - 6 hours or longer.

6.    Take out the jerky from the smoker and cool completely. Transfer into an airtight container or Ziploc bag. You can use it after one day because the meat will soak in the smoke.

# Brined and Smoked Wild Boar Shoulder Roast

**Ingredients:**

- 8 – 12 pounds wild boar shoulder roast
- 2 cups brown sugar
- 1 cup soy sauce or tamari
- 4 tablespoons cracked pepper
- 4 bay leaves
- 2 gallons filtered water
- 1 ½ cups kosher salt
- ½ cup Worcestershire sauce
- 2 tablespoons dried rosemary
- Apple cider for smoking

**Directions:**

1.   Pour water into a large stockpot and bring to a boil over a high flame. Remove the pot from heat. Add salt and sugar into the pot and stir until the sugar dissolves completely.

2.   Let the mixture cool completely.

3.   Stir in soy sauce, pepper, bay leaves, Worcestershire sauce, and rosemary. Add the meat into the pot. Now transfer the meat along with brine into a large, food-grade plastic bag that can be sealed. You can also keep it in a container but make sure that it isn't aluminum.

4.   After sealing the bag, place it in a cooler or refrigerator for 6 – 8 hours.

5.   About 25 minutes before starting the smoker, take out the meat from the refrigerator.

6.   Take out the grill rack from the smoker. After rinsing the meat under cold running water, pat it dry with paper towels. Discard the brine.

7.   Place the meat on the rack.

8.   Add apple cider to the bowl of water in the smoker.

9.   Start up your smoker and preheat it to 275°F. Keep the top vent open. Place the boar on the rack. Place rack in the smoker and smoke the boar until the internal temperature of the meat in the thickest part shows between 145°F - 155°F for sliced meat, or 160°F - 165°F for pulled boar on an instant-read thermometer or meat thermometer, depending on how you like it cooked. Add wood chunks or wood chips, water, and apple cider as and when required. (Follow the manufacturer's instructions on how to use the wood chips). See that the temperature of the smoker is maintained between 260°F and 275°F. It should be cooked in 4 – 5 hours.

10.  Once cooked, place the boar on your cutting board. Cover loosely with foil.

11.  After 20 – 25 minutes, cut into thin slices or shred with a pair of forks and serve with a side dish of your choice. You can also serve it with BBQ sauce.

# Smoked Whole Quail

**Ingredients:**

- 3 whole quails, skin-on, cleaned
- 1 teaspoon sea salt
- ½ teaspoon garlic powder
- ¼ teaspoon dried oregano
- ¼ teaspoon dried thyme
- ½ apple, cored, cut into 3 equal slices
- 4 teaspoons extra-virgin olive oil
- ½ teaspoon cracked black pepper
- ½ teaspoon smoked paprika
- Zest of 1/8 lemon, grated

**Directions:**

1. Place thyme, oregano, pepper, paprika, lemon zest, garlic powder, and sea salt in a container.

2. Place quails in the container and turn them around in the brining mixture. Rub the brining mixture into the quails.

3. Cover and chill for 4 – 6 hours in the refrigerator.

4. About 25 minutes before starting the smoker, take out the quails from the refrigerator.

5. Take out the grill rack from the smoker. After rinsing the quails under cold running water, pat them dry with paper towels. Discard the brine.

6. Place the quails on the rack.

7. Add apple cider to the bowl of water in the smoker.

8. Set up your smoker and preheat it to 220°F. Keep the top vent open. Fill a slice of apple in the cavity of each quail. Keep the quails on the rack. Place a rack in the smoker and smoke the quails until the internal temperature of the meat in the thickest part shows between 145°F - 155°F on an instant-read thermometer or meat thermometer, depending on how you like it cooked. Add wood chunks or wood chips as and when required. (Follow the manufacturer's instructions on how to use the wood chips). See that the temperature of the smoker is maintained between 200°F and 220°F. It should be cooked in 4 - 5 hours.

9. Once cooked, place the quails on your cutting board. Cover loosely with foil.

10. It is best served with wild rice or brown rice, or a mixture of both. You can also serve it with a salad made of wild rice.

# Smoked Pheasant Breast

**Ingredients:**

- 2 pheasant breasts
- ½ cup chopped fresh basil
- ½ tablespoon salt
- 2 rashers middle bacon
- Ground black pepper to taste
- 1 cup water

**Directions:**

1. Combine water and salt in a bowl. Stir until salt dissolves completely. Place the pheasant breasts in the bowl in the refrigerator for 4 to 6 hours.

2. Set up your smoker and preheat it to 225°F.

3. Place the pheasant breasts on the cooking plank. Sprinkle pepper over the breasts and scatter basil on top. Place bacon slices to cover the breasts and tuck the ends beneath the breasts.

4. Smoke for 2 hours. Add wood chunks or wood chips as and when required. (Follow the manufacturer's instructions on how to use the wood chips). See that the temperature of the smoker is maintained between 210°F and 225°F. Once cooked, take it out of the smoker and place it on your cutting board.

5. When cool enough to handle, cut into pieces and serve.

# Smoked Duck Breast

Ingredients:

- 1 duck breast half (about ¾ pound)
- 2 cups apple juice or apple cider
- ½ bay leaf, crushed
- ¼ teaspoon whole peppercorns, cracked
- 2 tablespoons kosher salt or 1 ½ tablespoons canning salt
- 2 small cloves garlic, crushed
- Melted bacon grease, as required

Directions:

1. Combine apple juice, bay leaf, peppercorns, kosher salt, and garlic in a bowl.

2. Drop the duck breast half in the brine and let it soak for 2 - 8 hours, depending on how much time you have.

3. Take out the breast half from the brine and rinse under cold running water. Now pat dry with paper towels.

4. Smear melted bacon grease all over the breast half.

5. Set up your smoker and preheat it to 225°F. Place the duck breast half in the smoker and smoke for 1 - 2 hours. Add wood chunks or wood chips as and when required. (Follow the manufacturer's instructions on how to use the wood chips). See that the temperature of the smoker is maintained between 200°F and 225°F.

6. Cook until the internal temperature of the meat in the thickest part shows between 155°F - 165°F on an instant-read thermometer or meat thermometer, depending on how you like it cooked.

7.   It is best served with wild rice or brown rice, or a mixture of both.

# Maple-Smoked Duck Breasts

Ingredients:

- 4 boneless duck breast halves, skin-on
- 4 teaspoons cracked black pepper
- 2 teaspoons maple syrup to brush
- 6 tablespoons maple syrup
- 4 tablespoons kosher salt

Directions:

1. Sprinkle salt and pepper all over the duck breast halves. Place them in a dish and drizzle 6 tablespoons of maple syrup over them.

2. Cover the dish and chill for 12 - 24 hours.

3. Set up your smoker and preheat it to 225°F. Place the duck breast halves in the smoker and smoke for 3 - 4 hours. Add maple wood chunks or wood chips as and when required. (Follow the manufacturer's instructions on how to use the wood chips). See that the temperature of the smoker is maintained between 200°F and 225°F.

4. Cook until the internal temperature of the meat in the thickest part shows between 155°F - 165°F on an instant-read thermometer or meat thermometer, depending on how you like it cooked.

5. Cool completely. Cut into slices. It is now ready to serve.

6. Store the leftovers in an airtight container in the refrigerator. It can last for 4 - 5 days.

# Goose Pastrami

## Ingredients:

- 4 skinless goose breasts

- ½ teaspoon pink curing salt (not Himalayan pink salt) for every 3 pounds of goose breasts

- ½ teaspoon celery seeds

- 2 teaspoons sugar

- 2 tablespoons +2 teaspoons ground black pepper

- 2 tablespoons ground coriander

- 1 teaspoon dried thyme

- ½ teaspoon caraway seeds

- ½ teaspoon crushed juniper berries (optional)

- ½ cup brandy or red wine or water or vinegar

- 1 tablespoon kosher salt for every pound of goose meat

## Directions:

1. You can use slightly lesser salt if desired. Once you weigh the goose breasts, use kosher salt and curing salt accordingly.

2. Combine curing salt, kosher salt, thyme, sugar, caraway, celery seeds, 2 teaspoons black pepper, and juniper berries in a spice grinder and grind until you get a powder consistency.

3. Cover the goose breasts with the spice mixture. Rub the mixture into the meat. Place them in an airtight container and keep them in the refrigerator for 24 – 72 hours.

4. Take goose breasts out of the refrigerator and rinse well with cold running water. Pat dry with paper towels.

5. Place a rack on a baking sheet and put the goose breast halves on it. Place it in the refrigerator and let it dry in the refrigerator for 24 hours.

6. Pour brandy or red wine or vinegar or water into a container. Place the goose breast halves in the container for a few seconds.

7. Take it out and sprinkle 2 tablespoons of pepper over the breasts. Also, sprinkle ground coriander.

8. Set up your smoker and preheat it to 225°F. Place the duck breast halves in the smoker and smoke for 3 - 4 hours. Add maple wood chunks or wood chips as and when required. (Follow the manufacturer's instructions on how to use the wood chips). See to it that the temperature of the smoker is maintained between 200°F and 225°F.

9. Cook until the internal temperature of the meat in the thickest part shows between 140°F on an instant-read thermometer or meat thermometer, depending on how you like it cooked.

10. Cool completely. Slice the meat against the grain.

11. Store leftovers in an airtight container in the refrigerator. It can last for 5 - 6 days.

# Smoked Cornish Game Hens

**Ingredients:**

- 1 Cornish game hen
- ½ tablespoon salt
- ½ tablespoon dried basil
- ½ teaspoon dried thyme
- ½ teaspoon dried oregano
- ½ teaspoon cayenne pepper
- 1 tablespoon butter, melted
- 1 teaspoon ground black pepper

**Directions:**

1. Dry the Cornish game hen by patting with paper towels.

2. Smear butter all over the hen and rub it well into it.

3. Set up your smoker and preheat it to 275°F. Place the Cornish game hen in the smoker and smoke for 1 - 2 hours. Add wood chunks or wood chips as and when required. (Follow the manufacturer's instructions on how to use the wood chips). See to it that the temperature of the smoker is maintained between 260°F and 275°F.

4. Cook until the internal temperature of the meat in the thickest part shows 180°F on an instant-read thermometer or meat thermometer.

# Wild Game Backstrap

**Ingredients:**

- 2 pounds elk or deer backstrap or tenderloin
- ¾ cup butter
- 3 sprigs rosemary
- 4 cloves garlic, sliced
- Coarse salt to taste
- Ground black pepper to taste
- 2 tablespoons olive oil or as much as needed

**Directions:**

1. Brush olive oil lightly all over the backstrap. Sprinkle salt and pepper over it.

2. Set up your smoker and preheat it to 225°F. Place the meat in the smoker and smoke for 1 – 2 hours. Add wood chunks or wood chips as and when required. (Follow the manufacturer's instructions on how to use the wood chips). See that the temperature of the smoker is maintained between 200°F and 225°F.

3. Cook until the internal temperature of the meat in the thickest part shows 100°F on an instant-read thermometer or meat thermometer.

4. Remove the meat from the smoker.

5. Meanwhile, make garlic herb butter: Combine ½ cup butter, half the garlic, and 2 sprigs of rosemary in a small pot.

6. Place the pot over low flame, let the butter melt, and cook for 3 to 4 minutes.

7. Turn off the heat and set it aside.

8. Place a cast-iron skillet over medium flame. Add ¼ cup butter, remaining garlic, and rosemary, and let the butter melt.

9. Place backstrap in the pan and cook the meat until you have a crust on the meat. Use the butter from the same pan to baste while cooking. Cook until the internal temperature of the meat in the thickest part shows 125°F on an instant-read thermometer or meat thermometer.

10. Take out the meat from the pan and place it on your cutting board. When it cools a bit, cut into about ¼ inch thick slices.

11. Spread the garlic herb butter over the meat. Sprinkle salt on top and serve.

# Sugar Cured Feral Hog

Ingredients:

- 4 – 6 pounds ham
- 1 cup sugar
- 1 cup sea salt or kosher salt
- 12 – 16 cups cold water

For basting:

- ½ jar Texas Gourmet's Mandarin orange Serrano jelly
- 1 ½ teaspoons finely chopped rosemary leaves
- ¼ cup olive oil
- 1 ½ tablespoons soy sauce
- ½ tablespoon ground ginger
- 3 ounces Crown Royal whiskey
- 2 tablespoons honey
- ¼ cup butter
- 1 tablespoon ground black pepper
- 3 cloves garlic, peeled, minced

Directions:

1. For curing: Combine sugar, salt, and cold water in a container and stir until sugar and salt dissolve completely.

2. Place the ham in a Ziploc bag or food-grade plastic bag. Take your turkey injector and inject 2 – 3 full injectors of the solution into the ham at different places and adjacent to the bone.

3. Pour the remaining solution into the bag. Remove air from the bag and seal it up tightly.

4. Keep the bag in the refrigerator for 24 – 48 hours, depending on how much time you have.

5. Take out the ham from the solution and rinse it well under cold running water. Pat dry with paper towels.

6. To make basting mixture: Combine jelly, rosemary leaves, oil, soy sauce, ginger, whiskey, butter, pepper, and garlic in a bowl.

7. Start up your smoker and preheat it to 275°F. Place the ham in the smoker and smoke the ham roast until the internal temperature of the meat in the thickest part shows about 160°F on an instant-read thermometer or meat thermometer. The approximate timing is about 45 minutes of smoking per pound of meat. Add wood chunks or wood chips as and when required. (Follow the manufacturer's instructions on how to use the wood chips). See to it that the temperature of the smoker is maintained between 250°F and 275°F.

8. As the ham is smoked, you must baste it as well. Baste with the basting mixture every 45 minutes. Turn the ham after every 1-½ hour.

9. Once cooked, remove ham from the smoker and place it on your cutting board. Cover it loosely with foil. Let it rest for 45 minutes.

10. Slice and serve with the remaining basting mixture.

# Smoked Mackerel Salad

**Ingredients:**

- 2 smoked mackerel fillets, flaked
- 3 - 4 cups baby spinach
- 4 cherry tomatoes, halved
- ½ large bag salad leaves, torn
- 4 boiled new potatoes, sliced

For dressing:

- ½ tablespoon balsamic vinegar
- ½ teaspoon honey
- 2 tablespoons extra-virgin olive oil
- ½ teaspoon Dijon mustard

**Directions:**

1. To make the dressing: Whisk together vinegar, honey, oil, and Dijon mustard in a bowl.

2. Place salad leaves, spinach, and potatoes in a bowl and toss well.

3. Pour half the dressing over the salad and toss well.

4. Distribute the salad between 2 plates, top with the mackerel and tomatoes and drizzle the remaining dressing on top. Serve immediately.

# Conclusion

Preserving food using different techniques is not a modern concept. Our early ancestors were known to freeze meats on ice in extremely cold climatic conditions and sun-drying foods in tropical and hot regions. Initially, food preservation was more about survival than taste or flavor. Food preservation techniques also reduce the risk of food spoilage or contamination. What more? Smoked and cured meats, fish, and poultry have proved to be incredibly delicious.

Smoking and curing are not difficult techniques. Once you get the hang of it, you will realize how simple it truly is. From understanding the basic elements of these techniques to their nuances, everything you need to know is given within this book. You can start making delicious mouthwatering meals quickly at home using the recipes in this book!

Now that you have all the information you need, what are you waiting for? Gather the required supplies and ingredients, select a recipe that strikes your fancy, and follow the simple instructions in this book. To master the art of smoking and curing, you need a little patience and the right information. Now that you have everything needed, it is time to learn and experiment!

Thank you, and all the best!

# Part 3: Root Cellaring

*The Ultimate Guide to Building a Root Cellar
and Keeping Food in Cold Storage*

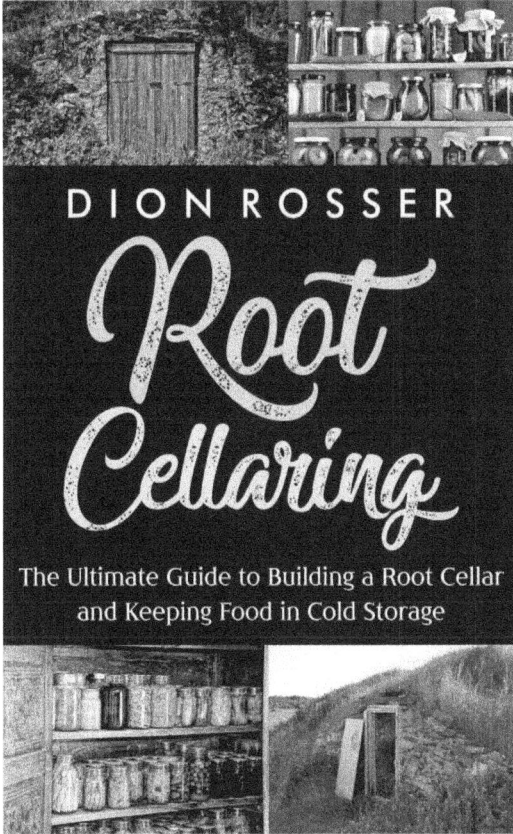

# Introduction

Welcome to the world of root cellaring. Some of you will be lost in nostalgia, remembering your grandparents' and parents' root cellars, while others will be wondering what they even are. The fact that you are reading this book shows that you want to know and are interested in root cellars.

This book will guide you through everything you need to know about the humble root cellar, from its origins right up to modern-day use. By the time you get to the end, you will have a solid plan in mind of what you want to do, how you will achieve it, and when.

This is where the excitement builds. All that fantastic, organic, healthy food you can grow in your garden—you can now store it and live off it all year! Forget buying vegetables wrapped in harmful plastic from the grocery store and food that you know has been sprayed in chemicals or imported from a foreign country at great expense. Instead, think of the rows of carrots and potatoes, the corn, onions, beets, and the dozens of other things you can grow in your garden and put away to live on over the winter.

Run an Internet search for books on root cellars, and you will find quite a few. However, this one is different. This one will teach you how to build a root cellar, not just one you dig into the ground, but how to make one from something else. After all, not everyone has a vast garden and space to start digging down to build a cellar. You might be surprised at what you can use to store your vegetables, and this book lists some exciting ideas for you to try out.

Now, time to dig in. Turn the pages and work your way through this incredibly easy-to-read guide on root cellars and follow the steps outline—you will soon be well on your way to becoming a master at it!

# Chapter 1: An Introduction to Root Cellars

Can you imagine what your life would be like without a refrigerator in the kitchen? Since the 1800s, technology has come a long way, and now virtually every household has at least one refrigerator working to keep their food cool and fresh. Imagine not having one. Picture going back to a time way before these cold units were even thought of.

Before the rise of modern, convenient home appliances, most people had a root cellar. Those who did not have one were looked down upon—considered too poor to even have a hole in the ground where they could store food. While root cellars lost ground many years ago, replaced by modern-day luxuries, they were essential in older times. Even as late as World War II people were still using them to keep precious food supplies fresh.

Today, root cellars are making a huge comeback. Keep reading to find out what they are and why they are, once again, so popular.

# What is a Root Cellar?

Technically, root cellars are rooms below the ground that use the earth's natural humidifying, cooling, and insulating properties. They are an old-fashioned way of storing and preserving food to get people through the winter months. While they were once rooms beneath the house, cellars nowadays are any type of storage that keeps food fresh for longer by controlling light, temperature, and humidity. Your refrigerator is the modern root cellar, but learning how to make a root cellar successfully is essential if you do not want to rely on electricity.

Every root cellar, regardless of design, functions in the same basic way. If properly constructed, it can keep your food up to 40 degrees Fahrenheit cooler than ambient summertime temperatures. During the winter, low temperature also has significant benefits, as storing food at temperatures just above freezing point can slow down rot and deterioration. Even in a basement, the temperatures are slightly warmer inside your homes, meaning stored foods will spoil much quicker. If the temperature rises above 45 degrees Fahrenheit, most vegetables will turn tough, start sprouting, and quickly spoil.

That said, root cellar temperatures are never the same in every corner. Near the top, the temperature is around 10 degrees warmer than the lower part of the cellar, so it is important to organize the root cellar efficiently. Place vegetables that tolerate warmer temperatures at the top.

Now, what if your garden is too small or you have no interest in growing your own vegetables? Not a problem—root cellars are designed to store produce that you don't have to grow yourself. If you can pick up great bargains from your local farm or farmer's market, you can just as easily store those in your cellar.

Root cellars were originally designed for root vegetables, which is where their name comes from—vegetables such as potatoes, carrots, parsnips, beets, and turnips are ideal for this type of storage. However, these days, people store much more, including apples, flower bulbs, canned goods, pears, pickled vegetables, etc. Think of a root cellar as a huge extension to your pantry.

# A Brief History of the Root Cellar

The root cellar has a long and interesting history, dating back at least 40,000 years. The first to start using the earth's natural insulation and cooling properties to store food were Indigenous Australians. Records show that over 40,000 years ago, they were growing vast amounts of yams and came up with a way of storing it long term, namely burying it in the ground. While developing their technique, they also discovered another process, fermentation, and that is why alcoholic beverages are commonly stored in cellars.

Iron Age storage rooms have also been discovered beneath the ground, which Etruscans still use to store immature wine. Although the first alleged use of a walk-in root cellar occurred in seventeenth century England, the most notable uses came from English colonists who settled in North America.

During ancient times, China and Egypt had already mastered preserving food using methods such as salting, pickling, using spices, and drying. However, cold winters and widespread famines are what drove the British to invent the walk-in root cellar.

Across the eastern parts of Canada and America, the land is scattered with old root cellars; thousands of them. Elliston, a small town in Newfoundland, has even claimed the title of "Root Cellar Capital of the World," with over 135 root cellars, some of them around 200 years old.

# Pros and Cons of Root Cellaring

Understandably, more and more people are now turning to their gardens to feed themselves, and the humble root cellar is an integral part of this. While you may choose to grow only a small amount and buy the rest from markets, proper storage remains essential. And there are a few reasons why they are suddenly becoming so popular again:

- They cost little to nothing to run. You don't need electricity unless you want a lightbulb in your root cellar.

- You can store your own home-grown produce or stock up on seasonal goods purchased from farmer's markets.

- Your food is guaranteed to be organic and free from the chemicals that most shop-bought vegetables are conventionally sprayed with.

- Recent and ongoing events worldwide have led people to become more self-sufficient. Building simple root cellars helps them get their bounty throughout the year.

- There may come a time when you cannot get to a grocery store to get your food—with a root cellar, you don't have to worry.

- The recent pandemic has shown how quickly people will empty grocery stores without a second thought—if you don't get there in time, there is nothing left. When you have your own produce stored in a root cellar, you can feed yourself and your family with reassurance and comfort.

## The Advantages

- You can have food stored seven days a week, 365 days a year

- No electricity is required

- It is a proven food storage method—even our ancestors knew it worked

- They are incredibly versatile—you can have one in any size or shape, and your budget can be as big or as small as you decide

## Disadvantages

- You need space—if you have none, this perhaps is not for you

- There are many different types, and each has its pros and cons

# What You Need to Know About Root Cellars

## What to Store?

As established, root cellars can be used to store just about anything these days. Traditionally, they were used to store root vegetables, mostly potatoes, turnips, and carrots. Today, people store other root vegetables, apples, pears, hard fruits, etc. In addition, you can store canned foods, medicines, salted meat and fish, and so much more. If you build one big enough, you can even use it as an emergency shelter!

### How They Function

Root cellars use the earth to maintain good humidity, light, and temperature levels. The optimum temperature is 32 to 40 degrees Fahrenheit, and the optimum humidity is 85 to 95 percent. For a successful root cellar, you need three essential things: humidity, darkness, and good ventilation.

Temperature is incredibly important. If properly controlled, the temperature helps the vegetables and fruits slowly release ethylene gas, allowing microorganisms to grow and stopping the decomposition process in its tracks. In parallel, high humidity prevents moisture from evaporating.

### Different Types of Root Cellars

In the olden days, a root cellar was a room built beneath a house or in the ground to store vegetables. Nowadays, just about anything can be used:

- Basements or space under the porch

- Holes dug in the ground

- Old refrigerators or freezers

- Garbage cans

- And much more— all that is required is your imagination!

# Common Mistakes When Building Root Cellars

Many people dive straight into building their root cellars without stopping to think about what needs to be done and how to do it. While they are a fantastic idea, they are hard work— even the simplest in design—and there are several things you should consider before you start.

- ## Lack of Ventilation

The most common mistake is not installing ventilation. If your room is airtight, humidity levels can build up very quickly, leading to excess moisture in the room. Ideally, you should have two vents as an absolute minimum, each a few inches in diameter. They should have a mesh screen over them to keep out mice and other unwanted pests, and one should be at the top of the room, helping to vent our ethylene gas and stale air as well. There should be one near the bottom of the room to allow fresh air in. How many you install will depend on how large your root cellar is.

- ## Not Enough Light

When you create a root cellar, you must consider exposure to the light. This must be controlled because light exposure is one of the biggest problems in food storage. There are several reasons for this, including bleaching food, which wipes out its nutritional content and value.

Some vegetables, especially potatoes, will turn green and begin sprouting if they are exposed to light. Therefore, if you opt to have lighting in the cellar, it must be the minimum amount possible, and it should never be left on. You could also cover your vegetables with cardboard or burlap to protect them from light and maintain optimum temperature.

- ## Tossing Fruits and Vegetables in Together

Vegetables and fruits should be kept separate in a root cellar. While they may need pretty much the same conditions for storage, some fruits produce more ethylene gas. In excessive amounts, it can compromise vegetable health and lifespan. Some of these fruits include blueberries, apples, avocados, apricots, bananas, cranberries, citrus fruit, and cantaloupe melons.

# Takeaway

If you want a natural method of storing your fruits and vegetables, consider building a root cellar. They may be hard work but are well worth the investment, and the benefits are amazing.

That was a very brief introduction to root cellars. So far, this book has not gone into detail because much of what you have read here will be covered in greater depth later. Thus, without further ado, it is time to get into how root cellars work.

# Chapter 2: How Does a Root Cellar Thrive?

Before you can even think about building a root cellar, there are many things to consider. Perhaps the most important thing is working out the conditions needed to store your fruits and vegetables, which all come into your design.

Basically, every root cellar, no matter what design you choose, works on the same principles—staying dark and cool all year and not freezing. Simple enough, right? You can use just about any cool space you have available, such as a space in your garage or basement. Or you can get right down to it and build one in your garden. However, there are two things to consider here. In regions where winters are mild, you may need to provide artificial cooling as the earth may not do the job sufficiently for you. In contrast, if you live where the weather is hot, such as the tundra, you might need additional insulation.

A quick Internet search will provide you with tons of plans in terms of building a root cellar. Do not just pick the first one—all root cellars are different, so it is important to choose the one that works best for you. The key things to consider are size and shape, which will determine how your root cellar thrives. How so? Because the size and shape determine how you deal with humidity and temperature.

# The Basics of Root Cellaring

As established, root cellars need to provide three conditions: humidity, ventilation, and temperature. The closer you can get to the ideal conditions, the more success yours will have.

### Humidity

Root cellars require high levels of humidity, around 85 to 95 percent. This stops your stored produce from drying out and shriveling up. There are three ways to achieve the right levels of humidity in your root cellar:

- *A dirt floor — Dirt floors retain moisture much easier than their concrete or stone counterparts. Suppose you built your root cellar into the ground. In that case, you already have an advantage because the soil will provide some humidity. The earth should be packed in solid, and then a layer of gravel placed over the top. This does two things: it keeps your feet dry when things get damp and helps retain moisture. If your cellar does get dry, you can spray a little water (carefully) over the gravel. The water will evaporate quickly, causing more moisture and humidity in the air.*

- *Adding water — If you do not want to add gravel or if your floors are made of concrete, there are other solutions. You can add water by spraying the floor lightly, spreading damp burlap bags over the vegetables (making sure they are not soaking wet), or placing a few pans of water on the floor. Measures like these are usually required in the fall season when you first put your produce into storage. Dug-in root cellars are less likely to require help with humidity, whereas basement root cellars will do. In areas where the air is very moist, you can keep root vegetables in bins, uncovered, so they are kept firm and smooth.*

- *Sawdust, moss, or sand — Now, if your humidity falls below optimum levels, there is a third option. You can use damp sawdust, moss, or sand to pack your fruits and vegetables in. This works especially well for parsnips, beets, and carrots, helping cut down on surface evaporation.*

One of the most important things to factor in is that warm air absorbs more moisture than cool air. If your root cellar is damp and cold, the environment will be somewhat unstable. For example, if your air temperature is 34 degrees Fahrenheit, it has room to absorb a bit more moisture. However, if the temperature drops a couple of degrees, the air will become saturated. This is known as the "dew point," where the air can no longer hold excess water. That water will start condensing on your ceiling, walls, and your fruit and vegetables. The safest way to ensure your humidity levels are correct is to invest in a hygrometer—you can get one from any hardware store or garden center.

## Ventilation

Equally important to humidity is proper ventilation. Air must be allowed into the cellar and able to circulate through it, keeping the temperature low. Adjusting the air intake is critical to help reduce extra humidity and preventing condensation from destroying all your hard work. When air moves efficiently, it eliminates the ethylene gas some fruits give off and other vegetable odors that could alter flavors in other vegetables and fruit.

Understanding how the air circulates through your root cellar requires you to remember basic science—hot air rises (lighter) while cold air falls (heavier). If you have a large or enclosed cellar, you need to have two things: an air intake system and an air outlet. The intake should be situated quite low in the room, bringing in the cool air from outside. The outlet should be higher up, allowing warmer air to escape. It is best to have the outlet and inlet on opposite sides of the room to allow the air to circulate efficiently.

Where your storage area is smaller, or where there are plenty of cracks to allow the air in—think old stone foundations—you may find it is enough to have one outlet situated high up to remove the warm air. When you store your produce, make sure it is elevated off the ground a couple of inches—this allows the air to circulate beneath them.

## Temperature

Temperature is, above all else, the vital variable to consider in a root cellar. Good root cellars do two things: they borrow cold, and they stay cold. How do you borrow cold? It is simple— dig into the ground. Below the frost level, the earth will stay at a steady temperature of around 52 degrees. This is because the deeper earth temperature takes much longer to be affected by the freezing temperatures above, offering your vegetables more protection. If you choose not to dig your root cellar into the ground, there are two other ways you can borrow the cold; with a window or an exhaust pipe that you can close off. These options will allow the cold night air into the cellar but should be shut off during the day when the temperatures rise.

Successfully maintain a temperature of 32 to 40 degrees, and you have the perfect place for food storage. If your temperatures are between 40 and 50 degrees, you can still use the root cellar as a short-term storage area for apples and root vegetables. Peppers, eggplant, and tomatoes can be kept for about a month.

Because there is a difference in temperature between the floor and the ceiling, you can take advantage of it by placing your fruits and vegetables per their storage requirements—more on that later.

Invariably, you need to invest in a good thermometer to monitor your root cellar temperatures.

## Tips on Keeping Your Root Cellar Cool

Creating the optimum atmosphere can be done by following these simple tips:

- *Your root cellar should be dug in about ten feet (or three meters), as this is where temperature stability is reached.*

- *Do not site a dug-in root cellar near large trees. Not only will you find it difficult to dig through the roots, but eventually, they will grow through your cellar walls.*

- *Use wooden platforms, bins, and shelves to store your produce on and in. Wood does not conduct the cold or heat as quickly as metal does, and plastic may turn brittle.*

- *Ensure your shelves are between 1 and 3 inches away from the walls—this ensures good air circulation, minimizing the chances of airborne mold.*

- *If your root cellar is outdoors, the best flooring is packed earth, whereas, in a basement cellar, concrete is more practical and works better.*

- *Make sure you have a hygrometer and a thermometer handy and check them every day.*

- *Use inlets and outlets to regulate heat and cold into and out of the root cellar.*

# More Tips on Storage and Root Cellar Conditions

- *If you need to preserve moisture in your cellar and create a humid micro-climate, place the vegetables that need that climate in individual bags with holes in them. Alternatively, you can use perforated, sealed plastic containers. Avoid regular plastic containers—although they do work for some things.*

- *Conversely, you can create dry micro-climates using sealed containers with materials that absorb moisture in them. For example, a cup of rice in a paper bag absorbs air moisture while the bag keeps the rice away from your vegetables.*

- *Start planning your root cellar storage at the start of the planting season. Choose varieties designed for long storage periods.*

- *When you harvest your vegetables, do not wash them before storing them. The cellar will have disease-fighting properties, and washing it off may be detrimental.*

- *Conduct enough research—some vegetables need to be cured before storing them, while others store better if exposed to frost. Proper research ensures you get the best lifespan for your produce.*

- *Do not store anything that is diseased or damaged. If you bruise or cut any vegetable or fruit during the harvest, put it to one side—this should be eaten first.*

- *Make sure you check your storage every couple of weeks to ensure nothing is going bad. If anything is, remove it immediately before it affects the rest of your harvest.*

## What a Root Cellar Can Do for You

Having a root cellar ensures that you enjoy vegetables and fruits out of season or produce you cannot get at the grocery store unless sprayed and imported. To achieve this, you do not have to bottle, can, boil, or freeze anything.

What is more, no longer will you be confined to storing only certain vegetables—carrots, potatoes, and turnips. Provided you plan your root cellar program well, you can store all kinds—nuts, fresh tomatoes, cantaloupes, sweet potatoes, and much more.

Don't worry if you find that you can't always fill your root cellar with what you grow. Visit the farmer's markets and purchase in-season vegetables or storage vegetables in the fall.

Here are some of the foods you can store along with useful indications:

| Food | Temperature | Humidity | Shelf-Life |
|------|-------------|----------|------------|
| Apples | 32 degrees F | 90 to 95% | Two to seven months, depending on the variety |
| Dried Beans | 50 to 60 degrees F | 60 to 70% | One year |
| Beets | 32 degrees | 90 to 95% | Three to five months |
| Broccoli | 32 degrees F | 90 to 95% | One to two weeks |
| Brussels Sprouts | 32 degrees F | 90 to 95% | Three to five weeks |
| Cabbage | 32 degrees F | 90 to 95% | Three to four months |
| Carrots | 32 degrees F | 90 to 95% | Four to six months |
| Garlic | 50 to 60 degrees F | 60 to 70% | Five to eight months |
| Jerusalem Artichokes | 32 degrees F | 90 to 95% | One to two months |
| Leeks | 32 degrees F | 90 to 95% | Three to four months |
| Onions | 50 to 60 degrees F | 60 to 70% | Five to eight months |
| Parsnips | 32 degrees | 90 to 95% | One to two months |
| Pears | 30 degrees | 90 to 95% | Two to three months |
| Potatoes | 40 to 45 degrees F | 90 to 95% | Four to six months |

| | | | |
|---|---|---|---|
| Pumpkins | 50 to 60 degrees F | 60 to 70% | Five to six months |
| Rutabagas | 32 degrees F | 90 to 95% | Two to four months |
| Squash | 50 to 60 degrees F | 60 to 70% | Four to six months |
| Sweet Potatoes | 55 to 60 degrees F | 60 to 70% | Four to six months |
| Tomatillos | 50 to 60 degrees F | 60 to 70% | One to two months |
| Tomatoes | 50 to 60 degrees F | 60 to 70% | One to two months—green tomatoes<br><br>Four to six months for those varieties bred for winter storage |
| Turnips | 32 degrees F | 90 to 95% | Four to six months |

The above list gives you some idea of the temperatures and humidity levels that certain foods need to be stored at. The next chapter goes into more detail about foods you can store.

# Chapter 3: What to Store in a Root Cellar

When deciding what to grow or purchase for storage in a root cellar, you need to consider a few things:

- What varieties you grow or buy
- If growing your own, your timing for each harvest
- The right conditions for storing each fruit and/or vegetable

All of this will ensure that your food supplies last as long as possible without spoiling and losing flavor or nutritional value. Typically, you will have some food that needs to be stored in damp, cold environments and others that need a drier and warmer environment. In the list below, the produce has been sorted according to their temperature requirements, providing information on how to harvest and store it, along with a few good storage varieties.

## Cold and Damp

All the fruits and vegetables listed must be stored at 32 to 40 degrees Fahrenheit and 90 to 95 percent humidity.

# Apples

Everyone you talk with will have their opinion on what apple varieties store the best, but the consensus is that heirloom and antique varieties do not store as well as newer ones. One exception is a variety called Winter Banana. It is also well-known that sweet apples don't store as well as the tart varieties.

## How to Store

1. *Pick your apples* — Choose unbruised, unblemished, fully ripe fruit. Any cut or bruised apples will quickly go bad, meaning it can destroy an entire box of fruit. Try to ensure they have the stems on, as these will store for longer than those without.

2. *Protect your apples* — If your apples are being stored long term, they must not touch each other. Wrap each one individually in newspaper—if using recycled paper, ensure you know what ink has been used. Most newspaper print is soy-based, but some still have toxic chemicals and metals—not something you want your apples to be in contact with. Do not use glossy papers, such as magazines or newspaper inserts. These are usually printed with toxic ink and do not have the same protective qualities as conventional newspapers. You could also use paper towels, butcher paper, or paper bags. If you prefer not to wrap the apple, place them in boxes with clean straw, damp, clean sand, or sawdust, ensuring the apples do not touch one another.

3. *Pack your apples* — Lay your apples in layers in a small/medium cardboard or wooden box. Be careful that you do not bruise them. Don't use large boxes as you need to check your apples regularly—too many apples in a box makes this hard.

Make sure you check your apples at least once a week for rot and use or dispose of any that look like they are going off.

Do not store near other fruits/vegetables because apples give off ethylene gas, which can cause other foods to overripen and spoil quickly.

### Varieties

The following varieties are ideal for long-term storage:

- Arkansas black
- Criterion
- Cameo
- Honeycrisp
- Fuji
- Northern Spy
- Newtown Pippin
- Rome Beauty
- Pink Lady
- Yates
- Winter Banana

### Shelf Life

Between two and seven months, depending on the variety.

## Beets

Beets should be harvested once the weather has been dry for a few days, provided the roots have a diameter of around 2 inches. Dig the beets up, cut the greens off, making sure to leave 1 to 2 inches on the root, and brush off the loose soil.

Do not wash the beets. Simply store them in a lidded bucket or a wooden box filled with peat moss, sawdust, or damp sand. Make sure your beets do not touch each other. If you are using a bucket, put the lid on as this will help retain moisture, but do not tighten the lid (you still need air circulation).

Check on your beets every now and then and remove any that look like it is going bad—like apples, one bad beet can destroy the lot.

### Varieties

The following varieties are ideal for long-term storage:

- Long Season
- Boltardy
- Lutz Green Leaf

### Shelf Life

Beets will store anywhere between three and five months.

## Broccoli

Broccoli is not well known for being a long-storage vegetable. That said, when stored correctly, you can make it last for a couple of weeks.

Dig up your broccoli and trim the stems. Now, you can store it in perforated plastic bags or hang it upside down in the cellar. However you do it, make sure you do not store it near any fruit, such as apples, that releases ethylene gas as this can dramatically shorten its storage life.

### Varieties

The following varieties are ideal for long-term storage:

- Green Comet
- Greenbelt
- Marathon
- Legacy
- Waltham 29

### Shelf Life

Between one and two weeks at most.

# Brussels Sprouts

Love them or hate them, Brussels sprouts are good for storing—although they do not have a long shelf life. To get the best flavor from your sprouts, wait until several frosts have passed before harvesting. If your cellar is large enough, carefully dig the plant up and plant it in a container. Place it in your cellar and carry on harvesting it. Alternatively, hang it in the cellar by the roots. If you don't have much space, harvest your sprouts and store them in perforated plastic bags.

### Varieties

The following varieties are ideal for long-term storage:

- Long Island Improved
- Jade Cross

### Shelf Life

Between three and five weeks.

# Cabbage

Red cabbage varieties will store better than their green or white counterparts, and late varieties are better than early ones.

Harvest your cabbages when the first frost has passed. Pull or dig the plant up and trim the leaves off. Choose cabbages with solid, unblemished heads to store.

These are best stored in bins or outside pits—if you store them indoors, the cabbage odor will go right through the cellar or house and can have a serious impact on how pears, apples, and celery taste. If you can only store them in the root cellar, each head should be wrapped in paper and stored on a shelf, with a few inches between each one.

## Varieties

The following varieties are ideal for long-term storage:

- Danish Ballhead
- Brunswick
- Red Acre
- Late Flat Dutch
- Storage No 4
- Red Drumhead

## Shelf Life

Between three and four months, depending on the variety.

# Carrots

Carrots are one of the best root crops for storing right where you grew them in the garden—but only if you do not have any pest issues and can mulch the carrots with one to two feet of straw or hay.

If you need to store them inside, harvest them from the ground when the season is over before the ground freezes. Cut the tops off as close to the carrot as possible, leaving just a tiny bit, or snap them off. Leaving too much green will only deplete the carrot's nutrients and moisture, and they will not last long.

Lay the carrots in boxes filled with peat, moss, or damp sand.

## Varieties

The following varieties are ideal for long-term storage:

- Danvers
- Kingston
- Chantenay
- Carson
- Bolero

- Nigel

- Kurota Chantenay

- Royal Chantenay

- Red Core Chantenay

- St Valery

**Shelf Life**

Between four and six months, depending on the variety and storage conditions.

## Jerusalem Artichokes

Jerusalem artichokes store better in the ground than in root cellars, lasting the entire winter long as the ground does not freeze. If you opt to leave them in the ground, you must take precautions because exposure to frost and freezing conditions will break the starches down. Their texture, color, and flavors will change, and if any are diseased or bruised, they will spoil very quickly.

If you want to store them in your root cellar, dig them up, remove the tops, and brush off the soil. Store them in plastic bags or damp sand in containers. They must not be stored in areas where they can dry and shrivel up, as they do not store as well as potatoes do.

### Varieties

The following varieties are ideal for long-term storage:

- Fuseau (most common)

- Coris Bolton Haynes (less common)

**Shelf Life**

All winter in the ground, provided the ground does not freeze. If stored in the root cellar, up to ten days in plastic bags and one to two months in sand.

# Leeks

Leeks are another vegetable that can survive in the ground over the winter or until the first hard frost. Mulch your leeks heavily and keep them that way until after the frost. Dig them up, making sure their roots stay intact.

Fill a deep bucket with soil or damp sand and plant the leeks upright in it.

## Varieties

The following varieties are ideal for long-term storage:

- Musselburgh
- Arena
- Elephant
- Nebraska
- Zermatt

## Shelf Life

Between three and four months in the cellar, all winter in the ground, provided you do not get frost.

# Parsnips

Like carrots, you can also leave parsnips growing in the ground over the winter. Cover them in heavy mulch and harvest them when needed. However, parsnips are not fond of freeze/thaw cycles; if your winters are cold, it is best to harvest them.

Lift them at the end of the season, before or just after the first frost, and cut off the tops. Store in boxes layered with sphagnum moss, damp sand, or peat.

### Varieties

The following varieties are ideal for long-term storage:

- Hollow Crown
- All-America
- Offenham

### Shelf Life

Between one and two months.

## Pears

Pears are incredibly sensitive to changes in temperature and should be stored at the lower end of 29 to 31 degrees. If you store them at higher temperatures or for too long, the pears do not ripen. Instead, they break down, turning brown and mushy inside, while the outside still looks fine.

Like apples, you should store only the unbruised and unblemished fruits, preferably with their stems on. Each pear should be wrapped in a paper bag or newspaper and stored in wooden or cardboard boxes with a perforated plastic lining. This allows air circulation while keeping moisture levels up.

### Varieties

The following varieties are ideal for long-term storage:

- D'anjou
- Comice
- Bosc

### Shelf Life

Between two and three months.

## Potatoes

Potatoes are one of the best root vegetables to store in a root cellar—unsurprisingly so, considering they were the original reason root cellars were built.

Wait until the foliage has died back, and then leave the potatoes in the ground for another two weeks. This helps cure the skin and harden it for storage. Dig up your potatoes carefully and sort through them.

Place any bruised or damaged potatoes to one side to be used straight away. If any have green spots, do not eat them—the green is a chemical that can cause digestive and intestinal upset.

Grade the potatoes by size—you want to store the same-sized potatoes together and brush off any dirt. Do not wash them. Now place the potatoes somewhere dark, at 45 to 60 degrees, for further curing for ten to fourteen days.

Once this is done, you can store the potatoes in bins, boxes, or burlap sacks. Boxes or bins should have shredded paper between each layer of potatoes and have air holes cut in the sides.

Do not store potatoes near any fruits that give off ethylene, and do not allow the temperature to rise as this will prompt the potatoes to start sprouting.

### Varieties

Most late potato varieties will store just fine (early and second early varieties are not meant for storage). The following varieties are ideal for long-term storage:

- All Blue
- Red Pontiac
- Kennebec
- Sangre
- Katahdin
- Yukon Gold
- Sebago

### Shelf Life

Between four and six months.

## Rutabagas

Rutabagas, like most root vegetables, can stay in the ground over winter. You can add a ten- to 12-inch thick layer of mulch to stop the ground from freezing, extending it about 18 inches on either side of the row. Even if you get a couple of feet of snow, the roots are protected. However, they must all be harvested before the spring; otherwise, new growth will start from the tops.

If you cannot leave them in the ground all winter, lift them at the end of the growing season, brush the dirt off, and twist off the tops—this will ensure you can store them for longer. You should not wash them, but they must be 100 percent dry before you put them into storage if you do.

Sort through the roots and put aside any that are damaged—these cannot be stored and must be eaten straight away.

Layer the good roots in a wooden box or bucket with sawdust, peat moss, or damp sand. The roots should be packed and covered but not touching one another, and the container should not be completely sealed to allow the moist air to circulate.

### Varieties

The following varieties are ideal for long-term storage:

- Laurentian
- American Purple Top

### Shelf Life

Between two and six months, depending on the variety.

## Turnips

These should be treated the same as carrots and kept moist. However, unlike carrots, turnips should be stored in an outdoor pit if possible. Otherwise, the smell permeates and taints the flavors of other foods.

### Varieties

The following varieties are ideal for long-term storage:

- Purple White Top Globe
- Navet des Vertus Marteau

### Shelf Life

Between four and six months.

## Winter Radishes

Winter radishes can withstand temperatures down to 28 degrees outdoors and can be left in the ground, provided they are mulched heavily. However, should you need to store them out of the ground, consider an outdoor ground pit or garbage bins as they give off a very heavy odor indoors.

If you store them in a root cellar, cut the tops off, leave an inch of stem, and place them in boxes or baskets layered with sphagnum moss or sand.

### Varieties

The following varieties are ideal for long-term storage:

- Chinese White
- Black Spanish
- Violet de Gournay

### Shelf Life

Between two and three months.

# Cool and Dry

The vegetables and fruits on this list should be stored at 50 to 60 degrees Fahrenheit at 60 to 70 percent humidity.

## Dried Beans

Once your beans have grown and fruited, leave the pods on the plant until they are dry—the beans should rattle in the pods, indicating that they have dried. Then, dig up the plant and leave it somewhere shady and protected for another one to two weeks. To test if they are ready, press your thumbnail into the pods; if it leaves an indent, they need to be left to dry for longer.

The beans should be shelled by hand or beaten against a wall to drop out. Then, use a compressor or hair dryer to blow the chaff away and place the beans in an airtight container.

As beans are prone to weevils, you can freeze-dry them for a few weeks before storing them. For this, place them in single layers on trays in the freezer and leave for several weeks.

### Varieties

The following varieties are ideal for long-term storage:

- Black Coco
- Adzuki
- Jacob's Cattle
- Brown Dutch
- Steuben
- Speckled Cranberry
- Yin Yang
- Repokeb (Tiger's Eye)

### Shelf Life

Up to one year.

## Garlic

Garlic is one of the easiest vegetables to store. First, wait until half of the leaves have begun dying, turning yellow or brown, yet still have green leaves at the top, and then dig up a bulb to check it. If the heads are loose but have not split, you can harvest them; if they are still tight, leave the rest a bit longer.

Dig the garlic up and brush off the loose soil. Be careful in your handling. Leave the garlic somewhere well ventilated to dry and cure, ensuring the bulbs cannot get sunburned or wet. Leave them for ten to fourteen days.

After this time, braid the leaves together, hang the garlic up, cut the tops off, and store the bulbs in a mesh bag. They must be kept in dry conditions; otherwise, they will begin sprouting and will not be nice to eat.

### Varieties

The following varieties are ideal for long-term storage:

- Marbled Purple Stripe
- Chilean Silver
- Porcelain
- Mother of Pearl
- Tipatilla

Be aware that the hard neck varieties are not so easy to store as their soft neck counterparts.

### Shelf Life

Between five and eight months.

## Onions

Lift the onions when the tops turn brown and fall. Dig them up during a dry day and spread them on hardware cloth, a screen, or newspaper. Let them sit somewhere cool, dark, and well-ventilated for ten to fourteen days, or until the roots have dried and the skin has turned papery.

Cut the tops off, leaving about an inch, and store them in paper bags, net bags, or even pantyhose. Do not use plastic containers or bags that are not breathable—if onions are not stored in dry conditions, they will begin sprouting.

### Varieties

The following varieties are ideal for long-term storage:

- Brunswick
- Australian Brown
- Copra
- Red Burgundy
- Bronze d'Amposta
- Newburg
- Red Creole
- Norstar
- Red Weathersfield
- Stuttgarter
- Rossa di Milano
- Yellow of Parma
- Yellow Globe

Sweet varieties do not store very well.

### Shelf Life

Between five and eight months.

## Pumpkins

Pumpkins should be harvested before the first frost; they do not like cold weather, and frost will kill them. Leave about an inch of stem on the pumpkin as this stops them from spoiling.

Leave them to cure for about ten days—the temperature should be 80 to 85 degrees. If your weather is warm and dry, you can leave them outside. The curing process hardens the skins, ensuring they store for longer. However, you should not store any that are bruised, damaged, or have broken stems.

The pumpkins can then be piled up in your root cellar, two or three deep, so long as they are in a dry area—off the floor may be best.

## Varieties

The following varieties are ideal for long-term storage:

- Winter Luxury
- Howdens

## Shelf Life

Between five and six months.

# Squash

Squash is cured and stored in the same way as pumpkins, except for acorn squash, which does not need to be cured.

## Varieties

The following varieties are ideal for long-term storage:

- Delicata
- Crown Prince
- Hubbard True Green Improved
- Golden Delicious Hubbard
- Waltham Butternut
- Uchiki Kuri

## Shelf Life

Between four and six months.

# Sweet Potatoes

Sweet potatoes should be harvested as soon as the vines have died back, usually in late fall. Dig the potatoes up carefully, putting any damaged tubers to one side for immediate consumption. Brush the loose soil from undamaged tubers and cure them for five to ten days, at a temperature of 80 to 85 degrees and 90 percent humidity.

After this time, you can move them into the root cellar, wrapping each tuber in paper and layering them in ventilated baskets or boxes.

## Varieties

The following varieties are ideal for long-term storage:

- Centennial
- Allgold
- Jewell

## Shelf Life

Between four and six months.

## Tomatoes

You do not have to wait for your tomatoes to ripen on the vines. You can pick them still green and allow them to ripen while in storage or choose varieties better suited to longer storage. Provided the conditions are right, some tomatoes store much better than others.

If you are storing green tomatoes, pull the whole vine from the ground and hang them in the cellar upside down. Alternatively, you can pick the tomatoes and wrap each one in paper. Store them at about 55 degrees so they ripen slowly—do not go below this temperature, or they will not ripen. At the ideal temperature, green tomatoes generally take ten to fourteen days to ripen.

## Varieties

The following varieties are ideal for long-term storage:

- Eva Purple Ball
- Green Thumb
- Fried Green Hybrid
- Old Fashioned Garen Peach
- Reverend Morrow's Long Keeper

- Red Siberian
- Red October
- Winter Keeper
- Ruby Treasure

## Shelf Life

Between one and two months for standard green tomatoes; up to six months for long storage varieties.

# Chapter 4: Easy DIY Root Cellar Alternatives

Not everyone has the room to build a root cellar, but did you know that you do not need one? If you only have a small space at your disposal and don't grow vast amounts of produce but still want to store it, there are tons of ways to do it. Try some of these neat, easy, and cheap ideas:

## Garbage Can Root Cellar

Materials:

- A metal garbage can with a lid
- A waterproof covering—a tarp or sheet of plastic
- A shovel
- Some straw

Garbage can root cellars are ideal for root vegetables such as carrots, potatoes, turnips, and parsnips. It is nothing more than a hole dug in the ground, the can buried, and your vegetables stored inside. Here is how to do it:

First, you need to choose your site. Trash can root cellars should be placed somewhere well-draining, so do not bury it where water can pool when it rains or runs off other parts of your garden.

Next, dig your hole. Evidently, your garbage can has to fit inside but ensure that the top of the can protrudes several inches from the soil.

Pop your root vegetables in and put the lid on.

Pile the straw on top of the can about one to one-and-a-half feet thick, ensuring all exposed parts of the garbage can are covered.

Lay your tarp or plastic sheet over the top; this ensures rain cannot get between the can and the lid and soak your vegetables. It also helps keep the straw in place.

Whenever you open the can to get vegetables out, check the others. If you spot any starting to rot, growing shoots, or beginning to shrivel, remove them and discard them. Leaving one rotten vegetable in there can destroy your entire storage.

If you do not intend to get vegetables out regularly, make sure you check the contents of the can at least once a week but never leave the lid off for long periods. Stored vegetables must not be exposed to the light for too long as it shortens their shelf life.

# Bucket Root Cellar

## Materials

- A five-gallon plastic bucket with a lid
- A drill
- A shovel
- Straw (optional)

Five-gallon buckets make the perfect miniature root cellar for onions, potatoes, and other root vegetables.

First, cut the bottom out of the bucket using a sharp knife or another cutting tool.

Next, dig a hole in the ground big enough to accommodate the bucket leaving its top flush with the soil line.

Fill the bucket with your vegetables and put the lid on.

If your vegetables need to be insulated from the cold, place a thick layer of straw over the top and, if necessary, cover with plastic to keep the rain out.

Although this holds fewer vegetables, you still need to check on them regularly to ensure none are going bad.

# Freezer Root Cellar

**Materials:**

- An old chest/upright freezer or refrigerator
- PVC piping
- A shovel
- A tarp or large plastic sheet

If you are about to replace your freezer with a brand-new one, do not throw the old one out—you can easily repurpose it into a root cellar. However, you may need to get a specialist out to remove the freon gas if there is any left in the freezer.

If you don't have a freezer or refrigerator to repurpose, head to your nearest scrap yard and scour for one.

Remove all of the working parts from the freezer or refrigerator. Make sure you strip the back off and remove all mechanical parts—you should be left with nothing more than a shell.

Now, you need to make some holes in the back of the freezer. Use a drill with a small drill bit—this seems to work well. Do not worry if the drill breaks the plastic back; air holes are critical to the success of this project as they allow the air to flow into the root cellar. In the ground, provided you dig deep enough, the air will remain at a temperature of around 55 degrees Fahrenheit, which stops your vegetables from freezing over the winter.

Attach a layer of fine-meshed bug netting over the back, covering the holes. Although your freezer will be in the ground, you have no way of knowing what creepy crawlies are down there—and you don't want them anywhere near your vegetables.

Punch a hole in the top and the bottom of the freezer. Again, this is to aid in air circulation, helping air coming in through the holes on the back to circulate out to the surface. Proceed cautiously; do this right, and it will not draw in the cold air—sufficient circulation will see to that.

Insert pipes into both holes. How long these are will depend on the depth of your root cellar in the ground. Ideally, you should try to have them extending two to three feet out of the ground and attach vents to the top—this will stop dirt and water from falling down the pipes and into your root cellar.

Now you are ready to dig your hole, and how large depends on what size refrigerator or freezer you are using. Some people use a backhoe—it is a lot of digging—but you might not have access to one. If you have to dig yours by hand, take it easy—there is no rush!

Line the bottom of your hole with bricks or rocks, making sure it is an even layer. This will help the air to flow better.

Carefully get your freezer or refrigerator into the ground, in its final resting place. Ensure you leave sufficient space to get the door open, especially if you are burying it near a building.

Fill in around the freezer with dirt but leave space around it. The easiest thing to do is place boards around the freezer a few inches out, making a box. This will stop dirt from being kicked into the freezer when you open it; it also makes it easier to put a heavy cover over the freezer later.

Now, while some regions have relatively mild winters, others have much colder and harsher ones. If yours is the latter, you will want to add some insulation over the top. This reduces the level of cold that can blow over the top, making it freeze.

Make your cover—this should be big enough to go over the top of the freezer and heavy. It will help stop your freezer from getting too cold and potentially freezing everything inside it.

You are now ready to fill your freezer with your vegetables. Layer them in, remembering to keep apples and other fruits that give off ethylene gas separate. Keeping the baskets in your freezer or refrigerator can help with this.

Remember, when you pull anything out of storage, you must check everything else to ensure it is not rotting or showing signs of spoiling.

Now, everything you do will have a learning curve, and this is one potential scenario. Say you fill your freezer with lots of fruits and vegetables, and everything is fine—until the temperatures plummet hard. Then, when you go to your cellar, you find that all your vegetables have frozen solid. Some can be salvaged, but all your squash and pumpkins are gone.

All you needed to do—and should have done from the beginning—was add a temperature sensor. A simple sensor plug will do, which switches a light on when the temperature falls below a certain level. A halogen bulb is sufficient—it will raise the temperature just enough to stop everything from freezing. That is your final step; adding your temperature sensor and bulb!

# Pallet Root Cellar

## Materials

- Six good-quality wooden pallets
- A tarp or thick plastic sheet
- A shovel
- Tools to cut the pallets

Pallets make a perfect underground cellar for root vegetables and dried goods. However, unless you can source your pallets for free, this might cost you a little.

Get your six pallets together—you can make it bigger or smaller as you wish. If you cannot find any, head to a garbage pick-up point, furniture movers, or builder's merchants—they usually have some on hand, but they may charge you for them.

Measure the pallets; standard ones are usually four feet by four feet.

Dig a hole a few inches bigger than the pallets, allowing sufficient space for the top pallet to be 6 inches beneath the ground. So, if your pallets are four feet square, dig the hole at least four feet in depth and width.

Use a tarp or a sheet of thick plastic to line your hole, making sure it is big enough to drape loosely in the hole.

Put the first pallet at the bottom of the hole—this is your floor—taking care not to tear or damage the plastic sheet.

Stand on the bottom pallet and place four more around to form the walls of your cellar. At this stage, because the pallets are all the same size, they will not support one another.

Cut two bits of 4" x 2". They should be the same width as your pallets. Attach them to the end or side pallets—it does not matter which—using thick, strong string, or bailing twine/wire. This will stop your pallets from falling in.

Use string or wire to attach the pallets to each other at the corners, giving you a strong, sturdy box.

Standing inside the box, pull the plastic inside, and then fill the gap between the outer walls of your box and the sides with loose dirt.

Pack the dirt in, ensuring the box is firmly planted in the ground before getting out. Then walk around it, tamping the soil down, and remove the plastic from inside the box by rolling it up—you will need this for the next step.

You can now put your food into the box. Use thirty-gallon plastic bins to store your food, fill the box, and put the final pallet on top. Place the rolled plastic on top, keeping it cool inside.

You can add hinges to your top pallet if you want, and you can even make shelves to put in the box. After all, this is just a basic root cellar—you can make it as big or fancy as you like.

Once your cellar is full and the lid is on, add at least 3 inches of newspaper on top and pull the plastic back over the top. Cover it with a tarp and weigh the tarp down using bricks, ricks, or whatever else is at your disposal.

That is all you need to build a basic root cellar for your food. Pack the food in carefully, and you can store it for months. The only natural disaster this type of cellar cannot withstand is severe flooding. So, it is not best if your land is permanently soggy or if you live where there are high water table levels.

# A Basement Cold Storage Room

Materials:

- Assorted pieces of wood
- Assorted tools
- Insulation
- Vents

If you have a reasonably sized basement and can afford the space, you can construct a cold storage room in one corner. This is not the easiest one to build. You will need to do plenty of research to learn how the air will circulate and manage humidity and temperature levels.

Simply select a corner in your basement, wall it off, and insulate it. The walls give you the cooling effect you need, and the insulation stops the cool air from circulating the rest of the basement. If you are not confident in doing this, hire a contractor specializing in this line of work to help you.

First, choose your corner. You need your room to have the best possible exposure to the exterior walls—the more concrete or stone there is, the better. Ideally, one wall will be exposed north.

Install a pair of dryer vents of approximately 4 inches. This will result in a kind of siphon, which allows you to regulate how the external air circulates the insulated room. If you can, get vents where the damper control is manual and with internal screens that stop insects and other pests from entering the room. They should be installed at least 10 inches away from one another and caulked in well.

Using PVC piping or dryer pipe, run some ductwork from one vent down to the floor—this will ensure the cold air goes downward. It flows through the vent, down the pipe to the floor, and the warm air will rise, exiting the second vent. Although it is optional, you can add a small exhaust fan to help with the airflow.

Build your wall and doorway frames.

Use 2-inch-thick extruded polystyrene boarding to add insulation to the interior walls. This type of boarding is resistant to moisture, relatively cheap, easy to work with, and works well with temperature changes in the evenings and at night.

Secure the board using polyurethane adhesive—construction quality is best—making sure to apply it in a continuous line.

The exterior walls will not be insulated as they do not need it, so don't make the mistake of thinking a double layer of insulation will help.

Add a vapor barrier on the warm side of the walls—plastic works best—and tap up the seams.

Use drywall or paneling to cover the external walls. However, do not put any finishing on the interior walls.

Use another vapor barrier to insulate the ceiling in your cold room, covered with rigid foam insulation.

Plan how your shelving will be arranged to allow the best air circulation—metal shelves mounted from the ceiling work well.

Lastly, install your door. It must be insulated and the base sealed with weather stripping.

Now, you are ready to stock your cold room. Ensure you clean this room regularly as debris or dust building up can stimulate mold, which you don't want anywhere near your produce.

# A Zeer Pot

## Materials

- A large clay pot
- A small clay pot with a lid
- Duct tape
- Sand

Zeer pots are fascinating and fun to make. You can use these to keep food cool, and it works thanks to the water that evaporates from the combination of two different-sized pots and the sand. They are also very easy to make, so if you have kids, you can use this opportunity to teach them some science!

Get your supplies together, and make sure your clay pots are big enough to store the food you want. Alternatively, make several pots if you cannot find one big enough to start with. There are no size limitations—you can scale this up to any size you want, so long as the outer pot is a few inches bigger than the inner pot.

For example, if you want a Zeer pot with an outer dimension of 10 inches, you need:

- One clay pot, 8-inch diameter
- One clay pot, 10-inch diameter
- Insulation or soil
- Cotton or burlap

- A 12-inch potting tray
- Silicone, cork, or another type of watertight material for the plug

Start by putting the larger pot on a flat, stable surface. Once built, this will be quite heavy, so it is best to place it where you plan to use it. The best location has a steady flow of natural air, like a walkway between two buildings or on a balcony or terrace. You can even use a table next to an open window in a pinch, so long as there is a cross breeze. Place it on a large potting tray.

If your clay pot has a hole in the base, it must be plugged. Use a cork, duct tape, a rubber stopper, or anything else that will prevent leaking and is watertight. Cut your plug off so it is flush with the pot's base, and then seal it off using glue, duct tape, or wax. Ideally, you should get solid pots with no holes—that way, there are no chances of leaks.

Add a layer of soil, vermiculite, sand, or another insulating material to the bottom of the pot—it should be 1 to 2 inches thick. The depth will depend on your pot size, but the two pots must be even and level at the top rim, giving you space for the next step.

Place the smaller pot inside the bigger one in a central position and make sure the two tops are level. Looking at it from the top, you should see something that looks like the bulls-eye on a dartboard—an inner ring and an outer one with an even cavity between them.

**Note:**

If your smaller pot has a hole in the base, wrap the entire pot in plastic to create a waterproof barrier. However, be aware that this may slightly alter the evaporative and insulating properties.

You can now begin to add the rest of the insulating material. Pour it carefully in the space between the inner and outer pot. If you spill any into the inner pot, remove it before proceeding.

If you notice any water entering the inner pot at any time during these steps, you must start over, ensuring the inner pot is fully sealed. It must be dry and cool, and if water comes in from the bottom, this creates the perfect conditions for mold to grow.

Using a funnel, add your insulating material to the bigger pot, ensuring it packs in around the small one.

Now you are ready to begin adding water—do this slowly, allowing the material time to settle and add more insulation as needed. Once your material is saturated, place a layer of pebbles or small rocks on the top. These are not just to make it look nice. When you pour water over them, the stones ensure the material is evenly distributed and doesn't cut a channel through your insulation.

When it comes to the water you use, if you collect it from a pond, stream, lake, or river, you will need to filter it. Otherwise, you could end up contaminating your food since you do not know what may be in that water!

Check the pot for any leaks and use silicone to patch them. The potting tray will catch any water that leaks out and the surface your pot is on.

You can now put your food in. Don't be too hasty—the pots need time to cool before you start adding the food. If you are making the pot to stand in your garden, add the food a little at a time as it ripens until you are ready to start preserving it. Carrots and tomatoes will last for up to three weeks in a Zeer pot, giving you more time to harvest and potentially increasing your haul.

Once your food is in, the pit must be covered. There are a couple of ways you can do this. Place a lid on the inner pot; it could be a clay lid or an old glass slow cooker lid, so long as it fits the small pot snugly. Measure this before you start, as you may need to sand the pot a little to ensure a good fit.

Alternatively, take some cotton, cheesecloth, burlap, or another type of woven cloth big enough to cover the pot completely. Do not use polyester, blended materials, or any other synthetic material.

Soak the cloth in water and wring it out to remove the excess moisture. Lay the cloth over the pot and secure it (especially important if you experience high winds). Use twine, rope, an elastic band, or whatever you have on hand. Repeat to add more layers as needed, but be aware that air needs to flow up through the top—too much material will stop this. Conversely, more layers also stop pests from getting into your pot.

As the cloth dries, it will need to be changed for wet ones. If you used several layers, remove the top one, soak it again, and place it at the bottom of the pile. Rotating the cloth this way helps stop mildew and mold from developing because the layers are exposed to the air.

Monitor your Zeer pot and refill it as needed. To keep an eye on the water levels in the pot, you may place a piece of tube into the insulating layer. That way, you can see the water level inside and know when it needs topping up.

### Cautions

While a Zeer pot is great for keeping food cool, it cannot substitute for a freezer. If you want to preserve frozen food, you can place it in a Zeer pot, where it will slowly defrost—much slower than leaving it out on your side.

These pots need two main things to be effective: moisture and airflow. If you don't have good airflow or it suddenly stops, your pot will not cool very well. In parallel, if you allow your clothes to dry out, evaporation won't be so effective. Also, consider the pot's location—whether there is any shade, the ambient temperatures, and humidity levels.

If you use your Zeer pot to store root vegetables or scallions, you could fill the inner pot halfway with damp sand. Your vegetables can then be buried in it, keeping it fresher for longer. With scallions, only the root part should be buried.

### Things to note:

Eventually, your pot will accumulate a buildup of minerals. Dip a clean sponge in hot water or use some lemon juice to wipe this away from the pot's outer shell.

Breeze is required for the chilling effects. If you have a decent breeze or rig up a small fan, the pot will stay cold.

If external humidity levels are high, the pot won't be as efficient, so try to keep it in a ventilated, shaded area.

Lastly, be aware that a Zeer pot will go through at least two gallons of water per day in dry, warm, and breezy weather. Rather than wasting water when running a shower, collect the clean water and use this instead of running the tap. Alternatively, collect clean rainwater.

# Build a Spring House

**Materials:**

- Assorted wood—2" x 4"
- Assorted tools
- A small stream or creek in your garden
- Cinder blocks
- A backhoe
- A shovel
- A measuring tape
- Hammer and nails
- Stone
- Cement
- Gravel
- Tin roof
- Windows
- A door
- Storm pipe
- A level

This method will only work if you have a source of fresh running water in your garden. Spring houses are a wonderful, traditional method of food storage, and the water ensures an even temperature throughout.

Your structure needs to be near a stream, creek, or another running water supply. The ideal location will have you build your spring house into the side of a hill with earth walls. If you cannot do that, make sure your location is level and beside the water. Try to avoid anywhere that is full of rocks and roots. The idea is to divert water from the spring, through the house, and back to the spring.

Measure the spring's depth in the center at several locations. You are looking for an average depth, so you know how deep to dig your trench through the house. Do not forget: Water will always find its level, so ensuring the trench is the average depth of the spring will enable the water to flow in and out of the structure easily.

Next, determine how long you want your spring house; this helps you work out where the spring will be diverted into and out of the building. The diversion point should be a few feet ahead of the walls.

Now, work out how far the distance is between the spring and the spring house. It should be close but not right next to it. If you dig your diversion trench too close to the spring walls, they are likely to collapse. Try to go for a width where you can walk safely between the spring and the house.

Time to decide on your structure. There are two ways to build a spring house: into a hillside or as a free-standing structure. Which one you choose will depend on your property layout. Building it into a hillside is deemed the most ecologically sound, using far fewer materials. However, there is always a trade-off—hillside houses take much longer to build than free-standing structures.

If you are building a hillside house, start by excavating the soil. Work out how wide and high you want the structure; it should be at least ten by ten feet and at least six feet tall to give you room to stand up. The entrance to your spring house should be on the opposite side of the diversion trench.

If you build a free-standing structure, you may use blocks, stone, bricks, or wood as per your preference. The most efficient method is to use a slip form construction with stone walls—it keeps the cost down because you can use materials around you. Blocks and bricks are also great choices if you are good at masonry, whereas wood constructions should be insulated to ensure the temperature is maintained.

Knowing how to build your spring house properly requires understanding how to get the floor right and why that matters. Once the walls have been determined, plan the spot where your structure will be built.

Start by digging a trench—it should be at least ten feet square and at least 6 inches deep. This depth will ensure the concrete does not crack when the ground contracts through seasonal changes.

The diversion trench should be built on the side near the spring, so dig a trench three feet wide, ensuring it is the average depth of the spring. Dig it from the side of the house to where it will return to the spring—at this stage, do not break through the spring bed.

Make your floor framework using 2" x 4" wood. You need two frames: a big rectangle and a narrow one. The big one frames the walkable space, while the smaller one frames the floor from the trench to the wall. The narrow rectangle should be the width of the wall as a minimum since one of the walls will rest on the concrete.

Place a 1-inch deep layer of gravel inside the frame and level it off. Fill the frame with concrete and level it off, removing air bubbles. The concrete will need a curing time of at least twenty-four hours.

While the concrete cures, decide if you want wood, stone, or concrete in the trench inside the house. Each has its pros and cons. While stone lasts longer, you need masonry skills. Wood is easy, but it rots quickly. Concrete lasts a long time, but you need to build a framework, and it needs time to settle and cure.

Use lumber to block the trench off and make the walls the required length for the water to flow through. Line the trench floor with a decent layer of gravel, eliminating the risks of any soil contaminants being picked up by the water.

The last thing to do is divert your water. You will need a covered trench for the entire length of the water coming in and flowing out of the house back to the spring. While the spring house will cover some of it, the inlet and outlet will not be covered.

Lay storm pipe in the trenches, ensuring enough to extend from the spring to interior walls, under the walls, and into your trench.

When the pipe is close to the spring, break through the bed and connect it so it extends into the spring. It must be at an angle that draws the water in and allows it to exit.

Check for leaks or weak spots in the pipe and, once you are happy, the storm pipe can be covered in soil. The entire line must be buried from the spring to the house, stopping the water from picking up contaminants.

Tips

Cinder blocks can be added at the trench sides inside the house. These should be half the trench height—tall items can stand in the middle of the trench, while smaller ones can go on the shelving at the side.

You can also build a wooden frame the same width but half the height of your trench—the length is down to your preference and need. The frame should fit snugly into the trench and be used to place storage items in so they do not get washed away.

The doors and windows should be in the north-facing wall; this allows sunlight to come in but stops direct sunlight from heating the room.

Finally, installing a tin roof will ensure a longer life span and keep heat out.

# Make a Storage Clamp

**Materials:**

- Straw
- A shovel

This is one of the easiest ways to store vegetables and was originally used to store potatoes, carrots, and other root vegetables. Storage clamps are highly efficient and cheap to build; all you need to insulate the vegetables is soil and straw.

First, choose where your clamp will be. The ground must be level, well-draining—you do not want water pooling around your vegetables—and be sheltered from strong breezes and high winds.

Once you have determined your location, you can dig a pit. It should be about four feet in diameter and shallow.

Layer a 6-inch thick layer of straw in the pit and fluff it—this will trap the air.

Place your vegetables on the straw, making sure you only use unblemished and undamaged goods.

Add another layer of straw on top of the vegetables and around them—make it around 6 to 8 inches in depth.

Layer soil carefully over the top, again about 6 inches deep, leaving a bit of straw poking up—this allows ventilation in the clamp.

You can use a vegetable clamp to store vegetables for a few months. However, if the temperatures drop below freezing for a long time, you may find some of your crops will deteriorate.

You can bring your vegetables out through the straw on the top, but you may want to consider building several storage clamps to keep a mix of vegetables or one for each type.

# An Outbuilding or Garage

If you do not want to build something and have another outbuilding on your property or in the corner of your garage, you can still create a root cellar.

However, these are only really good as seasonal cellars; even if you have insulation in the room, you will need to add more to ensure stable temperatures.

Garages are one of the best places because, typically, they are unheated, staying cool all year round. The most important things to consider are:

### Ventilation

Your garage must have the correct ventilation—one of the most important factors in a root cellar. Regardless of the weather outside, you want to choose somewhere where the temperature remains stable.

The best ventilation is an airtight space. This ensures that your food stays fresh, but don't confuse airtight with little or no ventilation.

Proper ventilation stops mold from developing and accumulating. While these grow as mildew is trapped in the cellar, you can use simple pipes to ensure it is right in a garage. You need the air flowing into the garage and out of it—cool air must come in while stale, warm air must flow out. This helps remove ethylene gas from the space.

### No Heat Insulators or Air Conditioning

Root cellars must withstand temperature variations, so it is unnecessary to add heat insulators or air conditioners to the garage. Plus, if you do that, you just bump up your electricity costs—and you do not need them in a root cellar anyway. Don't forget; root cellars have been around far longer than refrigerators or freezers!

Get the conditions in your garage right, and your food will stay fresh for weeks or even months.

### Food Shelves

While ventilation is a key consideration, you also need to consider other things to keep your food fresh for as long as possible. One of those is making the best use of your space, as this will help your food last longer. Some foods are very sensitive to changes in temperature, so putting in a proper shelving system will help you get the right foods in the right places. Food that needs to be kept cool can go on the lower shelves, while foods that do well in warmer temperatures can go on the upper shelves.

### Humidity

Provided you keep the humidity high in the garage, your food will not dry out. The humidity should be kept at around 80 to 95 percent, ensuring your fruits and vegetables retain their moisture. However, you must check on any food stored in lidded jars as these can rust due to the moisture in the air. Do not allow humidity to go above 95 percent, as that will destroy your fresh foods.

All in all, it is just a case of finding the right corner, putting up your shelves, optimizing your space, and going for it!

# Container Root Cellar

If you can lay your hands on a large steel container, you can use it as a root cellar. All you need to do is bury it! However, before you go ahead and dig your hole, there are some things you need to consider:

## 1. Zoning

Before you can even think of using a steel container as a root cellar, you need to check if any zoning laws (city, county, or state) stop you from doing it or restrict where or how you do it. This will vary from region to region and may depend on what the ground is like and how far you intend to sink the container. You can choose to bury it completely, dig it into a hillside, or just bury it halfway. In any case, zoning laws may apply. First, run a quick search of your local and county websites and then start making calls—when a decision is made over the phone, ask them to confirm it to you in writing just to be on the safe side.

## 2. Placement

Chances are you already decided this when you checked out the zoning laws. When you decide this, think carefully about how you are going to use your container. If you build it into a hill, you will want a door and steps to access it. It is also worth noting that the deeper the container is buried, the more planning it will require.

## 3. Structure

If you choose to bury your container, you need to think carefully about how it will stand the pressure on it from the earth. Containers are not exactly designed to be buried; they were designed to be stacked on a ship or at the docks. The only load-bearing parts of a container are the four corner posts—the sides are strong enough to support the roof, and that is it. You may need to plan on erecting a retaining wall around where your container is located without forgetting to include drainage. If you do, heavy downpours could submerge your container, fully or partially. If you are completely burying your container, you will need a platform that pushes the earth's weight onto the four corner posts. The one thing you should never do is dig your hole and bury the container without planning—it will most certainly collapse.

### 4. Moisture

While containers are watertight and windproof, you need to consider how you will stop the earth's moisture from getting in. The floor is built of steel cross-members with treated plywood on top. You need to think about sealing underneath the floor and possibly pouring a cement base first. Your container also needs to be sealed with plastic tarps, roofing tar, or truck bed liners. Do your research and find the most cost-effective way of sealing your container for optimum results.

### 5. Ventilation

Your container cellar must have good ventilation and air circulation; otherwise, anything you store in it will be destroyed. The principle here is the same as any other type of root cellar.

Once your container root cellar is in place, you can follow the same rules for any type of root cellar. You can even add an extra door and use it as a storm shelter—at least it will have food in it!

# Food Storage Shelves

If you have spare walls in your pantry or a spare room in your house, you can make a food storage system. Here, you can store fruit, some vegetables, and canned and dried foods—so long as your shelves are kept in a dark, cool place.

Later, you will read step-by-step instructions on building shelving units.

# Crawlspace

If you have a crawlspace, you can certainly convert it, or part of it, into a storage room. Choose an area away from furnaces, water heaters, and other heat sources. Add sturdy shelving to give you more space; if it has a dirt floor, even better, as these are best at regulating humidity. Concrete floors are not ideal but will still provide a longer lifespan for most vegetables. Bring out your creative side without forgetting to include enough ventilation.

# Plastic Tote

Plastic totes can easily be used to extend the life of your root crops. All you need to do is bury the vegetables partially in sawdust, which will help with moisture regulation and stop the vegetables from touching one another. Using a tote also means you can keep your vegetables in the dark. This method works well for potatoes, beets, and carrots, and you can also use straw if you cannot get sawdust—while it will need to be dried out, you can reuse sawdust or straw the following year.

# Under Your Porch

If you are really clever and creative, you can use the space under your porch. One design is a hole in the basement wall leading to the under-porch space. Rigid foam is used to line it, adding insulation from external temperatures, and the entrance is designed to blend in with the room it came from.

These spaces are not huge but can be used to store several pounds of potatoes or other root vegetables in a space that would otherwise be unexploited.

# Basement Window Well

If you have no extra space but have a basement window well, you can turn it into a miniature root cellar.

Ideally, your window well should be on a north wall. Cover it with orientated strand board (OSB) and a layer of straw bales. This keeps it cool but does not promote freezing. And if your window well is layered with gravel at the bottom, it will help regulate the humidity levels.

You can stack milk crates in there to hold your vegetables, and as these stack together well, you take full advantage of your space. You can also put dark curtains up at the window to keep the light out.

This type of storage works well for winter squash and potatoes. However, it is not ideal for those who are not very mobile, as accessing it can be quite challenging.

# Earth Pit

This was another common method used to store root vegetables—this one is similar to clamp storage. All you need to do is dig a pit somewhere shady and well-drained, ensuring water can drain away and not into it.

Layer sawdust or sand over the bottom of the pit, add your root vegetables and cover them with more sawdust or sand and a thick layer of straw or leaves. Add a black plastic sheet and weigh it down using logs, rocks, bricks, or other heavy items.

# Using Cardboard Boxes

If you have space in a room or even under your bed, you can use cardboard boxes to store your vegetables. The concept is simple: Place your vegetables in the box and cover them with something that will stay damp but not soaking wet. This makes your vegetables feel as though they are resting under the ground, just waiting to be picked.

You can use any size cardboard box appropriate for the vegetables you want to store. The filling should be sand, peat moss, or wood chips for most vegetables (make sure your wood chips are not toxic) or newspaper for potatoes.

Most vegetables do not need to be washed before being stored—simply rub the dirt off potatoes, but most other things are fine being stored dirty. In fact, they should be, as the soil can help fight off diseases and protect the vegetables. The best way is to pick your vegetables or dig them up and place them straight in the boxes.

All root vegetables should be trimmed, leaving a couple of inches of top greenery on them to prevent them from deteriorating and drying out.

### Potatoes

Lay some newspaper sheets in the bottom of the boxes.

Dig up your potatoes, sort out the ones for storage, and rub off the dirt. Be careful not to damage the skins.

Sort your potatoes by size or variety and place a single layer in the bottom of the box. Layer more newspaper and then add another layer of potatoes. Repeat until the box is full.

### Other Root Vegetables

Spread a thin layer of filler material on the bottom of the box and add your vegetables. Try to lay them as per their shape—carrots are horizontal while turnips are upright. Add a layer of filler and then another layer of vegetables, and so on. Make sure the filler is moistened—this will act as a humidifier. Close the box and put it into storage.

Check on your vegetables regularly and remove any that are deteriorating or drying out. Beets are one of the worst for drying too quickly, but you can still use them if you get to them swiftly enough. Simply pop them into a pan of simmering water to revive them a little.

Provided you dry the filler out thoroughly, you can reuse it many times over.

## Storing Vegetables in Sand

You can do this with just about any container you have on hand and a supply of fine sand (the type used in kids' sandboxes).

There are a couple of ways to go about this. First, you can use the crisper drawer in your refrigerator. Put a few inches of play sand in it and tuck in your root vegetables. You can also use this method for firm fruits like pears or apples. Cover with more sand, leaving a bit of space between the fruits/vegetables so they can breathe and the air circulate. You should leave about an inch between fruits.

Make sure you do not wash anything you store this way, as that will just hasten the decomposition process. Simply brush the dirt off and cut off green bits, like carrot tops or beet greens.

Another way is to add sand to wooden or cardboard boxes and store them in basements or cellars, even a garage—so long as it is not heated. It does not matter where as long as the temperature doesn't go below freezing.

The same procedure applies for the crisper drawer. Keep your fruits and vegetables separate, especially those that give off ethylene gas, such as apples. This gas speeds up the ripening process and can taint other vegetables and fruits. Store root vegetables vertically in the sand and the rest lying down.

# In-Place Storage

There are a couple of methods for in-place storage; just pick which one suits you:

## Garden Rows

Carrots and beets will store perfectly through the winter in this way, and in some cases, their taste may even sweeten over time.

The idea is to ensure the rows are insulated against sub-zero temperatures. You can do this by poking holes in a black garbage bag and filling it with wet leaves. Place it over the top and simply lift it off when you want to harvest your vegetables. Try to harvest enough to last you a couple of weeks so that you do not have to keep disturbing the rows, exposing them to the cold air. What is more, those leaves are perfect for adding to your compost heap when spring rolls around.

Another way is to cut the carrot tops off. Use the carrots—freeze, bottle, or whatever you want. The carrot tops can then be piled on another row of vegetables as insulation. After that, layer black plastic over the top and weigh it down with bricks.

Another method is mounding. Several pockets are dug into the earth and vented to allow the air to circulate. A drainage trench will ensure water is drained away from the pockets. The downside is that all the food in a pocket needs to be harvested at once, so it is best to create several small ones. The pockets are covered with straw and dirt layers to insulate them, and this method works for onions and potatoes, and any other food that requires storing in dry conditions.

Hay bale storage requires a structure made of hay bales to be built around your rows of vegetables. This is topped off with a large sheet of plexiglass or a recycled storm door, effectively turning it into a cold frame. A blanket or tarp can be used for extra insulation in very cold weather. This method allows you to harvest food as you need, not necessarily all at once, and works for crops that like moist conditions, such as carrots, winter radish, and beets.

The final method involves building mini hoop-houses over your rows. These are made from lengths of PVC piping and clear plastic sheeting. You can find many different ways of doing this online, they are pretty easy to construct, and they allow your crops to be harvested as you want them.

# Chapter 5: Planning Essentials

Root cellars may well be considered a luxury nowadays, but back in the old days, they were as necessary as modern freezers and refrigerators.

If built properly, root cellars are a lifesaver, especially if you live somewhere remote, off-grid, or where power outages are common. Losing your refrigerator or freezer contents to a power cut can be devastating; a well-stocked root cellar means you will not starve.

With a root cellar, you can also bring your utility bills down. You can store as much in a decent root cellar as you do in a big walk-in refrigerator without the power bills that go with it!

And root cellars do not just give you a place to store your food; they can also provide shelter from adverse weather conditions.

So, as you know, a root cellar is a space that uses the earth's natural humidifying, cooling, and insulating properties to help preserve food. That said, for a root cellar to work, it needs three things: stable temperatures of 32 to 40 degrees Fahrenheit, ventilation, and 85 to 95 percent humidity.

You need stable temperatures to stop microorganisms growing on your food and to slow down how fast ethylene gas is released. Both of these will aid in the decomposition process, destroying your food stores.

The humidity stops vegetables, roots, and tubers from drying out and shriveling up.

Part of the planning process requires deciding what type of root cellar you want. Most people will try to dig a root cellar beside their house, alongside the foundations, thinking they will already have one wall for their cellar made from cement. However, this has one big problem—doing this runs the risk of undermining your house foundations, all for the sake of building something that could cost you little to nothing.

The ideal distance is around twenty feet, at the very least, from your house. Not only will you avoid upsetting your house foundations, but you can also avoid running into any issues with groundwater.

One of the best types of root cellars is the hillside option, where the root cellar is dug into a hillside, and the floor sloped toward the cellar opening to aid drainage. Sure, you can add drainage pipes to help keep your root cellar dry. However, bear in mind that, in the old days, people did not have PVC piping and drain pipes—they kept their root cellars dry by designing and building them properly.

If you opt for a pit-style cellar, the pit should be square and sloped at one end, allowing you to add steps over the slope.

Now, if you opt for the garbage can, make sure your can has holes in it—metal cans cannot breathe, and if you omit the holes, your food will spoil quickly.

# Basic Tips

All households are different in their eating habits, and the design and contents of all root cellars will be wildly different depending on the household's needs. For most people, root cellars offer a great place to store root vegetables and tubers, such as carrots, potatoes, parsnips, beets, and so on.

You might ask why you cannot just go and buy these as you need them. Well, you can if you want; however, take a careful look at the quality of the vegetables in your grocery store. They are often damaged, bruised; some are already going off and are generally tasteless. If you have the room to grow your own or have a farmer's market nearby, a root cellar is the way to go—and face it, homegrown vegetables always taste better and more satisfying than store-bought.

You also have the added benefit of knowing that your food has not been sprayed with chemicals, pesticides, and whatnot. Besides, when the shelves are stripped bare and food shortages loom, you know you will not starve in times like the current pandemic—if it ever comes down to that.

As such, these are the basic principles that you need to follow in planning and building your root cellar successfully.

- **Check with your building department** – The last thing you need is to fall foul of any building regulations. Your local building department can tell you any requirements or regulations you must comply with before you begin constructing your root cellar. You must follow all construction or building codes that apply to your construction and ensure you have the permits you need—if applicable before you begin.

- **Draw up a plan** — Design your root cellar to meet your food storage goals and consider any physical disabilities you may have. For example, if you struggle to use a ladder or stairs, opt for a more accessible root cellar design.

- **Choose your size** — Your root cellar must be big enough to store all the food you want in there. For example, if you grow an acre's worth of food, it is no good building a tiny root cellar that will barely hold a fraction of what you harvest. Conversely, do not build a massive one if you only have a small amount to store. If you choose to build underground, bear in mind some precautions for building in enclosed spaces. Some potential risks include structural failure, unwanted gases building up, cave-ins, and so on. The last thing you want is to build a death trap by accident! Remember that immense weight is pressing down when you build anything underground, not just from the top but also from the sides. That is why it is critical to get your design and build right. So, design your cellar from the ground up, ensuring it is safe, sound, and has adequate ventilation.

- **Think about the location** — You must consider every aspect of the land where you want your root cellar. Some places have very high water tables, and some have septic systems—both of these can be catastrophic as the root cellar will flood and fail. Also, consider how far away from your house the cellar will be. If you locate it a long way off, it will not be very convenient to keep going down there for some vegetables for dinner; it needs to be close and accessible. Some people have even constructed their root cellars beneath a garden shed, with access inside the shed. When it snows heavily in the winter, they can still access the storage without shoveling snow away first.

You also don't want to build in rocky soil or where there are tree roots. Not only do you need to chop through these, but they will start to grow again, which can compromise your cellar.

- **Factor in the important aspects** – When drawing your design, factor in controlling temperature, drainage, ventilation, and humidity. All of these are important and will affect how long your food will last in storage. Commonly, people approach building a root cellar based on what food they are storing. So, when you draw your plan, ask yourself these questions:

o Does my food need to be stored in a warm and dry environment, a moist and cool environment, or a dry and cool environment?

o Does my food require ventilation to remove excess ethylene gas, saving my food from rotting or starting to sprout?

Perhaps the best way to design your root cellar is with flexibility and the option to control its climate as per your storage needs. After all, you may not grow the same things every year.

- **The foundations** – Next, you need to plan your cellar's foundations. You will need to dig a minimum of ten feet down—this will take you to the ground level, where the temperature stabilizes. If your soil is loamy or sandy, you might need to dig a bit deeper.

- **Lining the walls** – Use cinder blocks if you can—they are cheaper, more malleable, and excellent for lining your walls. Do not forget that your walls must be built on the foundation to ensure they stay up; you might be surprised at the number of people who put the floor in and then build their walls to the sides!

• **Plan your floor** — Many people think that pouring a cement floor is the best way to go, but in reality, the best flooring for a root cellar is gravel and natural dirt. This works to retain moisture better than a concrete floor. The idea is to keep humidity high; the more moisture you can keep in, the better.

• **What about the roof?** — Graded ceilings are far better for keeping the rain out, along with other external elements, and stopping them from resting on the cellar roof. Heavy rain or snow piled on the roof can add a lot of extra weight, all bearing down on your cellar foundations.

• **Ventilation** — This is a critical step in constructing your root cellar, as ventilation will stop too much humidity and moisture from spoiling your crops. Excessive moisture forms condensation, which, as you well know, means you will have water running everywhere, causing your crops to rot and spoil.

If you decide you want to convert an existing building or space, ensure you follow the same guidelines for location and make the right alterations to fit what you want.

## Maintaining Your Root Cellar

While root cellars are relatively easy to maintain, you need to be on top of monitoring it, especially when yours is newly built at the start of the season. Two of the most important things you can invest in are a hygrometer and a thermometer. As established, you must maintain the following conditions in your cellar:

• Humidity — 90 to 95 percent

• Temperature — 32 to 40 degrees Fahrenheit

• Ventilation — Constant and properly installed

Keeping the temperature stable is possibly the hardest thing to do. Most root cellars rely on the soil temperature to keep the cellar cool. Based on your climate, you may need to consider digging your cellar in a bit deeper—this is why research is critical.

It is fairly simple to raise humidity levels—just leave a few water bowls in the cellar. Then, do some experimentation with humidity and see how many bowls you need to use to get the humidity at the right level. However, be mindful of ensuring your root cellar is secured—water can attract insects and other unwelcome creatures.

By contrast, if you need to lower the humidity level, make your ventilation a bit bigger or angle it to where the winds prevail from in your region. Make sure your ventilation is covered with a screen; otherwise, you will get insects, dirt, rain, and all sorts in your cellar.

Adequate ventilation will stop ethylene gas from building up and destroying your food or causing it to sprout too early. Ethylene is odorless and is typically associated with fruits like bananas and apples.

## Ventilation Methods

All root cellars are different and will require their own methods for regulating ventilation and humidity. The critical thing to monitor is the conditions inside your root cellar and ensure you can alter your design if needed, preferably before you start building. Alternatively, ensure your design allows for alterations to be made at a later date.

Perhaps the easiest way to vent your cellar is with two vents, about three to 4 inches wide. The first should be located near the top of the room and the second near the bottom to ensure optimum air circulation.

Lastly, you need to consider the lighting in your cellar. Essentially, a root cellar should be as dark as possible—too much light can lead to rotting and sprouting. By all means, have a single light bulb in your cellar but do not leave it on any longer than necessary. You can also cover your fruits and vegetables with burlap to keep the light out while allowing sufficient air circulation and ventilation. If you are using a window as your ventilation, cover it with dark material.

# Organizing Your Space

How you design your space mainly depends on what you are storing. If you are only keeping one type of produce, ensure the humidity and temperature levels are even throughout the cellar.

Build shelves for the walls and other storage units using wood—they will not conduct the heat or cold the same way metal does and ensure the temperatures remain steady. Also, make sure your storage options are a couple of inches away from the walls to keep them dry. Using shelving means storing foods that need different temperatures, too—colder at the bottom, warmer at the top.

Lastly, load in your produce, and don't forget to check it weekly. Discard anything going bad and reap the rewards of all your hard work.

In the next chapter, you will be walked through building a simple, beginner-friendly underground root cellar.

# Chapter 6: How to Build a Simple Root Cellar

Your garden is overflowing with fruit and vegetables, and while you can give some away to your friends, family, and neighbors, that still leaves you a ton of it. So, since you can only eat so much, what will you do with the rest?

You could spend days and inflate your electric bill canning some of it. You could shove it in your freezer, but what do you do when you run out of space? Plus, not all fruits and vegetables fare very well in the freezer or canned. So, the best answer is to build a root cellar.

There are plenty of options, and many have been covered in a previous chapter. Here, you will be walked through building an underground root cellar and a barrel-in-the-ground cellar, step by step.

# Building an in-Ground Root Cellar

Building an underground root cellar requires time and commitment—in abundance—so if you do not have either of these, you will need to consider another type of root cellar. If you are not handy at building or don't have the right equipment, consider hiring an expert contractor to help you.

First and foremost, you need to choose the materials you will build your root cellar from. Some options include:

- Natural stone
- Cinder/concrete block
- Cedar logs
- Tires packed with dirt

Most people tend to choose cinder blocks as these are inexpensive and easy to come by in most builder's yards or DIY stores.

If you want to go down a different route and let your creative side have free rein, you could consider using a water tank made of fiberglass. These can easily be modified to your requirements and are easier to bury than digging out an entire room and building walls. Just make sure it is ventilated and has at least one foot of soil covering it.

For the in-ground root cellar, you will also need to consider your flooring. Most people use concrete, flat stones or leave it as a packed earth floor with a layer of gravel. That is the cheapest option and is often the best, as it ensures humidity can be better controlled.

### Step One

Consider the location of your root cellar. It must be in an area that has well-draining soil—the last thing you want is water running in. You must also consider the water table—you cannot build an in-ground root cellar where the water table is high. Lastly, ensure that the opening is on a north-facing side—this limits the exposure to the hot sun during the day. Remember that you will need to factor in ventilation, temperature, and humidity wherever your root cellar is located.

### Step Two

Dig that hole!

Depending on how large your root cellar is, you may need to use a backhoe or hire a contractor who has one to help you dig it.

### Step Three

Dig down further for the footings all around the cellar and pour in the concrete. Now, you will need to leave this for at least twenty-four to forty-eight hours to harden.

### Step Four

When the concrete has hardened off, you can begin building your walls. Take your time with this step—it is a substantial job, and trying to lay all the bricks in one go will result in disaster. Again, if you are not a confident bricklayer, consider hiring someone to do it for you.

At this stage, you should also ensure your ventilation is added. You want a PVC pipe, approximately 3 to 4 inches in diameter, inserted at the bottom of the cellar, drawing in the colder air. A second one, of the same size, needs to be installed near the top to vent the hot air and ethylene gas. Ensure your vent pipes have breathable screens over them—the air can still flow while keeping pests out.

As you are building the wall, frame your entrance. After all, you need a way to get in! Build the footings five brick rows high where the door will be.

## Step Five

Make your roof. You could just pour a flat slab of concrete for the top, but you would have serious trouble with condensation. So, the best option is to build an arched roof. This requires great carpentry skills (or someone to do the job for you!).

You will need ½-inch plywood and 2x4s to build a strong enough structure; it will need to be built, taken apart, and reassembled on your cellar walls.

First, build your skeleton using 2x4s and plywood as shown below:

Next, use plywood to cover the roof of your structure.

Reassemble it on the cellar walls.

Place the plywood cover on top, cover it in a tight plastic sheet, and affix it to the structure before covering the entire roof with rebar.

Now, pour your concrete. It should cover the entire structure and the wall bricks and be around 6 inches thick. You will probably need to do this in sections unless you have a contractor helping you.

Now comes the time for patience! That concrete needs to be cured and dried before you can remove the wooden form from the inside. Leave it at least two to three days before you attempt to remove the form. You should also brush a waterproof sealant over the concrete.

### Step Six

The next step involves building your stairs. This is best done with concrete—although you can construct wooden ones if you wish. Add a door at the top, one at the bottom, and your root cellar is ready.

Two doors are recommended because they help keep creatures out of your root cellar and the cooler air in—just make sure to shut the top door before opening the bottom one. You will also want a light of some sort atop the stairs so that you can see your way down.

If you have chosen to keep your cellar floor as packed earth, you can also layer gravel over it.

### Organize your Cellar

Use wooden shelves on your walls; these are not so fast to conduct heat and cold and help you regulate your temperatures. All that is left to do is install a hygrometer and thermometer and start stacking your food in.

# Building a Barrel Root Cellar

This is a much simpler way of building a root cellar, and this book provides the plans for two different types—a small and a larger one. First, the small one:

### Materials

- A five-gallon barrel or trash can
- A drill and drill bit
- A shovel
- A hay bale

### Step One

Determine where your barrel is going to be located. It should be somewhere shady and north-facing, as this will help keep your vegetables cool with minimum light exposure. If you have natural hills in your ground, use them, or you could pile soil up about six feet; these make perfect locations for barrel root cellars. If not, you can dig your barrel in—do be careful that you will not fall foul of water issues in the ground.

### Step Two

Gather your supplies. You can use plastic buckets, metal trash cans, or anything that suits your needs, so long as it has a sealable lid.

### Step Three

Get drilling. The earth is what regulates the humidity in a root cellar, and air circulation is a must. Drill some holes into the bottom of the barrel. You could cut off the entire bottom; either way, it will work.

### Step Four

Dig the hole. This is straightforward—just make sure the hole is large enough for the barrel. Keep checking the size against your barrel and, when it is the right size, pop the barrel in for good. Fill in the edges using the earth you dug out and ensure that the barrel protrudes a couple of inches out of the ground.

### Step Five

Fill it up. Pop your vegetables in, ensuring you do not mix vegetables and fruits that are not happy together. It may be best to build separate ones for each type of produce—that way, you eliminate the issue of ethylene gas. Do not wash your vegetables before you put them in as this can draw moisture out of them; simply dig them up, brush off loose soil, and put them in.

### Step Six

Seal it up. Put your lid on, ensuring it seals tightly, and put a thick layer of hay or straw over the top. You can simply put a whole bale on to prevent your vegetables from freezing.

## 50-gallon Barrel Root Cellar

This is just a larger version of the previous design, which you can do in two ways depending on what you are storing.

### Materials

- A large wooden barrel or a steel drum
- Sawdust
- Burlap sack
- Straw or piles of dead leaves
- Rocks

- Wooden leaves

If you only have apples to store, you can use the first method below.

### Step One

Dig a hole in the ground, about half the depth of the barrel or drum—you only want it buried halfway into the soil. Put the barrel in and pack the earth around it.

### Step Two

If you are using a steel or metal drum, you will need a layer of sawdust at the bottom and between the fruit and the sides of the barrel—freezing metal will quickly destroy your harvest.

### Step Three

Fill the barrel with your apples. Cover the barrel with a burlap sack filled with dead leaves or straw and then heap soil up around the exposed sides of the barrel, leaving just the sack visible.

### Step Four

Around the barrel, dig a drainage ditch. It should be about 6 inches deep and run around the outside of the heaped soil. Place some rocks on top of the bag to hold it down.

When you want apples from the barrel, simply remove the bag and take what you want. Be sure to watch out for any fruit going bad and discard it immediately.

# For other vegetables

You can also use your barrel to store other vegetables besides apples, but the method is slightly different.

### Step One

Ensure your barrel is going in a well-drained space and dig a hole. The barrel will be laid on its side and tilted down into the earth. This will ensure that any moisture can run out of the barrel.

### Step Two

Layer the hole with dead leaves or straw to provide insulation, and lay the barrel in the hole. Place a piece of board over the bottom end to stop your vegetables from falling out. Then, pack the soil behind it to hold the board there.

### Step Three

Cover the top end of the barrel and the sides with soil. The top end and side should be covered in about 18 inches of soil, tapering down to 3 inches at the lower end, up to the board.

### Step Four

Cover the whole barrel with a thick layer of straw and top it off with heavy boards to stop the straw from being blown by the wind. You can do this in two ways; lay the boards on top, or construct a roof-like structure over the top, buried in the earth on either side.

The three types of root cellars have been covered here, and a previous chapter gave you many more ideas. Ultimately, you are bound to find a design that will suit your budget, space, and storage requirements, however big or small.

# Chapter 7: DIY Shelving Systems for Produce

Once your root cellar is built and you are happy with it, the next step is to put in some storage options. Sure, you could just pile your vegetables in, but that would be a recipe for disaster. As you have seen, not all fruits and vegetables go together well, and some definitely should not be stored near others. Some require colder temperatures, while others like it a bit warmer. This chapter looks at ways to organize your root cellar, but first, you need some ideas on building easy DIY storage shelving. Here are three different ideas—feel free to adapt them to your requirements.

## Slide-Out Shelving Racks

With a slide-out shelving rack, you can easily store and access your fruits and vegetables as you need them. These also make great racks for curing produce like potatoes or apples or ripening pears before putting them into storage for the winter. This easy slide-out rack also solves the problem of not having enough floor space to store everything you want.

## Materials

- Four pieces of 2 x 2 wood, eight feet long
- Fourteen pieces of 1 x 3 wood, eight feet long
- Seven pieces of 1 x 2 wood, eight feet long
- Brad nails – 1 ¼-inch and 2-inch
- Self-tappet screws – 2-inch
- PH screws (pocket-hole screws) – 2 ½-inch

The first step is to cut your wood to the desired lengths. This will make it much easier for you to put it all together—you will not have to keep stopping to cut a bit here and there. Cut the following pieces of wood:

### For the Vegetable Rack Frame:

- Legs – 4 pieces of 2 x 2, 41 ½ inches long
- Slide Drawer Gliders
- – 16 pieces of 1 x 3, 23 ½ inches long
- 2 pieces of 2 x 2, 41 inches long. Cut both ends at 60 degrees off square, keeping the ends parallel.
- 4 pieces of 2 x 2, 41 inches long. At the longest points, cut one end at 60 degrees off square and the other end at 30 degrees off square. Cut the ends in the same direction, making sure they are not parallel.
- Front and Back Supports – 4 pieces of 1 x 3, 25 ¼ inches long

### For the Drawers

- 14 pieces of 1 x 2, 23 ½ inches long
- 14 pieces of 2 x 2, 20 ½ inches long
- 49 pieces of 1 x 3, 23 ½ inches long

Make sure to keep the pieces for the frame and drawers separate—you do not want to get them muddled up, or else it will make the job much harder!

**Tools**

Get all your tools together before you start:

- Good tape measure
- A speed square
- Pencils
- Safety glasses
- Ear protection
- A drill
- A circular saw
- A brad nailer
- A sander
- Stainer and brush

**How to Make Your Vegetable Rack**

Read through the following tips to make sure you understand all that is required.

First and foremost, ensure that you take all the right safety precautions and wear protective clothing/goggles/gloves where needed.

Ensure you are working on clean surfaces that are level, not chipped or cut, and have no other debris or imperfections. Make sure your boards are straight when you buy them—bent or twisted wood is not easy to work with, and the result will be less than desirable.

After every step, check that your build is square. If you don't and the finished project is not square, it will be a tough job to go back and find out where it went wrong.

Predrill your holes before you put screws in. This makes it easier to get the screws in, and you are less likely to split or damage the wood.

Your finished nails should be put in with glue, which provides a much stronger hold. If you intend to stain your vegetable rack, make sure to wipe off any excess glue—dried glue makes it hard for the stain to take.

Lastly, be safe and have a lot of fun with this project! Do not forget: If you don't know how to do something, get someone to help you who does—it may cost you a few dollars, but it will be much safer and more rewarding in the end.

**Instructions**

*Step One*

Starting at the top, work downward, attaching your 23 ½-inch pieces of wood to the two pieces of 4-inch long wood you cut for the frame. The pieces must be dead even on either side and be spaced at 2 ½ inches between them. That will make it 5 inches between the top of one piece of wood and the next. When you measure your diagonals from top to bottom (opposite corners), they should both measure 47 ¾ inches exactly. That way, you will know your build is square.

One important thing to ensure is that the ends are square and identical. Your side rails will work as drawer guides, so these must attached square. Otherwise, the drawers will not work. The side rails can be attached using glue and 2-inch brad nails.

*Step Two*

Now, you want to add your cross-braces—the two pieces of 41-inch 2 x 2 wood. These will add great strength to the rack and hold it square, so attach them diagonally to the back of the rack. You do not have to use both—one will do unless you opted to build a much bigger rack, in which case you will need both. Attach these from the inside of the rack, using glue and 1 ¼-inch brad nails.

If you use both, your center angles should be 30 degrees off square, and you should use PH screws to join them in the center.

*Step Three*

Add your front and back supports using the 25 ¼-inch pieces of wood, affixing them using glue and 2-inch screws.

*Step Four*

Time to build your trays—these must be completely square, or they will not slide correctly. Trays are built using 23 ¼-inch wood for the fronts and 20 ½-inch wood for the sides. Leave a ¾-inch gap between your slats (23 ¼-inch) to allow for good airflow. Check your diagonals—they should measure exactly 32 ¼ inches.

Build the first one and ensure it slides properly before you build the rest.

*Step Five*

Put your trays in, and your rack is complete! At least the build is. Now it is time to finish it off. First, add a little candle wax to the drawer slides and the drawer bottoms to ensure a smooth glide.

Go over the rack, filling all the screw and nail holes with wood filler, and then leave it to dry. Apply more as needed. When the filler has dried completely, you can sand your wood using 120-grit sandpaper, making sure to follow the wood grain direction. Next, vacuum it down to get rid of the mess and wipe it over with a damp, clean cloth.

If you are going to stain the wood, do it now and leave it to dry.

Fill it, and enjoy!

# Multi-Purpose Flexible Storage

If you have gone to the trouble of building a fantastic root cellar, you do not want to spoil it —and your haul—by using second-rate storage shelves. By keeping in mind that your harvest is likely to be unpredictable from one year to the next and that you may have different produce each year, you can build flexibility into your storage. This flexible storage project includes bins, drawers, and shelves, all ventilated to allow airflow for all sorts of vegetables and fruits. This build is also fully customizable to your needs.

## Materials

These quantities are for the basic build. If you want to customize it to your requirements, scale the materials up or down as needed.

- ¾-inch plywood in 4 x 8 sheets
- 1 x 2s pinewood
- 1 x 3s pinewood
- ½-inch plywood
- 1 x 10s pinewood
- Wood glue
- L brackets
- ¼-inch drywall screws
- 3d and 6d finish nails

## Instructions

### Step One

Cut the large sheet of plywood into strips—the length is based on how high your root cellar is, and the width should be 16 inches. Each shelf upright will require two strips.

Spread wood glue on one strip's face and then apply the other strip on top. Use drywall screws to secure them together.

### Step Two

Make a story stick*—this will help you ensure all the cleats on your shelf uprights are equally spaced. These will hold your shelves and should be 1 ½-inch wide, with a 1 ¾-inch wide space between them, allowing room for the shelves and bins to slide out.

The top of the story stick should be held flush to the top of an upright, and the tick marks transferred to the edges of the panels. Using a framing or drywall square, extend the marks across the entire width of the panel. The story stick should be used on both sides to ensure your spacing is uniform throughout, and the uprights should all be marked in the same way.

(*A story stick is one of the simplest yet most valuable tools you can use when designing complex projects from wood. It is a rod or board used for checking the measurements that are repeated throughout the project. Graduated marks are made on the stick with a pencil, related to the specific project, and then used to ensure your measurements are correct. Using a pencil to make the marks, you can use your stick repeatedly for all your woodwork projects. How convenient!)

*Step Three*

Cut the 1 x 2 wood in cleats of 16 inches. Install them to the upright faces using drywall screws and glue. It is a good idea to drill pilot holes before putting the screws in—this stops your wood from splitting.

*Step Four*

Use L brackets, concrete anchors (if needed), and screws to attach your uprights to the walls, floor, and ceiling in your root cellar. Each pair should have a gap of 24 to 28 inches between them.

The spacing between the uprights determines the bin, drawer, and shelf dimensions.

*Step Five*

First, find or make a spacer to use as your spacing guide. It should be the same thickness as the spacing between your slats—16d nails tend to work well.

Make your ventilated shelves. The 1 x 3 side supports and slats should be cut to length to fit your gap—although the slats should be ¼-inch shorter than the space you left between your uprights.

The slats should be positioned on top of the side supports, about ⅛-inch apart, to ensure sufficient air circulation. Ensure your slats are square to the supports by using a framing square. Use wood glue and 3d finish nails to assemble the slats on the supports.

*Step Six*

Now you can build the drawers. Cut plywood bases from ½-inch plywood to fit the gap between the uprights, ensuring the width is ¼-inch narrower. Cut some oval finger grips along the front—this is best done with a 1-inch spade bit in your drill and a jigsaw, allowing you to create the straight edges.

Build the drawer box from 1 x 4, making it narrow enough that the plywood will go 1 ½ inches beyond the front and sides. Assemble the frame using screws and glue.

Now spread glue on the base of the frame and put the plywood base on top—use 6d finish nails to secure it to the drawer box.

*Step Seven*

To build your bins, use 1 x 10 wood for the sides, and cut it so that the top edge is 19 inches long and the bottom edge is 15 inches long. Cut 16-inch runners from 2 x 2 and use glue and screws to secure them to the sides at the top. Cut slats from 1 x 3, 3 ½ inches shorter than the gap between your uprights.

Turn your side pieces upside down and install the slats on the back, front, and bottom using screws and glue. Use a spacer to ensure your gaps are even.

Put it all together, and you have one of the most versatile and flexible storage units, ideal for all sorts of produce!

# 2 x 4 Basic Shelving

One of the first things you should do when you organize a root cellar is get everything off the floor. The best way to do that is with a good set of shelves. Sure, they may end up cluttered with stuff, but you will soon sort it out and get everything in order.

Rather than making shelves, you could just go and buy some—there is nothing wrong with that. However, some people feel they have put so much work into building their root cellar that store-bought shelves just would not do it justice. And, to be fair, homemade shelving is more cost-effective. As an example, you could pay upwards of $80 to $100 for a 48-inch by 24-inch by 72-inch unit, while you could build one at least twice that size for the same price—and it will probably be assembled in less time!

## Materials

- Thirteen 2 x 4s, 8 feet long (It might be wiser to get a couple extra, just in case something goes wrong.)

- Two sheets of 23/32 OSB subfloor, 4 x 8 (If you cannot get this, use plywood.)

- 3-inch screws—try not to use drywall screws

- A saw

### Instructions

*Step One*

The first step is to do your measuring and cutting. The OSB sheets should be cut in half lengthwise, giving you four shelves of 2 x 8. There are a few reasons why you might want to consider having the store cut them for you:

1. It may fit easier in or on your car
2. It is far easier to unload and get to your root cellar
3. Less sawdust

Now for the corner posts. Cut your 2 x 4s to six feet. Cut one into four pieces 21-inches long for your end pieces, and use the 2-foot cut-offs from your posts to make a further four pieces 21 inches long.

In the end, you should have eight 2 x 4s, eight 21-inch long pieces of 2 x 4, and 44 2 x 4s, 6-feet long.

*Step Two*

The next step is to pre-drill and pre-screw. Make a drilling template, one for the end bits and another to attach the long bits of 2 x 4 to those end pieces, making your skeleton. Now, you can pre-drill all your holes and get the screws ready to go in.

*Step Three*

This is why you cut and pre-drill first—assembly time is dead simple.

Put your corner posts on the floor and mark the point where the shelf supports will go across them all. Use a tape measure or scrap wood to mark where your shelf heights will be.

The end brackets can now be attached to the corner posts. Do not forget that they should all be 21-inches long, so the total width with the side brackets is 24 inches.

Now comes the tricky part. First, you need to determine if your end brackets will be toward the inside or outside of the shelves. If you put them inside, you will need to cut some off-the-shelf pieces so they slide in; if you put them outside, the shelves will need to be notched.

Put the end pieces on their sides, spaced about eight feet apart, and then place your top support across them. That way, you can get the distance right. Do the same with the bottom support, and once you are happy, attach the supports. Repeat the operation with the middle supports, and it should be square.

Once your OSB has been cut or notched, you will need the patience to get the shelves to go in. If you notch it, cut them a bit larger. You could also consider cutting the shelves in half and fitting them that way, but you may need to add a center support depending on whether there is any sag.

Congratulations! Your shelving unit is ready to go into your root cellar and be stocked with all your fruit and vegetables.

# Chapter 8: 8 Best Methods to Organizing a Root Cellar

Your root cellar is built, and you have even DIYed your storage shelves. All that is left to do is stock it. Many people will get excited at this stage and start piling in their vegetables without considering what they are doing.

If that is you, stop—right now!

Organizing a root cellar requires a great deal of thought and planning. Not all foods are happy together, and not all foods like the same temperatures. So, the next thing you will learn is how to organize your cellar, section by section. When you built your root cellar, you built it with its own temperature zones, whether you realized it or not. Working with those temperatures ensures that you can keep your food fresh for as long as possible, and proper organization means accessing your food quickly.

## Method 1 — Using the Drawers

If your root cellar is equipped with drawers, you can at least use them to store certain vegetables and fruits. First, the drawers in the colder area of your root cellar can be used for fruit storage as these do much better in colder temperatures. Kept in high humidity and higher temperatures, fruits tend to break down very easily and rot. As such, dry, cooler temperatures are much better.

Vegetables prefer higher humidity because it stops them from drying out. Drawers in warmer parts of the root cellar can store broccoli, lettuce, carrots, and other produce. The higher the humidity level for these, the better. Some vegetables, such as spinach and cauliflower, are spritzed daily with water to keep them fresh in some grocery stores.

However, using drawers for storing produce does come with a warning—you must never mix fruits and vegetables in the same drawer. This is because every food type needs a specific humidity and temperature level, and storing them together will result in the loss of both fruits and vegetables and can cause mold to start growing.

# Method 2 — The Upper Shelves

The upper shelves are best for food that you intend to eat fairly quickly. That includes ready-to-eat foods, leftovers, and drinks. These shelves are best because they are eye-level, and you see them straight away and are within easy reach. Obviously, if your root cellar is very tall and your upper shelves are above eye level, you will need to rethink that and use those you can see straight away.

# Method 3 — The Middle Shelves

In any root cellar, the temperature around the middle shelves is the most constant, and that is where you should keep foods that must be kept cool but will not spoil so quickly. These may include eggs, cream, soft cheese, deli meats, and so on. Vegetables you can store on these shelves also include peppers, pumpkins, squash, sweet potatoes, and tomatoes.

# Method 4 — The Lower Shelves

Down near the floor, the temperature is at its coldest, which is where spoilable foods need to go, such as chicken, fish, and other meats. This also prevents juices from dripping down onto other foods. Vegetables suitable for storage include potatoes, cabbage, cauliflower, dried beans, onions, and parsnips.

# Method 5 — Keeping a Journal

When you first start a root cellar, you must keep a journal. That way, you will know what you have in storage at any time and where it is in the cellar. Information to put in your cellar journal includes:

- The date.
- The item stored.
- The quantity at the start of storage—this must be kept updated as you take stuff out.
- Other information regarding the food you consider important, including notes on storage techniques, whether it needs to be moved to a different part of the cellar, and so on.

The same applies to any foods that you choose to can for storage.

# Method 6 – Keep Similar Foods Together

This applies to all foods, whether root vegetables, fruits, canned products, jars, or more. For example, keep all canned fruits, pie fillings, etc., in one place and tomato-based canned or bottled foods in another. Potatoes, beans, carrots, beets, etc., should be stored near one another. At the same time, fruits should be kept separate from the vegetables but stored in another area together. There are some exceptions, and it has all to do with ethylene gas—more details are provided later.

# Method 7 – Rotate Your Food

One habit you must adopt is regularly checking your food, and this is where your journal comes in handy. If you have filled it in religiously, you will know what dates everything went in. Canned foods, bottled ones, cheeses, meats, dairy, etc., must be rotated to ensure that you use the oldest first—that way, things do not spoil and go to waste. With vegetables and fruits, they must be checked regularly, and anything that is going bad must be removed immediately. If something looks like it is beginning to spoil but is still edible, remove it for immediate use—in some cases, you can freeze what you salvage. Anything that has definitely gone off should be discarded, and all fruits and vegetables nearby checked carefully. These should also be wiped over—if one fruit or vegetable has gone moldy, it may have started spreading to others.

# Method 8 – Store in Containers

Another way of storing your vegetables in a root cellar is in containers or bags, and one of the most common is plastic tubs. You can usually find five-gallon or larger tubs at fast food places, restaurants, supermarkets, and so on—simply go in and ask if they have any. More often than not, these are only going to be thrown away so you can put them to good use. Some of these containers will have lids—although they are generally single-use lids. That said, you can extend their use by cutting a few slots in the lid edge to fit it onto the container. These are ideal for storing many different fruits and vegetables, but you should cut air holes into the bottom and/or sides to ensure the air can circulate.

The second type of container you can use is wooden pallets. These are great for standing things like squash and pumpkins as they provide plenty of air circulation. Alternatively, you can build crates out of a series of pallets. By layering newspaper or straw between layers of vegetables, you can easily store large amounts in one place.

You can also use feed bags or burlap sacks. Feed bags are usually made from woven plastic and are breathable, ideal for storing food. They suit cabbages or apples layered with straw or leaves to keep them apart.

Cardboard boxes or wooden crates are also superb for storage. Some of these can be filled with sand and used to store carrots and other root vegetables. Make alternate layers of vegetables and sand until you reach the top.

# Top Storage Tips

This chapter finishes with some other tips on storage and general information to help your storage organization go much smoother, ensuring better chances of success.

While proper storage is absolutely critical to success, there are other things you need to do. Otherwise, all your careful planning will go to waste.

### Manage the Climate

As you have already learned, the climate in your root cellar is critical—that includes humidity, temperature, and ventilation. Most crops require a temperature between 32 and 40 degrees Fahrenheit and humidity of 90 to 95 percent. Others need warmer temperatures, between 50 and 60 degrees, with humidity of 60 to 70 percent. Root cellars with packed dirt floors are better than those with concrete floors because they ensure higher humidity. Again, humidity can be increased by using a humidifier or placing bowls of water on the floor.

### Air the Cellar

Proper ventilation is essential to keeping odors out, slowing rotting and spoilage by evacuating ethylene gas, and regulating humidity and temperature. In that regard, ensuring you have adequate inlet and outlet pipes is the best guarantee of all.

### Keeping Your Root Cellar Cool

With the following tips, you can ensure the best climate in your root cellar:

- Digging your root cellar at least ten feet (three meters) down ensures you reach complete temperature stability.
- Not digging your root cellar near big trees. The roots are not only tough to dig through, but they will also grow and crack the walls in your carefully dug root cellar.
- Use wood as far as possible for your storage as it does not conduct heat and cold like other materials.
- Stand your storage shelves, bins, etc., about 1 inch away from the wall to ensure proper air circulation.
- Have a packed earth floor rather than concrete.
- Ensure you install a hygrometer and thermometer to monitor temperature and humidity.
- Ensure adequate ventilation.

### One Last Tip for Now

- *Keep the lights off.* If your root cellar has windows, make sure they are shaded. Lights should be kept off as much as possible since too much light can cause a loss of quality, and some vegetables may begin sprouting.

# Root Cellar Ventilation and Ethylene Gas

Not having the right or adequate ventilation is one of the more common mistakes in designing and installing a root cellar. Most people are under the impression that food storage areas should be kept airtight to remain cold, but this is the fastest way for food to spoil.

This is by no means a good idea. Some foods will give off a gas known as ethylene. You cannot smell this gas, but it is the leading cause of food over-ripening and rotting in root cellars. Airtight areas can also be too humid, leading to excess water, which leads to the formation of mildew and mold.

You already know that you should have two vents in your cellar, one near the top of the room and one near the bottom. The bottom one allows the colder air in, while the top one vents out stale, warm air and ethylene gas.

If your room is around six by eight feet, you will get away using a 4-inch PVC pipe. Any larger, and the pipes need to be larger. All ventilation pipes should be covered in mesh to ensure animals and pests cannot get in, and they should be curved or angled so that debris, snow, or rain can't fall into the cellar.

Ethylene gas has been mentioned in this book several times, which tells you how important the subject is.

When some fruits ripen, particularly pears and apples, they give off this gas, which reduces the shelf life of other produce around them. It can cause early sprouting, mold, rotting, shrinking, yellowing, soft or tough skins, a bitter taste, and lots of other damage.

To curb this phenomenon, vegetables and fruits that produce the gas must be stored separately from those that can be affected. Foods that can emit excess ethylene gas include:

- Apricots
- Apples
- Avocados
- Yellow bananas
- Cantaloupes
- Blueberries
- All citrus fruit except for grapefruit
- Figs
- Cranberries
- Grapes
- Guavas
- Honeydew melons
- Green onions
- Ripe kiwifruit
- Melons
- Mangoes
- Nectarines
- Mushrooms
- Papayas
- Okras
- Passion fruit
- Watermelon
- Tomatoes
- Persimmons
- Peppers
- Pears

- Quince
- Plantains
- Prunes
- Pineapple
- Plums

Fruits and vegetables susceptible to damage by ethylene gas are:

- Broccoli
- Asparagus
- Cabbage
- Brussels sprouts
- Cauliflower
- Carrots
- Cucumbers
- Chard
- Eggplant
- Escarole
- Endive
- Green beans
- Kiwifruit
- Lettuce
- Kale
- Florist greens
- Cut flowers
- Peas
- Parsley

- Peppers
- Romaine lettuce
- Sweet potatoes
- Watercress
- Potatoes
- Leafy greens
- Yams
- Spinach
- Squash
- Potted plants

# 10 Final Tips to Store Your Harvest

- Leave it as late in the season as you can to stock your root cellar. If possible, keep the produce chilled somewhere, perhaps your refrigerator, before you place it in your cellar.

- Some vegetables, like pumpkins, winter squash, potatoes, and onions, must be cured for several days before they are placed into storage. This must be done in warm temperatures and helps the skin to harden off, ensuring they last longer in storage.

- Do not wash vegetables before storing them; simply brush off any loose dirt. Your vegetables will store much better, and wet vegetables are more susceptible to rotting. Regarding vegetables with top foliage, like beets and carrots, the foliage should be clipped back to about an inch above the top, and they are best stored in peat moss or damp sand.

- Be careful when handling your vegetables during the harvest and storing process. Even the slightest rough touch can cause invisible bruising, leading to early decomposition and rot.

• Turnips and cabbages should be stored away from other food—their odor can taint everything else.

• Fruit can breathe, especially pears and apples. Those that produce ethylene gas should be individually wrapped in paper to slow down its release.

• Space your vegetables out on their shelves or trays for optimum freshness—when you heap them together, they can generate heat, speeding up the rate of decomposition.

• Check your produce regularly and remove anything that is going off.

# Chapter 9: Troubleshooting Common Problems

While owning a root cellar should be fun, there are likely to be problems in any place where you store food. Be it mold, pests, or whatever, food storage is a magnet for problems. This chapter deals with some of the worst ones and provides effective solutions.

## Tips for Root Cellar Success

### Rodents

Wherever there is food, there are mice and rats, even in a root cellar. The trick to keeping them out is to stop them from accessing your root cellar in the first place, and the easiest way to do that is to block off their access points. Metal wire mesh is one of the best ways to go about this. Place it over anywhere these creatures can access your storage, including vents. If you struggle to keep mice out of your cellar, you may need to consider placing your storage off the ground. Just keep in mind that many rodents can climb, and if their prize is your food, they will stop at nothing. Later, we will explore some natural ways to repel rodents and other pests from your root cellar but, for now, keeping it clean will help. You may also need to consider laying traps along the walls—these must be checked at least once a day and any dead rodents removed immediately.

## Rot

Another common issue in root cellars, inevitably, is rot. You might have heard the saying "one rotten apple spoils the barrel," and this could not be more true. But how do you stop it from happening? You cannot entirely stop it, but you can minimize its occurrence considerably:

• When you harvest your vegetables, be extra careful. Sort through your produce before storing it—anything that has been damaged during the harvest, i.e., cut with a fork or space, should be put to one side. Anything that has been bruised, put aside. If you drop something, such as an apple or potato, it will probably have an invisible bruise even if it does not look damaged. Put it aside as well. Only undamaged, blemish-free foods should be stored in your root cellar. Those damaged can either be used immediately or stored in another way, such as freezing or canning.

• Another mistake many people make is to wash their root vegetables before storing them—however tempting it might be, do not do this. Root vegetables store much better the way they come out of the ground, with their roots, stems, and soil intact. All you need to do is gently brush off any excess dirt and place them straight into storage. Washing vegetables draws the moisture out of them and precipitates their decomposition.

• Ensure any canned or bottled foods are stored with airtight lids. Before you decide to can or bottle anything, the containers and lids must be sterilized beforehand—even the slightest bit of contamination can spoil the contents.

- When you store your produce, put the largest ones at the back and the smallest first—these are more likely to go off quickly and should be used early.

- If your cellar has high humidity, check for condensation. When water begins dripping from the ceiling or running down the walls, it can get onto your produce, and they will begin to rot. Before you store your food, pretreat your cellar ceiling with disinfectant, something like chlorine, as this slows down diseases transmitted by dripping water.

As a cardinal rule, check your root cellar regularly. Any foods starting to wither, rot, or show signs of decomposition should be removed immediately.

## Insects

This seems to be more of a problem where nuts and grains are stored, and since you have other food in your root cellar, it means you should never use chemical sprays or insecticides—ever. The best way to keep insects out of your root cellar is to have a tight-fitting door, all cracks sealed up, and insect mesh over the vents and drainage. Alternatively, you can scatter bay leaves around—insects hate these with a passion—or other herbs with a strong smell.

## Sprouting Vegetables

If you notice that your vegetables are starting to sprout in your root cellar, it means something is wrong, and it typically comes down to one of three things:

- *Ethylene gas* — Look at where you have stored the vegetables that are sprouting. What other fruits or vegetables that give off excess ethylene are nearby? If so, move them. Also, inspect your ventilation system—is it adequate? Is it working? Have you got it in the right place? If you answer "no" to any or all of those, it is a sign that something needs adjusting in your cellar.

- *Too warm* — If the temperature is too warm, it can force vegetables into growing, which is not something you want in your cellar. Once a plant begins to grow again, it will need to be consumed fairly quickly. To stop any others from sprouting, once again, check your ventilation system.

- *Too much light* — Do you leave the door open when you visit your root cellar? Are the windows covered? Do you leave a light on for long periods? The only way to stop vegetables from growing again is to keep them in the dark for as long as possible.

## Frozen Produce

If your produce is freezing in your root cellar, this simply indicates that the temperature is way too low. First, check your thermometer. If the temperature is below freezing, you need to raise it. However, at this stage, you may already have lost much of your stored foods. Most vegetables will go mushy and rot when they freeze, making them unusable for anything. The second thing to check is what vegetables are frozen. If it is only those at the bottom, the air coming in through the inlet is too cold, meaning you most likely did not dig your root cellar deep enough. There is little you can do about that except emptying it and digging deeper. Don't forget that constant temperature stability is reached at around ten feet or three meters underground.

## Produce Going Off Too Quickly

Did you open the door of your root cellar and get knocked back by the smell? Yes, your food is going off quickly, and the smell is quite distinct. So, what would make that happen? Simply put, it is down to the climate in your root cellar. The main culprits are moisture, light, air, temperature, and microbial growth.

One of the fastest causes of fresh food going off is damage caused by microorganisms, such as yeast, mold, and bacteria. However, this can only happen when the conditions are right—they need nutrients and water to grow and reproduce. Most fruits and vegetables have an average of 90 percent water content, making them the perfect target.

Light is a serious enemy of fresh food in storage. Too much exposure and the outer layer of the vegetable of fruit will begin to spoil. This process is called photodegradation, and it leads to discoloration and a loss of flavor, proteins, and vitamins.

The one thing you must not do is store any vegetables or fruits wet or in an airtight container. In fact, a lack of air circulation will do nothing more than hasten decay. If your humidity levels are too high, you run the risk of water pooling on the produce, once again resulting in rot.

Lastly, the temperature is a major consideration, and getting it right is critical. Bear in mind that some vegetables like it cool, whereas others like it warmer. Extremes of temperature can cause significant problems—cold to the point of freezing, and the food begins to form ice crystals inside. These expand and break through the cell walls, causing discoloration and, in some cases, a slimy texture.

As such, one of the most important things to do is get your climate right on point before you start storing food. Once your cellar is full, use your thermometer and hygrometer to measure temperature and humidity. Using a notebook to record your results daily can give you an early warning when something is not right.

## Mold

When your root cellar is working as it should be, it will be cool the whole year, and humidity levels will remain steady. However, one thing can affect all root cellars, whether underground, in a basement or garage, under the porch, or a simple barrel in the ground: mold. While you may think you have sealed your cellar properly, construction flaws or inadequate maintenance can lead to mold growing where you do not want it.

If your root cellar is attached to your home or inside it, mold growth in the cellar can have a detrimental effect on the air you breathe. When mold forms in a cellar or cold storage, it is because condensation has formed. It may be due to warmer air seeping into the room in the summer months, usually because the door has not been sealed properly.

When that warm air hits the cold surfaces in your cellar, such as the roof or poorly insulated walls, it forms condensation. This creates the perfect conditions for mold to develop. In a short time, that mold will spread to your produce or onto the containers your food is stored in, and within a few days, your entire crop is ruined—that is how quickly it can happen.

Your root cellar should have air vents, and these are one of the best tools at your disposal to control humidity. In turn, that helps you control the conditions and prevent mold growth—these air vents will keep the fresh air moving through your cellar and keep it dry.

However, that is not the only source of mold. You can introduce it into your cellar on the food you take in there. In that case, it does not matter how well your root cellar functions—once the mold is there, it will grow and spread to other food and your root cellar structure.

Now, if you suspect or can clearly see mold growing in your root cellar, you need to do something about it immediately. If left unchecked, mold can quickly spread to other areas, especially if your root cellar is attached to your home. Professional help will be needed to remove the mold and repair the damage already done in some cases.

What damage, you might ask?

First off, and most important, is the damage it can do to your health. This is more likely to affect those with respiratory diseases, weak immune systems, or allergies, but long-term exposure can also affect people with no underlying problems. It can lead to infections, asthma, bronchitis, allergic reactions, and more. Some of the common symptoms of mold exposure include:

- Sneezing
- Coughing
- Constantly fatigue
- Eye and throat irritation
- Headaches
- Skin rashes and irritation
- Nausea
- Breathing problems
- Nosebleeds

In any case, it is strongly recommended that if any of these symptoms manifest, you seek immediate medical advice and not just assume they are caused by mold.

Second is the damage it can do to the structural integrity of your house or root cellar. It can infest your walls and ceilings, turn into fungus, cause decay in wooden structures, and lead to wet and dry rot. If left untreated, you will end up with some pretty hefty structural repairs in the future.

Many people think that the onset of winter will kill off the mold growing in their cellar, but in reality, this is not the case. While colder temperatures can slow the growth and freeze mold, they do not dry out the mold spores. As such, the mold simply lies dormant, and when the temperatures warm up again, off it goes, growing fast and hard.

So, clearly, you must not wait for winter to set in and hope it will solve the problem for you. There are two things you can do. If the mold is confined to the root cellar and has only just started growing, you can strip everything out and thoroughly wash the walls, floors, shelves, etc., with a solution of diluted chlorine bleach. Alternatively, you can use hydrogen peroxide, diluted to a solution of three to ten percent, distilled white vinegar, or baking soda and borax. When you use these solutions, do not wipe them all off—leaving a little on the surfaces can help counteract future growth.

As an aside, if the mold is growing on a concrete surface, you cannot clean it yourself. Concrete is made using water, and when you add additional water to the surface to clean it, the water is drawn deeper into the structure. It takes the mold and bacteria with it, making the problem worse.

Generally speaking, if the mold covers about ten feet or more or is on concrete surfaces, you need to call in professional help, which is your second option. Professional mold specialists have the right products to remove the mold, identify the source, and fix the damage. They can also tend to air circulation issues or advise you on what to do to stop the problem from occurring again.

### Preventing Mold in Your Root Cellar

Once again, it comes back to proper air circulation and ventilation. This must feel like the thousandth reminder, but that should tell you how important these aspects are in a successful root cellar.

Make sure you have adequate ventilation in place and that it is in the right place. The inlet vent should be near the bottom of your cellar, while the outlet should be near the top. Hot air rises and will be taken out of the room via this outlet pipe. Correct ventilation and sufficient air circulation can also regulate humidity and optimize air quality, removing the conditions mold needs to develop.

Check that your cellar has no air leaks in it other than your ventilation system. Cracks in the walls and gaps in the window or the door frames can all let warm air in, causing major problems. Again, your cellar should be at least ten feet down in the ground. Your inlet pipe will only draw air at the same temperature as outside—ten feet down is the constant temperature. Any imperfections need to be fixed immediately to stop the problem from occurring and leading to expensive mold removal specialists being called. It will also stop the food in your cellar from being destroyed.

## Effective Tips to Keep Critters Away

Mice, rats, and other pests can get into just about anything. The smallest of holes is an invitation, and once one is in, you can pretty much guarantee they will invite their friends, family, and long-lost relatives to enjoy the feast!

To that end, here are some tips to help you keep them away from your precious storage supplies.

• **Avoid Excess Moisture**

Rodents do not just need food to survive; they also need water. Therefore, when they look for somewhere to feed, they will always look for somewhere moist, so you must not allow excess moisture to pool in your root cellar.

Also, consider storing food off the ground—there is less chance that rodents will get at it. Sometimes, if the area is moist, the rats and mice may pass through, and you will not even notice they have been there. By adding easily accessible food into the equation, you open the floodgates to destruction.

- **Eliminate Water and Food Smells**

Leading on from the previous tip, if your root cellar smells of food and/or water, you can guarantee the ultra-sensitive noses of rats and mice will pick up on them. This is why it is imperative to keep your root cellar clean, free of water, and free of food smells. Proper air circulation will help with this, but strong food smells will be carried into the air. By minimizing these smells, you can use other smells, such as those that deter rodents, to cover trace odors.

Rats and mice do not just look for food and water—they want nesting material. Therefore, leaving piles of newspaper, sawdust, and other materials lying around will attract them. If there is enough, you may even find the rodents building their nest right there in your cellar.

Mildew and dust also tip rats and mice off to the fact that the area is relatively undisturbed. That tells them they are safe, and that is when they start nesting—and multiplying. Fast.

- **Peppermint and Spearmint are Great Deterrents**

If you have ever grown mint in your garden, you know how invasive it can be. This is why many people choose to grow it in pots. Rats, mice, and other rodents detest the smell of mint because it irritates their noses and throats. You can do two things with that knowledge. First, if your root cellar is outdoors, plant mint around the perimeter. It will grow quickly, spreading into the available space and surrounding the cellar. Second, you can sprinkle mint leaves in your cellar, scattering them around the produce. If you use bins to keep your food in, chuck a few leaves in—they will not hurt the vegetables or fruit, and they will keep them safe from invasion.

Replace the leaves twice each week. The smell will stay strong enough to keep the rodents out, and it will mask any water or food odors.

One more thing you can do is boil up some mint leaves in water and put it in a spray bottle. Then, spray around your cellar regularly to provide an extra layer of protection and freshness.

## • Use Mothballs

Yes, they do smell strong, but that is the idea. Sprinkling mothballs in the root cellar can deter rodents and snakes; they hate it and will avoid it as much as they can. This could be the one thing that keeps your cellar free of pests. At first, the smell may overwhelm you, but you will get used to it. You have a (pretty obvious) choice—

a strong smell in the root cellar or no produce because the mice, rats, and snakes have taken over and eaten it all.

While snakes will not eat your fruit and vegetables, they are attracted by the mice and rats. So, if you do not get rid of the rodents, you won't get rid of the snakes.

## • Get a Cat or Two

Most cats are excellent mousers and will certainly help curb the presence of rodents. Allow cats to roam around the outside of your root cellar—any rodents that approach are likely to lose the battle or will be deterred from coming closer. When you enter your root cellar, let a cat or two in with you. If there are any rodents around, the cats will sort them out. Cats will also tell you if rats or mice have been in there—they can smell their scent and will alert you to their presence. Some cats will also go after moles, chipmunks, squirrels, rabbits, and other small creatures that might have taken a fancy to your root cellar.

## • Don't Run Away

When you enter your root cellar and mice or rats are scurrying around, do not back out. This works for snakes, too. Most of these creatures prefer to be alone and are not happy to stay where there is a human presence. Make a noise, stand your ground, and they will be the first to back down.

You should also ensure you enter the root cellar a few times each week, even if you don't need anything. You can use it as an excuse to check your crops over or do a bit of cleaning—a regular presence will cause some critters to vacate the area permanently. And when you do go in to check on things, make some noise. Rattle food bins, move them around, anything to tell any hidden creatures you are there and that they should leave.

- **Set Some Traps**

This is not a good idea if you let cats or children into your root cellar. Rat or mouse traps are easily set with a little peanut butter, as most rodents are attracted to this. You should also have a few bigger traps, just in case you get anything larger than a rat in your cellar. Alternatively, small spring traps can be modified with nail boards on the metal bars, making it easier to catch rodents of various sizes.

Place your traps along the cellar walls—this is usually where the rodents run. You should secure the traps to the ground as larger rodents can run off with them still attached. Inspect your traps daily. If there are any caught, you need to dispose of them at once. If sadly they are still alive, it is kinder to put them out of their misery immediately, rather than letting them suffer for a long time.

You can also put poison bait down—although you run the risk of cats eating poisoned rodents.

Lastly, if you want a more humane method to keep them out of your cellar, invest in an ultrasonic repellent device.

### • Keep a Steel Rod or Wooden Pole Handy

Never enter your cellar without a hoe, steel rod, or a large, heavy wooden pole. Why? Because you do not want to be caught unprepared if there are mice, rats, or snakes in there. If your food is stored in bins, in sawdust, sand, or straw, never put your hand in—lots of things can hide in there, and you don't want to be bitten. Instead, use a hoe to dig through to get your vegetables out. Poke around using a rod or pole to investigate anything alive or waiting to pounce on you.

Rats can grow to a foot and a half in length if the conditions are right, so make sure your rod is at least two or three feet long—you may need to lash out the rat with it, and you don't want to be too close.

### • Hardware Cloth

Mice and rats struggle to chew through hardware cloth, so it is a good idea to wrap your bins and crates in it, stretching it across the tops. That said, you still should not just stick your hand in without checking—mice are crafty, and any chink in your armor is their way in.

Hardware cloth also makes a good layer of protection, which is why many people line their walls with it to stop pests from getting in. As it is made from flexible wire mesh, it's tough for most rodents to chew through, and those who use it claim great success.

### • Lock it Down

One of the most important things you can do to keep pests out of your root cellar is to keep it all secure. Your door should be sturdy, and it must be secure enough to keep the outside world from getting in. However, you do need to ensure proper ventilation. Place hardware cloth over your ventilation pipes to allow air to enter and exit while preventing anything else from getting in.

Inside your root cellar, store your produce in chew-proof bins. You can use wooden or plastic containers where you do not have an issue with mice and rats, but these offer little deterrents. Rodents will even use chewed plastic to build their nests.

You may also want to consider other options, such as metal, cinderblock, or cement, where you have a problem. If you can get hold of them, metal ammo containers work fine, or you can weld or solder metal together to make your own. Whatever you use, ensure it has a tight-fitting or protective lid on it.

- **Guinea Fowl**

Last but not least is the often under-rated guinea fowl. Sure, they are loud, and yes, they will boss any other poultry you may have around. That said, when it comes to pest deterrents, they are one of the very best.

The best way to keep mice, rats, snakes, and other critters out of your root cellar is to remove them from your property, and that is where the guinea fowl will come into play. They are excellent hunters and will also eat bugs and ticks. Besides, they are a fantastic alarm system, and adding a few to your flock will ensure you have a much better chance of keeping pests away.

All in all, pest control in a root cellar is a tough job and an ongoing one. However, it is well worth the fight, and if you do not stay on top of things, all your hard work will most likely go to waste.

# Chapter 10: Cleaning and Sanitizing a Root Cellar

The last thing worth discussing is cleaning your root cellar. This should be done twice a year, the first time in March or April and the second before storing your next harvest.

Come the spring, most of your remaining root crops will have gone past their best limits for storage. Whatever you did not use must be consumed or discarded, depending on whether they are fine or going off. If you store potatoes, garlic, or onions, while these are probably still okay to eat, it should be done soon, or you need to plant them in the garden to produce a new crop.

If you have too many good vegetables left and cannot use them straight away, find another way of storing them. Potatoes, garlic, and onion can be turned into a lovely pan of scalloped potatoes! Use your vegetables for cooking up a batch of meals that you can freeze for another day.

If you have vegetables that can still be stored for a couple of months, move them out of the cellar. Ensure they are stored in burlap sacks or dark, ventilated containers while you do your spring cleaning. That way, they will not be exposed to the light, and the air can still circulate, keeping them fresh. Put canned and bottled foods to one side—you will read more on this below.

Once you have cleared all your food out of the cellar, remove any storage bins, crates, and boxes. Cardboard boxes may not be usable for another year; if not, discard them. It is best to burn them, just in case there are any bacteria or spots of mold growth on them.

Reusable containers should be scrubbed out thoroughly. Use a weak bleach solution to kill off any bacteria and wash them out in boiling water. Leave them to dry naturally.

Back into the root cellar, give it a good sweep. Clear up any dust, dirt, and debris from the shelves and the floor.

Now it is time to clean your shelves. Start at the top and work down, washing each one in hot soapy water. Rinse them off thoroughly with clean water and then spray them over with a kitchen disinfectant or a diluted chlorine bleach solution. You can make this with a teaspoon of water diluted in a quart of water. Leave it to dry. While cleaning, make sure you still have adequate ventilation.

Once your root cellar is cleared out, leave the doors open to air out for a few days. If the cellar still smells musty, run a fan in there for a few days to help evacuate the stale air.

Before you store your next harvest in the autumn, go back in there, have a final sweep out, rewash your storage containers and close down your vents. You do not want the warmer summer air getting in. Now you are ready to start over.

As a side note, you can use your root cellar in the summer months to keep early fruits and vegetables cool when you don't have time to process them straight away. However, do not leave them in there for more than a few days.

### Canned and Bottled Foods

Anything stored in jars, bottles, or otherwise preserved needs to be dealt with differently. When you began with your root cellar, you should have started a notebook detailing the dates each item was preserved and placed into storage. You should also have labeled each container with the date of preservation.

Your first job is to go through everything. Check for anything that has expired or gone off, and discard it in the garbage. Go by the dates on your containers or in your notebook—the earliest products should have been used first, so all you should have in storage are those stored later. However, if your system went awry, you may be left with old food—you really should not eat this unless it has been pickled. Dairy products are way past their "best by" date by now, unless they have only just been placed into storage.

Also, dispose of any rusted, dented, or bulging cans and any foods with torn or broken packaging.

Now, you can deal with what is left.

Wipe down all jars, cans, bottles, etc., to get rid of any dirt, dust, or sticky residue that may be on them.

Restock your cellar using a FIFO system—First In, First Out. The older stuff should be used first, or else it will go off soon.

Organize your food by type and label your shelves.

Ensure the conditions in your storage cellar are right, with proper ventilation, air circulation, and humidity.

### Maintenance

During your spring clean, you should check everything in your root cellar and make a note of any repairs, improvements, or upgrades that need to be made. If you used wood in any of the structures, check it for rot or damage—this needs to be replaced first.

Check the seals around your ventilation pipes and renew if necessary. Do the same with doors and windows and make sure any drainage issues are dealt with straight away.

When it comes time to start storing your new harvest, you need to ensure the right conditions in the root cellar. Over the summer, the temperature will rise and fall again as the nights draw in and the outside temperatures begin dropping. Once your cellar has been aired out after the spring clean, keep the door shut as much as you can.

Ensure you have sufficient storage containers and bags—buy new ones if you need to. Check that your old ones are in good condition, with no nails or loose bits sticking out.

Check your ventilation covers are in place—if necessary, replace them. When the outdoor temperatures are low enough, open your vent covers.

Your root cellar is finally ready to start working for you again.

# Conclusion

As you can see, building a root cellar is hard work, but it must be done right if you are to be successful. Putting in the time and effort to ensure your ventilation, temperature, and humidity are right will save you a lot of pain and headaches in the winter months.

Keep in mind that you do not have to go for a traditional root cellar if you don't want to. You may not have space or time, or it may be that this is your first time, and you want to start simple and see how it works before you decide to go all in on building a full root cellar at home.

Whichever type of root cellar you choose, make sure you follow the various tips provided in this guide, as it is the best way to ensure your success. The last thing you want is to bring in a huge harvest and store it all the way, only to find it goes rotten, or the mice and rats are happily enjoying the fruits of your labor.

Sure, root cellaring is a serious commitment, and you must be on the ball at all times. That said, it is also meant to be fun and a great way for you to make the most of what you grow or can buy at farmer's markets throughout the year. It's also a fantastic way to ensure that you eat healthy, organic food all year round and that you are set when unfortunate circumstances hit and stores run low.

All this book can encourage you to do now is to get out there, build your cellar, and have some fun.

Good luck!

# Part 4: Fermenting

*An Essential Guide to Culturing Food to Create Kombucha, Sourdough, Kimchi, Sauerkraut, Yogurt, and More so You Can Grow Probiotics at Home and Improve Your Gut Microbiome*

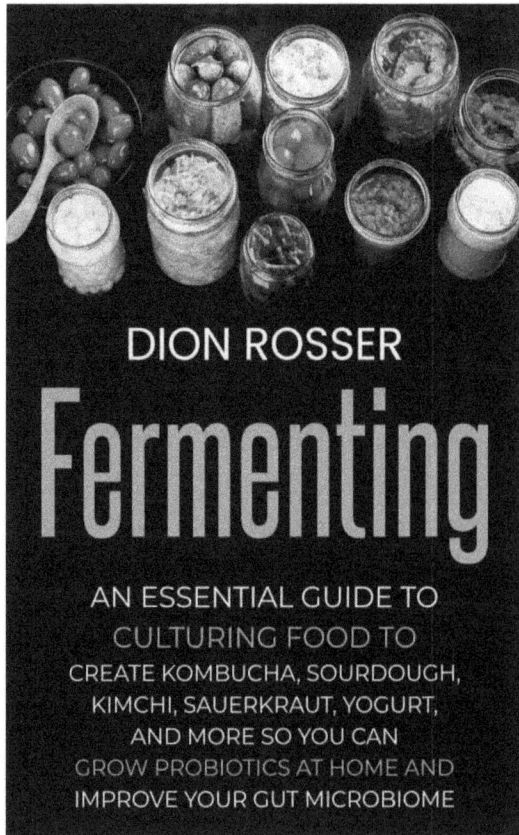

DION ROSSER

# Fermenting

## AN ESSENTIAL GUIDE TO CULTURING FOOD TO CREATE KOMBUCHA, SOURDOUGH, KIMCHI, SAUERKRAUT, YOGURT, AND MORE SO YOU CAN GROW PROBIOTICS AT HOME AND IMPROVE YOUR GUT MICROBIOME

# Introduction

Gut health is an essential aspect of your overall health and well-being. However, given the modern diet and lifestyle, most people have compromised their gut health and suffer from its side effects. If you want to improve your health and get your gut biome back to its healthiest state, this is the book for you. You might have heard about fermentation and the benefits of eating fermented foods. If not, you will soon discover the wonders of fermentation. Humans have been consuming fermented foods for a long time, but people have only recently started paying more attention to this type of food. Your beer, bread, salami, etc., are all fermented foods. They all have their own unique textures and smells and are a great addition to your diet.

Probiotics are one of the best things you can put into your body, and making your own at home is an invaluable skill. As you read on, you will learn about fermentation, its history, the process, benefits, and how to ferment various foods. This book will help you learn more about probiotics and how they can improve your gut health.

Kimchi, for instance, is a great probiotic that is a staple of Korean cuisine. Koreans seem to know enough about fermentation and its various benefits because they regularly consume kimchi. Throughout this book, you will learn how to make authentic Korean Kimchi at home too. Similarly, you will soon be making your own yogurt, kombucha, sourdough, and more. Learning how to culture your food will benefit your health and that of those around you.

This fermentation guide is different from others on the market. You may have found those challenging to follow or lacking crucial information. Here you will get easy-to-understand guidelines on how you can get started with fermentation. It contains hands-on instructions to make it easy for beginners to make the best sourdough, kimchi, yogurt, etc. This book provides you with simple recipes to help you make the best fermented foods. There are variations for each recipe that should suit every taste.

So, if you are ready to start growing your own probiotics and improving your gut health, let's get started.

# Chapter 1: Introduction to Fermenting

First, let's familiarize you with what fermenting foods means and why it is used. We will start by giving both the historical and the cultural background to fermenting foods. You will also learn how beneficial gut bacteria can be for your health. This section discusses the three fermentation types: lactic acid fermentation, acetic acid fermentation, and alcoholic fermentation.

Fermentation is a fascinating process, and this book is all about it. Also known as culturing, the basic and most important aspect of fermentation is a microbe. These microbes are tiny organisms present all around us, including your body, soil, and home. Many people think bacteria of all types are harmful to us and cause diseases. However, some microbes are actually beneficial for the body and even protect you against various illnesses. The important thing is to have a good balance of microbes in your body.

# History of Fermentation

Fermentation has been around as long as man. Its exact origins have not been determined yet, but evidence shows fermentation being used as far back as 7000 BC. In Chinese history, there is evidence they used fermentation to create rice wine around 4000 BC. The word itself comes from "fervere," a Latin word meaning "to boil." It probably referred to the conversion of fruit juice to wine after yeast was introduced to it.

Initially, our ancestors depended on fermentation for survival. They did not have easy access to food, and they needed to find ways to preserve it. They also had to prepare their rations so they could survive from one season to another.

Preserved food was especially important during winters when they couldn't grow or hunt for food as easily. They needed an option for when the harvest season had passed or when they couldn't hunt. These needs were how grapes were turned into wine and milk was made into cheese. Most countries in the world have their own traditions of fermenting food.

Egyptians made beer and bread with controlled yeast. Fruit juices were fermented to make tonics, wines, and cordials. The Romans made garum by fermenting fish guts. The Norwegians discovered the salted salmon buried and left for a while tasted different from fresh salmon but was still edible and delicious. In Russia, they left vegetable scraps in a barrel to age in winter, and this was how the original borscht was prepared. In Korea, cabbage was buried to last through the winter, resulting in the discovery of kimchi.

The western equivalent of this was sauerkraut in Europe. As our ancestors adapted to their environment and made new discoveries, they provided us with many different food options. The techniques and tools have been refined over the years, and we have better control over the process. The basics of the traditional methods lie at the core of preparing good, fermented foods. You can use accurate tools and techniques to get the desired results, but you also need to depend on your senses of taste and smell when it comes to fermentation.

In every culture, you can see traces of fermentation being passed over for generations. Humans have been using natural microbes for their health benefits for a long time. The beginnings of fermentation are unknown, but it is believed it might have started on accident. Someone might have dropped wild yeast or microbes in some grape juice, grain, or other food. This would have allowed for the fermentation process to spontaneously occur if the surrounding temperature was right. Ideally, temperatures between 40 and 70 °F can easily support fermentation.

The benefits of fermented foods have led people to embrace the process for a long time. In the next chapter, you will learn more about why fermentation is important and how it is beneficial. Many different techniques vary from culture to culture.

For instance, dairy farmers used fermentation to store milk for longer by turning it into cheese. Cheese is one of the earliest and most basic fermented products we know of. The core ingredients used for fermentation vary according to what was available in certain places. It could simply be dependent on what local microbes liked to consume.

The fermentation of certain foods is usually referred to as culture. This is because cultures or communities of microbes colonize a food. These microbes use the naturally occurring sugars in food for energy and simultaneously cause the fermentation process in food. This process takes place without the presence of oxygen and is thus called anaerobic digestion. It results in the creation of products like kombucha, cheese, sauerkraut, etc.

Wine, leavened bread, and beer are some of the earliest fermented foods. East Asian fermented foods like kimchi, pickles, vinegar, yogurt, etc., soon followed. In recent times, fermentation is also used for making vitamins B-12 and B-2, antibiotics, gluconic acid, and citric acid. Modern industrial fermentations also create microalgae and nutritional yeast.

In ancient times, the process of fermentation was somewhat of a marvel and mystery to humans. They did not really understand what caused or allowed fermentation to occur, and some even attributed it to the work of divine forces. In Japan, early breweries often had a small shrine where daily prayers were offered. In Greek mythology, Bacchus was proclaimed the god of wine.

One of the most significant contributors to the science of fermentation was Louis Pasteur. He was a French chemist and physicist who made discoveries that left a lasting impact on science, including the subject of fermentation. His germ theory, the Pasteurization method, and the creation of vaccines are some of the most significant contributions to science.

Around 1856, he connected fermentation to yeast, which made him the first zymologist in the world. An accident took place in a sugar beetroot distillery, and he was asked to investigate it. He discovered the spoiled batch had high levels of lactic acid instead of alcohol, which was why it tasted sour. The sour batch had a large amount of lactic acid bacteria, and this observation played a fundamental role in what we now know about the role of bacteria and fungi in fermentation. His observations allowed him to understand that the process took place in an anaerobic environment.

Later, Eduard Buechner discovered that fermentation could also occur with cell-free yeast extracts driven only by their enzymes. Fermented foods were considered a health benefit only around 1910. At this point, Elie Metchnikoff, a Russian bacteriologist, determined that Bulgarians have a longer lifespan than others because their diet had a larger amount of fermented milk. Over the last few decades, more research has been conducted to study and understand fermentation. This research has shown a clear link between improved digestion and friendly bacteria. Therefore, probiotics became a widely recommended part of the diet.

# What Is Fermentation?

It is a process where organic substances are chemically transformed into simpler compounds due to the action of enzymes produced by bacteria, yeast, and other microorganisms. The enzymes break down complex organic molecules into smaller compounds and nutrients. In the case of food, fermentation makes the end product more digestible for humans and creates distinct texture, aroma, and flavor, which improve the initial product. Fermentation processes are usually activated by yeasts, molds, or bacteria, either in groups or singularly.

All microorganisms have their own unique metabolic genes, and these produce enzymes that will break down specific types of sugar metabolites. In the process of fermentation, different kinds of microbes are present in various proportions. They work together to give you your desired fermented byproduct. The taste of certain fermented foods will vary depending on the numbers and types of microbes used in the process.

# Various Types of Fermentation

## • Alcoholic Fermentation

Yeasts break down pyruvate molecules in sugars and convert them to alcohol. The most well-known kind of fermentation is alcoholic fermentation. The byproducts in the form of wine, beer, etc., have been enjoyed by humans for thousands of years.

- **Acetic Acid Fermentation**

Sugars from fruit or grains are converted to sour vinegar and other condiments. This process starts when alcoholic fermentation ends. Vinegar is the most common byproduct of acetic acid fermentation. This is why apple cider is different from apple cider vinegar.

- **Lactic Acid Fermentation**

Sugars or starches are broken down, and lactic acid is produced. This is considered the oldest method of fermentation. Fermented milk products are found in most cultures worldwide, and these have been consumed for centuries.

When you start working on fermenting your foods, you must remember that it is essentially a sort of controlled decay. Fermentation leads to the creation of intense flavors and aromas that might be appealing to some and not to others. Such foods are not fresh, but they aren't rotten either. The consumption of fermented foods is a way to improve the digestion of other foods and create an unsuitable environment for undesirable bacteria in the body. The type of fermented food you consume will depend on your taste. Use this guide to try a few different fermentations and see what suits your palate. Add these to your diet for their health benefits and also as a way to waste less food.

# Popular Fermented Foods

Some popular fermented foods in this guide include:

- **Kimchi and Sauerkraut**

Kimchi is a Korean side dish that is made by fermenting vegetables like radish and cabbage. Typically, kimchi contains radish or cabbage with chili, garlic, pepper, ginger, green onion, and salt. Other ingredients like pear and apple may also be used. There are substantial amounts of Leuconostoc bacteria in it, and these produce lactic acid. Sauerkraut is made by fermenting cabbage and was originally from Northern China but may have been brought by the Mongols to Europe. It can be wild fermented or made with a starter culture. In wild fermented versions, you will find high levels of Pseudomonas and Enterobacter. In sauerkraut with a starter culture, there are higher levels of Lactobacillus, Leuconostoc, and Pediococcus.

- Miso

It is a popular Japanese paste obtained through the fermentation of mashed soybeans, grains, and salt. This richly fermented bean paste is made with Aspergillus oryzae, which is a type of mold. While any legume or even a mixture of legumes can be used, soybeans are the popular choice.

- Cheese

Cheese is one of the earliest fermented products, made from fermented milk, and is produced by the coagulation of casein, a milk protein. During the process of fermentation, microbes like lactic acid-producing bacteria acidify the milk. Enzymes like rennet then coagulate the milk. After the dairy solids are separated, they are pressed down into certain shapes, and they then go through the process of aging. This promotes the growth of molds in the cheese. The cheese's flavor, color, texture, and aroma are determined by the type of milk, environmental factors, and the types of mold and bacteria involved in the fermentation process. Probiotic starter cultures usually initiate cheese production, but the bacteria don't always survive the lengthy aging process. In cheeses like cheddar and Gouda, small numbers of probiotic bacteria survive and will be present in the final cheese product.

- Kombucha

It is believed that kombucha originated around 220 BC in China, Eastern Europe, or Russia. The fermentation of green or black tea gives you this healthy drink. It is slightly alcoholic and effervescent. The mixture of sugar and tea acts as a fermentation medium for the symbiotic culture of yeast and bacteria in a rubbery disk shape. This is a biofilm of many microbes like Komagataeibacter xylinus and Zygosaccharomyces bailii. Spices, fruit, and juices are also added to kombucha for flavor. Jun kombucha is a variation of the drink where green tea and honey are used as a medium for fermentation. The honey provides additional probiotic benefits to the kombucha. Traditionally prepared kombucha is more beneficial than the processed ones available in stores these days.

- **Mead**

Honey and water are fermented to produce mead. It can also include spices, fruits, or grains.

- **Natto**

Natto is another Japanese fermented dish. It is made from soybeans and has an intense aroma and flavor. The soybean is fermented with Bacillus subtilis var. natto. It is usually eaten with breakfast.

- **Kefir**

Kefir originated from the Caucasus Mountains and is a fermented milk product. Kefir grains made of bacteria, sugars, lipids, proteins, and yeast are used for fermentation. A symbiotic microbial culture is created when the yeast and bacteria feed on the nutrients present in the grains. Milk from goats, cows, or sheep can be used to make kefir. It gives a sour and effervescent product that is good for the gut.

- **Tempeh**

Cooked soybeans are fermented to produce this cake-like form that is good for digestion. It is traditionally an Indonesian dish made by boiling, dehulling and fermenting soybeans. Usually, a starter culture of a type of mold called Rhizopus oligosporus is used to make tempeh.

## • Chocolate

The seeds from the Theobroma cacao tree are fermented to make chocolate. This tree is native to the Amazon rainforest but grows elsewhere as well. The cacao pods from the tree are harvested, and the pulp and seed are left to ferment. The microbes that participate in this fermentation include Acetobacter pasteurianus, Lactobacillus fermentum, S. cerevisiae, Hortaea thailandica, Pichia kudriavzevii, and Hanseniaspora opuntiae. The first two are bacteria, while the rest are yeast species. During the drying and roasting of the beans, most of these microbes are killed. Many bioactive microbes remain, and these are responsible for the aroma and flavor of chocolate.

## • Yogurt

Yogurt is obtained from the fermentation of acidified milk and thickened using probiotic species like Streptococcus thermophilus and Lactobacillus bulgaricus. This fermented food has been consumed for thousands of years. The term yogurt was coined from "yogurmak," a Turkish word that means coagulate. Ancient Ayurvedic texts contain mentions of yogurt and its health benefits as well. This fermented product can be produced from the milk of many different animals like goats, cows, camels, and yaks. Yogurt was even sold as a medicinal substance at the beginning of the 20th century. Yogurt production in the food industry became more common after the Danone yogurt factory was established in France in 1932.

## • Sourdough Bread

Throughout history, bread was primarily made with the help of sourdough fermentation. Quick rise bread and industrial yeast were not invented until later. This transition to the latter meant that we now consume bread that is harder for the body to digest and is filled with antinutrients. For sourdough bread, a starter is created and mixed with water and flour. This is left out at room temperature for a few days. The lactic acid-producing bacteria in the air and yeast will colonize the starter and initiate the fermentation. There are no active probiotic cultures in sourdough bread, but it has a lower glycemic index and other benefits compared to modern bread.

- **Beer**

Beer is produced using a starch source, water, and yeast. Usually, some cereal grains are steeped in water, and the liquid is then fermented using yeast. Grains have to be malted before they can be fermented for producing beer. The cereal grains germinate during malting and release enzymes that will break down complex carbs present in the grains into simple sugar. The yeast feeds on the simple sugars and then produces alcohol. Hops and brewer's yeast are used to ferment most types of beers. Beer is, in fact, the most widely consumed alcohol and fermented drink in the world.

# Chapter 2: Why Fermentation Is Important

In this chapter, you will understand why fermentation is an essential aspect of overall health. It underlines the importance of bacteria in the human body. You will soon see how devoid your food supply is of vital nutrients due to commercial farming and pesticide use. It is important to be aware of the damaging results of fast-food diets and the use of antibiotics in farming. Eating fermented foods can improve the absorption of vital nutrients, provide a healthy gut microbiome and build a stronger immune system.

## Why Fermented Foods Are Good for You

You may be wondering why fermented foods are good for you. The answer is bioactive compounds. The probiotic content in fermented foods is usually responsible for all their benefits. Not every fermented food contains viable probiotics. Despite this, even fermented foods that lack those probiotics are beneficial for your health because of the various bioactive compounds found in fermented foods.

## Bioactive Peptides

Bioactive peptides are produced by certain lactic acid-producing bacteria that are present in fermented foods. These bioactive peptides are small organic molecules that are joined by peptide bonds. Some bioactive peptides like bacteriocins are antimicrobial in nature.

## Phenolic Compounds

These are small molecules that have a ring-shaped chemical group called phenol. Polyphenols are phenolic compounds present in blueberries, blackberries, and other colorful fruits. Fermentation increases some phenolic compounds with antioxidant properties that also balance the microbiome in the gut.

## Prebiotics and Micronutrients

Fermented foods act as a bioavailable delivery system for micronutrients and prebiotics like calcium.

## Easier Digestibility

Compounds that are usually difficult to digest for the body are broken down through fermentation. This includes FODMAPs in grains, vegetables, and legumes, as well as the lactose in dairy.

# Benefits of Fermented Foods

## Improves Gut Health

The first and most important benefit of fermented foods is that they support the gut microbiome. Many studies have been conducted to understand how the gut is affected by the consumption of fermented foods. Kefir is a fermented milk product that increases the concentration of friendly bacteria like Lactococcus, Lactobacillus, and Bifidobacteria in the gut, thus benefiting it. The consumption of tempeh will increase the concentration of Akkermansia muciniphila. It also increases immunoglobulin A levels, which is important for immune response in the intestines. Chocolate supplies prebiotic fibers and short-chain fatty acids that support beneficial microbes in the gut as well.

- **Better Bowel Regulation**

Healthy bowel movements are a crucial aspect of good health. Including fermented foods in your regular diet will support digestion and bowel regulation. Kefir is known to improve stool frequency and consistency in people with chronic constipation. Yogurt is also helpful when dealing with constipation that is caused by slow intestinal digestion. Certain foods are easier to digest when fermented. For instance, if you consume sourdough bread instead of non-fermented bread, you will see reduced gas production, less bloating, and less abdominal discomfort.

- **Easier Weight Management**

Fermented foods help with weight management. Kimchi does this by affecting the genes that are involved in fat cell creation. Yogurt consumption has long been linked to lower BMI and fat percentage in the body. Many nutritionists suggest fermented food for people suffering from obesity or those who are overweight. Fermented foods also tend to be high in dietary fiber, which keeps you feeling full for a longer time. They don't contain too much sugar or cholesterol, and they can be consumed in larger amounts without worrying about gaining weight.

- **Better Mental Health**

The gut is linked to your mental health, and fermented foods have a beneficial effect on both. When there is an imbalance in the gut microbiome, it affects mental health disorders like depression or anxiety. This is because gut dysbiosis may trigger an inflammatory response. By reducing the levels of such inflammatory microbes, fermented foods support mental health. They also increase the bioavailability of phenolic plant compounds that will modulate neurotransmission. Probiotics have a beneficial effect on the gut-brain axis too.

## • Antimicrobial Properties

Fermented foods supply the gut with a better concentration of friendly bacteria and also have antimicrobial effects that reduce undesirable bacteria. These antimicrobial properties help in fighting against pathogenic and opportunistic microbes in the gut. Kefir grains also have antibacterial and antifungal properties that fight against common pathogens like Salmonella typhi, Salmonella enterica, Shigella sonnei, and Candida Albicans. In the Helicobacter pylori infection, kefir can be consumed as an added defense along with antibiotics. The growth of Helicobacter pylori, Campylobacter jejuni, and Salmonella typhimurium is also inhibited by kombucha consumption. Regular consumption of yogurt introduces lactic acid-producing bacteria that have antimicrobial properties in the gut.

## • Improves Cognitive Function

Some research suggests that fermented foods may help in improving cognitive function. A study done on mice showed that Lactobacillus pentosus inhibits drug-induced memory impairment. This probiotic is present in kimchi. Another human trial done with functional MRI showed that the consumption of fermented milk products modulates brain activity.

## • Boosts the Nutritional Value of Food

Fermentation affects the nutrient content of food. It reduces antinutrients that diminish or stop the absorption of beneficial nutrients in the body. Fermented foods will boost the supply of healthy micronutrients instead. For instance, phytic acid is an antinutrient that reduces mineral absorption. Fermented grain and soybean products will provide microbial phytase that catalyzes phytic acid breakdown and prevent the negative effect on mineral absorption. Sourdough is a fermented food that promotes gluten breakdown and makes it easier to digest for those sensitive to gluten. Beta-galactosidase in kefir reduces the lactose content in it. Fermented foods increase the bioavailability of nutrients like iron, B vitamins, calcium, and zinc by promoting the breakdown of substances that otherwise inhibit their absorption. They also increase dairy product acidity, transforming micronutrients like calcium in these dairy products into bioavailable forms. Specific vitamins like vitamin K2 are synthesized by fermented foods too.

- **Stronger Bones**

For better bone health, fermented milk products are a great option. These products tend to be rich in protein, calcium, vitamin D, phosphorus, and vitamin K2. All of these nutrients are crucial for stronger bones in the body. Studies show that the consumption of kefir helps in bone turnover and better bone mineral density. Fermented milk products may also protect against bone loss that is linked to estrogen deficiency. This may be beneficial for post-menopausal women.

- **Improved Cardiometabolic Health**

Cardiometabolic risk is increased by insulin resistance, hypertension, high triglyceride levels, and many other factors. These factors increase the risk of diabetes type 2, strokes, or cardiovascular disease. Most research suggests that these risk factors may be reduced by increased consumption of fermented foods. Kefir can support healthy blood pressure in a way similar to drugs used for relaxing blood vessels. Adding kimchi as a side dish to each meal for a few months can help lose abdominal fat and reduce body mass index. Insulin resistance is also reduced. Kombucha can help lower blood lipids and blood sugar, thus lowering the risk of fatty liver disease not linked to alcoholism. The risk of blood clots is reduced by consuming natto. Fermented foods help maintain healthy cholesterol levels without having to depend on medication. Tempeh is particularly helpful in this since it provides protein, vitamin B, and fiber that reduce cholesterol build-up in your blood vessels. Studies show that people who consume tempeh regularly have a lower risk of high cholesterol issues.

- **Cell Growth Regulation**

Some preliminary research suggests that fermented foods help with cell growth regulation. This may help in reducing the risk or spread of cancer in the body. In vitro studies have also shown that kombucha has a toxic effect on cancer cells in the colon. Kombucha consumption may help in preserving the normal epithelial cells in the colon. Certain kimchi-based probiotics can also help in fighting the formation of cancer cells. Consumption of fermented beet juice can inhibit intestinal crypt formation that is considered an early symptom of intestinal cancer.

- **Immunity Boost and Reduced Inflammation**

Fermented foods have a positive impact on the immune system and can reduce inflammation. Kefir has a probiotic bacterium that has an inhibitory effect on immunoglobulin E production. This molecule takes part in allergic responses. A sugar in kefir called *kefiran* can help prevent allergies since it suppresses mast cell degranulation. Women who consume fermented foods during their pregnancy can help prevent atopic dermatitis in their children.

- **Healthier Skin**

A healthy gut is reflected in healthy skin. By improving the gut microbiome and reducing inflammation, fermented foods benefit the skin as well. People with acne may benefit from consuming fermented dairy products instead of non-fermented variants. This is because fermentation will reduce insulin-like growth factor 1, responsible for sebum production and inflammation. These foods modulate the gut skin axis and can benefit the skin due to this.

- **Protection From Toxins**

Promising studies have shown that fermented foods may enhance the ability to detoxify. Lactobacillus is a common species in fermented foods, and it can bind heavy metals and help remove them from the body. Sauerkraut and similar fermented foods contain L. rhamnosus that reduces organophosphate absorption in the gut. The levels of mycotoxins in foods like grains can also be reduced through fermentation. Daily consumption of such fermented foods will help fortify the body against environmental toxins and help cleanse the body.

- **Increased Energy Levels**

For higher quality of life, you need to be healthy and have high levels of energy. If you feel sluggish or lazy, it affects everything that you do. Processed and packaged foods tend to be high in hidden sugars and other additives that leave you feeling tired and lethargic halfway through your day. Fermented foods may help in maintaining higher energy levels. Kombucha is one example of fermented food that is recommended for increasing energy. It has several nutrients like vitamin B that will decrease energy combating factors.

- **Better Food Absorption**

The body needs to be able to absorb important nutrients from the food you consume. However, many factors may affect this. Nutritionists suggest that fermented foods can help in encouraging better food absorption in the body. In particular, foods like tempeh, miso, and kefir will help your body absorb the vitamins and minerals from the other foods you consume. This is why these are regularly consumed as side dishes during meals in Korean and Japanese cuisines.

- **Preservation of Food**

Most of us waste food regularly. We either buy too many vegetables or cook more than we can consume. This food changes when you leave it out on the counter or in your fridge for too long. You will notice that it looks withered or moldy. The food may look like it has melted or gathered colorful mold on its surface. You will also notice a strong unpleasant smell. Once the food is spoiled, you notice these signs and the awful smell. Fermented food smells quite strong as well, but it is not the same as rotten food. Fermentation is a point of balance between the food being spoiled and being preserved. It allows the good microbes to survive and the bad ones to be removed or killed. If you can carry out the process correctly, you preserve the food and are left with something edible that lasts longer than its original form. Salt often plays a significant role in it since it destroys microbes that usually cause the food to rot or spoil. This allows healthy microbes to thrive in your fermented food, and you can preserve your food for longer.

# Points to Remember

### • All Fermented Foods Are Not Equal

If you want fermented foods to benefit your body, you need to consume those fermented with natural processes and probiotics. Live cultures are found in kefir, yogurt, kimchi, etc., and so you have a lot from which to choose. The pickled vegetables that you buy from the grocery store may have been pickled with vinegar. Fermented products available in packaged form are often devoid of probiotics since they aren't prepared with the natural fermentation process. To ensure that you are purchasing fermented foods with probiotics, check the label to see if it mentions "naturally fermented." When opening jars of naturally fermented foods, you will usually see some telltale bubbles. These bubbles are a sign that living organisms are present inside. Preparing your own fermented food is the best option, but the next best thing is store-bought if you can find naturally fermented products.

- **Moderate Consumption**

When it comes to food, everything should be consumed in moderation. You don't have to cut out every food you like to lose weight or get healthy. You shouldn't be overeating something just because you enjoy it, either. Moderate consumption will allow you to enjoy your meals and maintain a healthy body. While we have mentioned numerous benefits of fermented foods, these should be consumed in moderation too. They don't harm your body but should be consumed in reasonable portions. Only then can you expect to benefit from them without worrying about the possible effects of overconsumption.

- **Food Safety in Fermentation**

Fermentation has been becoming popular again for a good reason. The process allows you to create new flavors from the same old foods and improve your health while you do this. In fact, fermented vegetables are more digestible than in their raw forms. This is because the living bacteria in the fermented vegetables help digest other food present in your digestive tract. People have been fermenting food since ancient times, even without having access to refrigerators or stoves. They managed to do this safely, which says a lot about whether fermented foods are safe for consumption. Most of us eat some form of fermented food every day, but when you are first introduced to the concept and think about fermented foods, you assume it will be pungent and possibly dangerous food. However, your bread, coffee, chocolate, etc., are all fermented foods. Food scientists advocate for the consumption of fermented foods because they are aware of the benefits.

As long as the food is fermented correctly, there is no danger. It is important to know how to ferment the right way to avoid any mishaps. Microbiologist Fred Breidt says that fermented vegetables might be safer to consume than raw vegetables. This is because the lactic acid in fermented foods can find and kill any harmful bacteria. Lactic acid bacteria consume sugars in food and convert them to lactic acid. This lactic acid will then be able to overpower almost any other pathogen nearby. Fermentation methods are easy to follow and similar all across the world. It is hard to mess them up, and although there is a slight possibility of mistakes, it is rare.

Almost all vegetables can be fermented, and cabbage, cucumbers, turnips, radishes, etc., are particularly suited for it. Leafy greens contain high amounts of chlorophyll, and most people don't like the fermented dishes prepared from these. Another thing to keep in mind is that fermentation and pickling overlap but are not the same. For instance, you can pickle cucumbers with or without vinegar and use salty brine instead. Vinegar and other such acids will be produced during fermentation, and this is why they have a vinegary aftertaste. There is still much research on fermentation needed, but most experts agree that the traditional fermentation methods are still as effective as before. People unfamiliar with fermentation are often scared of preparing fermented foods at home because they fear bacteria or assume that the pungent smell means the food has gone bad. But these fears will subside when you realize how common food fermentation is around the world and just how long it has been practiced safely. Sauerkraut has been a constant part of the German diet, especially in winter, since it provides vitamin C and has a high nutritional value. Humans relied on fermentation to preserve food and survive with good health even when food was scarce. The practice of fermenting foods is widespread across the world, and each place has its own fermented food recipes. Some, in particular, have found their way to different places other than their origins and became wildly popular. This book has recipes that will help you safely prepare these fermented dishes without worrying about food safety.

If you are genuinely concerned about food safety, you should know that the basics are the same as preparing any other kind of food. It is better to use vegetables or any other raw ingredient that has been grown organically. If the vegetables you use had come in contact with compost or manure, then they might still have pathogens like Salmonella or E. coli. In such cases, the raw ingredient you use will set you up for failure and harm your health even if you follow the proper fermentation process. Handling the food well and having proper sanitary practices can make a big difference. All produce should be washed thoroughly whether you buy it at a store or grow it in your garden. Wash your hands well before handling food. The surfaces on which you prepare the dish or the utensils you use should also be clean and uncontaminated. For higher quality fermentation, use vegetables that are as fresh as possible. These should help ease your mind on any food safety issues before the preparation of any fermented foods. Handle the food with clean hands or utensils. Don't let it come in contact with any meat or fish that might be contaminated as well. Overall, fermented vegetables have been known to be safer than raw vegetables for consumption. But practicing food safety guidelines helps avoid any possibility of getting sick from fermented food preparation or consumption.

Fermentation alone cannot eliminate every possible health risk associated with food. The correct temperature is crucial. The temperature will determine how much or how little time your food needs to be fermented. For instance, sauerkraut will ferment well in approximately four weeks if the temperature is around 70 degrees. If the temperature goes above 75 degrees, it may get soft. This means that the correct temperature facilitates proper fermentation and allows harmful pathogens to be destroyed while the good microbes thrive.

Salt plays a very important role in the fermentation of foods, so it is essential to measure and add the exact amount of salt mentioned in a tried and tested recipe. Pickling or canning salt is used for fermentation, and these cannot be substituted with kosher salt or table salt. Remember to use salt without added iodine since it may inhibit the fermentation process. The amount of salt appropriate for a dish will depend on what is being fermented.

Certain foods may need nearly 13 percent of their weight in salt, while some might only need around 2.25 percent. The best way to get this right is to follow recipes that are already tested. Someone else's trials and errors will save you time. The salt content will affect the kind and amount of microbial activity taking place while fermenting. It will also prevent your vegetables from getting too soft.

The amount of time you store the fermented food also affects its texture. The vegetables are firmer when they are kept for a shorter time. When you keep fermented food in the fridge, the fermentation rate slows down. This is why you can store fermented foods for a couple of months without their taste or quality being affected. The fermented food should be acidic enough for safe consumption, so check that the pH level is 4.6 or lower.

If the process of fermentation is carried out correctly, this acidic level will be attained easily. Temperature control and following the proper food safety precautions can help avoid any issues like botulism poisoning that bad fermented foods might cause. Using recipes created by food experts or other reputed sources is your best bet. The fermented food recipes in this book are a great way to get started. One of the easiest ways to get started is sauerkraut fermentation.

The basic procedure used for this dish can be used for fermenting many other vegetables too. The fermentation time and salt volume may vary accordingly. For vegetables like carrots that are dense, chop, grate or shred so the lactic acid can easily get inside them. The fermentation is better and safer when the surface area is more. This does not apply to cucumbers since they have a 90 percent volume of water, and the lactic acid bacteria can enter easily.

Another thing to consider when it comes to food safety is mold. A little mold on the surface can happen, and it can be easily removed. If the mold goes down into the solution or food, it increases the risk of disease. Toss out any batch where you notice excess mold formation. It is better to be careful to maintain good health than take undue risks by consuming moldy food.

If you keep all these simple points in mind, you can safely enjoy fermented foods and improve the health of your gut and body.

# Chapter 3: Supplies You Will Need

This chapter will cover the supplies you will need to begin fermenting. It will help you understand the importance of using the proper containers for fermenting. It will also act as a guide to buying "starter" cultures or finding them locally.

Although fermenting can be done with minimal supplies, a vast array of tools make the process safer and easier. Below, we've made a list of the most important items and explain how they could be used.

## Fermentation Supplies

### Fermentation Jars

There are many different kinds of containers that you can use for fermentation. It could be an old pickle jar or even a water-sealed ceramic crock. Any of these will help get the job done. Some make the process easier for you and show better results than others. Getting the suitable jars might make a little bit of a difference after all.

### Canning Jars

Canning jars are a great container for you to start with fermentation. They usually come under the labels of Mason, Kilner, Ball, etc., and are readily available. If you are a beginner, the quart-sized jar is perfect for you. It will be just enough for you to make a small batch of kimchi or sauerkraut. You can use these jars to experiment with many fermentation recipes and develop your skills along the way.

When you use different recipes for the same dish in small batches, you can determine which one turns out the best or more to your liking. You can use that recipe to make a bigger batch in the future. These jars are usually relatively cheap, and you can even buy them in bulk. You just need to make sure that the jars you get have wide mouths. Canning jars are handy for many things, so there can never be enough of them in the house.

### Clamp Jars

Wire bale clamp jars are another great option for fermentation. They are usually called Fido jars, and many people swear by them. These clamp lids are the perfect way to ensure that your food ferments in an anaerobic environment. An airtight seal is created with the thick gasket and strong wire bale that holds down the lid.

Some people ferment food in these jars with the airlock because they believe that the built-up gases from the fermentation will exert enough pressure on the lid to lift it a bit and allow them to escape through the space between the lid and rubber gasket. If you want to ferment without the airlock, it is better to stick with branded jars made from hardened glass. Instead of cheap knockoffs, buy brands like Fido and Bormioli Rocco. The knockoffs are usually from China and are made of thin glass and low-quality gaskets. These jars can explode if there is too much $CO_2$ build-up once the fermentation process begins. The hardened glass will help you avoid that.

### Choosing between Different Materials for Jars:

- **Glass Containers**. Glass is the most common and best option for fermentation. It does not contain harmful chemicals like BPA and is not easily damaged or scratched like plastic. Glass containers are fairly inexpensive. This makes them a viable option for most people.
- **Ceramic Containers**. Fermentation crocks are usually made of ceramic, and these are an excellent option for fermenting large batches. These ceramic jars can be found at supply stores or local potters.
- **Porcelain Containers**. For fermenting food, you have to get food-grade porcelain jars. Don't use porcelain pieces that are meant for decors like vases or pottery. These are not suitable for food fermentation.
- **Plastic Containers**. Plastic is a cheap option and can technically be used, but it is not recommended for many reasons. Plastic gets damaged, and the scratches in it can

harbor harmful bacteria. You need to use food-grade plastic if you choose plastic containers, but even these have undesirable chemicals that should be avoided.

## Mixing Bowls

If you want to make large batches of fermented foods, you need large bowls to help you prepare. Most people already have a large mixing bowl in their kitchen, but you need to get one if you don't. A glass or stainless-steel bowl is best, but you can get a plastic one too. It is better not to use copper or aluminum bowls since these metals will react with salt that you might use. You need a wide bowl where you can easily mix your ingredients using your hands. Get a large bowl that is big enough for preparing large and small batches of fermented food.

## Fermentation Weights

Another key tool in fermentation is fermentation weights. These weights help keep everything airtight. If you want to pickle vegetables, you will want to use fermentation weights. They will protect your food from yeast and mold growth. There are three kinds of fermentation weights with which you need to be familiar.

Fermentation weights rely on weight to hold the fermented food below the brine. However, these weights are often not heavy enough to do the job, which is a drawback. For instance, when you are fermenting sauerkraut, many air bubbles are created within the jar, which causes the cabbage to expand. The weight is moved up, and the fermenting cabbage will be exposed to air. This prevents fermentation in anaerobic conditions and will prevent you from achieving the best possible results.

Fermentation gates are devices that lock into the neck of a jar and prevent the contents from moving upward. It can be a challenge to pack the jar perfectly when you use a fermentation gate. If you pack it too high, you might get brine overflow. If it is too low, the gate cannot apply force at all and won't be helpful.

Fermentation springs rely on pressure from the coiled spring made of stainless steel to push the ferment under the brine.

## Fermentation Lids

Fermentation takes place in an anaerobic environment. This means the process occurs without the presence of air. To allow this, you should ideally use a lid that will seal your jar in a way that will reduce the chance of any yeast or mold growing on the surface. You can simply use the lids that usually come with the canning jars you purchase. You can also get special fermentation lids that have a one-way valve, airlock, or water-sealed moat. There are many different kinds of fermentation lids from which you can choose.

## Fermentation Lids with No Airlock

Plastic storage caps are a better option than the metal lids on canning jars. Plastic lids don't corrode like metal ones and do a much better job. A lid with a seal will work better to keep the air out from your ferment. Lids without airlocks should not be screwed on too tightly because the active fermentation stage causes a build-up of gases and may cause the jar to explode. Silicone gaskets or lids with silicone gaskets can be used to make the jar airtight and leakproof.

## Fermentation Lids with Airlocks

Lids with an airlock may allow gases to escape but will prevent any new air from entering the jar. Many fermenting experts say that this allows a better ferment with higher levels of good bacteria. You can get these lids in stainless steel, plastic, or silicone for your jars. Some lids even have an extractor pump that will allow you to suction out air from the jar. This should be done before the fermented product is refrigerated or right after the first week of fermentation.

## Cloth Covers

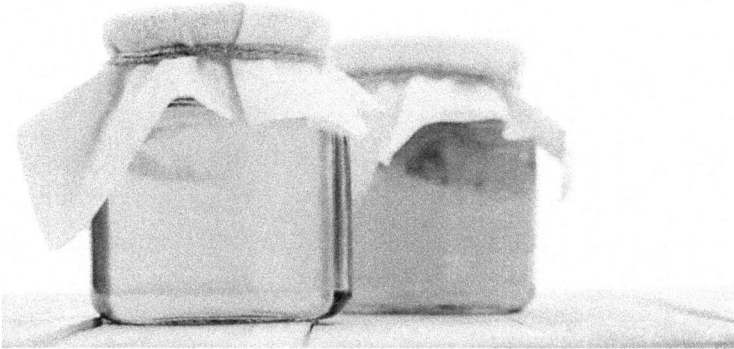

Some people choose to use cloth covers for fermenting certain foods. If you have a small container, you can use a coffee filter to cover the top and secure it with a canning lid ring or just a tight rubber band. This will keep out any pests and will let fermentation gases escape. For jars that are a little bigger, you can use a tight weave dishcloth or some butter muslin.

Secure this around the mouth of the jar with a rubber band. The advantage of using cloth covers is that you can easily taste or sneak a peek at the fermenting food whenever you want. The disadvantage is that the surface of the fermented food will likely form some mold or kahm yeast. Although this surface formation can be removed easily and is harmless, it is better to avoid this risk and use other lids. Cheesecloth is one of the best options to use as a cloth lid. It is a breathable fabric that will keep contaminants out of your jars.

### Digital Scale

Another important fermentation tool is a digital scale. Using the correct amounts of each ingredient for your fermentation recipe can make a huge difference in how it turns out. If you are making kimchi or sauerkraut, you need to measure out the right amount of salt required for fermentation. Using the correct amount of salt will ensure that the lactobacilli can do their job well. This is important for preserving the ferment safely.

When you buy a digital scale, you need to check for a few things. See if the display is clearly visible when you place a large bowl on the scale. The scale should also be capable of weighing at least ten pounds or more if you make large batches. It will also be helpful if you can get a scale that can be programmed not to shut off automatically. There are all kinds of scales available these days, and you can have your pick. Try to get one with high-precision sensors and multiple weighing modes to make your job easier.

### Water Sealed Fermentation Crocks

Quart jars are for beginners or smaller portions. Once you have enough experience, you can move on to a large crock specifically meant for fermenting larger quantities of food. Specialty crocks have a more stable environment that allows better fermentation. They come with water-sealed lids that enable fermentation gases to escape without allowing air to enter. This helps in maintaining an environment ideal for anaerobic fermentation. A 5-liter crock is usually enough for a small family. If you want to make kimchi or sauerkraut, this jar would easily pack ten pounds of cabbage. It is also not too big and can be picked up easily. A crock that is any bigger would be too heavy to move around and difficult to clean in the sink as well.

### Mineral-Rich Fermentation Salt

For sauerkraut, the cabbage is fermented in brine, which is prepared with salt. The salt pulls out water from the cabbage and other vegetables, creating an environment where gut-friendly bacteria grow and proliferate. The harmful bacteria will die in this brine. Using mineral-rich salts that retain their natural mineral profile is often a better choice. Fermentation makes the minerals bioavailable, and this is why your sauerkraut will be more nutritious.

Himalayan pink salt is a great option that is mined from deposits in the Himalayan Mountains. It contains high amounts of trace minerals, and the pink color is due to the iron oxide that is naturally present in this salt. This pink salt is dug from deep within the mountains, crystallized nearly 200 million years ago. It is not affected by any impurities and pollution from the modern world.

### Mandolin

Mandolins are stainless steel or plastic devices that are used for slicing fruits and vegetables. They have interchangeable blades depending on the kind of slicing you want to do. Blades made of surgical steel are the sharpest and best option for preparing your vegetables. Getting consistent texture and evenly sliced pieces will make your sauerkraut taste even better. When you have uneven pieces with some thick and others thin, the sauerkraut does not turn out the way it should. Making thread cuts for sauerkraut is recommended since it exposes more of the cabbage cells, releasing more lactic acid bacteria.

As long as you keep the mandolin clean, you won't have to replace or sharpen the blade very often. Mandolins are also easier to clean than most food processors.

### Redmond Real Salt

In Central Utah, there are ancient sea beds from which Real Salt is mined. You can buy this from most grocery stores or specialty health food stores. Unlike other salts, it is subtly sweet and has high amounts of trace minerals. Look for the unprocessed and unrefined kind with no additives.

### Safety Gloves

You might want to get right into it with your hands, but safety gloves might be a better option. Especially when you want to slice vegetables or fruits with tools like the mandolin, it is better to be safe than sorry. Safety gloves will protect your hands and are also comfortable enough to use while mixing. You can use your bare hands through most of the fermentation preparation process but use gloves when dealing with sharp tools or reactive ingredients.

### Kraut Pounder, Funnels

Not everyone has the hand strength required to crush the cabbage leaves thoroughly. This is where the kraut pounder comes in. Kraut pounders help you mix and pound your vegetables quickly in a large bowl, so the natural juices are released. This tool is also helpful for pressing down vegetables into a jar when the mouth isn't too wide. When your hand doesn't fit into the jar, the pounder is the easier alternative.

You can use it to pack fermented foods into small jars. This tool isn't a complete necessity since you can just use a large spoon, meat pounder, or rolling pin for the same purpose. It's always nice to have separate tools for your fermentation recipes. Getting a wide-mouth funnel will also make the packing part a little easier. This tool is helpful if you intend to use a kraut pounder but will only get in the way when you use your hands to stuff the jars.

**pH Test Strips**

# pH scale

| 0 | 1 | 2 | 3 | 4 | 5 | 6 | 7 | 8 | 9 | 10 | 11 | 12 | 13 | 14 |

**acidic**          **neutral**          **alkaline**

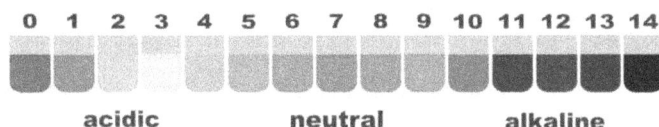

It can sometimes be hard for beginners to tell if they have a good ferment or just spoiled food. The pungent smell is not always a good indicator. In such cases, pH strips can be used to see if the ferment is safe for consumption. Buy pH strips that are in the lower range between 0.0 and 6.0. Just ladle out a little bit of your brine or any other fermented solution and dip a pH strip into it. The ferment is safe to eat if the pH level is 4.0 or lower. These strips are easy to read and can be pretty useful.

**Thermometers**

Fermentation takes place in a specific ideal temperature range. You have to check if the temperature is just right or if you have to make some adjustments to the duration of fermentation. The temperature can determine whether you need to let it ferment for a shorter or longer time. This is where a thermometer may be useful. Get a room thermometer that you can use for monitoring the humidity and temperature.

## Auto Siphon

Auto siphons will allow you to transfer liquid from one vessel to another in a sanitary way. This tool will come in handy when transferring your fermented food from a large vessel to smaller containers. It is useful when bottling something like kombucha, does not disrupt the liquid, and you don't risk contaminating it.

## Specialty Spices

Depending on what fermented dish you want to prepare, you will need to buy some ingredients. For certain dishes like kimchi, you need specialty spices. Korean red pepper powder or Gochugaru is one spice that you should purchase in bulk and keep. It adds an authentic flavor and color to kimchi and can even be used in sauerkraut. These days it is easy to buy spices online or in Asian food stores. Buy a lot so you can use it whenever you run out of kimchi. This spice is made from coarsely ground red pepper, and the texture is a mix of powder and flakes.

The flavor is more complex than your regular red pepper flakes, and it adds beautiful color to the dish. Sun-dried chili peppers will give you the best Gochugaru. You can extend the shelf life of this spice by storing it in the freezer. The amount of gochugaru you use will determine the heat in the dish.

## Bottle brush

When you are done with a batch of fermented wine, kombucha, etc., you need to clean the bottles out. Clean jars or bottles are a must when you want to ferment a new batch of food. If not, these can harbor foreign bacteria that will spoil the food and harm your gut. Get a brush with bristles that will clean the necks and corners of your containers thoroughly. Scrub them out and wash them thoroughly to prepare for the subsequent fermentation batch.

## Fish Sauce

Yet another ingredient that is a must for some fermented Asian dishes is fish sauce. It is especially important for preparing kimchi. Don't worry about getting a fishy taste or smell in the dish because it goes away once the fermentation happens. Instead, it will add a richness that will make your kimchi more authentic. Fish sauce will also be useful in cooking other Asian dishes at home, so you can get a bigger bottle and store it in the fridge.

## Refractometer

A refractometer with Auto Thermal Compensation (ATC) is not essential, and not everyone uses one, but if you are serious about fermenting foods, this might be useful. This tool will help you identify components and levels of ingredients in your fermentation solutions. This will allow you to calculate the alcohol percentage of a beverage. For instance, you can read sugar levels when you make drinks like tepache, a fermented drink made from pineapple. It will also be helpful when making kombucha, beer, wine, etc.

## Saniclean

When it comes to food, keeping things clean and hygienic is very important. This is more so when fermenting foods since the kitchen is always exposed to bacteria and yeast. The counter on which you ferment should be extremely clean. Saniclean is one of the best food-safe and affordable disinfectants out there. Saniclean is in line with industry standards, and you can even wash your utensils with a diluted solution. This will ensure that all your counters and utensils are completely clean and safe for storing or fermenting foods.

# Starter Cultures

Now let's talk a little more about starter cultures. You have to know when you need to use starters, when you don't and why whey is unnecessary.

Fungi and bacteria play a crucial role in the process of fermentation. Fungi usually produce alcohol, while bacteria produce acids. Certain foods require their use separately, but with others, you will need a mixture of both. Fungi are used for preparing bread, cheese, and wine, while bacteria are involved in yogurt or sauerkraut preparation.

When lactic acid-producing bacteria metabolize sugars in food and convert them to lactic acid, it is called Lacto fermentation. The bacteria are isolated in milk first, and this is why they are called lactic acid-forming bacteria. Lactobacillus is found in many places and not just exclusively present in milk or other dairy products.

Lacto fermentation is used for preparing many foods like sauerkraut, kefir, yogurt, and beet kvass. Unlike ethanol fermentation, alcohol is not created with Lacto fermentation. Lactic acid bacteria are microbes that primarily consume carbohydrates that are naturally found in cucumber. This is how you prepare sour pickles.

Many beginners assume that the fermentation process to make foods like sauerkraut will require dairy products like whey. This is just a myth, and you don't need whey at all. Whey was popularly used before for preparing fermented vegetables, but this method is not as popular now. The bacteria that cause lactic acid fermentation are present everywhere, from your skin to your food and even on your countertops. This is why it is not necessary to inoculate foods with starters like whey. In fact, fermented foods will turn out even better without them.

## Starters Are Not Required for Most Fermented Foods

Most fermented vegetable recipes don't require the use of starter culture and were traditionally prepared without one. Salting the vegetables will do the same job, and you can just pack them into your fermentation containers for the native bacteria to do their job. This will allow the vegetables to naturally sour and be preserved without needing any starter. You can store them for a long time with salt once they are fermented. Traditionally, vegetables were fermented without any starter culture, and this method is called wild fermentation. It involves using wild strains of bacteria for fermentation and not domesticated strains found in starter cultures.

Some fermented preparations require a starter culture, while others do not. Fermented vegetables like kimchi, sauerkraut, sour pickles, sauerruben, etc., do not need starter cultures. You also don't need them for preserving limes, lemons, or bonny clabber.

Certain foods require a starter to ensure that they can be safely consumed and have consistent texture and flavor results. Sourdough bread is one example that requires a starter. You can make this starter with wild fermentation or get a starter from another baker. A mother culture has to be used if you want Jun tea or Kombucha to be brewed properly. Water kefir grains are needed for preparing water kefir. Yogurt preparation requires a starter culture as well. Homemade sodas like probiotic lemonade and root beer depend on starter cultures.

For making kombucha, you need to use sweetened black tea. If this tea is left in a container on some shelf, it won't turn sour on its own and is likely to mold. Once you add a mother culture to the tea, the yeast and bacterial strains from the culture will consume the sugar in the tea and turn it into acids. This will give the kombucha a pleasantly tart flavor and added B vitamins.

If you leave raw milk in its own container, it will turn sour, and a bonny clabber will be formed. This is a wild-fermented product that has an inconsistent flavor and texture in each batch. If you want consistent results from your raw milk, use a yogurt starter culture. This will allow you to make batches of Bulgarian-style yogurt that is sweet and tart or villi yogurt that is ropy and viscous. Using a starter gives you the ability to make consistent batches of fermented food.

Then there are fermented foods that don't require a starter but benefit from the use of starter culture. This means that you get better results by using the starter rather than by depending on wild fermentation. These are usually foods that only ferment for a short time, like high sugar fruits or condiments.

Adding a starter culture to foods fermenting for short durations kickstarts the process and gives you reliable results. If you want to make homemade fermented condiments like mustard or ketchup, a few days of fermentation will give you maximum flavor. It is challenging to keep these submerged in a brine solution since they are pastes. They remain exposed to oxygen and tend to get contaminated by mold. When the starter culture is inoculated, it shortens the time needed and reduces the chances of mold contamination.

Fruits with high amounts of sugar usually turn alcoholic if they are fermented for a long time. If you don't want an alcoholic fermentation and just want to prepare a relish, condiment, or sauce, the fermentation time needs to be shorter. This can be achieved by introducing a starter culture. It will speed up the process and give you a rich fermented product with many beneficial bacteria without being alcoholic. Certain fermented foods like beet kvass have been traditionally prepared using starter cultures. The use of a starter is a choice and not a necessity. Following the traditional way of using a starter, in this case, will give you better results.

## Which Starter Do You Use?

Some popular fermentation guides recommend the use of whey in preparing most fermented foods. This is why beginners tend to use this as a starter for all their fermented food recipes. They use whey drawn from clabbering raw milk or making yogurt as a starter. This is a good option since it is abundant and inexpensive. You can use most liquids rich in beneficial bacteria as a starter culture. You can also purchase a store-bought packet of starter culture if you want.

If you want to consume a particular strain of bacteria for its benefits, you need to look for a starter culture that contains those strains.

The following are some starter cultures you can try using:

- Kombucha or Jun tea
- Brine from fermenting vegetables like sauerkraut juice
- Water kefir
- Commercial packaged starter culture
- Probiotic supplements
- The whey is obtained by straining kefir, yogurt, or clabbered raw milk.

Fermented foods usually don't need a starter, but using the right equipment can make all the difference in the end. You can try a starter for the foods that call for it in the recipe. These starter cultures are easy to get, but you should only use them for fermented foods that really need them.

Once you learn the basics of fermentation, it gets easy to experiment and to prepare new fermented dishes. You can virtually ferment any fruit or vegetable you like and make sodas from juices or teas. Try the recipes in this book and learn how to make your favorite fermented foods to improve your overall health.

# Chapter 4: How to Make Kombucha

Kombucha is an incredibly healthy fermented drink that can be dated back, through China, Tibet, and Japan, at least a couple of thousand years. However, we cannot determine its exact origin. Made from sweetened tea, kombucha grew fast in popularity, spreading through Russia, the USA, and Europe.

Most standard fizzy drinks you buy these days are made from sugar, artificial flavoring, and carbonated water. Kombucha differs in that it is *alive* – the natural fermentation process causes the carbonation, and its flavors are also natural. Seriously, take a sip of a shop-bought fizzy drink and then a sip of kombucha – the difference is amazing, especially when you make your own kombucha.

Making kombucha is a fantastic project – you get to dabble in microbiology and produce whatever flavor you want, using ingredients of your choice. The only limit is here is your imagination.

## What Is Scoby?

Making kombucha requires scoby, an acronym for Symbiotic Culture of Bacteria and Yeast. Scoby is shaped like a disk, a necessary culture to help the fermentation process convert the sweet tea into the kombucha. Typically, scoby floats on the top of the batch, but don't panic if yours should sink! It is still active and doing its job.

Where do you get this scoby? If you've got friends already making kombucha, the easiest way is to ask if you can have some scoby. If not, you can purchase it online or make your own. I've provided a step-by-step guide on making your own scoby below – try it; it's all part of the process.

If you purchase your scoby or get it from a friend, it will have liquid with it, which goes into your first batch. You must make sure this liquid goes in because it has large amounts of yeast and bacteria and a great deal of acid that creates the proper environment for subsequent batches.

Every scoby is different and is a result of the environment in which it was created. It contains many different yeasts that go far beyond your standard Saccharomyces cerevisiae – a beer and bread fermenter. These yeasts include Brettanomyces bruxellensis and Schizosaccharomyces pombe (also called "fission yeast), along with lots of bacteria species responsible for limiting alcohol content and increasing acidity.

# Equipment

You don't need to purchase expensive equipment to make kombucha. The chances are you already have some of what you need. The important thing is to use glass jars or ceramic if its glaze is food-grade, but *not metal or plastic*. Wide-mouthed jars are much better as the larger surface area ensures a faster fermentation process.

### Important Considerations

• Use de-chlorinated water because chlorine negatively affects the microbes we want to grow. Tap water is chlorinated, and a standard water filter will not receive the chlorine either. Boil and cool the water or leave it in a bowl overnight so the chlorine dissipates.

• Use black tea as it has all the nutrients required by the scoby. However, you may prefer a mixture of green and black or white and black tea; it's entirely up to you. Use loose tea or tea bags and avoid using tea like Earl Gray, which has added oils. You can also use plant-based tea, such as chamomile, raspberry leaf, nettle, rooibos, etc. However, try to make at least a quarter of the tea black in every batch or couple of batches. Lastly, use organic tea where you can.

• Try to use ordinary cane sugar. You can use less refined sugars, but they will change the flavor. You cannot omit the sugar because it feeds the bacteria and yeast to reproduce, creates new scobies, and processes the tea into carbonation, vitamins, and acids. Once fermentation is complete, most of the remaining sugar has been broken down into glucose and fructose. The bacteria transform it into healthy acids, and then the enzymes get to work, breaking the sugars down further. If you don't use enough sugar, your scoby will starve. Do not use honey as it contains different bacteria cells and yeasts, and do not use sugar substitutes or artificial sugars, as they won't feed the yeast or bacteria.

• When you begin your second or subsequent batches of kombucha, make sure you use starter liquid taken from the previous batch – this should be 10% of the new batch and is used to lower the tea's pH. Typically, kombucha has a pH of 3.5 to 2.5, whereas tap water is 7. Lower pH numbers indicate acidity, but you don't have to measure it – you'll taste it. The starter liquid is essential to protect the tea from kahm yeast, mold, or other harmful microorganisms.

All the equipment should be clean and dry.

• 1 to 2 glass jars (2-quart glass jar or 2 one-quart glass jars) or bigger if required, with airtight lids
• Stock pot
• Glass bottles or jars with plastic lid for storage
• Tightly woven cloth or lint-free cloth
• Funnel
• Strainer
• Rubber band
• Container to keep Scoby (symbiotic culture of bacteria and yeast) which is used for fermentation
• Kombucha and Scoby

Makes: 6 cups

Preparation time: 10 minutes

Fermenting time: 2-4 weeks

**Ingredients:**

**For Scoby:**

• 2 cups water
• 4 tablespoons granulated or raw sugar

- 2 tablespoons unflavored loose leaf black tea or 4 black tea bags
- 2 bottles (16 ounces each) unflavored, raw, unpasteurized, good quality kombucha with sediment

**For Kombucha:**

- •6 cups water
- •6 tablespoons granulated or raw sugar
- •4 tablespoons loose-leaf black tea leaves or 8 black tea bags
- •1 cup kombucha starter tea
- •1 scoby for every jar (¼ to ½ inch thick)

**Directions:**

**To Make Scoby:**

1. Boil water in a stockpot. Turn off the heat. Drop the tea bags or tea leaves into the water. Let it brew for 5 to 10 minutes. Remove the tea bags or strain the tea into a jar. Add sugar and stir until sugar dissolves completely.

2. Set aside to cool completely. Add kombucha with the sediment and mix well.

3. Keep the jar covered with cloth and tighten with a rubber band. Place it in an area without direct sunlight, at a temperature between 75° and 80°.

4. Slowly, in a few days, scoby will start forming on top of the liquid. You may find string-like things or some dots of mass. It will slowly grow into one big mass. This can take anywhere between 2 to 4 weeks until the scoby is at least ¼ inch thick.

5. The scoby can be used now.

6. The liquid remaining in the jar is the starter tea you can use to make kombucha.

## To Make Kombucha:

1.      Boil water in a stockpot. Turn off the heat. Drop the tea bags or tea leaves into the water. Let it brew for 5 to 10 minutes. Remove the tea bags or strain the tea into a jar. Add sugar and stir until sugar dissolves completely.

2.      Set aside to cool completely. Add kombucha with the sediment and mix well.

## For the First Fermentation:

1.Place scoby in the jar, making sure your hands are clean before adding scoby.

2.Keep the jar covered with cloth and fasten with a rubber band. Place it in an area without direct sunlight, at a temperature between 75° and 80°.

3.Let it ferment for 3 - 4 days. Start tasting it after 3 to 4 days. Keep an eye out for the scoby. New scoby will begin to form on the surface of the kombucha. It should be cream-colored. It generally tends to form on top of the old scoby.

4.If you think it is not good enough, ferment it for longer, around 7 to 10 days. When you find the taste pleasant, your kombucha is ready. It should have a sweet, though pungent (strong).

5.When the desired taste is achieved, you need to start with the second fermentation.

## For the Second Fermentation (Carbonation):

1. Clean your hands and take out the scoby from the jar. Keep the scoby in a clean container. If you are going to brew more kombucha soon (in a couple of days), place the scoby at a temperature between 75° and 80°.

2. If you are going to brew after 2 to 3 weeks, place it in a glass jar or airtight container Ziploc bag in the fridge. Pour some of the kombucha so it's immersed in the kombucha. Place one scoby per jar. Place it in the fridge. Do not keep it for longer than three months.

3. Stir the prepared kombucha and retain about a cup of kombucha to make a new batch of kombucha.

4. Pour the remaining kombucha into storage bottles using the funnel. Do not fill right up to the top. Leave neck space of at least 2 inches.

5. The flavorings can be added now (below are some flavoring options, but you can make your own flavorings). For this much quantity of kombucha, use about ¼ to ½ cup fresh fruit juice or fresh fruit puree, or some chopped fruit. You can also add 2 - 4 tablespoons of fresh herbs. If you are using chopped fruit, make sure the fruits are immersed in water as they may end up getting moldy if they float on top. The choice is ultimately yours to use chopped fruit, puree, or juice. You can add any other spices or flavorings of your choice. After adding flavorings, stir well.

6. Fasten the lid and keep it in a place with no direct sunlight for about 2 to 3 days. You can ferment it for longer if desired. Make sure to open the bottle once daily, to remove extra carbonation.

7. When you get the desired taste, place the bottles in the fridge until use. Below are some flavor options.

## Ideas for Flavored Kombucha

Now for the flavoring. Your options are endless, and you can use all different vegetables, fruits, and herbs, frozen, fresh, dried, or even juiced. How much you use depends on whether you want a subtle flavor or something more intense, but 5 to 10% is normally sufficient if using fresh fruit. That equates to 2 to 3 tablespoons per liter.

The easiest way to do it is to cut your fruit, veg or herbs into small chunks and add them to an empty bottle. Then fill the bottle with kombucha, but be sure to leave four fingers of space at the top because carbon dioxide will build up - if you don't leave the space, the whole lot will explode. Leave it at room temperature for 24 hours to allow the yeast to turn some of the sugars into carbon dioxide and then place it in the refrigerator. This will stop the entire process and prevent the bacteria from creating even more acid.

## Some flavor ideas:

You can use pretty much any fruit you like, either on its own or a few combined.

• **Berries** - a mixture of berries, such as blackberries, strawberries, and blueberries,

• **Stone fruits** - plums, peaches, and cherries. These will give your kombucha a stunning flavor and beautiful color.

• **Citrus fruits** – use chunks of fruit, the zest, or the juice. If you use the zest, make sure the fruit has not been waxed.

• **Exotic fruit** – such as goji berries, cranberries, figs, and dates. Do not use raisins or any oil-soaked fruit, or apricots, and any other fruit containing sulfur dioxide, as this can make your kombucha taste of rotten eggs.

• **Frozen fruit** –the ice crystals created during the freezing process break the fruit's cell structure down, which means the kombucha benefits from more flavor and color. However, you can also use puree or juice.

• **Herbs** – lemon balm, mint, lavender, and other herbs work well on their own or with fruit, such as strawberries paired with thyme, mint, and apple, raspberries with basil, and so on.

• **Spices** – mild spices can be used alone or blended or with a fruit pairing. You can use burdock, turmeric, allspice, cloves, coriander, star anise, peppercorn, cinnamon, cardamom, licorice, or juniper, to name a few. Hot spices you can use include ginger, jalapeno, or cayenne.

• **Vegetables** – carrot, cucumber, and beetroot provide lovely flavors, while garlic provides a kick and pairs well with lemon. You can even use mushrooms.

- **Other** – you can try cacao powder, brewed coffee, maca powder, tamarind, coconut water, rose petals, rosehips, and so on.

Here are some recipes you can try out:

**(for about 6 cups prepared kombucha)**

You can puree, juice, or finely chop fruits and add them to the bottles or jars

### Watermelon

Ingredients:

- 6 – 8 small watermelon cubes, deseeded

### Lime and Lemon

Ingredients:

- 3 – 4 teaspoons lime juice
- 3 – 4 tablespoons lemon juice
- 2 thin ginger slices
- 2 thin lemon slices

### Blueberry Ginger

Ingredients:

- 6 – 7 peeled, thinly sliced ginger, pricked with a fork
- A handful of blueberries, pricked with a fork

### Blackberry Mango

Ingredients:

- 4 – 5 small mango cubes (about ½ inch cubes)
- A small handful of blackberries, pricked with a fork

## Lemon Ginger & Honey

**Ingredients:**

- 4 - 5 tablespoons lemon juice
- 1 tablespoon honey
- 3-inch piece of ginger, peeled and grated

# Chapter 5: How to Make Sourdough Bread

Sourdough bread has recently risen in popularity - if you'll pardon the pun - and many think it is a far tastier bread than standard, not to mention healthier. Some even go so far as to say it is much easier to digest and won't send your blood sugar spiking. But, what is it, and how is it so different from conventional bread?

Sourdough is one of the most ancient forms of grain fermentation, believed to have begun around 1500 BC in Egypt and remaining as the primary method of leavening bread until a few centuries ago, when baker's yeast came into the picture.

Leavened bread rises as a result of gas produced while the grain is fermenting. These days, commercial baker's yeast is used in most leavened bread, but traditional methods still use two things found naturally in flour - lactic acid and wild yeast.

Wild yeast resists acid better than baker's yeast, and this is why it works well with the bacteria producing the lactic acid to help the bread dough rise. You will also find lactic acid in kefir, sauerkraut, yogurt, kimchi, and pickles, all the best-fermented foods on the planet.

Sourdough bread requires a "starter," a mixture of lactic acid bacteria, wild yeast, water, and flour. This mixture ferments the sugars present in the dough, which helps it rise and gives it its unique taste. Also, sourdough bread takes longer to ferment and rise than conventional bread, giving it a specific texture.

You can buy sourdough bread in many stores these days, but the traditional methods are not used to make it, and they are nowhere near as healthy as what you make at home. So don't do things the quick way - make your own; I promise you won't regret it.

Let's look at how the starter and sourdough bread are made.

Weigh all the ingredients on a weighing scale, including the water. The containers used should be made of glass or plastic (make sure it is not made of any metals) and should be clean and dry.

**Equipment Required:**

There are different methods of baking, so all these may not be needed. Some of these items are used in each recipe.

- Oven
- Dutch oven
- Mixing bowl
- Glass jar
- Kitchen towels

- Rubber bands
- Roasting pan
- Baking stone
- Bench scraper

# Sourdough Starter

It takes a minimum of five days to make the starter, depending on the temperature of your kitchen. It can take up to seven days. So you need to start making the starter at least 5 – 7 days before making the bread. If it's cold out, it will take around seven days. If it's warm out, it will take about five days.

### Feeding Your Starter

Everyone who bakes sourdough bread will find their own method of feeding their starter, but this is the basic method.

- Pour around half the culture off, and then add equal weights of water and flour to the remaining starter.

- Whisk thoroughly with a fork until there are no more lumps

- Leave it at room temperature or somewhere warm, at about 75 to 80°F, until it begins bubbling and becomes active.

You will know it is ready when it bubbles and has expanded to double its size. This may be 2 to 12 hours, depending on the temperature – warmer temperatures are better – and also depends on your starter's condition. The most important thing is to be patient.

If you are still not sure your starter is ready, drop a teaspoon of it into water. If it floats, it's ready. If it sinks, it needs feeding again.

Here's how to make it.

Makes: About 1 ¼ cups of starter

**Ingredients:**

For the first day:

- 1.4 ounces whole-wheat flour or rye flour
- 1.4 ounces all-purpose flour
- 1.4 ounces water

For each following day:

- 1.4 ounces whole-wheat flour or rye flour
- 1.4 ounces all-purpose flour
- 1.4 ounces water

**Directions:**

**First day:**

1. Step 1: Weigh the ingredients for the first day and add them into a glass jar. If you want to make a rye sourdough starter, use rye flour instead of whole-wheat flour. Stir constantly for a few minutes until well combined. The mixture will be thick and sticky.

2. Step 2: Cover the container loosely with a plastic wrap or clean kitchen towel. If you are using a kitchen towel, put a rubber band around the container to keep it tight. Place at constant room temperature at about 75° F to 78° F. You can keep it on top of your fridge. Make sure the jar isn't exposed to direct sunlight.

**Second Day:**

1. Step 3: Make sure you feed the starter around the same time every day.

2. Step 4: After 24 hours, a few bubbles may be visible at some places on the dough, and it shows the presence of wild yeast in the starter. You should be able to get a fresh, mild, and sweet smell. If the bubbles are not visible, that is okay. It may be because of the temperature. It takes longer in cold weather.

3. Step 5: You have to activate the starter (also called feeding the starter): For this, retain about 1.4 ounces (3 tablespoons) of the starter in the container and discard the rest.

4. Step 6: Weigh the other ingredients for each following day, i.e., whole-wheat flour, water, and all-purpose flour. Add the weighed ingredients into the container with the starter and stir until well combined. Keep the jar covered loosely with plastic wrap or a kitchen towel.

**Third Day:**

1. More bubbles should be visible all over the starter mixture.

2. Try stirring the starter, you can hear tiny bubbles popping, and the batter will be thick. The batter will smell sour and stale. Repeat steps 5 - 6.

**Fourth Day:**

1. Many more bubbles should be visible all over the starter mixture.

2. When you stir the starter, the batter will be looser to touch, and the smell will be more pungent and sourer than day 3.

Repeat steps 5 - 6.

**Fifth Day:**

1. The starter will be filled with bubbles, and it will look frothy. The dough should be nearly twice the size of the previous day.

2. The dough will be looser to touch compared to the previous day. Repeat steps 5 - 6.

**Sixth Day:**

1. The starter is now ripe and can be used to make sourdough bread.

2. To check for ripeness, drop a tablespoon of the starter in a bowl of lukewarm water. If the starter floats, it is ripe and can be used to make sourdough bread. If it does not float, you need to feed the starter again. Repeat steps 5 - 6.

## To Maintain the Starter:

1. If you are not making the sourdough bread on the 6th day and you want to make it in the next 2 - 3 days, you need to maintain the starter. Repeat steps 5 - 6 daily until you make the sourdough bread.

2. If you want to use the starter after 2 - 3 weeks, store the jar in the fridge (after covering with cling wrap loosely) and feed the starter once in 6 - 7 days (Repeat steps 5 - 6).

## To Dry the Starter:

If you want to store the starter for a longer time, you need to dry the starter:

1. Spread the starter on a Silpat and allow it to dry naturally.

2. After it dries, crumble into smaller pieces.

3. Transfer into an airtight container. It can last for months. Place it at room temperature in a dry area.

## To Activate the Dry Starter:

1.    Mix dry starter and some water in a bowl. Cover it loosely and set it aside for 6 - 12 hours.

2.    Start feeding the starter daily (Repeat steps 5 - 6) until the starter is ripe.

Note: If you live in a warm place, you have to feed the starter twice a day, every 12 hours. Also, instead of discarding the starter, you can use it for other recipes like pancakes, etc.

# Sourdough Bread

## Ingredients:

- 1 cup + 1 tbsp. water
- ¾ cup bubbly, active sourdough starter
- 25 g olive oil
- 2 ¼ cups bread flour
- ½ tbsp. fine sea salt

## Directions:

1. Whisk the water, starter, and olive oil in a bowl using a fork.

2. Add the flour and salt and use your hands to squish it together until the flour has been completely absorbed. You should have a dry, shaggy, rough dough.

3. Cover it with plastic wrap, a damp kitchen town, or wax wrap, and leave it to autolyze (rest) for about half an hour.

4. Work the dough into a rough ball in the bowl.

5. Cover it and leave it at room temperature, around 68 to 70°F, and leave it to rise. It will take up to 12 hours and is ready when it is twice the size and not dense anymore. It will take three to four hours in warmer temperatures, while it will take 10 to 12 hours in colder temperatures. However, *don't clock-watch* - your dough is ready when it has properly risen.

6. About half an hour into the rising session, you can stretch and fold the dough if you want. This process gives it more strength, height, and better structure - but only do it if you want to.

7. Once the dough has risen, tip it onto a lightly floured cutting board.

8. Divide it in half using a sharp knife or dough cutter if you are making two loaves, or leave it as is if you only want one.

9. Fold the dough into the center, turn it slightly and fold the next bit over. Repeat for an entire circle.

10. Once your dough is shaped, it must be left to rise again, and this is done in the Dutch oven you will cook the bread in.

11. Line the Dutch oven pot with non-stick parchment paper or a generous cornmeal coating and place the dough in it. Alternatively, use an 8-inch bowl or a proofing basket lined with cloth - that way, the dough is contained and holds the shape.

12. This time, we are only leaving for between 30 minutes and an hour - when it is puffy and not dense, it is ready - don't wait for it to double in size (it won't.)

13. In the last half of the second rise, preheat the oven to 450°F

14. Once the second rise is done, slash a 2 to 3 inch cut along the center of the dough using a paring knife or a small, serrated knife - this will let the steam out of the bread and let the dough expand while baking.

15. Time to bake - we use Dutch ovens because they keep the moisture and heat trapped in, providing the artisan style we've come to know and love. Steam also plays an important role in opening the bread up while baking, and Dutch ovens control this very well. That said, you can use any pot, so long as it is oven safe up to 450°F, including the handles and lid.

16. Place the lid on the pot and turn the temperature down to 400°F. Bake the bread in the center of the oven for about 20 minutes.

17. Remove the lid, and your bread should look shiny and pale

18. Leaving the bread uncovered, bake for about 40 minutes or until it is a deep gold-brown color. The internal temperature should be 205 to 210°F. If you want a crisp crust, crack the over door open slightly during the final 10

minutes of cooking time or turn the bread out and bake it on the wire rack.

19. Turn the bread out onto a wire rack and leave it for at least one hour or until cool before you slice it. *Patience is required here* – if you cut it too soon, it will be gummy.

# Blueberry Sourdough Muffins

Makes: 24

## Ingredients:

- 2 cups unbleached all-purpose flour
- 1 ½ teaspoons salt
- 3 teaspoons ground cinnamon
- 2 cups whole-grain yellow cornmeal
- 2 teaspoons baking soda
- 1 cup maple syrup or molasses or honey
- Coarse sugar to sprinkle
- 2 cups sourdough starter, ripe or discard
- 2 large eggs
- ½ cup milk
- ½ cup melted butter or vegetable oil
- 4 cups blueberries, fresh or frozen

## Directions:

1. As you preheat your oven to 425°F, take two muffin pans, 12 counts each, and spray cooking spray into the cups. Place disposable liners in the cups as well.

2. Combine flour, salt, cinnamon, cornmeal, and baking soda in a bowl.

3. Place starter, eggs, maple syrup, butter, and milk in another bowl and beat with an electric hand mixer until well combined.

4. Pour the egg mixture into the bowl of the flour mixture and beat until just combined, making sure not to overbeat.

5. Add blueberries and fold gently. Do not thaw the blueberries if you are using frozen blueberries.

6. Pour the batter into the muffin cups. Fill up to 2/3.

7. Sprinkle coarse sugar on top.

8. Put the muffin pans in the oven for baking and bake for 25 minutes. To check if the muffins are done, insert a toothpick in the center of a muffin and pull it out. If you find that some particles are stuck on it, then you need to bake for another 5 - 7 minutes.

9. Take out the muffin pans from the oven and let them cool in the pan for 5 to 6 minutes.

10. Remove the muffins from the pan and cool on a cooling rack.

11. Store in an airtight container in the fridge. It can last for 6 - 7 days. You can wrap individual muffins in cling wrap and freeze them.

12. Warm slightly in the microwave and serve.

# Double Chocolate Sourdough Bread

Instead of throwing off sourdough discard, you can use it in making other recipes like pancakes, double chocolate sourdough bread, scones, granola bars, etc.

Makes: 2 loaves

**Ingredients:**

- 3 cups all-purpose flour
- 1 teaspoon salt
- 1 teaspoon baking soda
- 1 teaspoon baking powder
- 1 cup cocoa powder, unsweetened
- 12 tablespoons butter, softened
- 4 eggs
- ½ cup chocolate chips
- 2 cups sourdough starter discard
- 1 ½ cups granulated sugar

**Directions:**

1.      If you do not have 2 cups of sourdough starter, discard, add some milk to make it 2 cups, and stir.

2.      Preheat your oven to 350°F. Take two loaf pans of 9 x 5 inches each and spray some cooking spray in it.

3.      Place butter and sugar in a mixing bowl. Set the electric hand mixer on medium speed and beat until creamy.

4.      Add eggs, one at a time, and beat well each time.

5.      Mix all dry ingredients in another bowl, i.e., cocoa powder, all-purpose flour, baking powder, and baking soda.

6.      Set the mixer on low speed. Add 1/3 cup mixture of dry ingredients at a time along with ¼ cup sourdough starter, discard and beat until just incorporated each time.

7.  Divide the batter into the loaf pans. Sprinkle chocolate chips on top. Press lightly to adhere. Place loaf pans in the oven and bake for around 45 minutes. To check if the bread is done, insert a toothpick in the center of the loaf and remove it. If you find any particles stuck on it, bake for another 5 - 10 minutes.

8.  Cool for some time before slicing.

# Troubleshooting Tips

Sourdough is sometimes quite daunting, even if you are experienced. This is because there is so much involved in it, and you are not expected to get it right on your first go - or even the next few. Here, we'll talk about some of the problems you might experience along the way and how to fix them.

### Sourdough Starter

Because the starter is a fermented culture, bringing it to life is not a quick job. While you may see bubbles in the first few days, it isn't unusual for it to go flat a week after you created it. Don't be disheartened - it does take time to get it right.

One of the main reasons this might happen is because your ambient room temperature is not correct. Sourdough starter is a live culture, and it requires the right temperature. Too cool, and the starter is sluggish. Too warm, and it could be overactive and not such a sour flavor.

Test your fed starter in several spots around the house until you find where it is happiest. You will know this because it will rise, fluffy, light, and bubbly, with a melted marshmallow-like texture, within 5 to 8 hours of you feeding it.

### Slow-Rising Dough

If your dough isn't rising as fast as it should be, it could be down to two things. The first is the temperature. If you have a cool or drafty house, the dough won't rise as fast as in a warm, draft-free area.

The second reason is down to the dough additions. Your bread will not rise so fast if you use eggs, butter, milk, or a vegan counterpart.

First, ensure your dough is in a warm, not hot, spot, with no drafts and a steady temperature. If you make additions to your dough, make sure they are at room temperature before you add them – if you use them straight from the refrigerator, they will cool the dough temperature and slow down the rising time.

### Proofing

Proofing refers to how long the dough rises before it is baked.

If you don't give your dough enough time to rise, your loaf will be under-proofed. While under-proofed dough can rise perfectly well, you may get a tight crumb rather than an airy, open one. It may also be dense and gummy inside when you slice the bread, and you risk large air pockets in the baked loaf. The only way to fix this is to let the dough proof for longer.

If you leave your dough to rise for too long, it becomes over-proofed. This results in the dough being a large puffy ball, and it won't rise when it bakes. Once baked, the crust will be pale, and it will have an unpleasant over-sour taste. To fix this, reduce the rising time by a minimum of an hour.

### Stickiness/Sticking

You can't get away from this – the sourdough dough is very sticky. The best way to handle it is to wet your hands lightly with water rather than using flour. If your loaves stick to the pot after shaping, use regular flour, rice flour, or corn flour to dust the pot first, or line it with a clean kitchen towel. When you remove it before baking, tap the excess flour out of the pot but do NOT wash it. Store it somewhere cool and dry, covered to keep it dust-free. Over time, the flour residue will build up lightly, helping reduce sticking.

### Scoring/Slashing

Are you struggling to get a nice cut on your loaf? There are three main reasons why this might happen:

Your bread's outer surface is slack and didn't get enough tension when you shaped it. You will know if this is the reason because your knife blade will feel like it is dragging rather than slicing cleanly through the dough.

You are using a blunt knife blade. Make sure you use a sharp blade and, if unsure, choose a different knife before you start.

Your cut wasn't deep enough. You should be able to score the dough cleanly without the dough trying to reattach itself.

### • Your Bread Bursts Through the Score

This could happen if your dough were over-proofed, and the only way to prevent it is to reduce how long the dough is bulk-fermented.

### • Crust Problems

There are a couple of problems you may encounter with your crust. First, it may be too dark or too light. The easiest way to fix this is to adjust your baking time – longer if it is pale, shorter if too dark. Keep the Dutch oven pot uncovered.

Second, the base of your loaf may be thick, dark, and tough to slice. This happens to experienced bakers as well as beginners, and one way to prevent it from happening is to place a metal baking sheet or pizza stone on the rack underneath the oven. This will absorb heat and stop your bread base from getting tough and dark.

# Chapter 6: Kimchi Basics

Kimchi is a delicious Korean dish of fermented vegetables. While there are hundreds of different types of kimchi, the most common one is Napa cabbage kimchi. Like most fermented foods, like yogurt, sauerkraut, or wine, kimchi results from a special fermentation process. The bacteria responsible for it can be found everywhere – in the air, on your body, in vegetable skins, not to mention mammal milk so, if you were breastfed as a child, you received some of that beneficial, healthy bacteria.

So, what is this bacteria?

It's good old-fashioned lactic acid bacteria, which is why the special fermentation is called Lacto-fermentation. The bacteria breaks the large flavor compounds down during the fermentation process, which refines the flavor molecules we can taste.

# How Does This Happen?

Lacto-fermentation turns vegetables into kimchi by metabolizing the sugars and carbohydrates in the vegetables into lactic acid. This process gives fermented food a sour taste and an increased acidity level, which, in turn, ensures they are safe to eat.

You might think this is much the same as what causes food to rot, so what is the difference? We can think of the difference between fermentation and rotting as an analogy between two parties.

The rotting party is where everyone can get it – the fungi and the bacteria, the safe and unsafe, the destructive and the flavor-enhancing. The fermentation party has a bouncer that keeps the unwanted "guests" out, only allowing the preferable guests in to make the party go with a bang.

Keeping this firmly in mind, the fermentation process is broken down into three separate stages:

### 1. The Bouncer – Brine

The first stage of the Lacto-fermentation process is to submerge the vegetables in a brine solution. This is the bouncer, the part that keeps the harmful pathogens out, like Salmonella – these pathogens cannot stand salt because the salt gets in through the cell walls and kills the pathogen. But lactic-acid bacteria is tough, and it survives the salt.

Lactic acid bacteria are anaerobic too, and they can survive without oxygen. When you submerge your vegetables in a brine solution, all the pathogens that love oxygen are eliminated, ensuring they can't spoil the party and make the preferred guests moldy, not safe to eat.

## 2. The Acid High

As the lactic-acid bacteria settles into the brine, it begins to weave its spells, consuming the carbohydrates and sugar in the vegetables, resulting in the lactic acid. This acid reduces the ferment's pH value, creating an extremely hostile environment, preventing further pathogens from growing, such as botulism (c. botulinum).

Aside from lactic acid, Lactic acid bacteria produces a second by-product, $CO_2$, better known as carbon dioxide. This is what gives your kimchi its pop when the jar is first opened and gives it a fizzy kick. $CO_2$ creates a buildup of pressure in your jar, so you must 'burp' the kimchi now and again to stop leakage. Just take off the lid for a second and then replace it.

## 3. The After-Party

Kimchi doesn't go bad because the fermentation process has broken down the minerals and nutrients, allowing our bodies to absorb them much better. The lactic acid bacteria carries on metabolizing the sugar until it's all gone and, at that point, the kimchi will become vinegar – hint, it can take years! Keep your kimchi in the refrigerator, as this will slow the process. You can use old kimchi in stews and soups, and the juice works well in a Caesar cocktail!

# Here's how to make basic cabbage kimchi:

**Equipment Required:**

- Large colander
- 2 large bowls or pots
- Large glass jar
- Gloves
- Fermentation weights

## Traditional Kimchi

Makes: About 1 ½ quart

**Ingredients:**

- 2 medium heads Chinese Napa cabbage
- Filtered water (non-chlorinated), as required
- 2 teaspoons grated ginger
- 4 to 6 tablespoons fish sauce
- 16 ounces Korean radish or daikon, and cut into matchsticks
- ½ cup kosher salt or sea salt
- 3 tablespoons grated garlic
- 2 teaspoons sugar
- 2 to 10 tablespoons Gochugaru (Korean red pepper flakes) or as per your taste
- 8 scallions, trimmed, cut into 1-inch pieces

**Directions:**

1. Cut the cabbage in half, halfway through with a knife, starting from the stem side. Separate the two halves with your hands. Do this with both the cabbages.

2. Similarly, cut each half into 2, halfway through with a knife. Separate each into 2 parts with your hands. Discard the core.

3. Now, cut cabbage into about 2-inch cubes.

4. Place the cabbage in a large bowl.

5. Sprinkle salt over the cabbage.

6. Using your hands, mix the salt into the cabbage, massaging the cabbage until it softens a bit.

7. Add water to cover the cabbage.

8. Place a weighted plate over the cabbage to keep it submerged in the solution.

9. Keep aside for about 1 to 2 hours. Place the colander over a bowl and drain the cabbage. Set aside the brine.

10. Rinse the cabbage thrice with cold water. Let the cabbage remain in the colander after the third rinse for 20 – 30 minutes.

11. Meanwhile, combine ginger, garlic, fish sauce, and sugar in a bowl. Stir until sugar dissolves completely.

12. Add red pepper flakes and stir until well combined. This is the seasoning mix.

13. Now wear gloves.

14. Combine radish, cabbage, and scallions in a large bowl and mix well. Add seasoning mix and mix well using your hands. Taste and add more salt if required. The mixture should be salty.

15. Transfer the kimchi into a large glass jar. Pour some retained brine into the jar and press the vegetable mixture, so the brine rises above the vegetable. If the brine does not rise, add some more brine. You should leave at least an inch of headspace on top of the jar.

16. Close the jar and place it on your countertop for 1 – 2 days, depending on the fermentation. If you are happy with the fermentation after a day, store the jar in the fridge, or you can ferment it for another before placing it in the fridge.

17. It should be ready to eat after 7 - 8 days but tastes better after 15 - 20 days. It can last for about 3 - 5 months.

18. When you see fizzing or lots of bubbles, it is time to discard the kimchi.

Don't forget - red pepper flakes are a traditional ingredient in cabbage kimchi, but make sure you only add to your taste - too much and you won't enjoy it; too little, and you won't taste it.

# Fruit Kimchi

Makes: 1 jar

## Ingredients:

- ½ fresh pineapple, peeled, cored, cut into bite-size cubes
- 4 pears, cored, chopped, cut into bite-size cubes
- 2 small bunches of grapes, stemmed, halved if desired
- 2 apples peeled, cored, cut into bite-size cubes
- 4 plums, pitted, cut into bite-size cubes
- Any other fruit of your choice, cut into bite-size pieces
- 1 cup cashews or any other nuts
- Juice of 2 lemons
- 2 - 4 jalapeño peppers, finely chopped
- 2 leeks or onions, finely chopped
- 5 -6 tablespoons grated ginger
- 2 - 3 tablespoons finely grated garlic
- 1 - 2 teaspoons Gochugaru (Korean red pepper flakes) or as per your taste
- ½ cup chopped cilantro
- 3 - 4 teaspoons sea salt

## Directions:

1. Combine all the fruits, nuts, lemon juice, cilantro, and spices in a large bowl.

2. Transfer into a glass jar. Press the fruits so that the liquid from the mixture rises above the fruits. If it does not, pour some water. Fasten the lid and keep it on your countertop for about two days.

3. Taste the kimchi after two days. If it is fermented to your liking, transfer it to the fridge.

# Kkakdugi (Korean Radish Kimchi)

Makes: 1 jar

**Ingredients:**

- 3.25 pounds Korean radish or daikon radish, rinsed, scrubbed, cut into ½ inch cubes
- 2 scallions, sliced into 1-inch pieces
- 2 ½ - 3 tablespoons Korean coarse salt

**For seasonings:**

- 5 - 6 tablespoons Gochugaru (Korean red pepper flakes) or as per your taste
- 1 tablespoon Korean fish sauce or to taste
- ½ teaspoon grated ginger
- 1 ½ tablespoons grated garlic
- 1 tablespoons sugar or to taste
- 1/8 cup finely chopped salted shrimp

**Directions:**

1. In a large bowl, combine ¼ cup salt and sugar. Add radish and mix well. Set aside on your countertop for an hour.

2. Place radishes in a bowl. Add salt and mix well. Let it rest for 35 – 40 minutes.

3. Drain the radishes in a colander.

4. Transfer the radish into a bowl.

5. To make seasoning mixture: Combine fish sauce, spices, sugar, and salted shrimp in a bowl. Let the mixture rest for 10 minutes.

6. Add the seasoning mixture into the bowl of radishes. Mix well. Taste the mixture; it should be salty. If it is not, add some more fish sauce or salted shrimp.

7. Stir in scallions. Transfer the mixture into a jar, and fasten the lid. Set aside on your countertop for 1 - 2 days to ferment. It depends on the temperature to ferment.

8. Transfer the jar into the fridge. It can be used after 8 - 10 days. It will last for about three months.

# Fermentation Temperature

It's worth noting temperature plays an important part in fermentation. Like humans, bacteria have an ideal temperature at which they survive. The warmer the temperature, the more active they are and the faster your kimchi will ferment, but too warm, and things will quickly go wrong. If you live in a colder temperature, bacterial activity isn't so high as in a warmer climate. That's no bad thing because if the temperature is too warm, your kimchi will quickly transform into a bowl of acid soup. Cooler temperatures lead to less activity which means the bacteria have more time to do their work. Warmer temperatures lead to much faster fermentation.

When fermentation is fast, though, it's generally because one strain of lactic acid bacteria is more dominant than the others, and your kimchi may have one sour, flat note. It all comes down to taste - if you like your kimchi more robust and sourer, stick to making it in the summer.

In colder climates, you need to watch the temperature carefully. If it drops to 39°F or lower, the bacteria will take far too long to acidify the food. If the environment isn't acidic enough, you risk mold or yeast forming on the kimchi. Fortunately, you can prevent this by leaving a new fermentation at room temperature for two or three days, giving the bacteria the best chance to thrive before moving it back to the refrigerator.

# Proper Storage of Kimchi

Kimchi rarely goes bad because the acidity levels stop bad bacteria from forming. However, there are ways to store it to maximize its lifetime.

 • **Vacuum packing** – if you own a vacuum packager, it's a great way of storing kimchi. Keep it in the refrigerator until you are ready to open it. Once open, you should consume it within a week but keep it refrigerated – this stops the cabbage from going soft too quickly.

 • **Jars** – make sure your jars are sterilized thoroughly before you use them, even brand new ones. Also, make sure the equipment you use to make the kimchi is sterilized before use. Submerge the vegetables completely in the kimchi liquid, or mold can grow. If there is insufficient liquid in the jar to do this, add some more seasoning mix or put a weight on the vegetables to keep them submerged.

Freezing is not recommended because it can kill off probiotics and beneficial enzymes, turning your kimchi bad and uneatable.

# Chapter 7: Sauerkraut for Beginners

Sauerkraut is one of the most popular fermenting projects, and there is a good reason for this - it is dead simple to make, doesn't require much equipment, and tastes delicious. All you do is add salt to shredded cabbage and pack it into a jar or crock. The cabbage will gradually release liquid which, when it mixes with the salt, creates brine. When the cabbage is submerged in this liquid for several days or weeks, it will ferment into the delicious sauerkraut we all know and love.

## How Is It Fermented?

In the same way kimchi ferments, sauerkraut ferments by way of lacto-fermentation. The surface of the cabbage contains beneficial bacteria, the same as you find in cultured products such as yogurt. When the bacteria are submerged in the brine, they start to convert the sugars from the vegetable into lactic acid, the natural preservative that stops harmful bacteria in its tracks.

Lacto-fermentation is a centuries-old technique used for preserving seasonal vegetables, thus extending their shelf life. Provided it is done right, it is a safe and reliable method, and you can store your sauerkraut for months in a cellar, at temperatures of around 55°F, or you can store it in your refrigerator.

# What Do I Need?

Making basic sauerkraut requires nothing more than cabbage, salt, and a container to ferment it in. One of the most important things to remember is to keep the cabbage submerged in the brine during the fermentation process. If you make large quantities in a crockpot, you should place a heavy plate or weight of some kind over the cabbage to keep it submerged and packed down. If you use a mason jar, place a small jelly jar filled with marbles, rocks, or other weights, into the mason jar's mouth to do the same thing.

Something else to be aware of is the top cabbage will float so, if you are using a mason jar, you will need to tamp the cabbage down a couple of times every day or put a sizeable raw cabbage leaf over the top to hold it down. You should also use cheesecloth or another clean cloth to cover the jar, ensuring dust and insects are kept out, but the air can still flow.

### Containers

The most common containers used for fermenting sauerkraut are stone crocks, glass jars, and containers made from food-grade plastic. If you are making large amounts, you can even use five-gallon plastic buckets. You must NOT use galvanized metal, iron, or copper containers or a crockpot glazed with lead. If you are unsure if your container is suitable, use a food-grade plastic bag to line the container with something like a turkey roasting or brining bag. Never use trash liners or garbage bags. No matter what container you use, you must ensure it is sterilized before use as it may contain bad bacteria that interfere with the fermentation process.

# Fermentation Time, Temperature and Management

While your sauerkraut is fermenting, keep the container stored at 70 to 75°F. This temperature ensures it takes about three to four weeks to complete the fermentation. If the temperature is 60 to 65°F, it will take longer than six weeks. Above 80°F, the cabbage will soften and spoil, and below 60°F, it will not ferment.

One of the most critical things to remember is following the exact ratios. Five pounds of cabbage requires exactly three tablespoons of salt to control the growth of pathogens. If you change the ratio, you could end up with a product not safe to eat.

The fermentation process will stop naturally when the acids have accumulated to a level where no more growth can occur. Once the cabbage is submerged in the brine, the container must not be disturbed until the fermentation has finished – the bubbling will stop. If you use jars as weights, ensure you check it two or three times a week and spoon off any scum formed on it.

Ideally, your sauerkraut should be tart and firm. The brine must not be cloudy or have any signs of yeast or mold growth. If you see any mold in or on the brine, it smells bad or is slimy, do NOT taste it.

Once your sauerkraut is fermented, you can store it for several months in the refrigerator.

# Let's make some sauerkraut.

**Equipment Required:**

- Large bowl
- 1 glass jar or wide-mouthed plastic container
- Fermentation weights
- Slicer

## Cabbage Sauerkraut

Makes: 1 jar

**Ingredients:**

- 1 tablespoon kosher salt for every 1 ¾ pounds cabbage
- 1 large head of green cabbage (about 4 – 5 pounds) or use as much as required

**Directions:**

1. Take out a few of the outer leaves of the cabbage and set them aside.

2. Quarter the cabbage first. Cut the cabbage into thin slices using a slicer. You can also slice with a sharp knife.

3. Measure out salt according to the weight of the cabbage. If your cabbage weighs 1 ¾ pound, you then need to use 1 tablespoon of salt.

4. Add salt and cabbage into a large bowl and toss well. Massage the cabbage using your hands for about 8 – 10 minutes. The cabbage will start getting softer, and it will release water.

5. Add the flavorings if using and mix well.

6. Transfer the cabbage into a jar. Press the cabbage down using your hands or spoon so the liquid comes up. Place 2 – 3 of the retained large, outer cabbage leaves on top of the sliced cabbage and place the fermentation weight on the cabbage leaves if necessary.

7. Keep the jar covered loosely with the lid. Set the jar aside for 24 hours, at a temperature of about 65 to 75°F, and it should be away from direct sunlight.

8. Press the cabbage every 2 hours or so. The cabbage should sink in the liquid.

9. Once 24 hours have passed, check for the liquid in the jar. If it is not over the cabbage, combine 2 cups water 2 two teaspoons salt in a bowl and pour as much as required to keep the cabbage below the water level. Generally, enough liquid is there in the jar, and it may not be needed to add some more brine.

10. Cover it loosely and ferment for 7 - 28 days. Make sure there is no sunlight falling on the jar.

11. Taste the sauerkraut daily, from the 7th day. When you are happy with the fermentation, remove the fermentation weights. Fasten the lid.

12. Transfer the jar into the fridge. It can last for 4 - 5 months.

13. Whenever you want to remove sauerkraut, remove it with wooden tongs.

14. If you see any scum or mold floating, it is time to discard the sauerkraut.

# Ideas for Different Flavored Sauerkraut

Add the flavorings in step 5 in the sauerkraut recipe. Choose any flavorings of your choice. The flavoring of sauerkraut is optional.

### Garlicky Carrots

Ingredients:

- 6 cloves garlic, minced
- 4 carrots, peeled, shredded

### Dill Flavor

Ingredients:

- 1 cup fresh dill
- 1 tablespoon caraway seeds (optional)

### Ginger and Carrots

Ingredients:

- 2 tablespoons freshly grated ginger
- 4 carrots, peeled, grated

### Spicy Beets

Ingredients:

- 2 medium beets, peeled, grated
- 2 teaspoons caraway seeds or ground cinnamon
- 4 cloves garlic, minced

### Turmeric Flavor

Ingredients:

- 4 carrots, peeled, grated
- 1 large beet, peeled, grated
- 1 cup grated radish
- 8 cloves garlic, peeled, minced

- 1/3 cup grated fresh turmeric
- 1/3 cup grated fresh ginger

**Kimchi Flavor**

**Ingredients:**

- 6 scallions, or green onions, thinly sliced
- 2 carrots, peeled, grated
- 1 cup grated radish
- 6 cloves garlic, peeled, minced
- 2 tablespoons grated ginger
- 2 teaspoons red pepper flakes

# Chapter 8: Yogurt Recipes

Do you ever stop to think about how yogurt is made? Have you ever thought about making your own yogurt?

Most yogurt contains live cultures, which means, yes, your yogurt has living bacteria in it. Before you spit it out in horror, *stop!* These bacteria are healthy and cannot cause you to fall ill. Instead, they turn milk into a creamy, delicious yogurt through a fermentation process.

Fermentation happens when microorganisms break complex substances down into simpler ones, changing the characteristics of your food – grape to wine, milk to yogurt, and so on. These microorganisms are known as "ferments" and are typically yeast or bacteria. They get their energy to grow and develop through the fermentation process.

## The Science of Yogurt Fermentation

When one strain of bacteria grows, it typically stops any other from growing. This is because they are all after the same nutrients. However, when you make yogurt, something different happens – two bacteria assist each other in their growth until a stable balance is reached. Those bacteria are Lactobacillus delbruekii ssp. bulgaricus and Streptococcus thermophilus; they work together to turn the lactose in milk into lactic acid. Thus, yogurt is created.

S. thermophilus is much better at growing in high-oxygen, neutral environments, such as milk, than Lactobacillus bulgaricus, so it tends to be the first to grow. It uses the oxygen to create new compounds, which, in turn, create the optimal conditions for L. bulgaricus to start metabolizing and growing.

Now, L. bulgaricus takes over, breaking some milk proteins down into amino acids. This ensures the S. thermophilus can easily collect the nutrients needed for its continued growth.

As both bacteria grow, they consume the lactose present in the milk, turning it into lactic acid. The more they consume, the more acidic the milk is and, once it reaches the right acidity, milk proteins, called caseins, begin clumping together. The milk consistency changes, gradually thickening into yogurt. The two bacteria stop any other bacteria from forming, specifically the bad ones that would cause the milk to spoil, which is why fermentation is one of the best ways of conserving food.

## Stopping the Process

When the milk has transformed into yogurt and has reached the texture and flavor you want, the process must be stopped. The simplest way to do this is to reduce the temperature, as cooler temperatures inhibit bacterial growth. Maintaining cooler temperatures also ensures your yogurt retains its flavor and texture by stopping it from increasing in acidity.

I shouldn't have to say this, but, as with everything, using the highest-quality ingredients equates to a higher quality of end product. Where you can, use organic, grass-fed milk and make sure you use a starter. You can use shop-bought yogurt as a starter, but you must make sure you only use one with the live cultures mentioned above. Alternatively, create your own starter

- it's easy to do, and it will ensure your yogurt is high quality and tasty.

# How to Make a Yogurt Starter

So simple - and it's much tastier and healthier than using shop-bought yogurt!

**Ingredients:**

- ¾ cup of raw cow milk (grass-fed, organic)
- Cardamom pods
- Glass measuring cup
- Thermometer
- Glass container to store the starter

**Instructions:**

1. Heat your milk to a temperature of 120°F
2. Pour it into a clean, sterilized container
3. Break a cardamom pod in half and place both in the milk, submerging them completely. If you cannot find the pods, you can use cardamom seeds – 20 is enough. Once the seeds or pods are submerged, leave it – do not stir as this can interfere with the curdling
4. Cover the container with a clean towel or cheesecloth and leave it somewhere warm, around 70°F. It will take around 10 to 14 hours to curdle, so it's probably best done late in the day and left overnight
5. Make sure your starter is curdled correctly – it should have a sweet smell, not pungent or sour, and be thick.
6. Pour it into a bowl through a strainer, removing the pods or seeds
7. Transfer it to another clean and sterilized container with an airtight lid and store it in your refrigerator. It will keep for up to three weeks.

Here's how to make your yogurt:

**Equipment Required:**

- Canning jars with lid
- Yogurt maker or instant pot or oven light or heating pad
- Fine wire mesh strainer lined with two layers of cheesecloth only for Greek yogurt
- Thermometer
- Saucepan
- Towels

# Yogurt

Makes: 4 1/8 cups

**Ingredients:**

- 2 tablespoons yogurt starter
- 4 cups milk (use whole raw milk if possible)

**Directions:**

1. To make yogurt with oven light: Pour milk into a saucepan and heat over medium flame. Check the temperature of the milk. Once it touches 180°F, turn off the heat.

   a. Pour the milk into a canning jar. Let the temperature of the milk come down to 115°F.

   b. Add a yogurt starter into the jar and whisk well. Close the jar. Turn on the oven light and place the jar in the oven, for 12 to 24 hours, until yogurt sets.

   c. Once the yogurt sets, place it in the fridge for a few hours until it chills and sets further.

2. To make the yogurt in an instant pot: Read the instructions manual of the instant pot before using it. Pour milk into the instant pot and select the "Yogurt" button. It should beep and show 'Boil.' The temperature of the milk should be 180°F.

a. Take out the cooking pot. Let the temperature of the milk come down to 115°F.

b. Add a yogurt starter into the jar and whisk well.

c. Place the cooking pot back into the instant pot. Select the "Yogurt" button and set the timer for 8 - 24 hours, depending on how tangy you want the yogurt to be. Make sure you do not set the timer for longer than 24 hours.

d. Once the yogurt sets, place it in the fridge for a few hours until it chills and sets further.

3.     To make yogurt in a yogurt maker: Pour milk into a saucepan and heat over medium flame. Check the temperature of the milk. Once it touches 180°F, turn off the heat.

a. Let the temperature of the milk come down to 115°F.

b. Add a yogurt starter into the jar and whisk well. Pour into the glass jars of the yogurt maker (read the instructions manual on operating the yogurt maker). Put on the timer for 7 - 15 hours, depending on how tangy you want it to be.

4.     To make yogurt using a heating pad: Pour milk into a saucepan and heat over medium flame. Check the temperature of the milk. Once it touches 180°F, turn off the heat.

a. Take a canning jar and pour the milk into the jar. Let the temperature of the milk come down to 115°F.

b. Add a yogurt starter into the jar and whisk well. Do not close the lid.

c. Set your heating pad to medium. Place a towel on it and place the jar with yogurt over the towel. Wrap the jar with towels as well.

d. After an hour, set the heating pad to low, check after 7 - 9 hours if the yogurt is set.

e. Now cover the jar and keep it in the fridge. Chill for a few hours.

5.     How to make Greek yogurt: Take a fine wire mesh strainer and line it with a double layer of cheesecloth. Place the strainer over a bowl. Add yogurt into the strainer. Place the entire setup, the bowl, and strainer with yogurt in the fridge for 6 - 24 hours, depending on how thick you want the Greek yogurt to be.

a. The liquid collected is called whey. The whey can be used in smoothies, lemonade, drink it as it is, in curries and gravies, as a starter culture for fermenting vegetables, Lacto-fermented drinks, etc.

# Tips for Making Homemade Yogurt

1. You can use whatever milk you want, but whole, 2%, or goat's milk are best. The more fat your milk contains, the thicker your yogurt will be.

2. Your first attempt at yogurt will have a tangy taste, regardless of how long it was incubated. There is nothing wrong with it - it's just that your tastebuds need time to adjust from the sweetened yogurts you buy in the grocery store. Give it a little time, and your tastebuds will adjust, and you won't want to go back to store-bought stuff again.

3. If you want your yogurt to be a little sweeter, add a couple of tablespoons of maple syrup and a scraped vanilla bean or vanilla extract. However, be aware that adding any type of sweetener can detract from the yogurt's taste and health properties.

4. If you want to add some fruit, only do it once the yogurt has incubated. If you add it before, the bacteria won't like it and cannot do the job correctly.

5. You can keep the yogurt for up to ten days in the refrigerator.

6. Before adding any fruit or sweeteners, take a few tablespoons of the yogurt and store it separately. This will help you start your next batch of yogurt, especially if you don't have a yogurt starter to hand

# Chapter 9: Turning Milk into Kefir

If you like yogurt, you'll love milk kefir. It's a tangy, thick, creamy yogurt-type drink packed with probiotics, and it's easy to make at home.

So, what is it?

Milk kefir is fermented similarly to yogurt but with one big difference – the milk is not heated and kept warm. Instead, all you need are something called kefir grains. For those of you who are gluten-free, please don't worry – these are not actual grains. Instead, they are small rubbery, knobbly cell structures where the bacteria and yeast responsible for fermenting the kefir live. They are the kefir equivalent of the scoby you use when you make kombucha.

## How It Works

It's a simple process. Add a teaspoon of grains to a cup of milk and over it. Leave it for about a day at room temperature, and the yeast and bacteria will go to work, fermenting the milk and turning it into kefir.

When it's done, it should have a consistency similar to buttermilk and taste tangy, like homemade yogurt. All you need to do is strain out the grains for use in the next batch and enjoy your kefir!

Your kefir grains can be used repeatedly, in batch after batch of kefir, so long as they are healthy. How do you keep kefir grains healthy? Easy – just keep making kefir! You can make a batch every 24 hours or so – your kitchen temperature will determine the exact time. Simply place your grains into another cup of milk and repeat the process. As time passes, the grains multiply – discard the extras or, even better, introduce a friend to the benefits of kefir. If you get to a stage where you don't want to make any more kefir for a while, put the grains in a cup of milk and refrigerate it – it won't start to ferment until you remove it and put it somewhere warm.

## What Are the Benefits?

Kefir provides many health benefits, the same as any fermented product. It is packed with probiotics, which lead to healthy gut flora and help in healthy digestion. During fermentation, part of the milk structure is changed, making it much easier to digest. Some people who struggle with milk often find kefir is better for them.

## What Milk Should You Use?

Kefir grains work better with full-fat cow, goat, or sheep milk. You can use low-fat or 2% milk, but you might find the grains are sluggish, and the milk takes too long to ferment. If so, place them in whole milk to revive them. Pasteurized or raw milk can be used, but do NOT use UHT (ultra-high temperature) pasteurized milk.

For non-dairy kefir, you can use full-fat coconut milk. However, coconut milk doesn't contain the nutrients and proteins found in animal milk, so your grains will lose some of their vitality over time. Use animal milk for a couple of batches to revive them or, if you cannot have any dairy, simply discard them and purchase new ones. Other plant-based, dairy-free milk, such as almond and soy, cannot be used for making kefir.

## What You Can Do With Milk Kefir

Milk kefir is perfectly drinkable on its own, but you can also add it to your lassis, smoothies, or any other drink you would add regular milk or yogurt to. You can also use kefir for baking. Simply replace buttermilk, milk, or yogurt in the recipe with kefir, and it will result in a fantastic baked product.

## Is It Safe? Can Anything Go Wrong?

Milk kefir can be dated back thousands of years. Traditionally, it was used to preserve fresh milk to last longer, so, yes, it is safe. The healthy yeast and bacteria in the grains stop unhealthy ones from growing and spoiling the milk when left at room temperature. You know what happens when you leave milk out of the fridge in a warm room – the grains prevent that.

The biggest thing you need to worry about is the room temperature. The kefir grains are happiest at an average of 60 to 90°F. Below that and the grains will be sluggish, even going into hibernation. While the grains are still okay, the kefir will take longer to make. Above, and the milk will spoil quickly, quicker than it can be cultured by the grains. This promotes an unsafe, unhealthy environment, so you need to avoid making the kefir when it is very hot, and air conditioning isn't available.

Lastly, store your kefir in glass jars. Metal containers can cause the grains to weaken and die; however, they are okay when exposed to metal briefly, such as using a metal strainer or metal spoon to stir the kefir.

## Where to Get Your Grains

If you know someone who makes kefir, ask them for some grains. They multiply after a time, and most people who make it regularly will have some to spare. If not, purchase them online but only from reputable organic sources.

# Time to make some kefir:

**Equipment Required:**

- Large jug
- Cheesecloth or coffee filters or paper towels
- Wooden or plastic spoon (slotted)
- Wide glass or plastic bowl
- Jar for storing
- Fine mesh strainer (plastic)
- Rubber bands

## Milk Kefir

Makes: About 7 ½ cups

**Ingredients:**

- 8 cups fresh, raw whole cow's milk, non-homogenized, at room temperature
- 2 tablespoons kefir grains

**Directions:**

1. Rinse the kefir grains with filtered water and place them in a jug.

2. Pour milk into the jug.

3. Cover the mouth of the jar loosely with cheesecloth for 2 - 3 layers of paper towels or coffee filter. Fasten with rubber bands.

4. Store the jar in a warm and dark place (65 - 85°F). It should be ready in 12 hours to 2 days, depending on the temperature of the place. The ready kefir will have a fermented smell and will be thick. It may be a bit separated, smelling tangy.

5. Place a strainer over a plastic or glass bowl. Add kefir into the strainer and strain into the bowl. The kefir grains can be used to make the next batch of kefir. Alternatively, you can rinse the grains and place them in a bowl of water in the fridge for a few weeks.

6. Add flavorings, if any now, and stir.

7. Pour the strained kefir into a jar. Seal the jar and chill until use. Consume within two weeks.

# Different Flavored Kefir

Flavors are to be added into the prepared kefir after straining and before storing. You can add fresh fruit juice, vanilla extract, dates, cocoa, carob, or any preserved or pureed fruits. The possibilities are endless. Mix and match until you find a favorite. Here are a few ideas.

### Fruit Juice

Ingredients:

- 1 tablespoon fresh fruit juice of your choice for every cup of kefir or add more to taste

## Flavoring with Extracts

Ingredients:

- 2 cups milk kefir
- ½ to 2/3 teaspoon pure vanilla extract or almond extract
- 2 teaspoons sugar or honey or maple syrup or stevia to taste

### Cocoa / Carob

Ingredients:

- 2 cups cocoa powder or carob or 1 – 2 tablespoons Nutella
- 2 cups milk kefir

### Fruit Preserve

Ingredients:

- 2 tablespoons fruit preserve of your choice
- 2 cups milk kefir

### Fresh Fruit

Ingredients:

- ½ cup chopped fruit of your choice
- 2 cups milk kefir
- 2 teaspoons sugar or honey or maple syrup or stevia to taste

### Citrus Strawberry

Ingredients:

- 2 handfuls of fresh or frozen strawberries
- 2 cups milk kefir
- 2 teaspoons lemon juice or lime juice or 2 tablespoons orange juice

Directions:

1. Place strawberries and lemon juice in a blender and blend until smooth. Add to the kefir after straining.

2. You can go for an all citrus flavor by adding a teaspoon of lemon juice, a teaspoon of lime juice, and 2 tablespoons of orange juice.

### Banana Berry Flavor

Ingredients:

- 1 cup frozen berries of your choice
- ¼ cup shredded coconut
- 3 to 4 tablespoons applesauce
- 2 cups milk kefir
- 1 large banana, sliced
- Honey or sugar to taste (optional)

Directions:

Place berries, coconut applesauce, banana, kefir, and honey in a blender and blend until smooth.

### Mango Flavor

Ingredients:

- 2 cups milk kefir
- ½ to 1 cup cubed mango

**Directions:**

Place mangoes in a blender and blend until smooth. Add to the kefir and stir.

### Pina Colada Flavor

**Ingredients:**

- ½ cup chopped pineapple
- 2 to 4 tablespoons shredded coconut
- 2 cups milk kefir
- 2 teaspoons lime juice

**Directions:**

Place pineapple, shredded coconut, lime juice, and kefir in a blender and blend until smooth.

# Chapter 10: Making Beet Kvass

Beet kvass has long been known as a wonder drink, heralding from Russia and the Ukraine thousands of years ago. All ranks and members of society drink it, and many people believe it is safer to drink than water. Across the world, ancient cultures dealt with contaminated water by transforming it into beer, wine, and other alcoholic drinks. Still, they created one of the most wonderous infusions in the North, a Lacto-fermented drink laced with numerous health properties. Not only is it incredibly thirst-quenching, but it is also known to help prevent hangovers, help with healthy digestion, and some claim it protects against infectious diseases.

Traditional kvass is made from sourdough-rye bread gone stale, producing a drink that tastes a lot like beer but without the alcohol. However, many people have had to eliminate grains from their diet for one reason and cannot partake of the health-giving drink. But all is not lost. Beet kvass made with sourdough bread may be the most traditional, but it isn't the only variety. Ever-resourceful, Russians will create kvass from just about anything, from raspberries and currants to cherries and lemons. But perhaps the best-known alternative is made from the good old beet.

Beets are one of the world's superfoods, packed with a nutritional unch rivaled by nothing else. Beets offer one of the best sources of potassium, sodium, calcium, phosphorous, iron, niacin, vitamin A, vitamin C, and fiber. And because they are also packed with folate and folic acid, they are perfect for pregnant women and those trying to fall pregnant. And this humblest and easiest to grow of all root vegetables has even been shown to help prevent some cancers, heart disease, and strokes.

Although beets are a nutritional powerhouse straight from the ground, Lacto-fermentation only serves to boost their nutritional value and benefits. By using a traditional preservation method, probiotics are added, and your body can easily absorb the nutrients in the beets. Cooking tends to destroy nutritional benefits in many foods, so keeping your beets raw throughout the entire process is a bonus.

On top of the benefits for pregnant women, beet kvass also has blood and liver cleansing properties that help stop morning sickness in its tracks. Likewise, because the nutrients in beets help play a critical role in assisting cells to function correctly, beet kvass has long been used across Europe to help treat cancer.

Any Lacto-fermented product chelates the body gently, flushing toxins and heavy metals out. Beet kvass is no exception. Recently converted people to the beet kvass craze tell us it's also an excellent heartburn remedy, chronic fatigue remedy, and helps people manage chemical insensitivities, digestive issues, kidney stones, and allergies. Lastly, it is believed kvass can improve regularity and alkalize the blood.

And that's not all. Some reports say it has been shown to reduce age spots, helps thicken up thinning hair, and makes gray hairs turn dark again.

So, how do we create this God of all drinks? The most basic version of beet kvass requires just three things – beets, salt, and water. The water and salt combine into a brine that pickles the beets. When the process is finished, the brine has turned into kvass. The beet juice saturates the liquid, and the fermentation provides a slight effervescence. However, like anything, the final product's quality is determined entirely by the quality of the ingredients you use.

Organic beets are preferred, but use whatever you can, so long as they are fresh if you can't get organic. And it's up to you whether you peel the beets or not – just make sure you scrub them clean. The beets are chopped into chunks, approximately one to two inches in diameter. Never shred the beets because they are high in sugar and, when you shred them, too much juice goes into the brine solution. Rather than Lacto-fermentation, you get an alcoholic fermentation instead, but don't be afraid to experiment – if you fancy trying your hand at a beet-based alcoholic drink!

Make sure the water you use is chemical-free, especially chlorine. Chemicals are added to tap water to kill bacteria. If you add them to your ferment, you can see what will happen – not only will they stop the bad bacteria, but they will also stop your good bacteria from growing, causing the beets to go rotten. If you cannot source spring or filtered water, boil tap water and leave it out overnight to ensure the chlorine dissipates.

The salt should NOT be regular table salt or iodized. Make sure only to use unrefined pure sea salt because additives can harm your ferment. Read the labels carefully – some salts labeled as pure contain anti-caking agents, which are a most definite no-no for fermented foods.

Sole plays an essential role in Lacto-fermentation – it stops the bad bacteria forming in the ferment. However, if you use too much, your kvass will be undrinkable. You can combat this by adding a fourth ingredient. Reduce how much salt you add and add some fermented whey instead; the whey kicks the fermentation into gear and provides the same protection as salt against harmful microorganisms.

Whey is easy to obtain if you decide to use it. All you need is plain homemade yogurt or kefir and a way to strain it. You can use shop-bought yogurt, but only if it has the live cultures in it. Homemade is best because the process used to make store-bought yogurt shelf-stable often eliminates the live organisms. If you opt for shop-bought, you can test if it is live very easily.

Heat a cup of milk in a pan on the stove, not allowing it to come to a boil. Mix a tablespoon of your yogurt into the milk and leave it somewhere warm overnight or for at least eight hours. If the milk has thickened noticeably, the yogurt is still live.

Line a strainer or colander with a clean towel or a few layers of cheesecloth and stand it over a bowl. Pour the yogurt into the strainer and leave it to drain. Cover the bowl with a plate or pull the cloth up over it – this keeps the dust and insects out of it. You should see a yellow liquid dripping through – that is the whey. When it's drained to your satisfaction, you can use your whey in the kvass.

# Let's make kvass:

**Equipment Required:**

- Large jar with lid
- Fine wire mesh strainer
- Masons jars or bottles to store

## Traditional Kvass

Makes: 1 jar

**Ingredients:**

- 12 cups water + extra if required
- 1 to 1 ½ cups sweetener like brown sugar, sugar, honey birch syrup
- ½ cup raisins (optional)
- 8 to 12 cups toasted, cubed stale bread (about 8 - 12 ounces)
- ¼ to ½ cup sourdough starter
- Herbs or fruit of your choice

**Directions:**

1. Combine sugar, water, raisins, herbs, or fruits in a pot and place over high heat. Stir often until the sugar dissolves. When it begins to boil, turn off the heat. Let it cool until it is about 85°F.

2. The bread needs to be cubed and toasted until brown but not burnt. This can be done in the oven.

3. Add sourdough starter and bread cubes in a jar. Drizzle the warm mixture over the bread cubes and stir. If the bread is not covered with water, add a little more.

4. Close the jar's lid loosely and place at room temperature for 2 - 7 days to ferment.

5. Start tasting the mixture daily after two days. When the desired fermentation is reached, strain the mixture into a bowl.

6. Pour into a storage jar and refrigerate until use. Consume within 7 – 10 days. It will not last longer than this.

# Beet Kvass

Makes: 1 jar

## Ingredients:

- 6 large beets, trimmed, scrubbed, cubed
- 4 tablespoons starter culture (basically 2 tablespoons starter culture for every quart of water)
- 2 teaspoons finely ground sea salt or kosher salt
- 8 cups water or more if required

## Directions:

1. Do not peel the skin of the beets. Just scrub them.

2. The different starter culture options are whey from yogurt (from making Greek yogurt), ginger bug, kombucha, juice from fermented pickles, or a commercial starter.

3. Add beets into a large jar of about 2 quarts.

4. Add the starter culture and salt into a bowl and whisk well. Add water and stir until well combined.

5. Place beets in the jar. Pour the brine over the beets. Close the lid tightly.

6. Store the jar at room temperature where there is no source of direct sunlight. Allow it to ferment for 3 - 7 days, depending on the weather. Shake the jar 2 to 3 times every day.

7. Open the lid on alternate days. Push the beets down and close the lid tightly again. When the kvass is ready, lots of bubbles will be visible in the jar. The kvass is ready when it has a pleasant, albeit sour taste. Strain and pour into bottles.

8. Place in the fridge until use. It can be served once chilled. Consume within a month.

# Lacto Fermented Fruit Kvass

Makes: 1 jar

## Ingredients:

- 2 handfuls strawberries or raspberries or blueberries
- 4 organic apples or pears, cored, sliced, peel if desired
- 1 cup whey liquid
- 2 tablespoons grated fresh ginger
- Filtered water, as required

## Directions:

1. Add apples or pears, berries, ginger, and whey into a jar. Pour enough water to fill the jar. Leave about 2 inches of headspace in the top of the jar. Cover the top of the jar loosely with a plastic bag. Place a pint-sized jar at the opening of the jar so the fruits are immersed in the liquid. Put a rubber band around the plastic bag to fasten.

2. Store the jar at room temperature without direct light on the jar. Let it ferment for 2 to 3 days. When the kvass is ready, lots of bubbles will be visible in the jar. The kvass is ready when it has a pleasant and slightly sour taste.

3. Strain and pour into bottles.

4. Place in the fridge until use.

5. To serve: If you do not like the strong fermented taste, dilute it with some cold water and serve.

# Chapter 11: Ferment Your Own Pickles

Before we talk about fermented pickles, you need to know there is a difference between fermenting and pickling. Both are excellent methods of preserving food naturally, producing wonderful results, but how are they different?

## Pickling vs. Fermenting

Both provide very different yet equally tasty results, but confusion occurs because of some overlapping areas. The main difference to remember is this – pickling is about soaking food in vinegar, or another acidic liquid, to produce a sour flavor, while fermenting is all about the chemical reaction between natural bacteria and the sugar in the food, with no additional acid needed.

### Pickling

With pickling, food is immersed in vinegar or another acidic solution. This solution changes the texture and taste of the food. Heat is also involved in the process, destroying microorganisms and stopping new ones from growing.

The quickest way is quick pickling, where vinegar, salt, sugar, and occasionally herbs and spices are heated in a pan and brought to a boil. This liquid is then poured over the vegetables or fruits, which are left to soak for a period.

While vinegar is a fermentation product, it does not ferment pickled foods because they do not produce the required enzymes and probiotics.

### Fermenting

With fermentation, it's all about chemical reactions, and no additional heat or acidic liquid is needed. Indeed, you can ferment foods with nothing more than salt and a container, although it does tend to be a little more involved than that. Fermentation is an older preservation technique than pickling and takes quite a bit longer to achieve. Ultimately, fermentation alters the food's color, texture, and flavor.

# Fermenting 101

Vegetables and fruits have natural bacteria that stop other microbes from growing when deprived of air. Those microbes could cause the food to spoil and promote the growth of mold.

The natural bacteria in the vegetables convert sugars and carbohydrates into lactic acid during fermentation, creating the ideal preservation environment. Lacto-fermentation starts when lactobacillus is present and provides fermented foods with their unique sour, tangy taste. But it does more than that. The fermentation process also creates probiotics to help aid digestion and promote healthy gut flora.

Given that fermentation produces acid, you could class homemade fermented vegetables as pickled too.

### Keeping Clean

Cleanliness is a critical part of homemade fermented pickles. That includes your hounds, all the equipment you use, your countertops, jars, everything. If not, you could introduce yeast, bacteria, or mold that spoils your food, leading to mushy, slippery, smelly, off-colored pickles.

### Ingredients and Recipes

Always follow a recipe *exactly*. Never leave anything out or reduce or increase any ingredients, especially salt, as it creates the right environment for the good bacteria to grow. Seasonings are usually optional. Your pickles should always be fresh, free of disease, unblemished, and, where possible, organic.

### Fermentation Environment

Your environment must be suitable for fermentation to be successful. The temperature should be 70 to 75°F, for a three to four-week fermentation time. Any higher, and you risk the pickles spoiling while lower temperatures slow the fermentation or even stop it altogether.

### Storage

You can refrigerate fermented pickles for up to six months but do check them weekly and remove any mold or scum starting to form. If you want to store longer than this, consider canning your pickles.

### What Type of Cucumbers?

You need to use pickling cucumbers, which are much smaller than normal salad cucumbers, usually four to six inches long. Their skin is bumpy, they have small seeds, and they are crisp in texture, with a light to dark green color. Try to get organic from your local farmer's market and only use good quality cucumbers. They should be roughly all the same size, so they ferment at the same rate.

HERBS AND SPICES YOU CAN USE

While herbs and spices are optional, they do make a lovely addition to your dill pickles.

- Mustard, fennel seeds, peppercorns, allspice, coriander, celery, and dill seeds go wonderfully with dill pickles. You can use the feathery fronds from a fennel plant (not too much) or chilies for an extra kick.
- Garlic - lots of it - and fresh dill
- Grape leaves or bay leaves - to stop their skins from softening, fermented pickles require tannin.

## Salt and Water in Fermentation

The salt and water ratio is the most important aspect of fermentation. Getting it right ensures you have the right environment for the healthy bacteria to grow while prohibiting the bad bacteria. You must be precise when you measure your salt and water:

- Too little salt and the bad bacteria will thrive
- Too much salt and all the bacteria may die, including the good ones, which stops fermentation from happening.

A safe ratio is 2.5% brine, which equates to 6 g of salt for every cup of water. This ratio allows you to drink it without it tasting like seawater! However, if you want your brine stronger, you can go up to 3.5%, which is 9 g of salt per cup of water.

Lastly, make sure you use unprocessed sea salt and filtered water with no chlorine in it.

## Tips

- If you require more brine, use a ratio of 1 teaspoon of salt per cup of water
- If you are using grape leaves to provide the tannin, lay it against the side of the jar before adding your vegetables and brine
- If you want to use a river stone as a weight in your jar, ensure you place it in boiling water for 20 minutes first to sterilize it.

Time to make some fermented pickles.

### Equipment Required:

- Jar or jars
- Fermentation weights*
- Bowl

*These are used to weigh the pickles down, so they are submerged fully in the liquid. You can buy fermentation weights or use a small glass jar filled with stones or marbles, a plate, or even a food-grade bag filled with water – do make sure this cannot break, though, or the fermentation environment will change, and your product will spoil.*

# Garlic and Dill Pickles

Makes: 1 jar

### Ingredients:

- 1 pound pickling cucumbers
- 1 teaspoon fine sea salt for every cup of water
- ½ teaspoon fennel seeds
- ½ teaspoon allspice berries
- ½ teaspoon dill seeds
- ½ teaspoon coriander seeds
- ½ teaspoon peppercorns

- ½ teaspoon celery seeds
- ½ teaspoon mustard seeds
- ½ to 1 fresh red chili or dried Arbol chili, sliced
- 3 cups non-chlorinated filtered water
- 4 to 6 cloves garlic, peeled, sliced
- Small handful dill sprigs
- 2 bay leaves

**Directions:**

1. Make sure the cucumbers are similar in size. Prepare an ice bath and place the cucumbers in it after rinsing. Let it sit for 15 - 20 minutes. This will help the cucumbers remain crisp.

2. Heat about ½ cup of water until warm. Add ½ teaspoon of salt and stir. Let it cool completely. Pour this brine into a bowl with the remaining water and mix well.

3. Place cucumbers in a jar. Sprinkle garlic, dill, all the spices, and bay leaves over the cucumbers.

4. Pour the brine into the jar. The cucumbers should be immersed in the solution. Place some fermentation weights over the cucumbers so they remain submerged in the brine.

5. Close the lid and tighten it a bit but not too tight. Keep a pan underneath the jar to collect any spills. Keep the jar in a cool and dark area without direct sunlight hitting it for three to seven days.

6. Keep a watch on the jar after three days for any bubbles. If you are satisfied with the taste, store the jar in the fridge and continue fermenting for a few more days until you are satisfied with the results. Make sure to taste the pickles daily starting from the third day.

7. If you want more fizzing on the top of the liquid, make sure to tighten the lid fully. Make sure to open the lid once every five to six days to release some of the gas.

# Mixed Pickles

Makes: 1 large jar

**Ingredients:**

- 6 tablespoons sea salt or pickling salt or kosher salt (3 tablespoons salt for every quart of water)
- 2 cups small cauliflower florets
- 2 cups red bell pepper chunks
- 2 cups carrot slices
- 2 cloves garlic, peeled, smashed
- 2 quarts non-chlorinated filtered water
- 1 teaspoon coriander seeds
- 2 bay leaves
- 2 grape leaves (optional but recommended to keep the vegetables crisp)
- ½ teaspoon black peppercorns

**Directions:**

1. Heat about ½ cup of water until warm. Add salt and stir. Let it cool to room temperature completely. Pour this brine into a bowl with the remaining water and mix well.

2. Place cauliflower, bell pepper, carrot, garlic, spices, and grape leaves in the jar.

3. Pour the brine into the jar. The vegetables should be covered with the liquid, so add more water if required.

4. Close the lid of the jar and tighten it. Place on your countertop for 2 – 3 days. Open the jar daily once to remove any built-up gas. If you see any scum or molds floating on top, remove them with a spoon.

5. If the pickles are to your liking, store the jar in the fridge.

6. It can last for about 1 – 1 ½ months.

# Pickled Green Tomatoes

Makes: 1 small jar

## Ingredients:

- 2 tablespoons kosher salt
- 4 sprigs dill
- 4 cloves garlic, peeled, sliced
- 2 teaspoons coriander seeds
- 4 green tomatoes, thinly sliced
- 2 green onions, thinly sliced
- 2 teaspoons whole black peppercorns
- 4 cups water

## Directions:

1. Combine salt and water in a bowl. Keep stirring until salt dissolves completely.

2. Take a jar and keep the tomato slices in it. Sprinkle garlic, peppercorns, coriander seeds, dill, and green onions on top.

3. Pour brine into the jar. The ingredients should be immersed in water. If necessary, place a cabbage leaf on top of the ingredients to keep the ingredients immersed. If necessary, keep something heavy over the leaf.

4. Close the lid and tighten it a bit but not too tight. Keep a pan underneath the jar. This is to collect any spills from the jar. Keep the jar in a cool and dark area without direct sunlight hitting it for 5 - 10 days.

5. Keep a watch on the jar after three days for any bubbles. Continue fermenting until bubbling stops. If, at any time, the liquid seems less in the jar, just stir a bit of salt in some water and pour it into the jar. Now the pickle can be placed in the fridge. It can last for 3 – 4 months.

# Granny's Pickle

Makes: 1 jar

## Ingredients:

- 2 tablespoons salt for every quart of water
- ½ jar chopped seasonal garden vegetables, cut into bite-size pieces
- 5 – 7 cloves garlic, peeled, sliced
- 1 onion, sliced
- 2 grape leaves or horseradish leaves (optional but recommended to keep the vegetables crisp)
- A handful of herbs of your choice
- ½ teaspoon each - pickling spices of your choice like peppercorns, coriander seeds, etc.
- 1 quart filtered, non-chlorinated water

## Directions:

1. Place garlic, pickling spices, and herbs in the jar. Spread vegetables over the spices. Place grape leaves as well. One grape leaf will do. You can also put in a few black tea leaves if you do not have grape leaves or horseradish leaves.

2. Pour water into a bowl. Stir in the salt. Let it dissolve completely.

3. Pour brine into the jar, and the vegetables should be covered with the brine. The ingredients should be immersed in water. Press the vegetables down. If necessary, place a cabbage leaf on top of the ingredients to keep the ingredients immersed. If necessary, keep something heavy over the leaf.

4. Close the lid and tighten it fully. Store the jar in a warm and dark place (65 – 85°F) without direct sunlight for 9 – 10 days. Make sure to loosen the lid once daily, to remove excess gas. Be quick in opening and closing it tightly again.

5. Once you are happy with the taste, store the jar in the fridge.

# Turnip Pickle

Makes: 1 jar

## Ingredients:

- 1 ¾ tablespoons sea salt
- 3 cups water
- 1 teaspoon red pepper flakes
- 6 medium turnips, scrubbed, cut into 1/8-inch-thick slices

## Directions:

1. Combine salt and water in a bowl. Add turnips and red chili flakes into the jar—drizzle brine over the turnips.

2. Keep the jar covered tightly and place at room temperature for 3 - 4 days or until you are satisfied with the fermentation. Open the lid for a few seconds daily to remove excess gas.

3. Store the jar in the fridge. It is ready to eat on the 5th day. It can last for 18 - 20 days.

# Indian Vegetable Kanji

Makes: 1 jar

### Ingredients:

- 1 pound carrots or radish or black carrots, peeled, sliced
- 3 tablespoons coarsely ground yellow mustard
- 5 - 6 cloves garlic, peeled
- 10 cups water
- 3 tablespoons salt
- 1 teaspoon turmeric powder
- 2 teaspoon red chili flakes

### Directions:

1. Combine salt and water in a bowl.

2. Place the chosen vegetable in the jar.

3. Blend garlic, turmeric powder, mustard, and chili flakes, adding a little of the brine in a blender until smooth.

4. Add into the brine and stir. Pour into the jar. Fasten the lid and place it in a warm area for about 3 - 4 days. If you can manage to place it in the sunlight, there is nothing like it. Initially, the vegetables will sink in the brine. As it ferments, it will begin to float. If you cannot place it in sunlight, it will take 5 - 7 days to ferment.

5. Once you are satisfied with the taste, store the jar in the fridge.

# Chapter 12: How to Make Apple Cider Vinegar (ACV)

When fall arrives, so do the apples, and households everywhere start to smell of apple pies. What do you do with your scraps? The peel, the core, and any other part leftover from baking? Whatever you do, don't throw them away because you can use them to make one of the healthiest ingredients on the planet – raw apple cider vinegar. It's really easy to make, and the benefits are enormous. Oh yeah, and because you are using leftovers, it's far cheaper than buying ACV from a store.

You can find apple cider vinegar all over the place. All grocery stores sell it, and everyone is talking about it. Is it hype? A new fad? Or is there more to ACV than first meets the eye?

I can tell you now, ACV is nothing new. It is one of the world's ancient remedies and has long been used in helping with health issues, but it seems we are only now starting to become more aware of the benefits.

These days, people are more aware of their health and do all they can to improve it by making natural, healthy choices. That is why ACV is seen everywhere and heard in just about every conversation about natural remedies and healthy foods.

And, in case you were wondering, most of the benefits attributed to apple cider vinegar are fully backed by science. So no, it isn't hype, and it isn't another fad.

However, you should note that apple cider vinegar can only do so much, incredible as it is. It isn't a miracle worker, and it doesn't take the place of a healthy, balanced diet and exercise program. Yes, it promotes good health, and it can undoubtedly help you maintain your health, but drinking it won't have a significant impact on your life unless you combine it with other steps towards a healthy life.

## What Is Apple Cider Vinegar?

Basically, it is vinegar made from apples, but it's fermented apple juice, to be more specific.

A good apple cider vinegar is not cheap to buy, but you can easily make your own from apples or apple peels and cores. The apples are crushed, exposing them to yeast, and natural sugar found in the apple is fermented into alcohol. It sounds much like making cider, and that's because it's a similar process. The only difference is, to make the vinegar, we ferment it *twice*. The first time makes the cider; the second time makes the vinegar.

### Why Drink it?

Apple cider vinegar is classed as a superfood, providing tons of health benefits, which we'll talk about in a minute. It is also an excellent weight-loss tool because it induces satiety, which reduces cravings. And it is packed with tons of nutritional benefits.

# The Benefits of Apple Cider Vinegar

So, what are these much-talked-about benefits? We'll start by listing them and then get into the details of the ones that can really help you with a healthy life:

- Apple cider vinegar aids digestion and is a natural laxative

- It helps lower your blood sugar

- It can improve insulin sensitivity

- It helps weight loss by increasing satiety and decreasing cravings

- It can reduce unhealthy belly fat

- It can help lower your cholesterol

- It improves your heart health by lowering blood pressure

- It can decrease the risks of cancer or prevent it altogether and slow cancer cell growth.

Well, all this sounds incredibly impressive, but it doesn't end there. Apple cider vinegar is also packed with nutrients, which goes a long way towards explaining why it has so many health benefits. Here's what ACV contains:

- Amino acids

- Antioxidants

- Iron

- Magnesium

- Manganese

- Phosphorus

And one tablespoon is just three calories.

Let's go deeper into those health benefits:

### Weight Loss

Losing weight is the primary reason people use ACV, but many don't realize all the other health benefits it offers. That's mainly because apple cider vinegar has long been used for weight loss. Some studies show it works, too - even if you don't make any changes to your diet. However, combine it with a healthy lifestyle, and the results will blow your mind.

How does this work? The main reason people eat so much is that they don't feel full, and keep right on eating. It takes 20 minutes for your stomach to send a message to your brain saying it is full - you can eat a lot of food in that time! ACV increases satiety, which means you feel full quicker, eat less, and stay on track with a healthy, balanced diet. This is even more important when you are just starting your weight loss journey.

### Diabetes

There are several things to know about apple cider vinegar and diabetes, mainly that it is a great tool to help prevent diabetes from starting. If you have a history of diabetes in your family, it may be worth consuming ACV to decrease your risks of getting it.

It works because it reduces blood sugar when you fast (when you don't eat). This is highly beneficial for anyone who struggles to regulate blood sugar, like those with diabetes. However, please do not stop taking medication - ACV cannot replace what your doctor has prescribed.

People with diabetes are urged to eat a healthy diet and exercise as much as they can. If you are on prescription drugs, you must seek advice from your doctor before consuming apple cider vinegar – it may cause a serious drop in potassium levels.

### Blood Pressure and Cholesterol

Apple cider vinegar has also been shown to reduce blood pressure and cholesterol, but how? ACV helps to control a hormone called renin; this hormone is produced by the kidneys and helps dilate and constrict blood vessels. When they constrict, blood pressure goes up and, when they dilate, it goes down. ACV helps the vessels to relax, keeping your blood pressure down and stable.

In terms of cholesterol, when you drink ACV before you eat, it can lower your cholesterol levels. The antioxidants in apple cider vinegar help reduce LDL (bad cholesterol) and raise good cholesterol (HDL).

### Digestion

Apple cider vinegar has long been shown to improve digestion by eliminating heartburn, reducing bloating, and improving your overall digestive health.

Pain and discomfort are not normal, and when we experience it after eating, we really should listen to what our bodies are telling us – something isn't right. We may have overeaten, or another issue is preventing the digestive system from working correctly.

The digestive system can only work properly when the correct acid levels are in the stomach, helping us absorb the nutrients from what we eat. When there is insufficient acid, the food isn't broken down properly, and the nutrients are not absorbed, leading to the digestive issues mentioned above or, in some cases, something much worse. When you drink apple cider vinegar, you increase acid production in the stomach, leading to your digestive system working as it should.

### Bacteria

Apple cider vinegar will kill bacteria, and in earlier times, it was used to disinfect wounds and kill fungus. It still is a good way of treating infections because of its ability to kill bacteria. It will also stop E-coli, and other bad bacteria, from spoiling your food, which is why ACV is often used to preserve food naturally rather than using artificial preservatives.

### Cancer

While it isn't clear exactly how it works because apple cider vinegar promotes health, it is thought to help prevent cancer. While it isn't a cure, and we know we have a long way to cure and prevent cancer, it has been shown to reduce the risks of getting it when combined with a healthy lifestyle. It has also been shown to slow down the growth of cancerous cells and tumors.

However, I must stress that remedies such as ACV should never be used to replace treatment in someone who has been diagnosed with cancer. Nor should it replace a healthy lifestyle for people wanting to reduce the risks of cancer. It is an addition, a supplement if you like, but if you are on any prescription drugs or treatment, you must seek advice from your doctor before using ACV.

### Hair and Skin

Apple cider vinegar doesn't just have health benefits. It can also improve your hair and skin health, and here's how:

- It can treat existing acne and reduce the frequency of outbreaks
- It can soothe and treat sunburn
- It contains anti-aging properties
- It can improve your hair health
- It can combat tangles in your hair
- It can reduce frizziness

- It can seal off the hair cuticles, helping your hair to retain natural oils and moisture
- It can treat dandruff

However, while it has all these wonderful properties, there is one thing I must tell you - never apply neat ACV to your skin. It must be diluted in water first.

# Best Ways to Consume Apple Cider Vinegar

With all its many benefits, you may be reaching for a bottle right now, preparing to take a swig. First, we'll look at the many other ways you can consume your freshly made ACV:

- Drink it but not neat - if you like the taste, go for it but don't down half the bottle in one go! A tablespoon or two is more than enough, mixed into a glass of water.

- Use it in your recipes - later, I will provide you with a couple of excellent salad dressing and marinade recipes you can use it in.

- Make a tonic - mix two tablespoons of ACV into a glass of fruit juice. This way, you still get all the benefits without the taste - along with the benefits of the fruit juice (make sure it is pure with no added sugars, flavorings, etc.) Add a touch of cayenne pepper or ground cinnamon to spice it up or a dash of raw honey to sweeten it.

### How Much to Drink Every Day

This is a critical point - overdoing it will NOT increase the benefits and can cause you additional health problems. Don't forget - *ACV is acidic.*

The ideal dosage is 15 to 30 ml per day - one or two tablespoons, that's all. If you have never consumed ACV before, start with one tablespoon diluted in a cup or two of water. It is strong so give yourself time to get used to it. From there, you can increase the amount of vinegar.

### Potential Side Effects

It is only vinegar made from apples, so, used in moderation, it is perfectly harmless. However, drink too much, and you invite problems. Plus, if you have kidney disease, other issues with your kidneys, or stomach ulcers, steer clear – it is far too acidic and can worsen some health problems. Always seek advice from your doctor first.

Just to remind you – always dilute ACV in some way before consuming it, be it in water, marinades, salad dressings, juices, etc. drinking neat ACV or too much of it can:

- Strip the enamel from your teeth and cause tooth decay
- Lower your potassium levels. If you already have low potassium, do not consume more than the recommended daily allowance
- Cause indigestion if you drink too much
- Cause worsening digestion issues in those with acid reflux or stomach ulcers
- Burn your skin if applied undiluted. For sunburn, add two tablespoons of ACV to your bath and, for acne, dilute a tiny bit in water before you apply it.

As with many things, a little bit of apple cider vinegar can go a very long way – moderation is key!

Let's make our first batch of ACV.

### Equipment Required:

- Large jar (2-quart size)
- Smaller jar
- Cheesecloth or coffee filter
- Rubber band
- Fermentation weights

# ACV Recipe

## Ingredients:

- 1 tablespoon cane sugar for every cup of water
- Organic apple scraps (chopped whole apples, peels, cores, etc.) preferably from a variety of apples
- 4 cups filtered water or more if required

## Directions:

1. Make sure your jar is clean and dry.
2. Place apple scrap in a 2-quart jar, enough to fill up to ¾.
3. Combine water and sugar in a saucepan. Stir until sugar has completely dissolved.
4. Pour the sugar solution into the jar. Press the apples until they are immersed in the sugar solution.
5. Despite pressing, if the solution is not over the apples, dissolve 1 - 2 tablespoons of cane sugar in 1 - 2 cups of water and pour into the jar.
6. Place some fermentation weights over the apples to keep them submerged in the sugar solution.
7. Keep the jar covered with cheesecloth and fasten it with a rubber band. Store the jar in a dark place at room temperature for approximately three weeks. Keep a watch over it and check for any mold growth. If you find some mold, remove it.
8. By now, you should be getting a slightly sweet smell.
9. Strain the liquid into another jar. Press the apples to extract as much liquid as possible. Discard the solids.
10. Cover with another cheesecloth and fasten with a rubber band. Store the jar in a dark place at room temperature for approximately 3 - 4 weeks.
11. Stir the vinegar every 4 - 5 days and taste it as well. When you are happy with the taste, remove the cheesecloth and put the lid on.

12. Remove a little of the vinegar floating on top (this is called "the mother") and store it for whenever you make ACV again. When you make a new batch of ACV, add a little of "the mother" so it can speed up the fermentation process.

# Apple Cider Vinegar Salad Dressing

Making a salad dressing with ACV takes just five minutes. It's delicious, cheap, and far healthier than what you buy in the shops:

**Ingredients:**

- 1 small shallot, peeled, cored, and chopped into quarters – if you can only get large ones, just use one lobe
- 1/3 cup extra-virgin olive oil
- 2 teaspoons honey
- 2 teaspoons Dijon mustard
- ½ teaspoon sea salt
- ¼ teaspoon ground black pepper

**Instructions:**

1. Put all the ingredients into a blender, mini chopper, or a jug with an immersion blender

2. Blitz to a smooth puree – it should take about 30 seconds

3. Use immediately or refrigerate in a sealed container for up to one week.

**Notes**

You can make this ahead and store it, but it will solidify after a couple of days. Remove it from the refrigerator and bring it to room temperature before using it. If you need it straight away, place the jar in a bowl of warm – not boiling – water.

# Apple Cider Vinegar Marinade for Chicken

This marinade is simple to make, taking just five minutes, and can be used for any meat, poultry, or fish.

**Ingredients:**

- 2 lbs. boneless, skinless chicken breast
- 1/3 cup extra-virgin olive oil
- ¼ cup fresh lemon juice
- 3 tablespoons apple cider vinegar
- 3 cloves garlic, pressed
- ¼ cup fresh chopped basil
- ¼ cup fresh chopped parsley
- 1 teaspoon fresh chopped rosemary
- 1 teaspoon fresh chopped thyme
- ½ teaspoon sea salt
- ½ teaspoon ground black pepper

**Instructions:**

1. Place all the ingredients in a bowl and whisk until combined

2. Poke the chicken (or whatever meat or fish you are using) with a fork all over and place in a dish or Ziploc bag

3. Pour the marinade in and cover the meat completely

4. If using a dish, cover with plastic wrap and marinate for between 30 minutes and four hours, depending on your taste

5. Use in your recipe

# Apple Cider Vinegar Marinade for Pork

Again, this marinade can be used for any meat or poultry and takes just five minutes to prepare.

**Ingredients:**

- ½ cup of fresh apple cider
- ¼ cup extra-virgin olive oil
- ¼ cup fresh apple cider vinegar
- ½ teaspoon garlic powder
- ¼ teaspoon mustard powder
- 1 tablespoon light brown cane sugar or Demerara
- 1 teaspoon sea salt
- 1 tablespoon raw honey
- 1/8 teaspoon ground coriander or 1/3 teaspoon finely chopped fresh

**Instructions:**

1. Place all the ingredients in a medium bowl and whisk until combined
2. Place your pork chops in a Ziploc bag and pour the marinade in. Make sure the meat is completely covered and then seal the bag, removing the air
3. Marinate for between eight hours and a day before cooking

This makes enough for about two or three medium pork chops – if you need more, adjust the recipe accordingly.

# Quick Tips

When you make your apple cider vinegar:

- Try to use organic fruit, free of chemicals
- Do not use fruit with any mold, soft spots, signs of rot, or fungi
- Rinse your apples under cold running water before using them
- If you are making your vinegar from whole apples, they should be soaked in a bowl of water first. Add a tablespoon of ACV to the water and leave them for five minutes. This simple addition will kill any bacteria, and if you can't source organic apples, it will also remove chemical residues.

# Conclusion

Now that we have reached the end of the book, I am sure you have all the information you need to start fermenting. Many people across the globe have taken to fermentation and have started drinking kombucha and eating kimchi to clear their gut. If you want to do the same, then use this book as your ultimate guide.

You now know that fermentation is the process of breaking down carbohydrates in foods into organic acids and alcohol using microorganisms, such as bacteria and yeast. This process only works if you have good bacteria in the mix since they can break the sugars and starch in food down easily. These microorganisms grow in number, and as they divide, they form lactic acid, preventing the growth of harmful bacteria in the food. The fermented food you end up eating has an acidic or tangy taste because of the lactic acid.

You can store fermented food for a long time. You can keep it for years as long as you store it in a dark and cool place. It is also essential to keep these foods in brine (a mixture of salt and water). Use the methods mentioned in the book to get started with fermenting. Once you finish the fermentation process, transfer the food to a cold storage area. You can store the food in a cold cellar or fridge, but make sure you maintain the temperature between 32 and 50 degrees. Do not use an airlock but a regular lid. The cold temperature will slow down the organisms' growth, which helps preserve the food while it continues to age. If you ferment vegetables, you can store them for a year. Consume fermented fruit within a week or a month at most to avoid alcohol formation.

It is okay to freeze any food you ferment, as well. This means the organisms stop growing altogether, which increases the shelf life of the fermented product. Make sure you double or even triple-layer the food to prevent freezer burns. Bear in mind that you need to follow the measurements given in the book to a tee. If you do not stick to these measurements, you may mess with the growth of the microorganisms. The book has everything you might need. Use this book as your guide. The recipes in this book are very straightforward and relatively easy to follow, and you can tweak them to suit your tastes. Few people will like the taste, but if you do, give these recipes a shot.

You will probably make some mistakes here and there, but this is normal. Learn from your mistakes and make sure you try new things. You will learn and get to the point where fermenting becomes just as easy as cooking.

Happy fermenting!

Here's another book by Dion Rosser
that you might like

# COMPOSTING

·····················AND·····················

# WORM FARMING

ALL YOU NEED TO KNOW ABOUT
CREATING AN ORGANIC COMPOST,
VERMICULTURE, VERMICOMPOSTING,
AND MAKING WORM BINS

## DION ROSSER

# Resources

Bilodeau, K. (2018, May 16). Fermented foods for better gut health - Harvard Health Blog. Harvard Health Blog. https://www.health.harvard.edu/blog/fermented-foods-for-better-gut-health-2018051613841

Clime, K. (2014). Beyond Sauerkraut: A Brief History of Fermented Foods. Lhf.org. https://www.lhf.org/2014/03/beyond-sauerkraut-a-brief-history-of-fermented-foods/

Coyle, D. (2019, January 15). What Is Fermentation? The Lowdown on Fermented Foods. Healthline; Healthline Media. https://www.healthline.com/nutrition/fermentation#benefits

Delany, A. (2018, January 29). 13 Fermenting Supplies to Buy Online Before You Start Making Kombucha or Whatever. Bon Appétit. https://www.bonappetit.com/story/fermenting-supplies-online

Fermentation: A History. (2017, December 8). EatCultured. https://eatcultured.com/blogs/our-awesome-blog/fermentation-a-history

Fermentation Supplies. (N.d.). Grow Organic. https://www.groworganic.com/collections/fermentation-supplies

Fermentation Supplies | Jars, Crocks, Pounders, Airlocks, & Kits. (n.d.). Retrieved June 1, 2021, from https://www.culturesforhealth.com/learn/natural-fermentation/fermentation-equipment-choosing-the-right-supplies/

Hooper, C. (2016, April 22). 10 Health Benefits of Fermented Food. Naturalife. https://naturalife.org/nutrition/health-benefits-fermented-food

Howe, H. (2017, January 12). The Best Fermenting Supplies for Sauerkraut & Vegetables. MakeSauerkraut. https://www.makesauerkraut.com/fermenting-supplies/

Kresser, C. (2020, June 25). The 13 Benefits of Fermented Foods and How They Improve Your Health. Chris Kresser. https://chriskresser.com/benefits-of-fermented-foods/

MacCharles, J. (1 C.E., November 30). Fermenting Tools/ Equipment/ Supplies. WellPreserved. https://wellpreserved.ca/fermenting-tools-equipment-supplies/

Marcene, B. (2020, July 9). 12 Amazing Health Benefits of Fermented Foods - Natural Food Series. Natural Food Series; Natural Food Series. https://www.naturalfoodseries.com/12-benefits-fermented-foods/

ResearchGuides: Fermentation Science: History of Fermentation Science. (2019). Lindahall.org. https://libguides.lindahall.org/c.php?g=242326&p=1616528

Shurtleff, W., & Aoyagi, A. (2020). A Brief History of Fermentation, East and West. Soyinfocenter.com. https://www.soyinfocenter.com/HSS/fermentation.php

Tay, A. (2019, July 18). The Science of Fermentation. Lab Manager. https://www.labmanager.com/insights/the-science-of-fermentation-1432

"Beet Kvass: The Miracle of Russia." Homestead.org, 12 June 2020, www.homestead.org/food/beet-kvass-of-russia/.

---

"How to Make Homemade Sauerkraut in a Mason Jar." Kitchn, Apartment Therapy, LLC., 6 Aug. 2013, www.thekitchn.com/how-to-make-homemade-sauerkraut-in-a-mason-jar-193124.Fermented Dill Pickles Video.

"How to Make Fermented Pickles!" Feasting at Home, 22 Aug. 2019, www.feastingathome.com/fermented-pickles/.

"How Does Kimchi Ferment? The Science of Lacto-Fermentation and Kimchi." Baechu Kimchi, baechukimchi.ca/kimchi-and-lacto-fermentation/.

"How to Make Kombucha." BBC Good Food, www.bbcgoodfood.com/howto/guide/how-make-kombucha."How to Make Milk Kefir." Kitchn, www.thekitchn.com/how-to-make-milk-kefir-cooking-lessons-from-the-kitchn-202022.https://www.facebook.com/asweetpeachef.

"19 Benefits of Drinking Apple Cider Vinegar + How to Drink It." A Sweet Pea Chef, 20 Apr. 2019, www.asweetpeachef.com/benefits-of-apple-cider-vinegar/.Moyano, Carolina.

"The Chemistry behind the Fermentation of Yogurt." Www.foodunfolded.com, 8 July 2020, www.foodunfolded.com/article/the-chemistry-behind-the-fermentation-of-yogurt."Science of Kimchi: What Affects the Taste of Kimchi? Take a Walk on the Wild Side." Baechu Kimchi, baechukimchi.ca/take-a-walk-on-the-wild-side/.

"Sourdough Bread: A Beginner's Guide." The Clever Carrot, 3 Jan. 2014, www.theclevercarrot.com/2014/01/sourdough-bread-a-beginners-guide/."Troubleshooting Sourdough Bread." Baked, 21 Jan. 2021, www.baked-theblog.com/troubleshooting-sourdough-bread/.

"What's the Difference between Pickling and Fermenting?" Kitchn, https://www.thekitchn.com/whats-the-difference-between-pickling-and-fermenting-229536.

Admin. "How to Clean out the Root Cellar." The Self Sufficient HomeAcre. March 12, 2013. www.theselfsufficienthomeacre.com/2013/03/cleaning-out-the-root-cellar.html

Bubel, Mike, and Bubel, Nancy. "The Fundamentals of Root Cellaring." Mother Earth News. Accessed March 20, 2021. www.motherearthnews.com/real-food/root-cellaring/fundamentals-of-root-cellaring-zm0z91zsie

Ellis, Lance. "The Advantages of Storing Produce in a Root Cellar and How to Build an Effective One." East Idaho News.com. June 22, 2020. www.eastidahonews.com/2020/06/the-advantages-of-growing-produce-in-a-root-cellar-and-how-to-build-an-effective-one/

Fazio, Pete. "DIY 2x4 Shelving for Garage or Basement." Dadand.com. Accessed March 20, 2021. www.dadand.com/diy-2x4-shelving/

Grow Organic. "Root Cellar Basics." February 20, 2015. www.groworganic.com/blogs/articles/root-cellar-basics

Inch by Inch Inspections Inc. "Minimizing Mold Growth in My Cold Room." Accessed March 20, 2021. www.inchbyinchinspections.com/blog/mold-growth-in-cold-room

Jones, Kylene. "Inexpensive Root Cellars: 13 Literally Cool Ideas to Chill With." The Provident Prepper. Accessed March 20, 2021. www.theprovidentprepper.org/inexpensive-root-cellars-13-literally-cool-ideas-to-chill-with/

Katahdin Cedar Log Homes. "Root Cellars Make a Comeback." March 13, 2013. www.katahdincedarloghomes.com/blog/root-cellars-make-a-comeback/

Moors, Debbie. "22 Foods You Can Store in Root Cellars." Hobby Farms. August 2, 2012. www.hobbyfarms.com/22-foods-you-can-store-in-root-cellars-2/

Neverman, Laurie. "Root Cellars 101 – Root Cellar Design, Use and Mistakes to Avoid." Common Sense Home. 8 February 8, 2020. www.commonsensehome.com/root-cellars-101/#Fruit_and_Vegetable_Storage_Chart

Newton, Sandy. "Root Cellars: Types and Storage Tips." The Old Farmer's Almanac. August 6, 2020. www.almanac.com/content/root-cellars-types-and-storage-tips

Robert. "How to Build a Root Cellar in 7 Steps." Walden Labs. September 24, 2015. www.waldenlabs.com/how-to-build-a-root-cellar-in-7-steps/

Rootwell Products Inc. "Everything You Need to Know about an Amazing Root Cellar." Rootwell. November 15, 2016. www.rootwell.com/blogs/root-cellar

Shelley, Patrick. "The 8 Fundamentals to Digging a Root Cellar." Off the Grid News. November 30, 2015. www.offthegridnews.com/how-to-2/the-8-fundamentals-to-digging-a-root-cellar/

Simple Family Preparedness. "Guide to Root Cellar Storage." April 5, 2018. www.simplefamilypreparedness.com/root-cellar/

Sperling. "Organize Your Root Cellar by 'Zone'." RootCellar. November 1, 2019.

Strawn, Heidi. "8 Ways to Prepare a Root Cellar for Food Storage." Hobby Farms. Last modified August 2, 2012. www.hobbyfarms.com/8-ways-to-prepare-a-root-cellar-for-food-storage-2/

Strawn, Heidi. "How to Customize Your Root Cellar Storage." Hobby Farms. April 4, 2014. www.hobbyfarms.com/how-to-customize-your-root-cellar-storage-2/

Thegreenlifefarm. "Tutorial on Storage Containers for the Root Cellar and Life." Thegreenlifefarm's Blog. November 27, 2010. www.thegreenlifefarm.wordpress.com/2010/11/27/storage-containers-for-the-root-cellar-and-life/

The Grow Network. "How to Plan Your Perfect Root Cellar." April 4, 2020. www.thegrownetwork.com/how-to-plan-root-cellar/

Tyrell, Carmela. "8 Tips to Keep the Mice out of the Stockpile." Survivopedia. June 5, 2014. www.survivopedia.com/how-to-keep-mice-out-of-stockpile/

Provident-Living-Today.com. "Root Cellar." Accessed March 20, 2021. www.provident-living-today.com/Root-Cellar.html

Winger, Jill. "13 Root Cellar Alternatives." The Prairie Homestead. September 2, 2016. www.theprairiehomestead.com/2015/10/root-cellar-alternatives.html

Carole, C. (n.d.). An overview of 10 home food preservation methods from ancient to modern. Retrieved from Homepreservingbible.com website: http://www.homepreservingbible.com/630-an-overview-of-10-home-food-preservation-methods-from-ancient-to-modern/

Christine Venema, Michigan State University Extension. (n.d.). Smoking as a food cooking method - MSU Extension. Retrieved from Msu.edu website: https://www.canr.msu.edu/news/smoking_as_a_food_cooking_method

Coppieters, K. (2014, April 23). The science of curing meats safely. Retrieved from Amazingribs.com website: https://amazingribs.com/tested-recipes/salting-brining-curing-and-injecting/curing-meats-safely

Curing and smoking meats for home food preservation. (n.d.). Retrieved from Uga.edu website: https://nchfp.uga.edu/publications/nchfp/lit_rev/cure_smoke_pres.html

Curing and smoking poultry. (2019, February 11). Retrieved from Tamu.edu website: https://agrilifeextension.tamu.edu/library/health-nutrition/curing-and-smoking-poultry/

Food preservation: History, methods, types. (2011, August 22). Retrieved from Schoolworkhelper.net website: https://schoolworkhelper.net/food-preservation-history-methods-types/

How to smoke fish – step-by-step guide. (2017, November 10). Retrieved from Cavetools.com website: https://blog.cavetools.com/how-to-smoke-fish/

Introduction and definition of food preservation. (n.d.). Retrieved from Brainkart.com website: https://www.brainkart.com/article/Introduction-and-Definition-of-Food-Preservation_33475/

Laurie Messing, Michigan State University Extension. (n.d.). The history of preserving food at home - Safe Food & Water. Retrieved from Msu.edu website: https://www.canr.msu.edu/news/food_preservation_is_as_old_as_mankind

MGConsults. (2017a, October 10). Advantages & disadvantages of food smoking - SmokeHouseReview. Retrieved from Smokehousereview.com website: http://smokehousereview.com/2017/10/10/advantages-disadvantages-of-food-smoking/

MGConsults. (2017b, October 10). Basic food smoking tips. - SmokeHouseReview. Retrieved from Smokehousereview.com website: http://smokehousereview.com/2017/10/10/basic-food-smoking-tips/

MGConsults. (2017c, October 13). Types of wood used for food smoking. - SmokeHouseReview. Retrieved from Smokehousereview.com website: http://smokehousereview.com/2017/10/13/types-of-wood-used-for-food-smoking/

PaulTM, & ARNIE. (2016, May 22). How is smoking used for food processing and preservation? Retrieved from Foodsafetyhelpline.com website:

https://foodsafetyhelpline.com/smoking-used-food-processing-preservation/

Proper processing of wild game and fish. (n.d.). Retrieved from Psu.edu website: https://extension.psu.edu/proper-processing-of-wild-game-and-fish

Restaurant Business Staff. (2010, May 1). The art and science of smoking foods. Retrieved from Restaurantbusinessonline.com website: https://www.restaurantbusinessonline.com/art-science-smoking-foods

Riches, D. (n.d.). Smoked fish: A centuries-old tradition. Retrieved from Thespruceeats.com website: https://www.thespruceeats.com/guide-to-smoking-fish-331552

Vuković, D. (2019, June 17). The 3 methods of curing meat with salt. Retrieved from Primalsurvivor.net website: https://www.primalsurvivor.net/salt-curing/

Waggoner, C. (2016, June 2). 5 ways to tell if food has gone bad, because no one trusts expiration dates. Retrieved from Spoonuniversity.com website: https://spoonuniversity.com/how-to/food-gone-bad-ways-to-tell

(N.d.-a). Retrieved from Suburbansteader.com website: https://www.suburbansteader.com/introduction-food-preservation/

(N.d.-b). Retrieved from Asgmag.com website: https://www.asgmag.com/prepping/smoke-em-6-steps-to-preserve-meat-through-smoking/

(N.d.-c). Retrieved from Masterclass.com website: https://www.masterclass.com/articles/what-is-a-bbq-smoker-6-types-of-meat-smokers-and-the-best-smoker-for-texas-style-barbecue#types-of-smokers-direct-vs-indirect-heat

Ashiya. (2011, May 17). *What Is the Importance of Food Preservation?* https://www.preservearticles.com/articles/what-is-the-importance-of-food-preservation/5187

*Approved Canning Methods: Types of Canners.* (n.d.)
https://extension.psu.edu/approved-canning-methods-types-of-
canners

Ewald, J. (2014, August 8). *What is Canning, and What Are the
Benefits?* 21, 2021. https://lifeandhealth.org/lifestyle/what-is-
canning-and-what-are-the-benefits/172324.html

Guerrero-Legarreta, I. (2004). *Canning. Encyclopedia of Meat
Sciences.* (pp. 139–144). Elsevier.

*National center for home food preservation.* (n.d.)
https://nchfp.uga.edu/publications/nchfp/factsheets/food_pres_hi
st.html

Neverman, L. (2021, January 16). *Home Food Preservation –
Ten Ways to Preserve Food at Home.*
https://commonsensehome.com/home-food-preservation/

Athearn, Kevin & Simonne, Amarat & Ahn, Soohyoun. (2018).
*Budget Template for Home Canning.* EDIS. 2018.

Christensen, E. (2010, July 30). *Canning Basics: What's the Deal
with Pectin?* https://www.thekitchn.com/canning-basics-whats-the-
deal-123192

Cook's Info. (2005, May 19). *Canning Funnels. Cook's Info.*
https://www.cooksinfo.com/canning-funnels

Food in Jars. (2010, July 28). *Canning 101: Why You Should
Bubble Your Jars.* https://foodinjars.com/blog/canning-101-why-
you-should-bubble-your-jars/

Healthy Canning. (n.d.). *Pickling Spice.*
https://www.healthycanning.com/pickling-spice/

Healthy Canning. (n.d.). *Sugar's Role in Home Canning.*
https://www.healthycanning.com/sugars-role-in-home-canning/

Healthy Canning. (n.d.). *Vinegar in Canning Water.*
https://www.healthycanning.com/vinegar-in-canning-water/

Helseth, R. (2021, 18). *Wide Mouth Vs. Regular Mouth Mason
Jars – The Same, But Different.*

https://masonjarlifestyle.com/wide-mouth-vs-regular-mouth-mason-jars-the-same-but-different/

Joachim, D., & Schloss, A. (n.d.). *The Science of Pectin. Fine Cooking.* https://www.finecooking.com/article/the-science-of-pectin

Loe, T. (n.d.). *Pickling Salt vs. Other Salts in Canning.* https://livinghomegrown.com/pickling-salt/

Michelle. (2012, September 12). *Canning Equipment 101: The Tools You Need to Start Canning.* https://rosybluhome.com/canning-equipment-101-the-tools-you-need-to-start-canning/

Sarah. (2021, 16). *Canning Supplies and Preserving Equipment List. Sustainable Thoughts.* https://www.sustainablecooks.com/canning-supplies/

*How to Select the Best Fruit for Jam/Jellies.* (n.d.) https://www.vigopresses.co.uk/AdditionalDepartments/Right-hand-panel/Vigo-Presses-Blog/How-to-Select-the-Best-Fruit-for-JamJellies

Lebert, A. (2017). *Fermented Meat Products. Current Developments in Biotechnology and Bioengineering* (pp. 25–43). Elsevier.

Sharon. (2020a, 14). *Canning Chicken: It's Great for Homemade Soup or Casserole Recipes.* https://www.simplycanning.com/canning-chicken/

Sharon. (2020b, 19). *Canning Venison – Raw Packed, Cubed, or Strips. It's So Easy!* https://www.simplycanning.com/canning-venison/

Sharon. (2020, May 5). *Ground Venison.* https://www.simplycanning.com/canning-venison-ground/

The Meadow. (n.d.). *Making Fermented Sausage.* https://themeadow.com/pages/making-fermented-sausage

Utah State University. (n.d.). *Canning Meats, Poultry, and Seafood.* https://extension.usu.edu/preserve-the-harvest/research/canning-meats-poultry-seafood

Winger, J. (2020, June 29). *How to Can Food with No Special Equipment.* https://www.theprairiehomestead.com/2020/06/canning-no-equipment.html

*Beyond Sauerkraut: A Brief History of Fermented Foods.* (2014, March 3). https://www.lhf.org/2014/03/beyond-sauerkraut-a-brief-history-of-fermented-foods/

Foodelicious. (n.d.). *Catherine's Pickled Blueberries.* https://www.allrecipes.com/recipe/206655/catherines-pickled-blueberries/

Imatome-Yun, N. (2015, January 24). *Save Your Pickle Juice for Pickletinis, Hangovers, & More.* https://food-hacks.wonderhowto.com/how-to/save-your-pickle-juice-for-pickletinis-hangovers-more-0159741/

Marisa. (2013, 10). *Preserving Spring: Spicy Pickled Asparagus.* https://simplebites.net/preserving-spring-spicy-pickled-asparagus-recipe/

*Pickled Fruit.* (2020, September 2). https://wavesinthekitchen.com/pickled-fruit/

Pruitt, S. (2015, May 21). *The Juicy 4,000-Year History of Pickles.* https://www.history.com/news/pickles-history-timeline

Sevier, J. (2017, August 11). *How to Can Pickles, Step by Step.* https://www.epicurious.com/expert-advice/how-to-can-pickles-weekend-warrior-article

Lang, A., BSc, & MBA. (2019, December 10). *Jam vs. Jelly: What's the Difference?* https://www.healthline.com/nutrition/jelly-vs-jam

Martens, M. F. A. (2020, June 29). *A Guide to Homemade Jams and Jellies.* https://asweatlife.com/2020/06/how-to-make-your-own-jam/

Beaty, V. (2018, June 26). *Thirty Homemade Fruit Jams and Jellies You Definitely Want to Make this Summer.* https://www.diyncrafts.com/41444/food/30-homemade-fruit-jams-and-jellies-you-definitely-want-to-make-this-summer

Chihak, S. (2018, July 26). *How to Use a Pressure Canner to Preserve Your Veggies, Meats, and More.* https://www.bhg.com/recipes/how-to/preserving-canning/pressure-canning-basics/

Meredith, L. (n.d.). *Boiling Water Bath vs. Pressure Canning.* https://www.thespruceeats.com/boiling-water-bath-versus-pressure-canning-1327438

Old Farmer's Almanac. (n.d.) *Pressure Canning: Beginner's Guide and Recipes.* https://www.almanac.com/pressure-canning-guide

Sharon. (2020, 29). *Pressure Canning, Learn How to Use Your Pressure Canner.* https://www.simplycanning.com/pressure-canning/

Autumn. (2018, October 25). *Pressure Canning Fish: A Basic Recipe.* 21, 2021. https://atraditionallife.com/pressure-canning-fish-basic-recipe/

*Canning Fish in Quart Jars.* (n.d.). 21, 2021. https://nchfp.uga.edu/how/can_05/alaska_can_fish_qtjars.pdf

*How to Can Fresh Fish for Beginners.* (2021, February 17). 21, 2021. https://www.anoffgridlife.com/how-to-can-fresh-fish-for-beginners/

Williams, T. (2016, 4). *How to Can Fish (Salmon, Tuna, and More!)* http://themasonjarsuite.squarespace.com/videos/howtocanfish

*Canning Meats & Poultry.* (2020, October 30). https://www.clemson.edu/extension/food/canning/canning-tips/51canning-meats-poultry.html

Tayse, R. (2014, July 3). *Nine Need-to-Know Tips for Canning Meat.* https://www.hobbyfarms.com/9-need-to-know-tips-for-canning-meat-2/

Thomas, C. (2020, January 30). *Step by Step Tutorial for Canning Meat* (Raw Pack Method). https://homesteadingfamily.com/step-by-step-tutorial-for-canning-meat-raw-pack-method/

Winger, J. (2015, January 27). *Canning Meat – Tutorial.* https://www.theprairiehomestead.com/2015/01/canning-meat.html

Winger, J. (2020, March 12). *Canning Chicken (How to Do it Safely).* https://www.theprairiehomestead.com/2020/03/canning-chicken.html

Cloudflare. (n.d.). *What is Fermentation – Masterclass.* https://www.masterclass.com/articles/what-is-fermentation-learn-about-the-3-different-types-of-fermentation-and-6-tips-for-homemade-fermentation#what-are-the-different-stages-of-the-fermentation-process

Coyle, D. C. (2020, August 20). *What Is Fermentation? The Lowdown on Fermented Foods.* https://www.healthline.com/nutrition/fermentation#safety

Cultures for Health. (2016a, May 16). *How To Prepare Your Vegetables for Fermentation.* https://www.culturesforhealth.com/learn/natural-fermentation/how-to-prepare-vegetables-fermentation/

Cultures for Health. (2016b, June 24). *Cross-Contamination: Keeping Your Cultures Safe from Each Other.* https://www.culturesforhealth.com/learn/general/cross-contamination-keeping-cultures-safe/

Cultures for Health. (2017, August 18). *Fermentation Supplies.* https://www.culturesforhealth.com/learn/natural-fermentation/fermentation-equipment-choosing-the-right-supplies/

Cultures for Health. (2018, June 14). *Salt vs. Whey vs. Starter Cultures for Fermenting Vegetables, Fruits & Condiments.* https://www.culturesforhealth.com/learn/natural-fermentation/salt-vs-whey-vs-starter-cultures/

Cultures for Health. (2020, November 9). *How To Ferment Vegetables: Everything You Need to Know.* https://www.culturesforhealth.com/learn/natural-fermentation/how-to-ferment-vegetables/

S. (2020, June 19). *Make Old-Fashioned Brine Fermented Pickles Like Your Great Grandmother.* https://simplebites.net/make-old-fashioned-brine-fermented-pickles-like-your-great-grandmother/

W. (2018, March 27). *Beyond Sauerkraut: A Brief History of Fermented Foods.* https://www.lhf.org/2014/03/beyond-sauerkraut-a-brief-history-of-fermented-foods/

*Drying Food at Home.* (n.d.) https://extension.umn.edu/preserving-and-preparing/drying-food

Farm, J. (2020, July 10). *Three Easy Dehydrator Jerky Recipes for Summer Hikes and Car Trips.* https://joybileefarm.com/dehydrator-jerky-recipes/

Fresh Off the Grid. (2020, May 21). *The Ultimate Guide to Dehydrating Food.* https://www.freshoffthegrid.com/dehydrating-food/

Reed, L. (2020). *Dehydrating food: The Beginner's Guide to Dehydrating Vegetables, Fruits, Meat, and Other Foods at Home with Easy Recipes.* Tonazzi Company.

Washington Post. (2020, March 22). *How to Freeze Fresh Vegetables.*

https://www.washingtonpost.com/news/voraciously/wp/2020/03/2
2/how-to-freeze-fresh-vegetables-while-preserving-their-best-
qualities/

A. (2021, January 4). *Why You Should Never Overload Your
Refrigerator or Freezer.* https://allareaappliancellc.com/why-you-
should-never-overload-your-refrigerator-or-freezer/

Crigger, D. (2021, February 2). *Brilliant Freezer Organization
Tips You Need.* https://www.onecrazyhouse.com/17-ways-
organize-freezer-probably-arent/

Fin, L. (2019, August 20). *Best Way to Efficiently Freezer-Store
Soups, Broths and Stews.* https://food52.com/recipes/16882-best-
way-to-efficiently-freezer-store-soups-broths-and-stews

*How Does Freezing Preserve Food and Maintain Quality?* (n.d.).
https://www.eufic.org/en/food-safety/article/chilling-out-freezing-
foods-for-quality-and-safety

Jennings, M. (2019, February 26). *How to Freeze Milk and Eggs.*
https://www.stockpilingmoms.com/frugal-friday-how-to-freeze-
milk-and-eggs.

Name, T. (2020, October 23). *How to Protect Your Food When
Your Freezer Stops Working.*
https://www.capitalcityapplianceservice.com/blog/how-to-protect-
your-food-when-your-freezer-stops-working/

R. (2020, January 9). *Tips for Freezing: A Guide to Proper Meat
Storage.* https://www.beststopinscott.com/freezing-meat/

*The Right Way to Freeze Fresh Fruits to Enjoy All Year Long.*
(2020, 14). https://www.stasherbag.com/blogs/stasher-life/the-
right-way-to-freeze-your-summer-fruits.

*Tips on Freezing Seafood.* (2018, July 13).
https://www.tourismpei.com/tips-on-freezing-seafood

Taraneh. (2021, March 1). *Best Canning and Food Preservation
Equipment for Preserving Local Bounty.*

https://www.kitsilano.ca/2016/10/11/best-canning-and-food-preservation-equipment